Realizing the Asian Century

Executive Summary

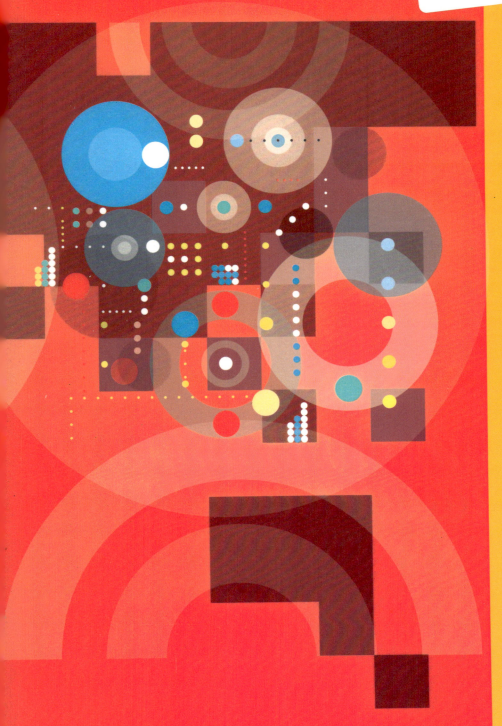

Asia 2050:
Realizing the Asian Century

Executive Summary

Asia is in the midst of a historic transformation. If it continues on its recent trajectory, by 2050 its per capita income could rise sixfold in purchasing power parity (PPP) terms to reach Europe's levels today. It would make some 3 billion additional Asians affluent by current standards. By nearly doubling its share of global gross domestic product (GDP) to 52 percent by 2050, Asia would regain the dominant economic position it held some 300 years ago, before the industrial revolution (Figure 1).

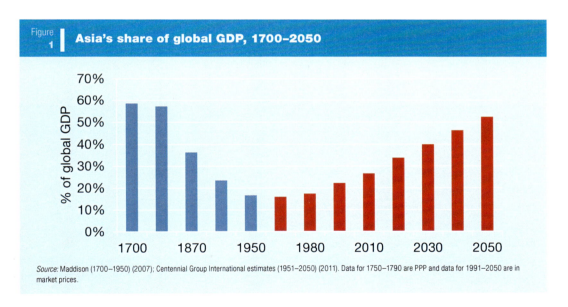

Figure 1 — Asia's share of global GDP, 1700–2050

Source: Maddison (1700–1950) (2007); Centennial Group International estimates (1951–2050) (2011). Data for 1750–1790 are PPP and data for 1991–2050 are in market prices.

But Asia's rise is by no means preordained. Although this outcome, premised on Asia's major economies sustaining their present growth momentum, is promising, it does not mean that the path ahead is easy or requires just doing more of the same. Indeed, success will require a different pattern of growth and resolution of a broad array of long-term challenges requiring strong political will.

To achieve this promising outcome Asia's leaders will have to manage multiple risks and challenges, particularly:

- Increasing inequality within countries, which could undermine social cohesion and stability.
- For some countries, the risk of getting caught in the "Middle Income Trap" (Box 1), for a host of domestic economic, social, and political reasons.
- Intense competition for finite natural resources, as newly affluent Asians aspire to higher standards of living.
- Rising income disparities across countries, which could destabilize the region.
- Global warming and climate change, which could threaten agricultural production, coastal populations, and major urban areas.
- Poor governance and weak institutional capacity, faced by almost all countries.

These challenges are not mutually exclusive. They can affect one another and exacerbate existing tensions and conflicts, or even create new pressures that could threaten Asia's growth, stability, and security.

This book postulates two scenarios of Asia's future growth trajectory: the Asian Century and the Middle Income Trap. These scenarios are only two possibilities of how Asia's future may unfold. They have a dual objective: to draw attention to the longer-term implications of the broad trends and to ask "what-if" questions.

Box 1 | The Middle Income Trap: Unable to compete

The Middle Income Trap is illustrated in the figure, which plots per capita incomes of three middle-income countries over 1975–2005. In a steadily growing economy per capita GDP rises continuously—the experience of the Republic of Korea. But many middle-income countries do not follow this pattern. Instead, they have bursts of growth followed by periods of stagnation or even decline, or are stuck at low growth rates.

They are caught in the Middle Income Trap—unable to compete with low-income, low-wage economies in manufactured exports and with advanced economies in high-skill innovations. Put another way, such countries cannot make a timely transition from resource-driven growth, with low-cost labor and capital, to productivity-driven growth.

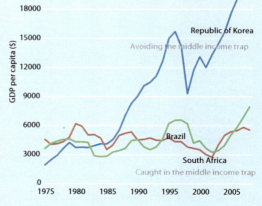

Makings of the Asian Century

The Asian Century scenario extends Asia's past success into the future, putting it on the cusp of a historic transformation. It assumes that Asian economies can maintain their momentum for another 40 years and adapt to the shifting global economic and technological environment by continually recreating their comparative advantages. In this scenario, Asia's GDP (at market exchange rates) increases from $17 trillion in 2010 to $174 trillion in 2050, or half of global GDP, similar to its share of the global population. Seven economies would lead Asia's march to prosperity (Box 2). With a per capita GDP of $40,800 (PPP), Asia in 2050 would have incomes similar to Europe's today. It would have no poor countries (those with average per capita GDP of less than $1,000), compared with eight today. The results of falling into the Middle Income Trap are outlined further below.

> **Box 2 | The engines of the Asian Century are the Asia-7 economies**
>
> Asia's march to prosperity will be led by seven economies, two of them already developed and six fast growing middle income converging economies: PRC, India, Indonesia, Japan, Republic of Korea, Thailand and Malaysia.
>
> These seven economies had a combined total population of 3.1 billion (78 percent of total Asia) and GDP of $14.2 trillion (87 percent of Asia) in 2010. Under the Asian Century scenario, their share of population by 2050 would be 73 percent and their GDP would be 90 percent of Asia. They alone will account for 45 percent of global GDP. Their average per capita income would be $45,800 (in PPP) compared with $36,600 for the world as a whole.
>
> Between 2010 and 2050, these seven economies would account for as much as 87 percent of total GDP growth in Asia and of almost 55 percent of global GDP growth. They will thus be the engines of not only Asia's economy but also the global economy.

Actions at three levels

In its march towards the Asian Century, the region must tackle daunting policy, institutional, and governance challenges. Given widely varying country conditions, the precise actions and their timing must vary. Still, it is possible to draw the contours of the major changes necessary for the region along three dimensions: national, regional, and global (Figure 2). The ability of countries to realize the promise of the Asian Century will be determined by their success in these three areas.

National action agenda

Seven overarching intergenerational issues require national action throughout the region.

Growth and inclusion. Growth and inclusion need not be mutually exclusive; indeed they

Figure 2. Strategic framework

can be mutually reinforcing. To sustain growth over the long-term, almost all Asian countries must give much higher priority to inclusion and reducing inequalities—rich/poor, rural/urban, literate/illiterate, and along gender and ethnic lines. Inclusive growth must not only address poverty, but also deal with aspects of equity, equality of access and opportunity, generation of employment and provision of protection to the vulnerable in the various facets of daily living.

Entrepreneurship, innovation, and technological development. The continuing rapid growth of Asian economies over the next 40 years will require a harnessing of the full potential of technology, innovation and, critically, entrepreneurship. More Asian countries need to emulate Japan, Republic of Korea, and Singapore, and come closer to (preferably achieve) global best practice. The fast-growing converging economies, particularly PRC and India, must move from catching up to frontier entrepreneurship and innovation to create breakthroughs in science and technology. A particularly fruitful area will be inclusive innovation to meet the needs of those at the bottom of the pyramid. A core requirement is a high-quality education system at all levels that promotes creativity.

Massive urbanization. By 2050, Asia will be transformed, as its urban population will nearly double from 1.6 billion to 3 billion. Asia's cities, which already account for more than 80 percent of economic output, will be the centers of higher education, innovation, and technological development. The quality and efficiency of urban areas would determine Asia's long-term competitiveness and its social and political stability. Asia must take advantage of being early on its urbanization growth curve to promote compact, energy-efficient, and safe cities.

Financial transformation. As its share of global GDP rises to 50 percent or more, Asia should also have about the same share of the world's financial assets, banks, and equity and bond markets, etc. In transforming its financial systems, Asia's leaders must remain mindful of the lessons of the 1997–1998 Asian financial crisis and the Great Recession of 2007–2009. Asia will need to formulate its own approach to finance, avoiding both overreliance on market self-regulation and excessive central government control of bank-dominated systems. It will also need to become more open to institutional innovation, also to support inclusive finance.

Radical reduction in the intensity of energy and natural resource use. The anticipated affluence of some 3 billion additional Asians will put tremendous pressure on the earth's finite natural resources. Asia will be the most affected by, and responsible for, excessive reliance on energy imports. Out of self-interest, it will need to take the lead in radical energy efficiency and diversification programs by switching from fossil fuels to renewable energy. Asia's future competitiveness will depend heavily on how efficiently it uses its natural resources and progresses to a low-carbon future.

Climate change. Climate change will affect everyone. With over half the world's population, Asia has more at stake than any other region. This has far-reaching implications for the way Asia needs to move forward: dramatically increasing energy efficiency and reducing reliance on fossil fuels; adopting a new approach to urbanization by building more compact and eco-friendly cities; relying much more on mass transit for urban dwellers and railways for long-distance transport; and changing lifestyles to alleviate pressures on finite natural resources.

Governance and institutions. The recent deterioration in the quality and credibility of national political and economic institutions (illustrated by rising corruption) is likely to become a binding constraint to growth in Asia. High-quality institutions will help fast-growing converging economies avoid the Middle Income Trap, and slow- or moderate-growth aspiring economies move towards a higher growth trajectory. Throughout Asia, an expanding middle class will exert new demands for greater voice and participation, greater accountability for results, and greater personal space. Although daunting, eradicating corruption is critical for all countries to maintain social and political stability and retain legitimacy. These common challenges all require effective governance, both at central and local levels. Asia must retool its institutions with an emphasis on transparency, accountability, predictability, and enforceability.

These intergenerational issues apply to most Asian economies, but their relative priority will vary over time, depending on the group a country belongs to at a given time.

High-income developed economies.[1] This group of seven economies should lead the rest of Asia in two areas: making the scientific and technological breakthroughs that are crucial to Asia; and moving beyond high economic growth toward promoting broader social well-being.

Fast-growing converging economies.[2] Avoiding the Middle Income Trap should be the main

---

1 Brunei Darussalam; Hong Kong, China; Japan; Republic of Korea; Macao, China; Singapore; and Taipei,China;
2 These 11 countries (Armenia; Azerbaijan; Cambodia; PRC; Georgia; India; Indonesia; Kazakhstan; Malaysia; Thailand; and Viet Nam) meet the criteria of the Commission on Growth and Development for sustained long-term success and hence convergence with best practice.

objective of this group's eleven countries. They should—in addition to further reducing inequalities and consolidating the fundamentals of development—train a world-class, skilled labor force and build credible and predictable institutions that protect property rights (physical and intellectual) and allow fair dispute-resolution. Constantly improving the business climate will be key.

Slow- or modest-growth aspiring economies.[3] The highest priority of this group of thirty one countries must be to raise economic growth toward that in their more successful Asian neighbors. They should focus on the fundamentals of development: faster and more inclusive growth by reducing inequalities through better education for all; infrastructure development; and major improvements in institutions, the business environment, and openness to external markets.

Regional cooperation and integration

Regional cooperation and integration is critical for Asia's march toward prosperity. It will become much more important for a number of reasons: it will cement the region's hard-won economic gains in the face of vulnerabilities to global shocks; it could be an important bridge between individual Asian countries and the rest of the world; with development assistance, it can help reduce cross-country disparities in income and opportunities (which, if left unchecked, could generate instability or conflict); it can be a stepping stone for poorer countries to move up the value chain and maximize their growth potential; in technological development, energy security, and disaster preparedness, it can help respond better to global challenges, and yield significant synergies and positive spillovers; and, through managing the regional commons, it can contribute to Asia's long-term stability and peace.

Given its diversity, Asia will need to develop its own model that builds on the positive experience of East Asia: a market-driven and pragmatic approach supported by an evolving institutional framework that facilitates free regional trade and investment flows throughout Asia, as well as some labor mobility. An Asian economic community must be based on two general principles—openness and transparency. Openness will be a continuation of Asia's long-standing policy of open regionalism, a key factor in East Asia's past success.

Crucial for increased regional cooperation is strong political leadership. Building Asia's regionalism will require collective leadership that recognizes a balance of power among participants. Asia's major economic powers, like PRC, India, Indonesia, Japan, and Republic of Korea, will be important in integrating Asia and shaping its role in the global economy.

Global agenda

Asia's growth and larger footprint in the global economy will bring new challenges,

---

3 Afghanistan; Bangladesh; Bhutan; Cook Islands; the Democratic People's Republic of Korea; Fiji Islands; Iran; Kiribati; the Kyrgyz Republic; the Lao People's Democratic Republic (Lao PDR); Maldives; Marshall Islands; Federated States of Micronesia; Mongolia; Myanmar; Nauru; Nepal; Pakistan; Palau; Papua New Guinea; the Philippines; Samoa; Solomon Islands; Sri Lanka; Tajikistan; Timor-Leste; Tonga; Turkmenistan; Tuvalu; Uzbekistan; and Vanuatu.

responsibilities, and obligations. The region will need to take greater ownership of the global commons. It will need to gradually transform itself from a passive onlooker in the debate on global rule making and a reticent follower of the rules, to an active debater and constructive rule maker. As an emerging global leader, Asia should act as—and be seen as—a responsible global citizen. When formulating its domestic or regional policy agenda, Asia will need to consider the regional and global implications. It will need to delicately manage its rapidly rising role as a major player in global governance non-assertively and constructively.

As Asia becomes the center of the global economy, it will be in its own interest that the rest of world also does well economically and politically. Peace and security throughout the world will be essential for its long-term prosperity. The Asian Century should not be Asia's alone but the century of shared global prosperity.

Asia's efforts to enhance regional cooperation must not be at the cost of its traditional openness to the rest of the world. Asia must adhere, as mentioned, to its long-standing strategy of open regionalism.

Need for enhanced resilience

Asia's rise will almost certainly not be smooth. Economic history tells us that there will be many ups and downs along the way. For example, in the past 40 years, financial crises have occurred roughly once every 10 years. It is most likely that between now and 2050, there will be major crises: financial or economic (even social and political). How countries navigate through them will decide Asia's fortunes. Fortunately, with each successive crisis, Asia has demonstrated a growing capacity to manage them. The region's much enhanced resilience to external shocks was demonstrated vividly during the Great Recession, as it became the first region to recover, with a V-shaped recovery.

But the region must not become complacent. It must continue to reinforce its resilience by following prudent fiscal and monetary policies and by making its financial systems more robust. Overall, the adaptability, flexibility and capacity to respond to the changing global economic landscape will carry a high premium.

Asian Century vs. Middle Income Trap

The agendas in this book—national, regional, and global—are wide-ranging and require far-sighted leadership. The region has to face up to the daunting task of realizing the opportunities that lie before it. How many countries will meet this challenge? The answer is unclear. Given this reality and uncertainties about the future, the book postulates two quantitative scenarios with very different outcomes.

Most of the discussion is based on the optimistic Asian Century scenario. This scenario assumes that: (i) the 11 economies with a demonstrated record of sustained convergence to best global practice over the past 30 years or so continue this trend over the next 40 years; and (ii) a number of modest-growth aspiring economies will become convergers by 2020. In this scenario, Asia will take its place among the ranks of the affluent on par with those in Europe today; some 3 billion additional Asians will become affluent by 2050. This is the desired or ideal scenario for Asia.

The Middle Income Trap scenario assumes that these fast-growing converging economies fall into that trap in the next 5–10 years, without any of the slow- or modest-growth aspiring economies improving their record; in other words, Asia follows the pattern of Latin America over the past 30 years. This is the pessimistic scenario and could be taken as a wake-up call to Asian leaders.

There will be a huge difference in the outcomes of the two scenarios. The economic and social costs of missing the Asian Century are staggering. If today's fast-growing converging economies become mired in the Middle Income Trap, Asia's GDP in 2050 would reach only $65 trillion, not $174 trillion (at market exchange rates) (Figure 3). GDP per capita would be only $20,600, not $40,800 (PPP). Such an outcome would deprive billions of Asians of a lifetime of affluence and well-being.

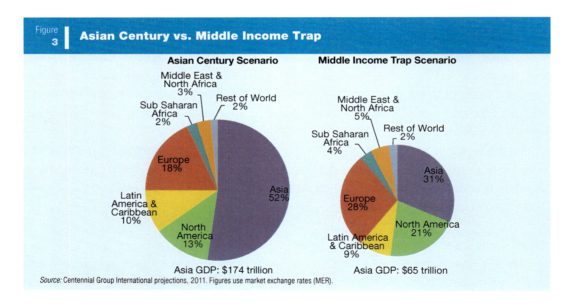

Figure 3 | Asian Century vs. Middle Income Trap

Source: Centennial Group International projections, 2011. Figures use market exchange rates (MER).

The possibility of a "perfect storm" cannot be ruled out in thinking about Asia through 2050. A combination of bad macro policies, finance sector exuberance with lax supervision, conflict, climate change, natural disasters, changing demography, and weak governance could jeopardize Asian growth. In this worst case—or doomsday—scenario, Asia could stumble into a financial meltdown, major conflict, or regionwide chaos well before 2050. It is impossible to quantify this scenario, but Asia's leaders must be aware of the potential for such a catastrophe and avoid it at all costs.

The intangibles

Four overriding intangibles will determine Asia's long-term destiny. First is the ability of Asia's leaders to persevere during the inevitable ups and downs and to focus on the long term. The region's ability to maintain the current momentum for another 40 years will require continual adjustments in strategy and policies to respond to changing circumstances and shifting comparative advantages. This will place a tremendous premium on far-sighted and enlightened leadership. Second is the willingness and ability of Asia to emulate the success of East Asia to adopt a pragmatic rather than ideological approach to policy formulation and to keep focused on results. Third is to continue Asia's success in building much greater mutual trust and confidence among its major economies, which is vital for regional cooperation. And fourth is to extend the commitment and ability of Asian leaders to modernize governance and retool institutions, while enhancing transparency and accountability.

Many of the required actions have long gestation periods that extend over many decades. Yet, their impact must be felt well before 2050 to allow Asia to continue on its path to prosperity. Asia's leaders must act with urgency if the promise of the Asian Century is to be realized.

ASIA 2050

Realizing the Asian Century

ASIA 2050

Realizing the Asian Century

EDITED BY
Harinder S. Kohli
Ashok Sharma
Anil Sood

$SAGE www.sagepublications.com
Los Angeles • London • New Delhi • Singapore • Washington DC

Copyright © The Asian Development Bank, 2011

The views expressed in this book are those of the authors' and do not necessarily reflect the views and policies of the Asian Development Bank (ADB) or its Board of Governors or the governments they represent.

ADB does not guarantee the accuracy of the data included in this publication and accepts no responsibility for any consequence of their use.

By making any designation of or reference to a particular territory or geographic area, or by using the term "country" in this document, ADB does not intend to make any judgments as to the legal or other status of any territory or area.

ADB encourages printing or copying information exclusively for personal and non-commercial use with proper acknowledgment of ADB. Users are restricted from reselling, redistributing, or creating derivative works for commercial purposes without the express written consent of ADB.

6 ADB Avenue
Mandaluyong City
1550 Metro Manila
Philippines
Tel +63 2 632 4444
Fax + 63 2 636 2444
www.adb.org

First published in 2011 by

SAGE Publications India Pvt Ltd
B1/I-1 Mohan Cooperative Industrial Area
Mathura Road, New Delhi 110 044, India
www.sagepub.in

SAGE Publications Inc
2455 Teller Road
Thousand Oaks, California 91320, USA

SAGE Publications Ltd
1 Oliver's Yard, 55 City Road
London EC1Y 1SP, United Kingdom

SAGE Publications Asia-Pacific Pte Ltd
33 Pekin Street
#02-01 Far East Square
Singapore 048763

Published by Vivek Mehra for SAGE Publications India Pvt Ltd, typeset in 9.5/14.5 pt Helvetica Neue and printed at Artxel, New Delhi.

Library of Congress Cataloging-in-Publication Data Available

ISBN: 978-81-321-0756-9 (HB)

The SAGE Team: Rudra Narayan, Swati Sengupta, Rajib Chatterjee, and Umesh Kashyap

Contents

xi	**List of Figures, Tables, and Boxes**
xix	**List of Abbreviations**
xxiii	**Foreword**
xxv	**Acknowledgments**

1 Executive Summary
- 2 Makings of the Asian Century
- 2 Actions at three levels
- 2 National action agenda
- 4 Regional cooperation
- 5 Global agenda
- 5 Asian Century vs. Middle Income Trap
- 6 The intangibles

9 Chapter 1. Introduction
- 9 Why an "Asia 2050" study?
- 10 What is "Asia"?
- 13 Is the Asian Century preordained?
- 14 Structure of the book

Part I: Makings of the Asian Century

19 Chapter 2. Asia in the Global Economy in 1700–2010: Setting the Scene
- 19 Decline and reemergence: 1700–1970

20   Reaping the globalization dividend: 1970–2010
24   Three country groups

29   Chapter 3. Asia in the Global Economy in 2011–2050: The Main Drivers of the Asian Century

29   Classic drivers of economic growth
33   New drivers of Asia's social transformation
38   From growth to social well-being

43   Chapter 4. Asia in the Global Economy in 2050: The Asian Century

43   Basic assumptions
46   The Asian Century
46   Asia's growing output footprint
48   The engines of the Asian Century: Asia-7 economies

51   Chapter 5. Realizing the Asian Century: Mega-challenges and Risks

51   Inequality within countries
52   The Middle Income Trap
55   Competition for finite natural resources
55   Disparities across countries and subregions
56   Global warming and climate change
57   Governance and institutional capacity
58   Risk of conflict
58   Asia's expanding global footprint

Part II: Realizing the Asian Century

63   Chapter 6. Realizing the Asian Century: A Strategic Framework

63   Three dimensions
65   National action
68   Regional cooperation
69   Global agenda

73   Chapter 7. Growth and Inclusion

73   Introduction

73	What progress has Asia made?
74	Import substitution, export orientation, poverty, and inequality
77	Poverty reduction and the Millennium Development Goals (1990 to date)
78	What is inclusive growth?
79	Why focus on inclusion and equity?
80	What is Asia's status?
88	Action agenda

99   Chapter 8. Driving Productivity and Growth

99	Introduction
99	Why focus on productivity and entrepreneurship?
102	Productivity and entrepreneurship in Asia
105	Getting entrepreneurship and innovation right: PRC and India
112	Key elements of the entrepreneurship and innovation ecosystem
122	Overall policy framework
125	Priorities and action agenda

129   Chapter 9. A New Approach to Urbanization

129	Looking back 40 years at Asian cities
133	Asia's urbanization avalanche
133	Rural development and urban development are complementary
135	Cities of the future
139	Major risks to be managed
142	Priority agenda for moving to a better urban future
148	Visionary leadership

151   Chapter 10. Transforming Finance

151	Asia's financial rise: Past and present
153	Alternative scenarios of Asian finance in 2050
155	Implications of the Asian Century for Asian finance
157	Conventional wisdom in finance: The Great Recession of 2007–2009
158	Current reform proposals and Asia
158	Asia in the international financial architecture
159	Global reserve currency
160	Future Asian financial system: Taming finance to serve the real sector
161	Transformational changes to serve the real sector
162	Transforming business models for Asia's financial institutional structure

172	Regional cooperation and Asia's global financial leadership
174	Priority action plan for Asian finance in 2050
176	The importance of using global best practice
178	Asian finance as a global leader

181 Chapter 11. Reducing Energy Intensity and Ensuring Energy Security

181	Introduction
182	Historical perspective: Evolution over 40 years
188	Implications for energy security
191	Implications for climate change
192	Improving energy security through efficiency and diversification
196	Minimizing damage from sudden supply disruptions
198	Priorities for domestic action
201	Priorities for regional cooperation

203 Chapter 12. Action on Climate Change in Asia's Self-Interest

203	Emerging economies' contributions to global emissions
204	Impact of climate change: Business-as-usual scenario
207	Impact of climate change: Mitigation by developed countries only scenario
208	Impact of climate change: Complementary mitigation actions by developing Asian economies scenario
210	Transition to low-carbon economies
216	Adaptation and risk management
217	Global burden sharing

221 Chapter 13. Transforming Governance and Institutions

221	Analytic framework
224	The past 40 years
226	Governance challenges in Asia today
230	The corruption dimension
233	Drivers for change in governance and institutions
237	Key actors of institutional change
239	Principles and priorities

Chapter 14. Regional Cooperation and Integration — 245

- 246 The importance of regional cooperation for Asia's future
- 247 Cooperation instead of conflict
- 249 The state of play 40 years ago: Asia in disarray in 1970
- 249 Forty years of progress with regional economic integration: 1970–2010
- 256 Drivers of economic integration
- 257 Prospects for further economic integration
- 258 Contours of future cooperation and integration
- 261 Priority areas to facilitate regional cooperation
- 268 Institutions for regional cooperation
- 269 Prospects and institutional options

Chapter 15. Realizing the Asian Century: Asia's Role in the World — 275

- 275 Dramatic change in Asia's global footprint
- 276 Implications of Asia's global role
- 277 Global commons
- 277 Global trading system
- 277 Global shipping lanes, trading routes, and communications channels
- 278 Global financial system
- 278 Climate change
- 278 Global peace and prosperity
- 279 Relations with other parts of world
- 279 Development assistance
- 280 Impact of national and regional policies on others
- 280 Global governance
- 281 Managing Asia's rise

Chapter 16. Conclusion: Cost of Missing the Asian Century — 285

- 285 Tackling transformation
- 285 National action agenda
- 288 Regional cooperation agenda
- 289 Changing Asia's role in the world
- 289 Priorities across countries
- 290 Need for enhanced resilience
- 292 Cost of missing the Asian Century

294	The intangibles
299	**Appendix 1. Demographic Changes in Asia's Regions by 2050**
305	**Appendix 2. Model for Developing Global Growth Scenarios**
311	**Appendix 3. Asia's Technology Landscape**
319	**Appendix 4. Driving Productivity and Growth**
321	**Appendix 5. A New Approach to Urbanization**
325	**References**
359	**About the Editors, Authors, and Contributors**
367	**Index**

List of Figures, Tables, and Boxes

Figures

Chapter 2
20	2.1	Asia's share of global GDP 1700–2010
22	2.2	World GDP growth rate is steadily increasing
23	2.3	Developing Asia GDP growth, 1990–2015

Chapter 3
30	3.1	Asian total factor productivity (1990–2050) is converging with best practice
32	3.2	Working age population (20–64) will begin to decline in all Asian subregions (1990–2050)
33	3.3	Asia will account for 70 percent of the world's added capital stock between 2030 and 2050
35	3.4	PRC's middle class is about to take-off
36	3.5	India's middle class is about to take-off
37	3.6	Mobile phone subscriptions still have room for growth in PRC and India

Chapter 4
44	4.1	Conflicts by region
47	4.2	PRC and India's rise is more dramatic than historical precedents: Average increase in percentage point share of global GDP per decade

Chapter 6
64	6.1	Strategic framework

Chapter 7
76	7.1	Thailand: Poverty falling, inequality growing

Page	Figure	Description
82	7.2	PRC: Urban income deciles
83	7.3	Urban Gini coefficients
83	7.4	Spatial inequality: Human Development Index for country's highest- and lowest-ranking regions
84	7.5	Average years of school (age 15–19), lowest and highest income quintiles
85	7.6a	Men's level of education in India (%)
85	7.6b	Women's level of education in India (%)
86	7.7	Philippines: Prenatal care provision (%)
87	7.8	Indonesia: Hepatitis B vaccination coverage (%)
87	7.9	South Asia sanitation (%)
88	7.10	Gender inequality in Asia
91	7.11	Action agenda

Chapter 8

Page	Figure	Description
100	8.1	High growth in converging countries is increasingly a result of TFP improvement
101	8.2	Entrepreneurship is correlated with TFP levels
102	8.3	Asia's TFP has been growing fast due to very high growth in converging countries
103	8.4	TFP levels and growth rates
111	8.5	Trends in PRC scientific publications
113	8.6	Asia's ranking on Ease of Doing Business indicators varies by region and income/convergence level
114	8.7	Asia's physical infrastructure leaves much room for improvement
115	8.8	Education index scores are correlated with TFP levels
116	8.9	Asia must try harder on different education indices
117	8.10	High-income countries in Asia have high secondary and tertiary enrollment, but others are far behind
120	8.11	Asia's share of global R&D expenditure has been growing significantly and has surpassed the US
121	8.12	Asia is home to a significant share of world researchers
122	8.13	Asia's innovation scores vary markedly by subregions and convergence stage

Chapter 9

Page	Figure	Description
133	9.1	Northeast Asia will be the most urbanized region of Asia

140	9.2	Urban Gini coefficient (by country)
140	9.3	Urban Gini coefficients over time

Chapter 10

153	10.1	Baseline, 2009
154	10.2	Asian Century scenario, 2050
155	10.3	Middle Income Trap scenario, 2050
155	10.4	Two-scenario projections for the Asian finance sector landscape, 2009–2050
156	10.5	Two-scenario projections for the US finance sector landscape based on Asia's shares, 2009–2050
156	10.6	Two-scenario projections for the EU finance sector landscape based on Asia's shares, 2009–2050

Chapter 11

181	11.1	Asia will lead world energy demand
182	11.2	PRC and India will see a huge increase in energy-related carbon emissions
194	11.3	Growth of wind power capacity in India and PRC (MW)

Chapter 12

204	12.1	Developing countries account for a greater proportion of current emissions than the G20 Annex 1 countries
205	12.2	Three-quarters of the growth in combustion-related global emissions between 2002 and 2007 came from developing countries
209	12.3	Asia has the ability and incentives to address climate change
209	12.4	Action by Asian countries can significantly mitigate damage from climate change
210	12.5	Emerging market action significantly reduces sea-level rise
212	12.6	Major developing economies are responsible for a rapidly increasing amount of low-carbon energy technology patenting

Chapter 13

227	13.1	Asia has worsened in voice and accountability as well as political stability, but it has improved in other areas: Asia governance indicators (weighted by GDP)
228	13.2	Asia-7 has outperformed the rest of Asia in governance: Governance

228	13.3	Asia-7 has outperformed the rest of Asia in governance: Governance indicators (weighted by GDP)
229	13.4	Asia-7 has lagged behind the rest of the world in governance: Governance indicators (weighted by GDP)
229	13.5	Northeast Asia outperforms other subregions in control of corruption
230	13.6	Asia, including Asia-7, has underperformed the rest of the world in control of corruption

Chapter 14

248	14.1	Mutual trust: From conflict to cooperation
250	14.2	Average GDP growth rates of selected Asian economies and subregions, 1958–2007 (%)
251	14.3a	Evolution of intraregional trade shares: World
251	14.3b	Evolution of intraregional trade shares: Asia and the Pacific
253	14.4	East Asian exports in sectors with increasing returns to scale
254	14.5	Parts and components trade in East Asia, 1990 and 2003
255	14.6	Evolution of South Asia's parts and components trade, 1992–2008
255	14.7	PRC's share of India's imports of manufactured goods, parts and components, 1995–2007
256	14.8	Intra subregional trade costs in Asia and other regions
257	14.9	Selected Asian countries in the tariff-freight plane

Chapter 15

275	15.1	Asia's share of global GDP 1700–2050

Chapter 16

293	16.1	Asian Century vs. Middle Income Trap
294	16.2	Population without access to improved water supplies
295	16.3	Increase in non-urban paved road network density, 2011–2050 (%)

Annex 1

299	A1.1	Population changes in Asia's subregions, 2010 vs. 2050

Tables

Chapter 3
Page	№	Title
34	3.1	The West currently accounts for the bulk of global middle class spending, 2010
34	3.2	The Asian middle class will grow sharply over the next 40 years
37	3.3	Internet usage is skyrocketing globally, picking up in Asia

Chapter 4
Page	№	Title
47	4.1	The Asian Century: Asia will account for more than half of global output in 2050

Chapter 7
Page	№	Title
74	7.1	Poverty reduction in selected Asian countries, 1980–1990 (percentage of population under the poverty line)
75	7.2	Population living on less than $1.25 (PPP) per day (%)
81	7.3	Rising inequality in Asia (Gini coefficients)
86	7.4	Nutritional status of children in Pakistan (% of children below 2 standard deviations of mean)

Chapter 9
Page	№	Title
135	9.1	Asia's urban population will nearly double by 2050

Chapter 10
Page	№	Title
152	10.1	Global finance sector indicators, 2009 (% of GDP)
152	10.2	Global finance sector indicators, 2009 (% of assets)
166	10.3	Global capital markets, 2001 and 2008

Chapter 11
Page	№	Title
183	11.1	Past and projected energy demand and supply in Asia
189	11.2	Past and projected oil demand and import dependency (million barrels per day)
190	11.3	Gas demand and import dependency
193	11.4	Asia's energy demand and supply scenarios

Chapter 12

206	12.1	GEM cities feature prominently in the list of cities most exposed to half-meter sea-level rise
214	12.2	Nine of the ten cities with the worst air pollution (particulate matter) are in Asia
216	12.3	Substantial abatement opportunities that reduce costs are available
218	12.4	Climate change adaptation types and examples by sector

Chapter 13

223	13.1	Analytic framework for governance and institutions
234	13.2	Working age population (%)
238	13.3	Pressures for governance and institutional transformation—domestic

Chapter 14

254	14.1	Uneven economic integration in Asia and the Pacific to date

Chapter 16

293	16.1	Economic 2050 outcomes in two scenarios—Asian Century and the Middle Income Trap

Appendix 1

300	A1.1	Population changes in Asia, 2010–2050
301	A1.2	Projected growth of Asia's elderly population (number of people, age 65 and above, in millions)
302	A1.3	Asia's differential-speed demographic inflection years
303	A1.4	Projected GDP per capita (PPP) vs. share of aging population, 2050

Appendix 4

319	A4.1	Asia: GDP growth and TFP growth, 1970–2010
320	A4.2	Asia: Composition of growth, 1970–2010

Appendix 5

321	A5.1	Fifth fastest growing cities in Asia
323	A5.2	World mega cities with population over 10 million for 2010, 2030, and 2050
324	A5.3	Rates of urbanization by country: 2010 and 2050

Boxes

Chapter 3
39	3.1	Economists of consequence

Chapter 5
54	5.1	The Middle Income Trap: Unable to compete
59	5.2	Conflict in Asia: Risk and deterrence

Chapter 7
77	7.1	Asia and the Millennium Development Goals
82	7.2	The two faces of Asia
90	7.3	Inclusive growth in policy planning: PRC, India, and Cambodia
92	7.4	Vocational education and training
95	7.5	Food security: Rising demands and shrinking resources

Chapter 8
106	8.1	e-Choupal—building on a traditional platform
116	8.2	Asia's creative thinking deficit
119	8.3	PRC's rapid progress in tertiary education and research
123	8.4	Republic of Korea's transformation into a center of science and technology

Chapter 9
132	9.1	Seoul 1970 and 2010
134	9.2	Jakarta 1970 and 2010
137	9.3	Vision for a successful Asian city of 2050
138	9.4	"Compact city" concept

Chapter 10
169	10.1	Infrastructure finance
177	10.2	Supporting domestic capital markets

Chapter 13
222	13.1	Evidence of the impact of governance and development outcomes
231	13.2	What is corruption?
232	13.3	Corruption and impact on the poor

Chapter 14

248	14.1	Moving toward cooperation without conflict: learning the lessons of history
252	14.2	ASEAN: An example of constructive regional cooperation
259	14.3	Central Asia's triple integration opportunity
270	14.4	Regional cooperation and integration in South Asia
271	14.5	Proposals for new regional institutions

Chapter 16

291	16.1	Avoiding the Middle Income Trap

List of Abbreviations

ABMI	Asian Bond Market Initiative
ADB	Asian Development Bank
AEC	ASEAN Economic Community
AFC	Asian Financial Crisis
AfPak	Afghanistan–Pakistan
AFTA	ASEAN Free Trade Area
AI	artificial intelligence
AMF	Asian Monetary Fund
AMRO	ASEAN+3 Macroeconomic Research Office
APEC	Asia–Pacific Economic Cooperation
APG	ASEAN Power Grid
A*STAR	Agency for Science, Technology and Research (Singapore)
ASEAN	Association of Southeast Asian Nations
ASEAN+3	ASEAN plus PRC, Japan, Republic of Korea
ASEM	Asia–Europe Meeting
ASX	Australian Stock Exchange
B2B	business to business
BAU	business as usual
Bcm	billion cubic meters
BCG	Boston Consulting Group
BIMSTEC	Bay of Bengal Initiative for Multisectoral Technical and Economic Cooperation
BIS	Bank for International Settlements
BOMCA-CADAP	Border Management Program in Central Asia–Central Asia Drug Action Program
CAREC	Central Asia Regional Economic Cooperation
CCS	carbon capture and storage
CMDA	Calcutta Metropolitan Development Authority
CMI	Chiang Mai Initiative
CMIM	Chiang Mai Initiative Multilateralization
CO_2	carbon dioxide

CSP	concentrated solar power
DAC	Development Assistance Committee
DMZ	demilitarized zone
ECA	Economics of Climate Adaptation (group)
EED	energy efficiency and diversification
EFSF	European Financial Stability Fund
EIU	Economist Intelligence Unit
EMEAP	Executives' Meeting of East Asia and Pacific Central Banks
ERPD	Economic Review and Policy Dialogue
ESCAP	Economic and Social Commission for Asia and the Pacific (of the United Nations)
EU	European Union
FAR	floor-area ratio
FDI	foreign direct investment
FSB	Financial Stability Board
FTA	Free trade area
GCC	Gulf Cooperation Council
GDP	gross domestic product
GE	General Electric
GED	Global Entrepreneurship and Development Index
GEM	G–20 emerging market (economies)
GERD	government expenditure on research and development
GFC	Global Financial Crisis
GHG	greenhouse gases
GMS	Greater Mekong Subregion Program
GW	gigawatts
HIV-AIDS	Human Immunodeficiency Virus–Acquired Immune Deficiency Syndrome
HNWI	high net worth individual
HVDC	high voltage direct current
ICP	International Comparison Program (of the World Bank)
ICT	information and communications technology
IEA	International Energy Agency
IEO	Independent Evaluation Office (of IMF)
ILS	insurance-linked securities
IMF	International Monetary Fund
IMS	International Monetary System
IOSCO	International Organization of Securities Commissions
IPO	initial public offer
IT	information technology
KEPCO	Korea Electric Power Corporation

KMDA	Kolkata Metropolitan Development Authority
KWh	kilowatt hours
LEED	Leadership in Energy and Environmental Design
LIH	life and health insurance
LNG	liquefied natural gas
Mb/d	million barrels per day
MDB	Multilateral Development Bank
MDF	Municipal Development Fund
MDG	Millennium Development Goals
MER	market exchange rate
MFSC	Monetary and Financial Stability Committee (of EMEAP)
MNC	multinational company
Mtoe	million tonnes of oil equivalent
NIC	newly industrializing countries
NIE	newly industrialized economies
NSTB	National Science and Technology Board
ODA	Overseas Development Assistance
OECD	Organization for Economic Cooperation and Development
OTC	over the counter
P&C	property and casualty
PFM	public financial management
PII	Physical Infrastructure Index
PISA	Program for International Student Assessment
PM_{10}	particulate matter less than 10 microns in size
PPP	purchasing power parity
P-PP	public-private partnerships
PRC	People's Republic of China
RIA-Fin	Roadmap for Monetary and Financial Integration of ASEAN
SAARC	South Asian Association for Regional Cooperation
SAFTA	South Asia Free Trade Agreement
SASEC	South Asia Subregional Economic Cooperation
SCO	Shanghai Cooperation Organization
SME	small and medium enterprises
SPR	strategic petroleum reserves
TAGP	Trans–ASEAN GasPipeline
TAPI	Turkmenistan–Afghanistan–Pakistan–India
Tcf	trillion cubic feet
TFP	total factor productivity
TWh	terawatt hour

UAE	United Arab Emirates
UNDP	United Nations Development Programme
UNODC	United Nations Office on Drugs and Crime
VET	vocational education and training
VoIP	Voice over Internet Protocol
WBES	World Business Environment Surveys
WEF	World Economic Forum
WHO	World Health Organization
WTO	World Trade Organization

Foreword

The rapid rise of Asia during the last three decades of the 20th century is the most successful story of economic development in recent times. In the 21st century, Asia's rise has been equally impressive, notwithstanding the global financial crisis. Per capita income in developing Asia reached nearly $5,000 in purchasing power parity terms in 2010. Investment rates averaged 35 percent of GDP over the decade. The number of people living below the $1.25-a-day poverty line fell by 430 million between 2005 and 2010.

Developing Asia's V-shaped recovery from the recent global financial crisis and recession further proved its economic prowess and resilience. These achievements accent the region's potential over the next four decades to reach the per capita income levels of Europe today. By the middle of this century, Asia could account for half of global output, trade, and investment, while enjoying widespread affluence.

Many see the ascendancy of Asia—or "the Asian Century"—as being on autopilot, with the region gliding smoothly to its rightful place in destiny. But complacency would be a mistake. While an Asian Century is certainly plausible, it is not pre-ordained. When examining the region's economic and social prospects, one cannot help but notice its many paradoxes.

The world's fastest growing region remains home to majority of the world's extreme poor. "Factory Asia" may be a global hub for manufacturing and information technology services, but vast numbers of its people are illiterate and unemployed. While parts of Asia are aging rapidly, others have booming populations. The region holds the largest savings pool globally, but urgently needs massive investment in infrastructure and social services. Its financial sector remains largely underdeveloped. Asia is urbanizing fast, but its cities are becoming unlivable. While Asia requires massive resources to maintain its rapid development, global stocks of resources are dwindling. The Asian paradox offers both major challenges and opportunities.

Asia 2050: Realizing the Asian Century, a study commissioned by the Asian Development Bank (ADB), identifies these challenges and suggests ways they can be tackled. The book is candid in saying that Asian nations must act now—individually and collectively—to forge solutions. Delays and inaction will only make solutions difficult and costlier. Policies that worked when Asia was low-income and capital-scarce are less likely to work today and unlikely to work in the future.

And, as an emerging global leader, Asia must embrace, promote, and advance global public goods—whether free trade, financial stability, climate change, or peace and security.

The book reminds us that challenges and risks are not mutually exclusive. They could impact one another, generate conflict, or build new pressure points within Asia, jeopardizing regional economic growth, and financial stability and security. Asia's paradoxes are neither new nor easily resolved. Widening inequalities, environmental degradation, and the threat of falling into a Middle Income Trap can only be overcome by well-integrated strategies and policies, coupled with the required institutional reforms. Effective regional cooperation is the bedrock for Asia's peace and prosperity. Building trust to assure shared interest in trade, financial stability, and access to natural resources will happen gradually and require leadership at country and regional levels.

These are long-term, generational challenges. Failure to meet them will deprive Asians from reaching potential affluence and greater well-being. We hope that political and economic leaders, the private sector, academia, development practitioners, and civil society will find this book useful when crafting long-term strategies and country-specific development programs.

A study on this scale could only come out of intensive consultations and pooling of expertise from an array of experts. ADB's Office of Regional Economic Integration led this flagship project and many individuals contributed to the book. The book benefitted greatly from extensive country consultations. ADB's management team and I joined many of these. Feedback from the Governors' Seminar at ADB's 44th Annual General Meeting in May 2011 and the Asian Wise Persons' Group in June 2011 was particularly valuable.

Asia's march toward prosperity and freedom from extreme poverty will require more than simply high growth. An Asian Century is plausible if Asia builds on its success and focuses on innovation, entrepreneurship, inclusion, sustainable development, and good governance. The Asian Century may well be a century of shared global prosperity. But future prosperity must be earned. I firmly believe Asia's leaders will take up the bold and innovative national policies needed—while pursuing greater regional and global cooperation—to make the Asian Century a reality.

Haruhiko Kuroda
President
Asian Development Bank

Acknowledgments

ADB President, Haruhiko Kuroda, provided vision and inspiration for the *Asia 2050* study. His stress on intellectual rigor helped present a stimulating yet balanced perspective of the multi-generational challenges and opportunities facing Asia.

ADB Managing Director, General Rajat M. Nag, gave conceptual shape to this study and provided overall guidance. Iwan J. Azis, Head of ADB's Office of Regional Economic Integration (OREI), brought in his intellectual strength to lead the ADB team.

Important contributions were provided by ADB Vice Presidents, C. Lawrence Greenwood, Bindu N. Lohani, Ursula-Schaefer Preuss, Lakshmi Venkatachalam, Xiaoyu Zhao, and ADB Institute Dean, Masahiro Kawai.

Harinder S. Kohli, President and CEO, Centennial Group, the principal author and study director, gathered an international team of experts and worked tirelessly to put together this study. He, together with his two co-editors, Ashok Sharma, Senior Director, OREI, and Anil Sood, COO, Centennial Group, guided the authors to shape the thematic chapters of the book. The three editors together produced the final manuscript. Ashok Sharma also managed the ADB staff team, comprising Jayant Menon, Principal Economist, and Sabyasachi Mitra, Senior Economist, who contributed significantly to this study.

The core authors of the book are: Homi Kharas (Asia in the Global Economy in 1700–2010: Setting the Scene; and Asia in the Global Economy in 2011–2050: The Main Drivers of the Asian Century); Homi Kharas and Harpaul Alberto Kohli (Asia in the Global Economy in 2050: The Asian Century); Homi Kharas (Realizing the Asian Century: Mega-challenges and Risks); Harinder S. Kohli, Ashok Sharma, and Anil Sood (Introduction; Realizing the Asian Century: A Strategic Framework; and Conclusion: Cost of Missing the Asian Century); Jayant Menon, Sabyasachi Mitra, and Drew Arnold (Growth and Inclusion); Yasheng Huang and Y. Aaron Szyf (Driving Productivity and Growth); Anthony Pellegrini (A New Approach to Urbanization); Andrew Sheng (Transforming Finance); Hossein Razavi (Reducing Energy Intensity and Ensuring Energy Security); Cameron Hepburn and John Ward (Action on Climate Change in Asia's Self-Interest); Shigeo Katsu (Transforming Governance and Institutions); Johannes F. Linn (Regional Cooperation and Integration); and Harinder S. Kohli (Realizing the Asian Century: Asia's Role in the World).

Other contributors to the study are Amitav Acharya, Vinod Goel, Ramesh Mashelkar, Natasha Mukherjee, and Hans P. Binswanger-Mkhize.

The study benefitted from Jong-Wha Lee, former ADB Chief Economist, and Srinivasa Madhur, former Officer-in-charge, OREI, who helped in shaping the study during its formative period.

Country consultations provided valuable insights and perspectives. The study team benefitted from the views of the following: **Bangladesh:** Abul Maal A. Muhith (Minister of Finance) and Atiur Rahman (Governor, Bangladesh Bank); **People's Republic of China:** Zheng Xiaosong (Director General, International Department, Ministry of Finance); **India:** Montek Singh Ahluwalia (Chairman, Planning Commission) and Kaushik Basu (Chief Economic Advisor, Department of Economic Affairs); **Indonesia:** Hatta Rajasa (Coordinating Minister for Economic Affairs), Armida Alisjahbana (Minister for National Development Planning), Mari Elka Pangestu (Minister of Trade), and Emil Salim (Chairman of Council of Advisors to the President and Former Minister of Environment); **Japan:** Takehiko Nakao (Director General, International Bureau, Ministry of Finance) and Tatsu Yamasaki (Senior Deputy Director General, International Bureau, Ministry of Finance); **Republic of Korea:** Yoon Jeung-hyun (Minister of Finance), Jong-ryong Lim (Vice Minister, Ministry of Strategy and Finance), and Sung-gul Ryu (Vice Minister, Ministry of Strategy and Finance); and **Viet Nam:** Nguyen Van Giau (Governor, State Bank of Viet Nam) and Tran Xuan Gia (Former Minister of Planning and Investment; Chairman, Asia Commercial Bank). The study team would also like to acknowledge the views offered by senior policy makers, eminent economists, private sector leaders, and civil society representatives during the country consultations.

The study team gained from discussions with several think tanks and institutions. These included the Federation of Indian Chambers of Commerce and Industry; Central Institute for Economic Management, Viet Nam; Viet Nam Institute of Economics; Shanghai National Accounting Institute; Asia-Pacific Finance and Development Center, Shanghai; China Development Research Foundation, Beijing; Korea Institute for International Economic Policy; and Graduate School of International Studies, Seoul National University, Republic of Korea.

The Governors' Seminar at ADB's 44th Annual General Meeting in May 2011, provided the invaluable views of eminent policy makers, including Abul Maal A. Muhith (Minister of Finance, Bangladesh); Christine Lagarde (Former Minister for Economy, Finance and Industry, France; and incoming MD, IMF); Pranab Mukherjee (Minister of Finance, India); Li Yong (Vice Minister of Finance, People's Republic of China); Nguyen Van Giau (Governor, State Bank of Viet Nam); and Motoyuki Odachi (Parliamentary Secretary of Finance, Japan).

The study also benefitted from discussions of the Asian Wise Persons' Group in June 2011. The Group included Cesar E.A. Virata (Former Prime Minister and Minister of Finance, Philippines); Anand Panyarachun (Former Prime Minister and Minister of Finance, Thailand; and Chairman of the Board of Directors, Siam Commercial Bank); Emil Salim (Chairman of Council of Advisors to the President, and Former Minister of Environment, Indonesia); R.K. Pachauri (Chairman, Intergovernmental Panel on Climate Change; and Director General, The Energy and Resources Institute, India); Young-Hoon Kwaak (Professor, Jeju National University of Korea; and Founder/Chairman, World Citizens Organization); Phisit Pakkasem (Former Secretary General of National Economic and Social Development Board, Thailand); and Noritada Morita (Chairman and CEO, Asia Strategy Forum).

The study team appreciates the valuable inputs of senior ADB staff including Philip C. Erquiaga, Klaus Gerhaeusser, Juan Miranda, Sultan H. Rahman, Kazu Sakai, Kunio Senga, Changyong Rhee, Robert F. Wihtol, and Xianbin Yao. The study team also acknowledges the inputs of several ADB and ADBI staff including Noritaka Akamatsu, Gambhir Bhatta, Biswanath Bhattacharyay, Sekhar Bonu, Richard Bolt, Jorn Brommelhorster, Giovanni Capannelli, Jin Cyhn, Jesus Felipe, Edimon Ginting, Rana Hasan, Paul Heytens, Zahid Hossain, Xinglan Hu, Abid Hussain, Kavita Iyengar, Hoe Yun Jeong, Thevakumar Kandiah, Jong Woo Kang, Hun Kim, Ayumi Konishi, Mario B. Lamberte, Werner Liepach, Carmela Locsin, Anouj Mehta, Hiranya Mukhopadhyay, Omana Nair, Kuniki Nakamori, Krishnadas Narayanan, Thiam Hee Ng, Cuong Minh Nguyen, James Nugent, Stephen Pollard, Ann Quon, Vivek Rao, Jason Rush, Lei Lei Song, Meriaty Subroto, Anil Terway, Woochong Um, Victor L. You, Shahid N. Zahid, and Juzhong Zhuang.

The team of editors, Bruce Ross-Larson, Natasha Mukherjee, Richard Niebuhr, and Kevin Donahue worked together to give this report its final shape. Kathryn Grober of Centennial Group was responsible for putting together the final manuscript, with the help of Charlotte Hess in organizing, formatting, and checking the document.

Kothandan Balaji, Nguyen My Binh, Sheila David, Lan Thi Tuyet Duong, Mohammed Easin, Keiko Hamada, Maruf Hossain, Meenakshi Jain, Keiko Kawazu, Ma. Criselda Lumba, Tanaka Miwako, Akiko Mochizuki, Ma Nan, Carol Ongchangco, Wilhelmina Paz, Ma. Rosario Razon, Ayun Sundari, Jennifer Tantamco, Meity Tanujaya, Pia Tenchavez, and Charisse Tubianosa (staff); and Michael Bon Albarillo, Santiago Martin Barcelona, Kevin Donahue, Layden Iaksetich, Ivan de Leon, Aldwin Mamiit, Carlo Monteverde, James Ong, Lilibeth Perez, and Theresa Robles (consultants) contributed variously to project administration and logistics, arrangement and coordination of workshops, and consultation seminars.

Executive Summary

Asia is in the middle of a historic transformation. If it continues to follow its recent trajectory, by 2050 its per capita income could rise sixfold in purchasing power parity (PPP) terms to reach Europe's levels today. It would make some 3 billion additional Asians affluent by current standards. By nearly doubling its share of global gross domestic product (GDP) to 52 percent by 2050, Asia would regain the dominant economic position it held some 300 years ago, before the industrial revolution.

But Asia's rise is by no means preordained. Although this outcome is promising, premised on its major economies sustaining their present growth momentum, it does not mean that the path ahead is easy or requires just doing more of the same. Indeed, success will require a different pattern of growth and resolution of a broad array of politically difficult issues over a long period.

This outcome is fraught with multiple risks and challenges, particularly:

- Increasing inequality within countries, which could undermine social cohesion and stability.
- The "Middle Income Trap" for a host of domestic economic, social, and political reasons.
- Intense competition for finite natural resources, as newly affluent Asians aspire to higher standards of living.
- Rising income disparities across countries, which could destabilize the region.
- Global warming and climate change, which could threaten agricultural production, coastal populations, and numerous major urban areas.
- Poor governance and weak institutional capacity, faced by almost all countries.

These challenges are not mutually exclusive. They can affect one another and exacerbate existing tensions and conflicts, or even create new pressures that could threaten Asia's growth, stability, and security.

This book postulates two scenarios of Asia's future growth trajectory: the Asian Century and the Middle Income Trap. These scenarios are not the only ones—they are only two possibilities of how Asia's future may unfold. They have a dual objective: to draw attention to the longer-term implications of the broad trends and to ask "what-if" questions.

Makings of the Asian Century

The Asian Century scenario extends Asia's past success into the future, putting it on the cusp of a historic transformation. In this scenario, Asia's GDP (at market exchange rates) increases from $17 trillion in 2010 to $174 trillion in 2050, or half of global GDP, similar to its share of the global population. With a per capita GDP of $40,800 (PPP), Asia in 2050 would have incomes similar to Europe's today. It would have no poor countries (those with average per capita GDP of less than $1,000), compared with eight today. All this assumes that Asian economies can maintain their momentum for another 40 years and adapt to the shifting global economic and technological environment by continually recreating their comparative advantages.

Actions at three levels

In its march toward the Asian Century, the region must tackle daunting policy, institutional, and governance challenges. Given widely varying country conditions, the precise actions and their timing must vary. Still, it is possible to draw the contours of the major changes necessary for the region along three dimensions: national strategic and policy action; collective regional action to bridge the national and global agendas; and Asia's interactions with the global community. The ability of countries to realize the promise of the Asian Century will be determined by their success in these three areas.

National action agenda

Seven overarching intergenerational issues and strategic challenges require national action throughout the region.

Growth and inclusion. Growth and inclusion need not be mutually exclusive; indeed they can be mutually reinforcing. To sustain growth over the long-term, almost all Asian countries must give much higher priority to inclusion and reducing inequalities—rich/poor, rural/urban, literate/illiterate, and along gender and ethnic lines. Inclusive growth must not only address poverty, but also deal with aspects of equity, equality of access and opportunity, generation of employment and provision of protection to vulnerable in the various facets of daily living.

Entrepreneurship, innovation, and technological development. The continuing rapid growth of Asian economies over the next 40 years will require a harnessing of the full potential of technology, innovation and, critically, entrepreneurship. More Asian countries need to emulate Japan, Republic of Korea, and Singapore, and come closer to (preferably achieve) global best practice. The fast-growing converging economies, particularly PRC and India, must move from catching up to frontier entrepreneurship and innovation to create breakthroughs in science and technology. A particularly fruitful area will be inclusive innovation to meet the needs of those at the bottom of the pyramid. A core requirement is a high-quality education system at all levels that promotes creativity.

Massive urbanization. By 2050, Asia will be transformed, as its urban population will nearly double from 1.6 billion to 3 billion. Asia's cities, which already account for more than 80 percent of economic output, will be the centers of higher education, innovation, and technological development. The quality and efficiency of urban areas would determine Asia's long-term competitiveness and its social and political stability. Asia must take advantage of being early on its urbanization growth curve to promote compact, energy-efficient, and safe cities.

Financial transformation. As its share of global GDP rises to 50 percent or more, Asia should also have about the same share of the world's financial assets, banks, and equity and bond markets, etc. In transforming its financial systems, Asia's leaders must remain mindful of the lessons of the 1997–1998 Asian financial crisis and the Great Recession of 2007–2009. Asia will need to formulate its own approach to finance, avoiding both overreliance on market self-regulation and excessive central government control of bank-dominated systems. It will also need to become more open to institutional innovation, also to support inclusive finance.

Radical reduction in the intensity of energy and natural resource use. The anticipated affluence of some 3 billion additional Asians will put tremendous pressure on the earth's finite natural resources. Asia will be the most affected by, and responsible for, excessive reliance on energy imports. Out of self-interest, it will need to take the lead in radical energy efficiency and diversification programs by switching from fossil fuels to renewable energy. Asia's future competitiveness will depend heavily on how efficiently it uses its natural resources and progresses to a low-carbon future.

Climate change. Climate change could affect every human being on the planet. With over half the world's population, Asia has more at stake than any other region. Climate change has far-reaching implications for the way Asia needs to move forward: dramatically increasing energy efficiency and reducing reliance on fossil fuels; adopting a new approach to urbanization by building more compact and eco-friendly cities; relying much more on mass transit for urban dwellers and railways for long-distance transport; and changing lifestyles to alleviate pressures on finite natural resources.

Governance and institutions. The recent deterioration in the quality and credibility of national political and economic institutions (illustrated by rising corruption) is likely to become a binding constraint to growth in Asia. High-quality institutions will help fast-growing converging economies avoid the Middle Income Trap, and slow- or modest-growth aspiring economies to establish the basic institutions for moving toward sustained economic growth. Throughout Asia, an expanding middle class will exert new demands for greater voice and participation, greater accountability for results, and greater personal space. Although daunting, eradicating corruption is critical for all countries to maintain social and political stability and retain legitimacy. These common challenges all require effective governance, both at central and local levels. Asia must retool its institutions with an emphasis on transparency, accountability, predictability, and enforceability.

These intergenerational issues apply to most Asian economies, but their relative priority will vary over time, depending on the group a country belongs to at a given time.

High-income developed economies.[1] This group of seven economies—especially Japan, Republic of Korea, and Singapore—should lead the rest of Asia in two areas: making the scientific and technological breakthroughs that are crucial to Asia; and moving beyond high economic growth toward promoting broader social well-being.

Fast-growing converging economies.[2] Avoiding the Middle Income Trap should be the main objective of this group's eleven countries. They should—in addition to further reducing inequalities and consolidating the fundamentals of development—train a world-class, skilled labor force and build credible and predictable institutions that protect property rights (physical and intellectual) and allow fair dispute-resolution. Constantly improving the business climate will be key.

Slow- or modest-growth aspiring economies.[3] The highest priority of this group of thirty one countries—which includes low- and lower-middle-income economies—must be to raise economic growth toward that in their more successful Asian neighbors. They should focus on the fundamentals of development: faster and more inclusive growth by reducing inequalities through better education for all; infrastructure development; and major improvements in institutions, the business environment, and openness to external markets.

Regional cooperation

Regional cooperation (including integration) is critical for Asia's march toward prosperity. It will become much more important for a number of reasons: it will cement the region's hard-won economic gains in the face of vulnerabilities to global shocks; it could be an important bridge between individual Asian countries and the rest of the world; it can help those Asian economies that are rebalancing growth toward "internal" (domestic and regional) demand to fully open their markets to neighbors in the region; with development assistance, it can help reduce cross-country disparities in income and opportunities (which, if left unchecked, could generate instability or conflict); it can be a stepping stone for poorer countries to move up the value chain and maximize their growth potential; in technological development, energy security, and disaster preparedness, it can help respond better to global challenges, and yield significant synergies and positive spillovers; and, through managing the regional commons, it can contribute to Asia's long-term stability and peace.

Given its diversity, Asia will need to develop its own model that builds on its past positive

---

1 Brunei Darussalam; Hong Kong, China; Japan; Republic of Korea; Macao, China; Singapore; and Taipei, China.
2 Armenia; Azerbaijan; Cambodia; PRC; Georgia; India; Indonesia; Kazakhstan; Malaysia; Thailand; and Viet Nam.
3 Afghanistan; Bangladesh; Bhutan; Cook Islands; the Democratic People's Republic of Korea; Fiji Islands; Iran; Kiribati; the Kyrgyz Republic; the Lao People's Democratic Republic (Lao PDR); Maldives; Marshall Islands; Federated States of Micronesia; Mongolia; Myanmar; Nauru; Nepal; Pakistan; Palau; Papua New Guinea; the Philippines; Samoa; Solomon Islands; Sri Lanka; Tajikistan; Timor-Leste; Tonga; Turkmenistan; Tuvalu; Uzbekistan; and Vanuatu.

experience: a market-driven and pragmatic approach supported by an evolving institutional framework that facilitates free regional trade and investment flows throughout Asia, as well as some labor mobility. An Asian economic community must be based on two general principles—openness and transparency. Openness will be a continuation of Asia's long-standing policy of open regionalism, a key factor in East Asia's past success.

Crucial for increased regional cooperation is strong political leadership. Building Asia's regionalism will require collective leadership that recognizes a balance of power among participants. Asia's major economic powers, like PRC, India, Indonesia, Japan, and Republic of Korea, will be important in integrating Asia and shaping its role in the global economy.

Global agenda

Asia's growth and larger footprint in the global economy will bring new challenges, responsibilities, and obligations. The region will need to take greater ownership of the global commons. It will need to gradually transform itself from a passive onlooker in the debate on global rule making and a reticent follower of the rules, to an active debater and constructive rule maker. As an emerging global leader, Asia should act as—and be seen as—a responsible global citizen. When formulating its domestic or regional policy agenda, Asia will need to consider the regional and global implications. It will need to delicately manage its rapidly rising role as a major player in global governance non-assertively and constructively.

As Asia becomes the center of the global economy, it will be in its own interest that the rest of world also does well economically and politically. Peace and security throughout the world will be essential for its long-term prosperity. The Asian Century should not be Asia's alone but the century of shared global prosperity.

Asia's efforts to enhance regional cooperation must not be at the cost of its traditional openness to the rest of the world. Asia must adhere, as mentioned, to its long-standing strategy of open regionalism.

Asian Century vs. Middle Income Trap

The agendas in this book—national, regional, and global—are wide-ranging and require far-sighted leadership. The region has to face up to the daunting opportunity that lies before it. How many countries will meet this challenge? The answer is unclear. Given this reality and uncertainties about the various drivers, the book postulates two quantitative scenarios with very different outcomes.

Most of the discussion is based on the optimistic Asian Century scenario. This scenario assumes that the 11 economies with a demonstrated record of sustained convergence to best global practice over the past 30 years or so continue this trend over the next 40 years and that a number of modest-growth aspiring economies will become convergers by 2020. In this scenario,

Asia will take its place among the ranks of the affluent on par with those in Europe today; some 3 billion additional Asians will become affluent by 2050. This is the desired or ideal scenario for Asia as a whole.

The Middle Income Trap scenario assumes that these fast-growing converging economies fall into that trap in the next 5–10 years, without any of the slow- or modest-growth aspiring economies improving their record; in other words, Asia follows the pattern of Latin America over the past 30 years. This is the pessimistic scenario and could be taken as a wake-up call to Asian leaders.

There will be a huge difference in the outcomes of the two scenarios. The economic and social costs of missing the Asian Century are staggering. If today's fast-growing converging economies become mired in the Middle Income Trap, total GDP in 2050 would reach only $65 trillion, not $174 trillion (at market exchange rates). GDP per capita would be only $20,600, not $40,800 (PPP). Such an outcome would deprive billions of Asians of a lifetime of affluence and well-being.

The possibility of a "perfect storm" cannot be ruled out in thinking about Asia through 2050. A combination of bad macro policies, finance sector exuberance with lax supervision, conflict, climate change, natural disasters, changing demography, and weak governance could jeopardize Asian growth. In this worst case—or doomsday—scenario, Asia could stumble into a financial meltdown, major conflict, or regionwide chaos well before 2050. It is impossible to quantify this scenario, but Asia's leaders must be aware of the potential for such a catastrophe and avoid it at all costs.

The intangibles

Four overriding intangibles will determine Asia's long-term destiny. First is the ability of Asia's leaders to persevere during the inevitable ups and downs and to focus on the long term. The region's ability to maintain the current momentum for another 40 years will require continual adjustments in strategy and policies to respond to changing circumstances and shifting comparative advantages. This will place a tremendous premium on mature, far-sighted, and enlightened leadership. Second is the willingness and ability of Asia to emulate the success of East Asia to adopt a (so far) pragmatic rather than ideological approach to policy formulation and to keep a laser-like focus on results. Third is Asia's success in building much greater mutual trust and confidence among its major economies, which is vital for regional cooperation. And fourth is the commitment and ability of Asian leaders to modernize governance and retool institutions, while enhancing transparency and accountability.

Introduction

Chapter 1 — Harinder S. Kohli, Ashok Sharma, and Anil Sood

Looking at the title of this book, readers may have three sets of questions. First, why a study that looks at Asia's future 40 years from today? Second, how is Asia defined? Is it a single region or entity, or an agglomeration of a very diverse set of people and nations that happen to be geographically linked? What binds these diverse people and nations? And third, given Asia's extraordinary performance during the past few decades, is an Asian Century not a given by now?

This introduction addresses these questions before laying out the structure of the book.

Why an "Asia 2050" study?

This book is targeted at senior policy makers, top business leaders, and key opinion makers in Asia. It aims to help forge a consensus on a vision of and strategy for Asia's potentially historic rise among the global community of nations by 2050.

The book offers a long-term perspective of the Asian region as a whole rather than a short- to medium-term perspective of selected countries, subregions, or issues. This approach brings into sharper relief multigenerational issues and tradeoffs that are crucial to the long-term growth and well-being of the region and its people.

The book attempts to add insights in the following five respects, particularly:

- It challenges the growing perception that Asia's rapid rise in the global economy is inevitable, as if the region is on autopilot. The book highlights the significant risks that could lead to economic, social, and even political instability and, in turn, derail economic development and growth. This extensive list of risks includes continuing or increasing social disparities and inequities; the Middle Income Trap capturing PRC, India, and many others; and a steady decline in the quality and credibility of institutions (political, economic, judicial, or law-enforcement). Given the economic history of other once-successful regions and countries (notably Latin America), it cautions policy makers and business leaders against complacency.
- The book highlights new challenges that current middle-income economies, such as PRC, India, Indonesia, Thailand, and Viet Nam, will have to overcome in the next 40

years and that the newly industrialized economies (NIEs)[1] of Hong Kong, China; Republic of Korea; Singapore; and Taipei,China did not have to face during the past 40. These include intense competition for finite natural resources; the adverse impact of climate change; and the need to go beyond current global best practice.

- It outlines the prerequisites and strategy for Asia as a whole to continue its rapid development (such as a new pattern of growth, as well as a greater focus on inclusive growth and urbanization) while avoiding the Middle Income Trap.
- It examines the prospects and options for Asian regional cooperation and integration. It argues for an unhindered flow of trade and investment throughout Asia based on a bottom-up market-based approach, as well as greater collaboration among countries, permitting them to prosper together.
- The book highlights the opportunities and obligations that would arise out of Asia's rapidly expanding global presence. Managing this rise in a peaceful and harmonious manner will require patience and humility on the part of all major Asian players.

In setting the scene for discussing the various mega-challenges and the policy agenda to tackle them, the book presents two scenarios of Asia's long-term outlook. But these scenarios must be treated as what they are: two out of many possible scenarios. They are not point estimates or definitive projections.

What is "Asia"?

Asia is a wide and heterogeneous region—physically, socially, politically, and economically. It includes some of the world's largest, most competitive, and most sophisticated economies, such as Japan; Hong Kong, China; Republic of Korea; and Singapore. PRC, India, Indonesia, and Viet Nam are fast emerging as important global players. All these countries coexist with numerous small, underdeveloped, and often fragile economies such as Afghanistan, Nepal, and some Pacific islands.

With such diversity, defining Asia as a region beyond a geographic unit is a difficult task, one debated often. Even with the growing recognition of Asia as a rising economic and political power—as a region in itself—it is often perceived as an economic community (particularly the subregion of East Asia) without a shared political and ideological identity.

So, what is Asia? The notion that, given its size and diversity, it is merely an idealistic concept incorporating distinct subregions and people rather than a homogeneous entity is not correct. "Regions can be endowed with different meanings and be made to perform different functions—which meanings and which functions at a particular moment will depend as much on the perspective of the observer as on the phenomenon to be observed" (Camilleri, 2003, pg.2). The

---

1 This name was coined in 1970 when Hong Kong, China; Republic of Korea; Singapore; and Taipei,China were growing fast on the basis of rapid industrialization. Today, they are not "newly industrialized" and are heavily services oriented, but the name has stuck.

endowment of meaning is an evolutionary process wherein the region's identity can be defined depending on how, when, and by whom the question "What is 'Asia'?" is framed.

Defining the boundaries of Asia at any given point is a reflection of history, politics, economic links, evolving institutional frameworks, shared cultures and values, and attempts to forge a collective identity. "Remapping" of Asia by scholars based on these characteristics has led to emergence of "webs of regional connectedness" ranging from trade networks to coalitions of various interest groups (Pempel, 2005).

Given that the region encompasses such a large area (Asia as a geographic entity was originally conceived by Europeans as everything to the east of their own borders), it is understandable that the region hosts a wide range of races as well as cultural and linguistic traditions, making it hard to identify a definitive Asian culture or set of values. Still, many common traits are discernible.

With highly evolved civilizations in place before the arrival of the Europeans, the region was the cradle of several religions (Langguth, 2003). The prevalence of irrigated rice agriculture in the region gave rise to another feature: the importance of the self-sufficient village community as a social and political unit at the center of agrarian societies (Miller, 2004). In such societies, the needs of the village were usually prioritized over those of the individual.

Most of the region fell under foreign control from the 1500s to the early 1900s, an experience that fueled the nascent concept of a common regional identity and value system. The beginnings of a pan-Asian identity grew out of intellectual exchanges across the region. Early proponents of an Asian identity included Okakura Tenshin, Rabindranath Tagore, and Sun Yat-Sen. The works of Okakura and Tagore called for a common Eastern civilization without Western cultural, political, and military interference.

The 1990s witnessed a revival of the concept of common Asian values, strengthened by the region's impressive economic success, referred to as the "Asian miracle" by many. The region's dynamic growth was attributed to respect for authority, hard work, frugality, discipline, social harmony, and the primacy of the group over the individual. However, the foundation of this characterization was weak as the region's economic success (which was initially limited to East Asia) was partly a product of its ability to learn and adopt certain Western practices, such as emphasizing the role of technological innovation and trade liberalization in economic development (Mahbubani, 2008).

Progress in institution building in the region demonstrates that shared norms (particularly the concepts of nonintervention, soft institutionalism, and consensus decision making) are emerging as key features of the Asian regional identity (Acharya, 2005).

In recent years, many have cited increased trade and investment links within Asia as the defining characteristic of Asia as a region. Such links are not new, though, and date back to the precolonial period, with the Silk Road connecting western PRC to Central Asia and Iran via India.

Southeast Asia, with its strategic location on the international maritime route connecting PRC and the West, also produced a strong network that drove regional exchange and intraregional trade involving PRC and India (Shanker, 2003).

Related to this regional trade network was the East Asian tribute-trade system, which gave rise to the overseas Chinese diaspora and led to the growth of extensive trading communities across the region. These merchants dominated commerce and finance in much of East Asia and interconnected the local economies of the region (Arrighi, et al., 1996).

Thus, the shared experiences of being occupied by foreign powers, the consequent struggles with nation building after independence, and—much more recently—the 1997–1998 financial crisis have brought Asia together to varying degrees and in different ways.

The current focus on fostering regional economic cooperation and integration is centered on creating a pan-Asian economic community, which would also expand links to include both Central and South Asia. The "variable geometry" of institutional architecture in the region brings out the fluidity of defining Asia. Institutions and arrangements like the Association of Southeast Asian Nations (ASEAN), ASEAN Plus Three (and its derivative groupings), the East Asia Summit, the ASEAN Regional Forum (ARF), and the Shanghai Cooperation Organization (SCO) illustrate how the region can be defined not on the basis of shared heritage, or even territorial proximity, but on shared objectives, including one overriding common trait—the pursuit of rapid economic and social development encompassing almost 60 percent of the world's population.[2]

The promise of rapid economic growth and the ability to realize such aspirations were first seen in Japan's transformation to a rich country within the span of a generation (a feat since emulated by Hong Kong, China; Republic of Korea; Singapore; and Taipei,China). Malaysia and Thailand, once among the poorest countries, have solidly established themselves as upper-middle-income economies.[3] And the region's largest countries—PRC and India—are now advancing at an impressive pace to join the ranks of the rich. Bangladesh, Indonesia, Kazakhstan, and Viet Nam are growing rapidly. It is therefore no surprise that all Asia, despite its heterogeneity, aspires to emulate these success stories.

When considering Asia's economic and social prospects, the region's many paradoxes stand out. The world's fastest-growing region, it is still home to nearly half of the world's absolute poor (with per capita income of less than $1.25 a day). It has become the global hub of manufacturing and information technology services, yet vast numbers of its people are illiterate or unemployed.

---

[2] In this book, Asia is defined to comprise three Asian subregions: East Asia and the Pacific (including the Democratic People's Republic of Korea); South Asia; and Central Asia (including Iran). The 49 economies covered are: Afghanistan; Armenia; Azerbaijan; Bangladesh; Bhutan; Brunei Darussalam; Cambodia; the People's Republic of China (PRC); Cook Islands; the Democratic People's Republic of Korea; Fiji; Georgia; Hong Kong, China; India; Indonesia; Iran; Japan; Kazakhstan; Kiribati; Republic of Korea; the Kyrgyz Republic; the Lao People's Democratic Republic (Lao PDR); Macao, China; Malaysia; Maldives; Marshall Islands; Federated States of Micronesia; Mongolia; Myanmar; Nauru; Nepal; Pakistan; Palau; Papua New Guinea; the Philippines; Samoa; Singapore; Solomon Islands; Sri Lanka; Taipei,China; Tajikistan; Thailand; Timor-Leste; Tonga; Turkmenistan; Tuvalu; Uzbekistan; Vanuatu; and Viet Nam.
[3] With per capita income of $3,946–$12,196.

The rapid aging of societies is a particular concern in PRC, Japan, and Republic of Korea, but Pakistan, the Philippines, and many Central Asian republics still have high population growth rates. The region is home to the largest savings pool in the world and is the largest net lender to industrial countries, but has simultaneous massive unmet investment needs at home, particularly in infrastructure and urbanization. And in contrast to its superiority in manufacturing and information technology services, its finance sector is underdeveloped: it finds it more efficient to intermediate its savings in European and North American financial centers than to rely on its own financial markets.

Despite these paradoxes, the speed and extent of Asia's economic and social progress during the past 40 years are undeniable. Indeed, it remains unprecedented. In many respects, the region has become an object of global envy.

Is the Asian Century preordained?

Asia is booming. On many dimensions, Asia's development performance in the 21st century has been its best decade so far. Per capita income in Developing Asia reached nearly $5,000 in purchasing power parity (PPP) terms in 2010, having grown at 9.4 percent annually over the decade 2001–2010. Investment rates reached new highs, averaging 35 percent of GDP over the decade, suggesting enormous confidence in the region's future. Average annual export growth was 11.4 percent. Net inflows of private capital into the region averaged $83 billion a year. External debt fell to 14.5 percent of GDP. And the region accumulated foreign exchange reserves of $3.5 trillion.

Asian countries may have reduced $1.25-a-day poverty by 425 million people in 2005–2010, representing 93 percent of the global poverty reduction in this period (Chandy and Gertz, 2011). Asia is becoming a middle-income region. According to the International Monetary Fund (IMF), only eight Asian countries had per capita incomes of less than $1,000 in 2010.[4]

The aggregate numbers are of course heavily influenced by the two population giants, PRC and India, but development performance is impressively broad-based. Eleven developing Asian countries have grown at more than 3.5 percent per capita a year since 2000, a rate that doubles incomes in 20 years.[5] Four of the five top performers in the most recent Organisation for Economic Co-operation and Development (OECD) Program for International Student Assessment are Asian: Shanghai, PRC; Hong Kong, China; Republic of Korea; and Singapore (OECD, 2010).[6] On another metric, PRC, Japan, and Republic of Korea are among the top countries in terms of the number of patents registered by the World Intellectual Property Organization.

The region's quick V-shaped recovery from the Great Recession of 2007–2009 (or the global

---

4 Afghanistan, Bangladesh, Cambodia, the Lao PDR, Myanmar, Nepal, Tajikistan, and Timor-Leste.
5 Afghanistan, Bangladesh, Bhutan, Cambodia, PRC, India, Indonesia, the Lao PDR, Maldives, Sri Lanka, and Viet Nam. Data are from the IMF *World Economic Outlook*, October 2010. Afghanistan's high growth has been driven by rising aid flows.
6 This program assesses reading, mathematics, and science among 15-year-olds.

financial crisis) is another indicator of Asia's economic prowess and resilience.

Perception of Asia as a region has evolved through the years as the social, political, and economic milieu has changed. The recent transformations in Asia's development path and its social and political outcomes will set the parameters as to how the region's story in the coming years will be told. The key difference this time is that Asia is on the cusp of defining the story on its own terms.

Against this backdrop, it has become common to talk about the Asian Century, giving the impression that Asia's ascendency is somehow a given and that the only question is when PRC and India will become the world's largest and second-largest economies—as if the countries are on autopilot, gliding smoothly to their rightful destiny.

Hence the importance of recognizing that Asia faces several mega-challenges: large, and in some cases, rising inequities within countries that could alter the political and social fabric of the region; the risk of some countries falling into the Middle Income Trap for a host of economic, social, and political reasons; intense competition for finite natural resources (energy, other minerals, water, and fertile land) that will be unleashed in the next 40 years as some 3 billion additional Asians become much more affluent and strive to achieve even higher living standards; the potential sharp rise in disparities across countries and subregions if past differentials in relative growth rates continue to 2050, possibly destabilizing some countries and subregions; and global warming and climate change.

Beyond these is the overarching challenge of governance, where improvements will be key to overcoming all other challenges. If current trends in the falling quality of institutions and in rising corruption continue unchecked, the ability to sustain the growth momentum will be jeopardized.

Asian countries thus face a long list of challenges that must be tackled at national or regional level (or both) if they are to realize and sustain rapid economic growth.

These challenges are not compartmentalized. They can affect one another and exacerbate existing tensions and conflicts, or even create new pressure points in Asia that threaten its growth, stability, and security. If leaders fail to address the intergenerational issues—many of them in a collaborative and collective manner—they increase the risk of failure.

The book highlights these issues. Its central message is that, although Asia is in the middle of fundamental economic and social changes, its sustained progress for another 40 years is far from preordained. Asian faces formidable challenges in their quest for an Asian Century. Asia's leaders must be aware that its future prosperity will need to be earned, in the same way that developed economies earned their success over the past 40 years. Asia controls its own destiny.

Structure of the book

The book is divided into two parts, followed by a conclusion. Following this introduction, the first part has four chapters devoted to Asia's reemergence over the past five decades and its possible evolution of the Asian Century over the next 40 years. To set the scene for discussing Asia's future, Chapter 2 briefly traces Asia's economic history from the advent of the Industrial Revolution in the 1700s to the present (2010). Chapter 3 discusses the main drivers—demographics, capital deepening, urbanization, growth of the middle class and communications revolution—that will likely drive Asia's growth between now and 2050. Chapter 4 then reviews the context and main assumptions for the global economic and geopolitical conditions under which the Asian Century is expected to unfold. Chapter 5 warns political and economic leaders against complacency and highlights the mega-challenges that countries need to meet, singly and jointly, in their march toward the Asian Century.

The second part starts off by presenting a strategic framework and key elements of the policy agenda for realizing the Asian Century. It has nine additional chapters on: promoting growth, inclusion, and equality; driving productivity, innovation, entrepreneurship, and growth; developing a new approach to urbanization; transforming finance; reducing energy intensity and enhancing security; managing climate change; transforming governance and institutions; securing regional cooperation and avoiding conflict; and expanding Asia's role in global economic and political governance. Each chapter starts, where relevant, with a brief description of how Asia looked 40 years ago and its evolution to today, before discussing the importance of the chapter's topic to Asia's long-term economic and social prospects, key issues, implications for other topics, and priority policy agenda to tackle the challenges.

The Conclusion highlights the key findings and suggestions offered in the two parts. It also presents a summary of the costs of missing the Asian Century, not only in economic terms but also along the human dimension. If Asia succeeds in maintaining its current growth momentum for another 40 years, some 3 billion more Asians will become affluent by 2050 and enjoy a quality of life similar to that in Europe today. But if Asia stumbles, if the major Asian economies fall into the Middle Income Trap, Asia's total GDP will be less than half that. Billions of Asians will have to wait for another generation, or more, before enjoying the fruits of affluence. The chapter highlights the strategic issues that policy makers need to confront in order to avoid the Middle Income Trap.

PART I
Makings of t

Asian Century

Asia in the Global Economy in 1700–2010: Setting the Scene

Chapter 2

Homi Kharas

This chapter briefly traces Asia's economic footprint from the 18th century. The period 1750–1990 saw Asia's share of the global economy decline from about 60 percent to less than 20 percent (in PPP terms). The two recent decades have witnessed the beginning of a reemergence as Asia has climbed back to 28 percent of global output.

Decline and reemergence: 1700–1970

Many outsiders call Asia's recent economic success the rise of Asia. A more accurate term would be the reemergence of Asia.

Asia accounted for roughly two-thirds of the world's economy from earliest records until about 1700. Throughout this period, PRC and India were the largest economies in the world by a wide margin (although India was fragmented into many princely states). This was not because Asia was the richest region in the world. Western European countries have long enjoyed that distinction. Asia's strength was drawn from its massive size and population. Before the industrial revolution, the differences in per capita incomes between countries was much smaller than today, so the size of an economy more closely followed the number of people. With one or two exceptions, the Asian giants of this period are recognizable today as still the largest economies in the region—PRC, India, Japan, Republic of Korea, Iran, and even Thailand. In 1700, Asian economies had averaged a per capita income growth of no more than one one-hundredth of a percent a year for a millennium.

Western European countries were the first to unlock the secrets of per capita income growth. Between 1700 and 1950, the West grew much faster than Asia. In the 19th century alone, Asia's global share fell by half to 28 percent in 1900 and continued to fall to a low of some 19 percent around 1950 in PPP terms (15 percent in market exchange rates) (Figure 2.1). This was not because Asia was getting poorer, but because the West had become steadily richer for two and a half centuries while Asia had stagnated in per capita terms.

Asia started to reemerge after 1950, spurred by Japan. Japan's income had fallen by one-third because of the devastation of World War II, but the country recouped these losses by 1956. Rapid growth continued. Japan was the first economy to double its per capita income

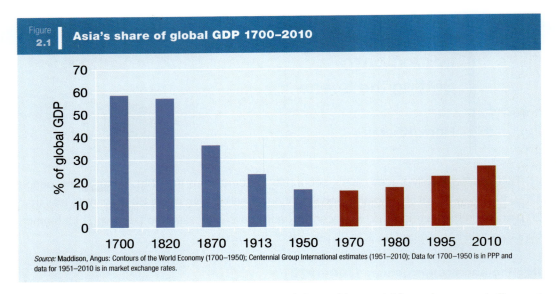

Figure 2.1 | Asia's share of global GDP 1700–2010

Source: Maddison, Angus: Contours of the World Economy (1700–1950); Centennial Group International estimates (1951–2010); Data for 1700–1950 is in PPP and data for 1951–2010 is in market exchange rates.

from previous highs in a single decade (1956–1965). It would repeat this performance in the next decade, but by then others were also starting to follow suit—the NIEs. The Asian miracle was already in full swing by 1970, although it would not acquire this name until the 1990s.

Reaping the globalization dividend: 1970–2010

By 1970, a few East Asian economies were driven by the ideas that economic growth was possible and that it should drive the national political agenda. Malaysia and Thailand—and PRC in the 1980s, followed by India, Indonesia, and Viet Nam—emulated the early globalizers, giving Asian growth a further boost. Today, Asia accounts for 28 percent of global output (at market exchange rates), almost double its low point in the 1950s.

Although the NIEs had authoritarian regimes, Japan did not, nor did many of the followers. Success appears to lie in the consistent, long-term focus on sustained economic growth, which the political leadership of all the fast-growing countries provided.

That long-term orientation was crucial for three reasons. First, East Asians saw exports, particularly labor-intensive manufacturing exports, as the primary engine of growth. But it is not easy to develop a strong export machine. Even though several of the early East Asian high-growth countries enjoyed trade preferences with the United States (US), many barriers to international trade remained. Companies incurred high costs in developing relationships with importing-country buyers, and only by amortizing them over years of sustained exports could they assure their profitability.

Second, the export-led strategy was complemented by significant spending on education at all levels. East Asian countries were among the first developing countries to achieve universal primary education, although they also heavily emphasized secondary and tertiary education. These investments, as with exports, paid off over the long-term, and it is a tribute to policy makers that they were prepared to take a long-term view of economic progress even when their countries faced great poverty.

Third, the Asian focus on long-term growth helped ensure that countries did not undergo frequent contractions. Unlike other developing economies (especially in Latin America) that had suffered from commodity-price and policy-induced booms and busts, the Asian miracle economies rarely saw their growth interrupted by recession—prudent macroeconomic policies made sure of that. And with little downside risk in the real economy and well-controlled inflation, fast-growing East Asian economies enjoyed high rates of savings, low interest rates, and high levels of capital accumulation. Investment in human and physical capital, in fact, was so high in many East Asian economies that Nobel laureate Paul Krugman dubbed the growth strategy as "all perspiration and no inspiration".

One other factor of the NIEs is noteworthy. They developed a significant middle class and this class sustained the growth initiated by exports.[1] The middle class in Asian countries more widely provided an important internal market to offset falling global demand, and was also a force for continuity in political and economic policies. The importance of the middle class is best illustrated by comparing the economic performance of Brazil and Republic of Korea. In 1979, Brazil's per capita income was $4,600 and it had grown at 9 percent annually for the previous 15 years. But from then, Brazil suffered a series of macroeconomic crises and was unable to sustain development. In 2005, its per capita income was still only $5,000—just 0.3 percent annual growth over 26 years. When Brazil got trapped and its economy stalled, its middle class was only about one-quarter of its population, thanks to the steep inequality of income distribution.

Republic of Korea reached an income level of $4,600 (the level at which Brazil stalled in 1979) in 1986. Since then, it has continued to grow rapidly, reaching over $18,000 in 2010, despite the shocks of the 1997–1998 Asian crisis, the 2001 dot com crash, and the recent Great Recession. Of course, Republic of Korea changed its growth strategy significantly, achieving a transition to a knowledge economy. But it could do this in part because of its sizable middle class. In 1986, its middle class represented 55 percent of the population, over twice Brazil's proportion at that income.

The same phenomenon of a large middle class has been seen in other fast-growing economies. Japan's middle class in 1965, when income levels were $4,900, was also 55 percent. Malaysia, Poland, the Russian Federation, and Thailand all have large middle classes. Among Asian middle-income countries, only PRC, India, and Indonesia have as small a middle class as Brazil did in 1979 (but India and Indonesia are still much poorer, so have time to develop it).

---

1 The initial impetus for equality in Republic of Korea and Taipei,China came from land reform. Following that, productivity increases in labor-intensive manufacturing allowed wages to rise rapidly contributing to growth with equity.

The Asian miracle was interrupted by the Asian crisis in the late 1990s. Through a combination of real GDP contraction and exchange rate adjustments, Asia lost almost 20 percent of its GDP at market exchange rates. It started to recover quickly before being hit again by the dot com crash that severely affected East Asia's substantial semiconductor industry. Asia's GDP did not recover to its previous level until 2004.

The more recent Great Recession promises to signal a turning point in Asia's fortunes relative to the rest of the world. Other economies slowed significantly, but Asia continued to grow. The NIEs, Thailand, and some small Pacific island economies had recessions in 2009, but virtually all rebounded strongly in 2010. Asia's share of global GDP at market exchange rates may increase by as much as 4 percentage points over the full cycle of the recession (2007–2011). The fact that Asia could continue to grow despite the huge impact on its exports suggests that the export-led model of Asia can already be balanced by domestic demand, at least in the short term.

In the wake of the Great Recession, there is a tendency to forget the extraordinary global boom that immediately preceded it and to wonder if the temporary stimulus measures adopted by Asian economies can sustain growth if the global economy does not recover. These fears may be overblown. Looking at the last 10 years and at IMF projections for the next 5 years suggests that, even taking the recession into account, global output is on a rising trend that should continue over the medium term (Figure 2.2). This is unsurprising. As the share of rapidly growing emerging markets in global output grows, so too does the average global rate. Trend growth in world GDP accelerated from 3 percent in 1990 to 4 percent in 2010, and based on IMF projections to 2015 is set to continue at that pace for the next few years.

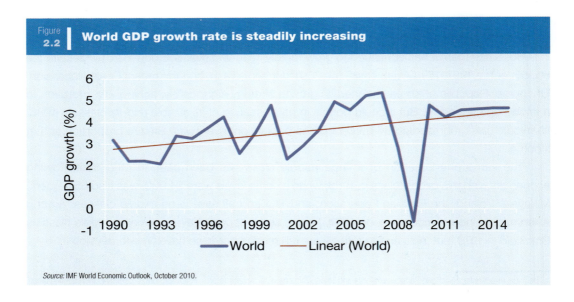

Figure 2.2 | World GDP growth rate is steadily increasing

Source: IMF World Economic Outlook, October 2010.

The same pattern holds for the developing countries of Asia (Figure 2.3). In 1990 trend growth was around 7 percent. By 2010 it had increased to around 8.5 percent, and actual growth was above this trend line. The period covers the Asian crisis, the dot com crash, and the recent recession. If not for these events the trend line would be even steeper, thanks largely to PRC's continued superior growth performance and India's acceleration of growth since 2004. But other emerging markets in the region—Bangladesh, Cambodia, Indonesia, Kazakhstan, and Viet Nam—have also been growing strongly.

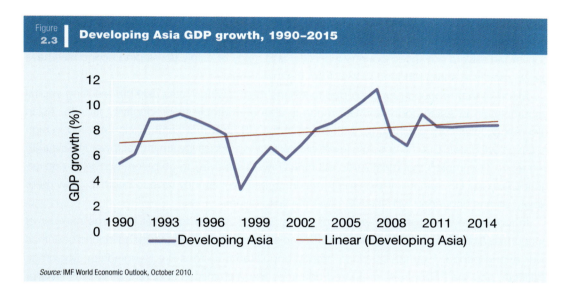

Figure 2.3 | Developing Asia GDP growth, 1990–2015

Source: IMF World Economic Outlook, October 2010.

Large structural changes in the world economy—spurred by globalization—are accelerating the pace of growth. These are being led by the integration of PRC into the world economy, symbolized by its accession to the World Trade Organization (WTO) in 2001, as well as the opening of formerly closed economies in the former Soviet Union and Eastern Europe. But globalization has not just been about expanding the global marketplace. The rapid development of information, communication, and transportation technologies has fostered faster growth, allowing an ever more granular division of labor, extending beyond goods markets into services. Indeed, services have been the fastest-growing component of global exports by a wide margin.

Capital flows have also fueled globalization. Net private financial capital flows from rich to emerging economies in 1990–2010 totaled $4.3 trillion (2010 dollars). Even though much of this was returned to rich countries through foreign exchange reserve accumulation, the gross flows are important. In the more recent years, many emerging economies have themselves become major investors in rich countries and in other emerging markets. They reflect the private sector's business flows and a more efficient global reallocation of capital.

One group of countries that has not seen growth accelerate despite globalization is the NIEs. Like other countries that have rapidly converged with advanced-country incomes, they have seen their growth level off. In 1990 they were growing at 8 percent a year, but by 2010 this was cut in half. In 1990, their per capita income was $9,550 (PPP), half that in the advanced countries. By 2010, the Asian NIEs had an average income of $34,120 (PPP), or 90 percent of that in the advanced countries. Having come so close to the global best practice economies, it is no surprise that their growth has slowed.

All these trends in the period of globalization since 1970 have therefore allowed Asia's share in the world economy to grow fast, to 28 percent. A small number of Asian economies have converged toward advanced-country incomes, and many of Asia's developing economies have grown rapidly. A sharp rebound indeed from the mid-1950s.

Much of that rebound has been due to Asians' high savings rates and the resulting capital accumulation in Asian countries. But much is also attributable to productivity growth. Asian technology levels are catching up with those in the US, and that catch-up is reflected in high Asian growth rates. But the absolute levels of total factor productivity are still far lower in Asia than in the US. This implies that most Asian countries have a long way to go before achieving convergence with the US, and it is therefore premature to believe that they have to begin to grow more slowly, as has happened with the NIEs over the last 20 years.

In looking at the aggregate weight of Asia's GDP, it is easy to forget the large number of economies that have yet to demonstrate they can successfully converge with advanced countries over a long period. Examples include heavily populated countries like Bangladesh, Myanmar, Pakistan, and the Philippines, mid-sized countries like Afghanistan and Iran, as well as smaller countries like the Pacific islands and most Central Asian economies. Asia has 31 of these economies. Their economic weight is small—only around 6 percent of Asia's total GDP—so their growth performance may not contribute significantly to Asia's overall rise, but they are nevertheless critically important for sustained Asian growth. As discussed below, although successful Asian economies have until now been able to grow thanks to their leverage of global demand, they will remain vulnerable to spillover from economic crises in the slow-growing and fragile Asian economies.

Three country groups

Based on Asia's economic record since 1970, it is possible to classify the region's 49 economies into three groups by economic performance.

- *High-income developed economies.*[2] These seven economies, led by Japan, triggered Asia's reemergence from the 1950s. They mastered the complex challenges of sustaining

---

[2] Brunei Darussalam; Hong Kong, China; Japan; Republic of Korea; Macao, China; Singapore; and Taipei, China.

high productivity and economic growth over an extended period and avoided the Middle Income Trap, as they steadily moved from low- to middle-income and, more recently, high-income status. Their productivity gap with global best practice (the US) is now relatively small. Their per capita incomes and living standards approach those of the developed economies of North America and Europe. These economies still account for a significant fraction of Asia's total economic output—$7.4 trillion, or 42 percent in 2010. For the rest of Asia, these economies are an important market, as well as the frontier locations for much of the region's research and innovation. In fact, as the region becomes increasingly dependent on productivity growth, the relevance of these seven rich economies for the region will only increase as a role model and pace setter, even if the rate of growth of their GDP remains well below that of the second group.

- *Fast-growing converging economies.*[3] These 11 countries, led by PRC and India, meet the criteria of the Commission on Growth and Development for sustained long-term success. Its Growth Report, along with many academic studies, concluded that development success could not be measured by performance over a single decade, but by long-term performance (Commission on Growth and Development, 2008). It suggested a 25-year horizon at least. Most of the countries in this group are middle-income countries and are still vulnerable to the Middle Income Trap. Their success in avoiding that trap will determine whether they join the first group, and in fact their current trajectory puts most of them in that group by 2030. These countries today account for 77 percent of Asia's population and 52 percent of GDP.

- *Slow- or modest-growth aspiring economies.* The largest group in number, these 31 countries encompass large and small, low- and lower-middle-income countries. Their average growth rate over the past 30 years has been well below that of the second group. A few countries have shown occasional bursts but these were followed by stagnation or decline. Some countries like the Philippines and Sri Lanka exhibit the classic signs of the Middle Income Trap. This group's overall share of Asia's total population and GDP is modest, at 17 percent and 6 percent. Yet improvements in their economic and social development are essential to reduce cross-country disparities and thus ensure the region's long-term peace and security.

These groups are not set in stone. Some aspiring economies may well join the ranks of the convergers in the not-too-distant future: Bangladesh, Kazakhstan, and Viet Nam are good prospects. Equally, some convergers may falter: Malaysia and Thailand have shown signs of vulnerability.

The three groups will have different imperatives and obligations in determining Asian economic outcomes over the next 40 years. The high-income economies will drive innovation and

---

3 Armenia, Azerbaijan, Cambodia, PRC, Georgia, India, Indonesia, Kazakhstan, Malaysia, Thailand and Viet Nam.

technology. Convergers will generate most of Asia's economic growth and provide an alternative to faltering demand in the West. And the performance of the aspiring economies will dictate, to a considerable degree, whether Asia's rise will be smooth or be disrupted by fragility, crisis, and possibly conflict.

Chapter 3

Asia in the Global Economy in 2011–2050: The Main Drivers of the Asian Century

Homi Kharas

This chapter discusses the main drivers of Asia's economic and social transformation to 2050. It first discusses the three classic drivers of economic growth: technological change, labor, and capital. It then elaborates on two other drivers of social transformation particularly relevant to Asia: the emerging middle class, and the communications revolution. These drivers are complementary and could, in fact, be mutually reinforcing. Finally, it draws attention to the debate on growth versus social well-being and personal happiness.

Classic drivers of economic growth

The basic dynamics of Asian—and global—growth depend on three fundamental factors: technical progress (total factor productivity growth), labor force growth, and capital accumulation.

Technological change and productivity

One useful way to view Asia's growth potential through technological change and productivity growth is to separate countries into the three groups based on their past performance described earlier:
- The first group contains the seven high-income developed economies.
- The second group comprises the 11 countries of demonstrated ability to converge with US productivity (taken here as representative of what advanced countries have achieved in technological growth) and can be expected to continue to do so, albeit at a pace that slows as they approach US productivity levels. Many of the larger economies (PRC, India, Indonesia, Kazakhstan, Malaysia, Thailand, and Viet Nam) are in this group.
- The 31 countries in the third group—mostly low-income—have not converged consistently. They may have grown faster than the US thanks to high levels of labor force growth and capital investment, but they have not shown sustained productivity growth. These countries could continue to have modest growth, especially once favorable demographic forces reverse or capital accumulation starts to slow. But they too can join the convergers' group if they improve productivity sustainably.

Of course, the global technology frontier itself is constantly improving, by around 1.3 percent a year (Appendix 2). So even the rapid adopters have much room to grow. By 2050 the global technology frontier could shift out by two-thirds, meaning that converging countries approach the frontier more slowly than otherwise. But by the time they have absorbed today's technology, they will have new possibilities to exploit (Figure 3.1).

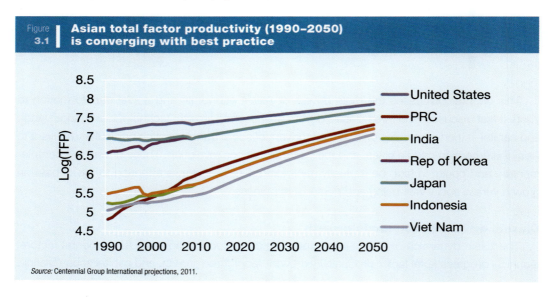

Figure 3.1 Asian total factor productivity (1990–2050) is converging with best practice

Source: Centennial Group International projections, 2011.

Modeling technological advancement in this way is highly stylized. The reality is that countries both adopt existing technology (adapting it to their own circumstances by changing production processes) in some areas, and leapfrog in others. In Asia, upgrading product lines (and discontinuing the outmoded ones) is the most common form of technological progress, followed by introducing new product lines or new technology (Gill and Kharas, 2007).

Much Asian research and development is conducted by the business sector, shortening the time between new ideas and their adoption in new commercial ventures. Many Asian economies spend a higher proportion of their GDP on research and development than countries elsewhere. This is especially pronounced in the advanced economies like Japan; Republic of Korea; Singapore; and Taipei,China, but is also increasingly true for PRC.

Asian technology has reached or is close to the global cutting edge in many areas of electronics, computers, information technology services, communications, pharmaceuticals, and biotechnology. The fact that in these areas technology is being increasingly developed in Asia raises the promise of technology's spread to other Asian countries. Patent citations suggest that knowledge spillovers are geographically concentrated. The closer to the source of innovation, the faster its adoption. This might appear surprising in an age of freely flowing written information and access to scientific journals. But it is consistent with the notion that what is written down is only a small fraction of useful knowledge for firms. The larger fraction, tacit knowledge, requires personal interaction to increase understanding and dissemination.

Demography and the labor force

Over the last two decades, the world has benefited from a demographic dividend. The number of people aged 20–64, traditionally taken as the potential labor force, has grown. About 560 million people joined the global labor force in the 1990s, and almost 640 million more in 2000–2010.

That dividend is now slowing, and will lose steam by around 2035. An ever smaller absolute number of workers will enter the global labor force, largely due to slower population growth rates in advanced and (some) emerging economies. By 2050, global labor force growth will be essentially flat, at perhaps 0.2 percent.

The labor force will reflect three offsetting trends. In some countries, especially emerging markets, a far higher proportion of youth will complete secondary school and get some tertiary education. Also, in countries such as India and Indonesia, the current large gap in participation rates of males and females will narrow, increasing the total number of workers. And in advanced countries, more of the elderly could remain in the labor force. Whether the global labor force expands or contracts depends on the sizes of these three trends. It does seem clear, however, that the rate of increase that has helped power the global economy is set to decline.

Asia reflects these trends. Its labor force has been growing at 1.8 percent a year over the last two decades. In the next two, that will fall to 1.0 percent a year. In the two following decades (2031–2050), Asian labor force growth will likely become flat.

This aggregate conceals vast differences between Northeast Asia, where the labor force is already peaking and about to decline, and other parts of Asia still seeing robust growth (Figure 3.2). In Japan, the labor force peaked in around 2000 and has been declining in absolute terms ever since, at about 800,000 workers a year. By 2050, Japan's labor force could be almost 25 million workers smaller than today's, a drop of one-third. Republic of Korea and Taipei,China are going through demographic transitions similar to Japan's, but with a lag of 15–20 years. For both, the labor force is likely to peak in the next 5–10 years and then start to decline at a pace similar to Japan's—1.3 percent to 1.5 percent a year.

The demography of Asia's giants is different. PRC is closer to Northeast Asia in that its labor force is still growing, albeit more slowly than before, and will also probably peak in around 2020. India, by contrast, still has a young population, and its labor force will continue to grow before reaching nearly 1 billion by 2050, when the country will have 41 percent more workers than PRC (versus 23 percent fewer workers today). This is one reason for India's projected higher economic growth than PRC over the longer term.

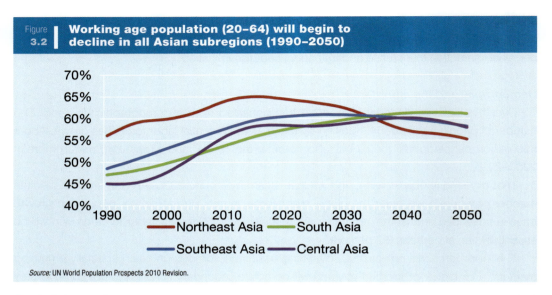

Figure 3.2 Working age population (20-64) will begin to decline in all Asian subregions (1990–2050)

Source: UN World Population Prospects 2010 Revision.

Capital deepening

Notwithstanding the huge investment rates of countries like PRC and India in recent years, most of the world's capital stock—about 70 percent—is in advanced economies. Small European countries, like Denmark, Finland, Norway, and Switzerland, have the world's highest capital stock per worker. Japan also has a capital stock per worker above the developed-country average.

But it is in the emerging Asian economies where the growth of this metric during the past two decades has been the fastest, with India at 8.3 percent, PRC 8.6 percent, Viet Nam 9.3 percent, and Cambodia 9.5 percent—among the fastest anywhere. Another tier of Asian economies, including Indonesia; Malaysia; Singapore; Taipei,China; Thailand; and Turkmenistan, are deepening capital at 5–6 percent a year, while Bangladesh, Kazakhstan, the Kyrgyz Republic, Pakistan, and the Philippines are showing only 2–3 percent growth in the capital–labor ratio.

As economies get richer and more capital intensive, it is harder to accumulate capital. Simply maintaining net capital levels requires an increasing proportion of investment to be used in replacing obsolete capital, leaving less to be added to new machinery. For rapidly growing economies, the rate of obsolescence is also greater.

But the world is entering an investment boom. Today, $5 trillion is added each year to the global capital stock.[1] In 20 years that could double to $10 trillion annually, and by 2050 it could double again. Most of this capital accumulation is in Asia (Figure 3.3). Already about 45 percent of net additions to the world's capital stock are in Asia. As PRC, India, and other dynamic Asian economies with high investment rates get richer, their absolute additions to the global capital

---

1 In 2007 dollars.

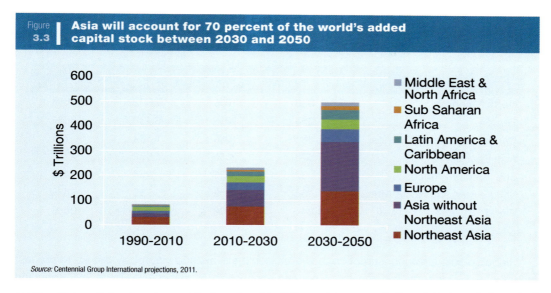

Figure 3.3 Asia will account for 70 percent of the world's added capital stock between 2030 and 2050

Source: Centennial Group International projections, 2011.

stock will rise. Asia already contributes about half the net increase in the global capital stock. If the trend continues, that proportion will be almost three-quarters by 2050.

New drivers of Asia's social transformation

Beyond the three classic drivers, Asia's economic and social transformation is expected to be driven by two other significant trends: the emerging middle class and the communications revolution.

The emerging middle class

The middle class will become a key driver of Asia's economic growth both because of its demand for goods and services and because it is the source of savings and of the entrepreneurship that drives new products and processes. Growth in today's advanced economies comes mainly from new products, and most growth happens when these new products are targeted toward and adopted by the middle class.[2]

Consumption by the global middle class accounts for almost one-third of total global demand, roughly divided between North America, Europe, and Asia, but heavily concentrated in advanced countries, which account for two-thirds of total middle class consumption (Table 3.1). These are the consumers at risk of retrenching their demand. In the Asian Century scenario (Chapter 4), middle class consumption in advanced countries rises by only 0.6 percent a year for the next 20 years and then declines.

---

[2] The middle class is defined here in the same way as in Kharas (2010) to include those living in households spending $10–$100 a day in PPP terms.

Table 3.1: The West currently accounts for the bulk of global middle class spending, 2010

	Number of People (millions and global share)		Consumption (billions PPP US$ and global share)	
North America	338	18%	5,602	26%
Europe	664	36%	8,138	38%
Central and South America	181	10%	1,534	7%
Asia Pacific	525	28%	4,952	23%
Sub-Saharan Africa	32	2%	256	1%
Middle East and North Africa	105	6%	796	4%
World	1,845	100%	21,278	100%

Source: The Brookings Institution, 2010.

Global middle class consumption, however, could still expand vigorously thanks to the fast growth of the middle class in dynamic emerging economies, mostly in Asia (Table 3.2). Spending by the Asian middle class could rise by 9 percent a year through 2030 (although Japanese middle class spending—one-third of all Asia's today—is forecast to rise by only 1 percent a year). This will be driven by the very strong growth in spending in the large Asian countries—PRC, India, and

Table 3.2: The Asian middle class will grow sharply over the next 40 years

	2030			2050		
	Middle Class Population	Upper Class Population	GDP per capita (PPP)	Middle Class Population	Upper Class Population	GDP per capita (PPP)
PRC	1110	45	$23,400	1100	205	$52,700
India	1280	15	$14,100	1485	205	$40,700
Indonesia	240	5	$15,100	240	55	$42,100
Japan	100	25	$53,000	40	70	$81,000
Republic of Korea	35	15	$56,000	15	30	$90,800
Viet Nam	80	2	$12,700	90	15	$34,200
World	5160	615	$20,300	5875	1625	$37,300
US	180	185	$65,800	125	280	$94,900
Germany	50	30	$51,500	25	50	$76,300

Note: Population figures given in millions.
Source: Centennial Group International projections, 2011.

Indonesia.

This growth has already started in PRC. Housing ownership in urban areas is over 80 percent, one of the highest rates in the world. College enrollments climbed to 26 million in 2009. Some 26 million automobiles were registered the same year, with sales of 13.6 million units. By the end of 2008, 150 million credit cards were in circulation. And there are an estimated 700 million cell phone subscribers.

But these anecdotal data conceal the modest role of PRC's middle class in the economy. In 2009, household final consumption expenditure was only 35.7 percent of GDP, well below the global average (61 percent) and that of Viet Nam (66 percent), Indonesia (63 percent), India (54 percent), and Thailand (51 percent). It is also much lower than the country's historical share. Since 2000, consumption growth has averaged 2.5 percentage points less than GDP growth. Finally, its middle class is small for an economy its size: no more than 12 percent of its people have living standards that would place them among the world's middle class.

PRC has long acknowledged the need to expand domestic demand, but so far has been unable to do this. Some changes are long term and structural, like improving public health, education, and pensions so that households do not need to save as much. Others are more immediate. The take-home pay of a PRC worker is only about two-thirds of total compensation. The remainder is taxed by the government through social insurance costs, government-mandated labor taxes, and insurance for health, unemployment, and the like (Bannister, 2005). PRC has the fiscal space to reduce these taxes using, perhaps, dividends and profits from state-owned enterprises. If the country achieves the new plan's target of increasing household expenditure at least as rapidly as GDP, the size of its middle class will explode. By 2030, if growth continues

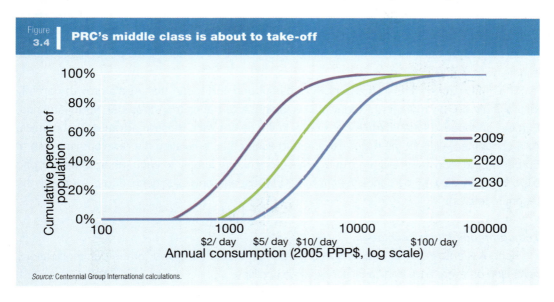

Figure 3.4 **PRC's middle class is about to take-off**

Source: Centennial Group International calculations.

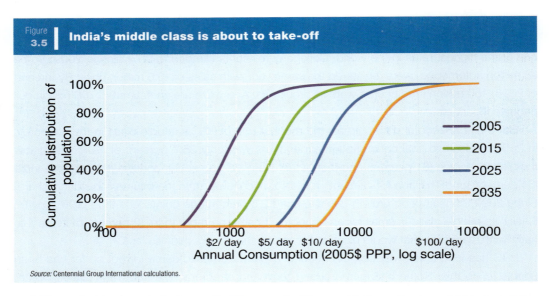

Figure 3.5 India's middle class is about to take-off

Source: Centennial Group International calculations.

and if households share in that growth, 75 percent of the population will enjoy middle class living standards, and $2-a-day poverty will be largely wiped out.

In the other dynamic Asian economies there is even more reason to believe that household incomes will expand by at least the growth rate of GDP and that this process will bring more households into the middle class. Combining growth with current income distribution parameters can be used to estimate the size of the middle class and the growth of its consumption for the next 20 years: India and Viet Nam (19 percent), Indonesia (13 percent), Thailand (8 percent), and Malaysia (7 percent). Low-income countries, like Cambodia, could also enjoy rapid increases in middle class consumption but from a very small base. Today, India has a tiny middle class by global standards, but if the economy continues its growth, 70 percent of the population could be middle class within 15 years.

These structural shifts in the pattern of global demand mean that Asia's growth can rely increasingly on the markets of today's Developing Asia rather than those of North America, Europe, or Japan. If Asian middle class consumers can replace those in advanced economies, Asian countries will become major exporters to each other, emulating the development path of Europe—European countries are significant exporters, but largely to each other, with eurozone exports growing by 4.5 percent a year from 2000 (Gasparini and Gluzmann, 2009), even with the recent recession.

The communications revolution

Recent events in Egypt and Tunisia have demonstrated the power of the communications revolution on even more traditional societies and politics.

Satellites, television, mobile telephony, and the internet—leveraged by the new social media—have already revolutionized the way in which information is gathered, stored, searched, and shared within and across national boundaries (Table 3.3). Witness the advent of Google, Facebook, and Twitter.

Table 3.3 | **Internet usage is skyrocketing globally, picking up in Asia**

Internet Users (per 100 people)	2000	2007	Average % change (annual)
PRC	1.8	16.1	37%
India	0.5	7.2	46%

Source: International Telecommunication Union ICT Indicators, 2010.

Until a few years ago, digital or electronic communications were primarily the preserve of developed countries. In the past 10 years this revolution has also spread to developing countries, especially in Asia (Figure 3.6). Just 10 years ago, only two or three of 1,000 Indians had access to a telephone (mainly fixed lines). By the end of 2010, India had some 700 million cell phone connections, for two-thirds of all Indians. Similarly, internet penetration has exploded, not only in high-income Asia, but also in middle-income PRC and India. The pace of change of this revolution is only likely to accelerate in the next 40 years.

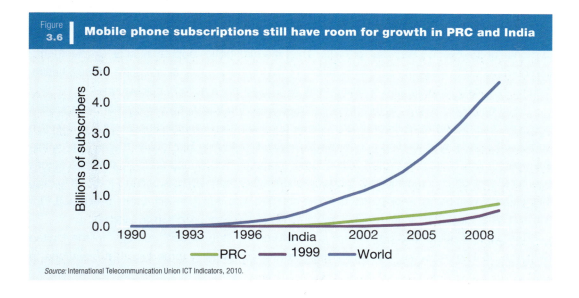

Figure 3.6 | **Mobile phone subscriptions still have room for growth in PRC and India**

Source: International Telecommunication Union ICT Indicators, 2010.

This revolution has major economic implications for Asia not only by sharply reducing the cost of information processing and sharing but also in the provision of both public and private services. Even more significantly, it could fundamentally alter relationships among the public at large, civil society, government at all levels, and private business. It has the potential to reduce the distance between the public and government. With a much more educated, affluent, and better informed citizenry holding middle class values, most Asian countries will witness far greater demand for more transparent, honest, and responsive governance.

From growth to social well-being

So far, Asian policy makers have emphasized social stability as the foundation of economic growth. Many have thought of social stability and economic growth as a virtuous circle. One underpins the other. That has certainly been Asia's historical experience, but it may need reconsideration as Asian societies become more affluent.

If governments could figure out what people really valued, they could construct better, more affordable social programs to maintain social harmony. But that is a complex process. For many years, the deficiencies of GDP as a measure of social progress or development have been known. Yet GDP remains the most convenient short-cut measure of well-being, hence policy makers' principal focus on GDP growth. But that is starting to change in some countries.

The first adjustment is to move toward counting nonmonetary aspects of the quality of life. Amartya Sen's "capabilities" approach focuses on the needs that people must meet to fulfill their potential as human beings. In addition to money, they may need education, health, a well-preserved environment, and other amenities. Conditional on these, however, more money expands people's choice set, and hence expands their welfare. And if individuals' welfare depends on the amount of money at their disposal, it follows that a nation's welfare depends on the amount of money at the nation's disposal, or GDP.[3] Thus the capabilities approach, in its simplest form, can be reduced to adding a certain number of measurable social indicators like literacy, health, income inequality, poverty, and environmental well-being into a nation's calculations.

These measures might still fail, however, to address the basic psychology that distinguishes personal satisfaction from income or material consumption—what is known as the Easterlin paradox. Easterlin was the first economist to suggest that while individuals' "happiness" within any country was clearly correlated with income, the same did not appear to be the case across countries. Well-off countries need to focus on issues other than GDP per capita if they are to raise their citizens' well-being. People may be more satisfied with less than with more. See Box 3.1 for this and other ideas that seem relevant and are influencing economic thinking today.

This type of subjective preference is measured by "happiness" surveys. In the United Kingdom, to take one example, policy makers are considering three types of questions to

---

3 This line of argument abstracts from distributional considerations, but those can be resolved, in theory, by appropriate government policy.

> **Box 3.1 Economists of consequence**

The ideas in this book draw on the thinking of a raft of economists who have only recently started to come to the fore. Some ideas are old, but seem particularly relevant to today; some are new and have promoted fresh thinking.

Easterlin pioneered the economics of happiness with a contribution on the declining marginal utility of money. His ideas are being acted on in the United Kingdom, as well as other high-income countries. Advanced Asian economies might find the ideas of greatest policy relevance, but many middle-income countries, like Malaysia, are already experimenting with such approaches.

Fujita formalized the spatial allocation of economic activity that underpins most current discussion of policy toward lagging subnational regions. His work is crucial for all economies striving to integrate domestically.

Glaeser's new book, *Triumph of the Cities*, develops the arguments for dense city planning rather than suburban sprawl. As Asia urbanizes, it will be critical that cities are as efficient as possible economically, environmentally, and socially.

Lomborg has argued that resource scarcity should not be feared, but must be managed. He highlights the role of the price mechanism for signaling scarcity, and concludes that distortions to prices in the name of stability only worsen long-term adjustments.

Minsky warns against the dangers of leverage and the common political vested interests of large banks and policy makers that create periodic crises and bailouts. He argues that a major focus for policy makers should be to avoid moral hazard in the banking system.

Romer models growth as an innovative process using knowledge. In this model, there is no mechanism driving convergence across countries. He provides an alternative to the Asian "flying geese" analogy by showing that countries can advance rapidly if they are more successful in adopting new technologies.

Saez shows that income concentration at the top level, by providing incentives for exceptional individuals, may not be necessary for growth. He proposes options for taxation to alter distributional outcomes.

Triffin warned of the fundamental conflicts between the short-term national policy interests of a reserve-currency country and the long-term international interests. In particular, such a country cannot increase its employment through exports at the same time as it exports dollars to satisfy reserve accumulation abroad.

Zhou Xiaochuan has reopened international debate on the future of the international monetary system and the role of dynamic emerging-economy currencies in the basket used for Special Drawing Rights.

ascertain happiness more broadly (Dolan et al., 2010). The first relates to the metrics of global life satisfaction or happiness as well as satisfaction within specific domains: health, crime, amount of leisure time, friendships, and family life. These evaluative measures can be particularly useful for revealing how people feel about collective issues like income inequality or quality of the environment. The second type has to do with subjective, cognitive evaluations of one's daily life experiences, including positive emotions such as joy and pride, and negative emotions like pain and worry. The third type relates to purpose in life and psychological well-being, and includes questions on autonomy, resilience, self-esteem, confidence, and optimism.

In an era when Asia is testing the world's limits to unfettered GDP growth, a more reasoned and scientific dialogue on how to improve Asians' happiness might be worth exploring. The Stiglitz Commission has already recommended that all national statistical offices incorporate subjective measures of well-being into their national surveys (Stiglitz, et al., 2009). Asian countries would do well to follow suit.

Asia in the Global Economy in 2050: The Asian Century

Chapter 4

Homi Kharas and Harpaul Alberto Kohli

Based on the previous discussion of the main drivers, it is possible to draw the broad contours of Asia's potential future trajectory through 2050. This chapter starts by laying out some basic assumptions and then presents two scenarios. But it must be reiterated that these scenarios are by no means exhaustive—they are two plausible, rough trajectories of how Asia's future may unfold.

The scenarios have a limited objective: to draw attention to the longer-term implications of the broad trends and to ask "what-if" questions, rather than focus on specific numbers or country rankings. Their range of outcomes is intentionally very wide and demonstrates the potential payoffs to proactive action—or costs of inaction—by policy makers and business leaders.

Basic assumptions

In developing any scenario, it is necessary to make some basic assumptions and to do so explicitly. The scenarios in this book have three: (1) the major structural changes in the world (notably Asia) will continue to remain relatively peaceful, and there will be no nuclear or other major armed conflicts, changes in current national boundaries, nor violent political transitions and upheavals in Asia over a long period; (2) the world will continue to have an open global trading system and a stable global financial system; and (3) there will be effective global action on climate change or adequate adaptation within Asia thanks to new, as yet unknown, technology.

If any of these assumptions were not to hold, the outlook for Asia would be radically different, but it is impossible to quantify either the probability or cost.

Peaceful and orderly restructuring

Asia has been the site of frequent clashes since World War II. Figure 4.1 reveals that Asia has more conflicts than elsewhere and that their frequency has not declined.

While devastating for individual countries or areas, these conflicts have not yet derailed economic development in Asia as a whole, but they serve as a reminder that the assumption of stability and lack of violence cannot be taken for granted. Asia has highly sensitive flashpoints. All these need to be managed if the Asian Century is to become a reality. Without peace and

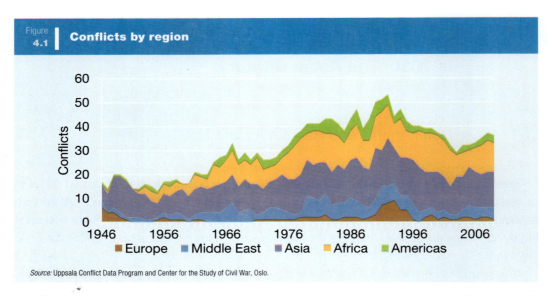

Figure 4.1 | Conflicts by region

Source: Uppsala Conflict Data Program and Center for the Study of Civil War, Oslo.

stability, the necessary transport and infrastructure to integrate Asian economies will not be built.

For the most part, the US has provided a security umbrella to ensure that Asian conflicts remain localized and do not spread into regional conflagrations. But as its relative economic power declines—the case in our scenarios—Asian rivals may contest the power vacuum.

Major transitions of economic power are often associated with war, but conflict is not inevitable. Indeed, the postwar rise of East Asia has been remarkably smooth. Still, the pace of the current global economic transformation is unprecedented. PRC's share of global GDP is growing four times faster than Japan's in its high-growth period and six times faster than the United Kingdom's during the industrial revolution. India is likely to display a similar increase in its global GDP share. Taken together, PRC and India could have global-share growth five times faster than that of the US in the first half of the 20th century.

An open global trading system and stable global financial system

It is far from assured that the world system of open trade and relatively stable financial arrangements will remain intact. Recent trade disputes and the failure to complete the Doha Development Round are testament to the strength of latent protectionist sentiments, which may well increase as the share of PRC and India in world trade expands. PRC is already the world's largest exporter, but as a developing country it is subject to different disciplines by the WTO than advanced economies are. PRC can be treated as a nonmarket economy by other WTO members until 2016. Large developing countries are resisting the push by major industrial economies to liberalize further in government procurement, services, and industrial policy and to forcefully implement intellectual property rights.

The difficulties involved in completing the latest multilateral trade round are mirrored by continued advances in regional trade agreements. Although conducted under WTO auspices, they are not consistent with each other in how rules of origin and other regulations are handled. As a result, their proliferation itself could become a barrier to open trade. Some have even argued that regional and bilateral trade agreements, by reducing the benefits of multilateral liberalization, have undermined the WTO. All this suggests that a continued open world trading system is not guaranteed. "Bicycle" theorists argue that if the WTO does not move forward with new rules and disciplines, it will become overshadowed by regional and bilateral agreements and overwhelmed by disputes in gray areas that should be clarified through multilateral negotiation rather than through case law.[1]

In a similar vein, despite progress with new rules to protect international financial stability through adoption of Basel III rules on bank capital and liquidity requirements, little has been done about two root causes of the recent global financial crisis: the moral hazard caused by "too big to fail" and the unregulated nature of the shadow banking system. The Financial Stability Board is reviewing principles for examining financial stability in emerging-market and developing economies, but based on the divergence of views expressed at the IMF April 2011 spring meetings on capital-flow monitoring, it might be hard to gain consensus on policy recommendations, especially as these economies are so diverse.

In short, the open global trading and stable global financial systems, taken for granted for most of the last 50 years, can no longer be automatically assumed for the next 40 years (although for the scenarios we assume the world will indeed continue to have open trading and stable financial systems). Many pressing issues have to do with accommodating Asia's rise, which is why Asian economies must develop a strategy for addressing these issues in concert rather than as individual countries. As a region, Asia must provide practical steps to ensure systemic integrity.

Effective global action on climate change

Asia is already the region most badly affected by natural disasters and most at risk if global climate change were to be significant. In the 10 years to 2008, Asia recorded 649 floods, affecting close to 1 billion people. Asia was home to 80–90 percent of all people affected by natural disasters over this period (OFDA/CRED, 2010). The glacier-fed rivers of the Himalayas–Hindu Kush, Kunlun Shan, Pamir, and Tien Shan mountains provide household water, food, fish, power, and other amenities for 2.8 billion Asians. These flows are at risk from climate change.

Climate change is unpredictable and a wild card for Asian development. Asia can influence global emissions, and must play a more active and constructive role in global risk-mitigation discussions. It can also invest more in adaptation. The assumption here is that the impact over 40 years will be manageable, but we do not quantify the opportunity costs of the investment

---

1 The theory asserts that if the bicyclist loses forward momentum, he or she falls off.

requirements or the direct costs of any increase in the frequency and intensity of natural disasters.

The Asian Century

Taking account of these assumptions, the drivers discussed in the preceding chapter, and the past performance of the three groups of countries, an econometric model is used to develop the two scenarios of Asia's economic trajectory to 2050. (Appendix 2 presents a summary description of the model.)[2]

- *Asian Century scenario.* This is the desired or ideal scenario for Asia as a whole. It makes two main assumptions: the 11 fast-growing converging economies, with a demonstrated record of sustained convergence to best global practice over the past 30-plus years, will continue this trend over the next 40 years; and countries accounting for roughly 40 percent of the GDP and population of Asia's slow- and modest-growth aspiring economies will become convergers by 2021. In this scenario, some 3 billion more Asians become affluent by 2050.
- *Middle Income Trap scenario.* This is the pessimistic scenario and could be taken as a wake-up call to Asian leaders. It assumes that the fast-growing middle-income converging economies fall into the Middle Income Trap in the next 5–18 years, without any of the slow- or modest-growth aspiring economies improving their record. In other words, Asia follows the pattern of Latin America over the past 30 years.

Where exactly Asia ends up within the two scenarios will depend primarily on how effectively the region tackles the policy and institutional agenda outlined in the following chapters. The result will have a tremendous impact on the well-being and lifestyles of future generations of Asians, as well as societies around the world.

Most of the remaining chapters discuss the Asian Century scenario. The implications of Asia becoming mired in the Middle Income Trap are discussed in the Conclusion.

Asia's growing output footprint

In the Asian Century scenario, Asia can be expected to steadily increase its global output footprint. In 2010, it accounted for about one-quarter of global output (Table 4.1). It this scenario, it seems to reach a rough equilibrium in its aggregate growth over the next 40 years at around 5.6 percent. This growth will not be even: the advanced Asian countries will grow more slowly, but the developing Asian economies will compensate with higher growth levels. Even the currently poor Asian economies should be able to achieve at least middle-income country levels. By 2040,

---

2 It is possible to construct alternative econometric models, including much more sophisticated and resource-intensive computable general equilibrium models. One may also construct models that explicity capture factors such as land, which appears to be a relevant constraint for the Indian economy, or human capital, which holds relevance in all economies but is difficult to measure. But for the limited purposes of this exercise—developing alternative scenarios to ask "what-if" questions involving 185 economies—the authors used the standard two-factor Cobb–Douglas production function approach without adjustments. Other bodies (Goldman Sachs, HSBC) have adopted a similar approach.

Table 4.1 — The Asian Century: Asia will account for more than half of global output in 2050

	2010	2020	2030	2040	2050
Global output (market exchange rates, US$ trillions)	62,910	98,320	148,261	224,318	333,347
Asian share of global output	27.7%	33.7%	39.9%	46.2%	52.3%
Global growth*		4.6%	4.2%	4.2%	4.0%
Asia growth*		6.7%	5.9%	5.8%	5.3%
Asian share of global growth*		44.5%	51.9%	58.6%	64.7%
Global GDP per capita (PPP)	$10,800	$14,800	$20,300	$27,800	$37,300
Asian GDP per capita (PPP)	$6,700	$11,200	$17,800	$27,600	$40,800

Note: * indicates growth or share of growth over the prior decade.
Source: Centennial Group International projections, 2011.

Figure 4.2 — PRC and India's rise is more dramatic than historical precedents: Average increase in percentage point share of global GDP per decade

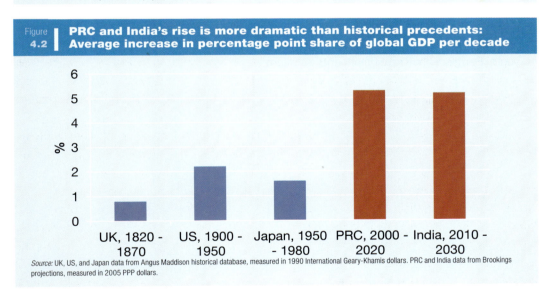

Source: UK, US, and Japan data from Angus Maddison historical database, measured in 1990 International Geary-Khamis dollars. PRC and India data from Brookings projections, measured in 2005 PPP dollars.

it is unlikely that any Asian countries will be poor by today's standards (that is, with a per-capita income of less than $995).

As Asia grows faster than the rest of the world, its share in global output will inexorably rise. The magnitudes are significant: by 2050, Asia's output footprint could be just over half the world's. That would represent a doubling of Asia's share to a level last seen in the early 19th century and mean that Asia would account for 60 percent of the change in world output in 2010–2050, and 65 percent of the growth in 2040–2050. It would also account for about 74% of the increase in the world's middle and upper classes. Little wonder that so much business attention is focused on Asia.

Asia's rapid growth implies that by 2050 it could converge with average global living standards. Asia would no longer be a poor region, but an average region, in income terms, with a range of advanced and middle-income economies. Asia could be about as prosperous as Europe today.

The engines of the Asian Century: Asia-7 economies

Asia's march to prosperity will be led by seven economies: PRC, India, Indonesia, Japan, Republic of Korea, Malaysia, and Thailand.

These seven economies had a combined total population of 3.1 billion (78 percent of Asia) and GDP of $15.1 trillion (87 percent of Asia) in 2010. In the Asian Century scenario, by 2050 their equivalent shares are 75 percent (population) and 90 percent (GDP). They alone will account for 45 percent of global GDP and 48% of the world's middle and upper classes.. Their average per-capita income will be $45,800 (PPP) compared with $37,300 for the world as a whole.

In 2010–2050, these seven economies will account for 91 percent of Asia's GDP growth and almost 53 percent of the world's. They will thus be the economic engines of not only Asia but also the world. Three other countries have the potential to join the Asia-7 over the course of the next 40 years: Bangladesh, Kazakhstan, and Viet Nam.

Chapter 5

Realizing the Asian Century: Mega-challenges and Risks

Homi Kharas

This chapter discusses the major challenges and risks that Asia must overcome to sustain its growth momentum and realize the Asian Century.

The region must confront five mega-challenges: large and, in some cases, rising inequities and disparities within countries that could alter the political and social fabric of the region; the risk of some countries falling into the Middle Income Trap for a host of economic, social, and political reasons; intense competition for finite natural resources (energy, other minerals, water, and fertile land) that will be unleashed in the next 40 years as some 3 billion additional Asians become much more affluent and strive to achieve even higher living standards; the potential sharp rise in disparities across countries and subregions if past differentials in relative growth rates continue to 2050, possibly destabilizing some countries and subregions; and global warming and climate change.

In addition, almost all countries face the overarching challenge of governance and institutional capacity, where improvements are a prerequisite for overcoming all other challenges.

These challenges are not compartmentalized. They can affect one another and exacerbate existing tensions and conflicts, or even create new pressure points in Asia that could threaten its growth, stability, and security.

Inequality within countries

Minimizing income and other inequality within countries will be a massive challenge. Many parts of Asia have seen huge increases in intracountry inequality as they unleashed—and gained from—the forces of globalization. Cities and coastal areas benefited first, while interior regions have lagged behind. Skilled workers have reaped a disproportionate share of the gains, leading to wide disparities in countries, as between the coastal and western provinces in PRC; eastern, southern, and western states in India; east and west Java; and north and south Sri Lanka.

Politically and socially, it is imperative to minimize the disparities of incomes and living conditions in countries. Otherwise, the large (and growing) disparities will generate rising social dissatisfaction and threaten peace and stability. This, in turn, would destroy the political support for the extraordinary discipline required to realize the Asian Century.

5 The Middle Income Trap

Few countries sustain high growth for more than a generation, and even fewer continue to experience high growth rates once they reach middle-income status.[1] Others reach middle-income status and are then caught in the Middle Income Trap (Box 5.1). The principal reason is that growth strategies are very different for low- and middle-income countries.

Low-income countries

Low-income countries generate rapid growth when they can move their labor force from low- to higher-productivity activities. The movement of surplus agricultural labor to become industrial wage earners is a classic example of this. Cities have three times the productivity of rural areas because of agglomeration economies. And fast-growing low-income countries always see rapid urbanization growth.

When women make the transition from rural farm to urban factory, the development and growth impact can be magnified because women in many rural settings have higher levels of underemployment (at least in terms of production of goods for the market) while employment of young women in factories is associated with later marriage and childbirth, better education for their children, and higher savings in the two-income households they form with their husbands. In other words, current income increases and investments in the human capital of the next generation are made at the same time.

What is crucial for this type of growth is the availability of jobs. Hence the attraction of an export-led strategy, whether in manufacturing or, as recently the case, in modern tradable services like business processing. Because demand for exports from any single developing country is relatively price elastic, once a successful niche is found it can be expanded rapidly without producers having to cut prices and profitability in a way that would otherwise stultify expansion and job growth.

Low-income economies grow fast by diversifying. They need to build domestic production capabilities in most goods and services. If they can save or borrow enough, they can achieve high rates of capital accumulation to build infrastructure, cities, and centers of education. The political leadership needs to marshal the resources of society and deploy them effectively. Planning, organization, management, and implementation are the critical skills in both the public and private sectors. Low-income-country growth is principally concerned with organizing the supply side of an economy for both maximizing factor inputs and ensuring enabling policies and institutions.

Middle-income countries

Growth strategies in middle-income countries are quite different. On the supply side, growth

---

[1] This section is based on the authors' article "Middle income trap: What it is and why countries fall in it" in the *Global Journal of Emerging Market Economies* (forthcoming).

tends to become more capital- and skill-intensive in manufacturing (sometimes referred to as "moving up the value chain") and to be more heavily oriented toward services. For many years, services have been considered by the economics profession as activities where productivity improvements were hard to sustain. But with the expansion of international service tradability, new information and communications technologies to digitize and store services, and easy and cheap transportability through modern telecommunications networks, services have become a powerful engine of growth for many middle-income countries. In fact, services have become the fastest-growing export sector globally and for many developing countries. And service productivity growth is outstripping industrial productivity growth in most developing and advanced economies.

The biggest difference between middle-income growth strategies and those of low-income countries is the need for the former to focus more on demand. In middle-income countries, exports cannot be as easily expanded as before because wages are higher and cost competitiveness has declined. Export growth depends on introducing new processes and finding new markets, not just on expanding sales of the same product to existing markets. To do this, exporters must understand the quality, price, and consumer-preference needs of the global economy—a demanding task. Most firms start by developing that understanding in domestic markets, and then, if successful, they can develop global brands.

Innovation and product differentiation to meet the needs of the market become more important in middle-income countries. These skills and firm capabilities also become important for the domestic market. Middle-income countries that successfully sustain growth develop sizable middle class populations that are prepared to pay a little more for quality and for differentiated products. That extra profit margin, in turn, spurs firms to invest in marketing, branding, and new product development—the ingredients of innovation and further growth.

In short, domestic demand and new export demand become more important engines of growth in middle-income economies and a transition must take place toward services firms. To avoid falling in the Middle Income Trap, middle-income countries need to develop modern and more agile institutions for property rights, capital markets, venture capital, and competition, as well as a critical mass of highly skilled people, in order to grow through innovation, as affluent countries do (Box 5.1). Such institutional development is often a multigenerational endeavor that presents a challenge for policy makers as the benefits are not immediately visible and may accrue indirectly and over the very long term.

One source of the Middle Income Trap may lie in connections between income distribution and macroeconomic growth. In advanced economies, there is a sense that the stagnation of the middle class and the growing concentration of income might have been important in the recent global financial crisis. Formal economic models show that if income distribution worsens, domestic demand can grow more slowly than potential GDP, and this either results in stagnation

> **Box 5.1 | The Middle Income Trap: Unable to compete**
>
> The Middle Income Trap is illustrated in the figure, which plots per capita incomes of three middle-income countries over 1975–2005. In a steadily growing economy per capita GDP rises continuously—the experience of the Republic of Korea. But many middle-income countries do not follow this pattern. Instead, they have bursts of growth followed by periods of stagnation or even decline, or are stuck at low growth rates.
>
> They are caught in the Middle Income Trap—unable to compete with low-income, low-wage economies in manufactured exports and with advanced economies in high-skill innovations. Put another way, such countries cannot make a timely transition from resource-driven growth, with low-cost labor and capital, to productivity-driven growth.
>
>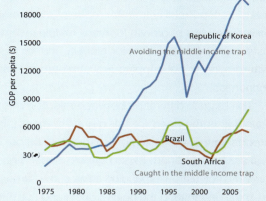

or is temporarily offset through more financial leverage and a growing debt burden of the middle and lower classes. If the latter continues for long enough, the debt levels eventually become intolerable and lead to widespread default and financial bankruptcies in the event of an adverse shock (Kumhof and Ranciere, 2010).

In much the same way, middle-income countries in Latin America have been through several cycles of growth based on credit granted during commodity booms, followed by crisis, and then recovery. This stop-go cycle has prevented Latin American countries from becoming advanced economies even though they have enjoyed several episodes of fast growth (Kohli et al., 2010).

Some analysts' current optimism for Latin America is based on its expanded middle class. Although Brazil's per capita GDP today is only 40 percent higher than what it was in 1978 (at market exchange rates in real terms), its middle class may be double the size it was then. This can be partly attributed to determined efforts by the recent administration to improve income distribution in the country. With a larger middle class, Brazil has been able to rebound rapidly from the recent recession, whereas in the past, it would have been badly hit by a global slowdown. The middle class provided a cushion of domestic demand to offset falling exports, and was a force for continuity in political and economic policies.

Political leadership

Perhaps more than any other factor, avoiding the Middle Income Trap requires political leadership in four main areas: to sustain the ambition to grow fast even when material well-being for the elite in society has advanced; to take a long-term, multigenerational view on growth; to engage in sustained institutional development that will bring returns in the long run (such as building high-quality higher education institutes and investing in improved governance and regulatory agencies); and to manage restructuring when some sectors lose their comparative advantage as they specialize (Kohli and Sood, 2010).

Competition for finite natural resources

Intense competition for scarce natural resources will be unleashed with growth and then exacerbated as some 3 billion additional Asians become increasingly affluent, especially if they emulate current Western lifestyles. Global supply cannot readily accommodate changes in demand of this size, especially for nonrenewable raw materials. That leads to a zero-sum game: more for one economy means less for another. Can Asian cities deliver water to their residents?[2] Can the region feed itself and, if not, will the rest of the world provide enough food? How will Asia's massive needs for energy and other natural resources be met? How will Asia sustain its rapid growth with limits on carbon emissions?

Such concerns about the sustainability of economic growth are not new. They date back to Malthus and reemerge whenever growth is rapid. But there are new features to today's debate. First, there is a backdrop of rapidly rising prices for food, fuel, and other raw materials. Higher prices signal scarcity in spot markets, and commodity stockpiles seem to be lower than many governments feel comfortable with. While few formal long-term growth models include commodity prices as a factor in explaining the pace of growth, conventional wisdom suggests that growth could slow if prices surge further—if for no other reason than the need to invent and disseminate new technologies to optimize resource use versus simply adapting off-the-shelf technologies in a process of growth catch-up. What can Asia, as a region, do to make sure that the "adding-up" problems of today follow the first cries of the Club of Rome in 1972 into the trashcan of history (Club of Rome, 1972)?

The new equilibrium will surely be found in a combination of adjustments: price increases to reduce demand and increase supply; new technologies to reduce unit consumption or substitute with more plentiful, renewable resources; and lifestyle changes that favor conservation and recycling to minimize waste.

Disparities across countries and subregions

Although most talk of Asian economics is upbeat, some Asian countries are falling well short of their potential, largely in South and Central Asia. Asia, as said earlier, is a region of paradoxes. The gap between its advanced and its least-developed economies is larger than in any other region. Most income inequality in Asia is explained by differences between countries, in sharp

---

2 Fatehpur Sikri, for example, the capital of the Mughal Empire, was abandoned in 1585 after only 14 years because of water shortages.

contrast to income inequality in Europe, North America, and Latin America, where most of it is within countries. Asia has so far given little thought as to how to manage intercountry inequality.

Countries in East Asia (and within PRC, the eastern seaboard) are the most developed and prosperous parts of Asia. For Asia as a whole to become developed and to provide a satisfactory lifestyle to the vast majority of Asians, the region must find ways to spread prosperity from east to west.

Two Asian borders already show very high disparities on either side. The Democratic People's Republic of Korea has lagged far behind Republic of Korea (and increasingly behind northeast PRC). Similarly, the income ratio between Singapore and Indonesia is stark, reaching 14:1 in 2010. In the future, as a growing number of Asian countries grow fast, border disparities could climb sharply if neighbors fall behind. If India, for example, continues to grow fast, the ratio between its real income and that of Nepal and Pakistan could widen from today's manageable 2.8 and 1.2, respectively, to as much as 11.5 (India–Nepal) and 4.8 (India–Pakistan) by 2050. For comparison, the income ratio between the US and Mexico today is 3.2 (in PPP terms). Other high income disparities could emerge in Central Asia.

Another factor changing the shape of Asia is that borders are no longer confined by geography. Migration has spread more broadly: Uzbek workers are in many other Central Asian countries, and Bangladeshis in East Asia and the Gulf. The Philippines has a long tradition of exporting skilled and unskilled labor worldwide. When income differentials across borders rise significantly, the chances are that migration, legal or illegal, will also rise in response.

These trends suggest that Asia faces a great risk if some countries are allowed to lag behind while others enjoy the benefits of global and regional expansion. This is the argument for why Asia as a whole should strive to achieve the Asian Century scenario.

Global warming and climate change

Global warming and climate change, as well as resultant severe water shortages, are mega-challenges that have assumed global visibility. They are perhaps the single most important long-term challenge facing humankind this century and beyond, possibly affecting every person on the planet, irrespective of country or income. Accounting for over half the world's population, Asians have more at stake in the well-being of the planet than any other people, particularly because these changes will affect not only Asia's vast populations that inhabit coastal areas but also areas that rely heavily on agriculture.

Mitigation of risks associated with climate change and measures to adapt to global warming will affect every aspect of the economy and way of life of all Asians: from the efficiency of energy use and weaning away from fossil fuels, to modes of transportation, to the design of buildings and indeed entire cities, to the care of forests and green areas; and, ultimately, to the need to transition to an economic growth model and much more eco-friendly and sustainable lifestyles of future generations.

While thousands of highly qualified and well-meaning experts and institutions—both public and private—have already produced many outstanding studies, until recently there was no independent study analyzing the economic self-interest of developing countries in Asia (or worldwide). But in late 2010 an independent international think-tank released an in-depth analysis of the economic impact of climate change on Asian and other major developing countries (Emerging Markets Forum, 2010). This analysis demonstrates that it is in Asia's self-interest to move decisively on the global commons. Asia needs to do so not because the West is asking it to, but because it is simply in Asia's own interest.

The analysis also makes clear that climate change has far-reaching implications for the way Asia needs to move forward in its march toward prosperity: dramatically increasing energy efficiency and reducing reliance on fossil fuels (coal and petroleum); adopting a new approach to urbanization by building more compact and eco-friendly cities; relying much more on mass transit (than private cars) for urban dwellers and railways for long-distance transport; giving priority to developing related technologies; and, perhaps more fundamentally, changing lifestyles to alleviate pressures on finite natural resources by using them much more efficiently.

These interrelated aspects are critical for Asia's long-term growth and development because the future competitiveness and prosperity of nations will greatly depend on how efficiently they use natural resources and progress in the race to a low-carbon future.

In the immediate future, Asian economies must take urgent steps to adapt to climate change given that some rise in average global temperature—2 degrees Celsius or more—appears inevitable.

Governance and institutional capacity

Governance and institutional capacity form the Achilles heel of most Asian economies. If recent adverse trends in the quality of institutions and corruption continue unchecked, the region's ability to realize the Asian Century will be jeopardized. All countries must improve governance and continually transform their institutions to realize the promise of becoming affluent societies by 2050.

Large improvements in the quality and credibility of national political and economic institutions (illustrated by falling corruption) are prerequisites for sustaining Asia's growth trajectory. High-quality institutions will help the fast-growing converging economies avoid the Middle Income Trap, and the slow- or modest-growth aspiring economies establish the basic conditions for moving toward sustained economic growth. Managing the common challenges—delivering high-quality social and infrastructure services, preventing crony capitalism, urbanizing rapidly, building a fundamentally sound finance sector, fostering entrepreneurship and innovation, protecting citizens' rights and maintaining the rule of law—requires effective governance, centrally and locally.

In this light, Asia will need to modernize governance and retool its institutions with an emphasis on transparency and accountability.

Risk of conflict

In addition to the above mega-challenges looms the risk of violent cross-border conflict—especially as some of the most violent conflicts since World War II have taken place in Asia. More important, most of the world's conflict hotbeds are in Asia. Similarly, the region's small and big countries alike have myriad domestic conflicts and insurgencies. Further are the distrust and tensions that characterize the relationships between Asia's major economies—and five countries are nuclear powers.

Any one or more regional or national conflicts can derail Asia's growth trajectory. This remains by far the biggest risk to the Asian Century (Box 5.2).

Asia's expanding global footprint

Beyond these challenges and risks, Asia's dramatically larger global output footprint will bring new obligations, as well as opportunities. The region's share of global GDP will not only exceed half but will also be more than twice that of the next largest geographic group—Europe. This will fundamentally alter Asia's role and mode of interaction with the global community (Chapter 15).

Box 5.2 — Conflict in Asia: Risk and deterrence

In the 1990s, Asia saw fewer conflicts, mirroring a global trend. Sadly, it appears that the Asian and global trends are now reversing.

Several internal conflicts (where one or more ethnic group seeks to break away from an existing state) have been brewing intermittently. The prime minister of India recently described the Maoist insurgency in eastern and central areas of his country as the most serious threat to national security.

Beyond national boundaries, there have been interstate conflicts that have flared up in the past, but could easily develop into full-scale wars.

A new type of conflict has entered the fray: climate change, a global threat, is increasingly feared to become a threat multiplier, especially in regions that are initially fragile and unstable. In turn, this could lead to widespread famine, chaos, and internal struggle, as well as conflict among neighbors for energy or other resources.

Several of Asia's major rivers—the Ganges, Indus, Mekong, Yangtze, and Yellow—originate in the Himalayas. If the massive snow and ice sheets in the Himalayas continue to melt, that will dramatically reduce the water supply of much of Asia, and could lead to conflict.

A major challenge for Asia is whether it is going to develop the necessary mechanisms to mitigate regional conflicts and ensure stability and order. Asia's regional security order is now in a state of flux. The unprecedented economic boom has had major—still unresolved—implications for how political power will be distributed throughout the region; it is generally agreed that the best-case scenario is a multipolar Asia.

So, what might ensure peace in a multipolar Asia? Economic interdependence, a key driver of peace, is steadily increasing, and serves as a powerful force for mutual restraint. But without stronger regional institutions, interdependence alone might not be sufficient. Asia's regional institutions, such as ASEAN, have been reticent in developing roles for themselves in dispute settlement or conflict resolution. The key question is whether Asia can manage its conflicts without external help.

Asia has yet to seriously institutionalize the necessary cooperation. Some foresee and advocate an "Asian NATO," which, like the Atlantic institution itself, might help the region to deal with traditional and nontraditional threats. But some analysts doubt that an Asian NATO will ever be formed for various reasons, ranging from Asia's long-standing aversion (one might even call it a norm) to collective defense, to its inability to articulate who or what exactly is the shared threat.

Asian Century

Realizing the Asian Century: A Strategic Framework

Chapter 6

Harinder S. Kohli, Ashok Sharma, and Anil Sood

This chapter presents a strategic framework and the contours of general strategies for Asia as a whole. The framework covers three dimensions: national action; regional cooperation; and collective action on the global agenda. A brief discussion of the three dimensions is followed by an elaboration of the priority actions within each.

Three dimensions

A distinguishing feature of Asia's economic story during the past 50 years has been the singular focus of most policy makers and political leaders on domestic economic and social development. This was appropriate as countries attempted to eradicate poverty and rapidly catch up with the developed world. It was also feasible when Asia's global footprint was smaller. But as the global economic center of gravity returns to Asia, this focus will no longer be possible or even desirable.

The national agenda will always retain its paramount importance, but Asian policy makers—particularly in the large economies—have six reasons to look beyond their borders:

- Many of the intergenerational issues have national, regional, and global perspectives.
- Asia has the most to gain (or lose) from the preservation of the global commons essential for future growth and prosperity: an open global trading system, a stable global financial system, mitigation of climate change, and peace and security. It must play an active role in any global discussions and negotiations.
- Large Asian economies increasingly need to consider the potential impact of their national policies and actions on the rest of the region and the world. Their much larger global footprint requires them to play a larger role in global governance.
- Diversifying export markets to reduce the heavy reliance on North America and Europe will require Asian leaders to work together to remove behind-the-border legal, administrative, and logistical barriers to the free movement of goods and finance within the region.
- Managing some of the biggest risks facing the region—particularly cross-country disparities that could lead to conflict—will require regionwide discussion and action.
- The actions (or inactions) of the Asia-7 countries will determine whether the less well-off

economies share the benefits of the Asian Century—or are left behind.

Given Asia's diversity and widely varying country conditions, the precise actions and timing of measures on the intergenerational issues must be country or subregion specific. They need to be formulated case by case. Even so, one can articulate a strategic framework and define contours for the region as a whole.

The strategic framework has three dimensions (Figure 6.1). Its central dimension covers national strategic and policy actions. These range from getting the fundamentals of development right for the slow-growth economies, to sustained improvements in productivity and shifting comparative advantage (to avoid the Middle Income Trap) for the converging economies, to sustaining growth and moving from pure growth to well-being in the high-income economies.

Figure 6.1 Strategic framework

The second dimension entails regional cooperation to pursue regional commons, maximize collaborative synergies, and work toward shared regional prosperity.

The third dimension is transforming Asia's interactions with the global community in line with its expanding global footprint. This dimension relies on collective action, particularly among the large economies.

Five criteria were used for keeping down the number of issues addressed: centrality to the objectives of ensuring faster and more inclusive growth; avoiding the Middle Income Trap; intergenerational nature of the issue and related solutions; horizontal interconnectedness; relevance to meeting the mega-challenges; and importance in light of Asia's fast-growing global footprint.

Many of the issues are interconnected and mutually reinforcing across the three dimensions, such as financial transformation, the efficient use of resources, and energy security. Similarly, urbanization, finance, energy efficiency, and climate change are closely interrelated at the national, regional, and global levels. Each issue should be seen as part of the overall agenda. In one sentence, Asian policy makers must address these challenges in a coordinated manner to realize the promise of the Asian Century.

National action

The focus of the proposed national economic and social policy agenda differs greatly among the three country groups. Still, overarching issues and contours of general strategies emerge.

Growth and inclusion

Growth and inclusion need not be mutually exclusive—they can be mutually reinforcing. To sustain growth over the long term, almost all Asia needs a strategy to deal with inequality if it is to maintain the social stability that has been so important for growth until now.

Asian countries must give much greater priority to inclusion and elimination of inequalities—rural/urban, educated/uneducated, or along ethnic lines—throughout their societies. Asia will have to rethink its policies toward distribution. Inequalities of opportunity can no longer be disregarded, nor can islands of poverty (either in countries or groups in society) coexist easily with growing affluence. Rural development, including agriculture, will remain important in all low- and middle-income economies. Urban inequity—rising in parts of Asia—will need to be addressed, and slums will need to be eliminated.

The range of policy instruments is limited, however. A sharper focus on education and development of human capital, with a particular focus on women, will be essential to fully realize the demographic dividend. This is an obvious area, followed by government redistribution policies. Governments must also increase access to high-quality infrastructure services and promote innovation that meets, affordably, the needs of those at the bottom of the pyramid. Supportive environments for domestic philanthropy can also play a significant mitigating role, as can various forms of insurance against risk, such as unemployment, disability, illness, or death of a family wage earner. Minimum-wage and active labor-market policies, such as guaranteed employment schemes, can make a difference (though they can be abused). Mobility of labor is important but that is best achieved when regulations ensuring migrant rights (domestic and international) are developed and respected.

Financial transformation

All else equal, as Asia's share of global GDP rises to 50 percent or more, it should have about the same share of global financial assets, banks, and equity and bond markets, to efficiently recycle and allocate its huge savings and foreign reserves.

In growing and transforming their financial systems, Asian economies must keep in mind the lessons of the Asian financial crisis and the recent recession. Above all, they must avoid falling prey to another bubble of excessively exuberant expectations.

Asia will need to formulate its own financial model, avoiding both an overreliance on self-regulation by markets, as well as the excessive central government control of bank-dominated financial systems present in many parts of Asia. It should become more open to institutional innovation. It must also, immediately, develop instruments and create an enabling environment to finance its massive infrastructure and urban development needs through public–private partnerships and public financial markets. Northeast Asia has to pay greater attention to the special needs of its aging societies.

National reforms must aim to create conditions to facilitate regional (and global) integration. Well before 2050, Asia should be home to one or more global financial centers and several global financial houses.

Managing massive urbanization

By 2050, Asia will be transformed as its urban population nearly doubles from 1.6 billion to 3 billion. This historic shift can be an unparalleled opportunity to increase productivity and improve the quality of life of its citizens. Asia's cities, expected to account for more than 80 percent of economic output, will be the centers of higher education, innovation, and technological development. Urban buildings and transport will account for the bulk of energy consumption and carbon emissions. Consequently, the quality and efficiency of urban centers will increasingly determine Asia's long-term competitiveness, as well as its social and political stability.

Asia must adopt a new strategy to manage urbanization by promoting compact, energy-efficient, green, safe, and livable cities, which will be more reliant on mass transit than on cars. It must also manage some significant risks, particularly those associated with inequality, slums, and a breakdown of social cohesion.

Better financing and management of cities will require governments to further decentralize responsibility to local levels, offer more local accountability, and move toward market financing of urban capital investment. Urban development takes many decades. Timely action will require visionary leadership.

Reduction in intensity of energy and natural resource use

The anticipated rapid rise in the living standards of some 3 billion Asians will put tremendous pressures on—and create intense competition for—the earth's finite natural resources.

Based on current trends, Asia will surpass the OECD long before 2050 to become the largest energy consumer grouping. It will be the grouping most affected by, and most responsible for, risks related to energy security and climate change. Out of self-interest, it will need to take the lead in securing and decarbonizing energy through radical energy efficiency and diversification programs. Many countries, for example, need to eliminate energy subsidies and switch from fossil fuels to renewables. Most other natural resources, including water and fertile land, have similar issues. The only way out is a combination of price increases (hence removal of subsidies), more stringent standards (for buildings and transport), technological breakthroughs, and adjustments in consumption patterns.

Remedial actions will be required nationally, regionally, and globally. There is a strong synergy between energy efficiency and total factor productivity growth, which is needed for sustained convergence and global competitiveness.

The key policy implication for all Asian countries is that their future competitiveness and well-being depend heavily on improving the efficiency of natural resource use and winning the global race to a low-carbon future.

Entrepreneurship, innovation, and technological development

The continuing rapid growth of Asian economies over the next 40 years will require the full potential of technological change, innovation and, critically, entrepreneurship to be harnessed.

The model in Asia, with a few exceptions, has been that of catching up with the more advanced economies and adapting the technologies developed there to produce for Western markets. This was appropriate when Asian countries were far from global best practice and on the lower rungs of the convergence ladder. But as more Asian countries emulate Japan, Republic of Korea, and Singapore and come closer to Western best practice, catching up will be inadequate.

The fast-growing converging economies, particularly PRC and India, must move to frontier entrepreneurship and innovation, and create breakthroughs in science and technology, if they are to become high-income countries. A particularly fruitful area, where India has already demonstrated notable success, will be inclusive innovation to meet the needs of millions of people on modest incomes.

The core requirement—where many Asian economies fall short—is high-quality education that promotes creativity at all levels, supported by a system that fosters innovation and entrepreneurship. The most critical element of the system will be an overall policy framework that promotes competition and enables private development.

Governance and institutional development

Asian economies in all three groups must improve governance and transform their institutions to meet the challenges of the coming decades.

The recent deterioration in the quality and credibility of national political and economic institutions (illustrated by rising corruption) is a key concern. High-quality institutions will help the fast-growing converging economies avoid the Middle Income Trap, and the slow- or modest-growth aspiring economies establish the basic conditions for moving toward sustained economic growth. Managing the common challenges requires effective central and local governance.

Throughout Asia, an expanding middle class—itself a desirable product of rapid socioeconomic growth—will demand increased voice and participation, transparent allocation of resources, accountability for results, and enhanced personal space.

Although daunting, eradicating corruption is critical for all countries to maintain social and political stability and retain the legitimacy of governments. As recent events in the Middle East illustrate, the quality of communication between the governing and the governed will be crucial as new social media and other tools as yet unknown (but certain to emerge) become available. Asia will need to substantially improve governance and its institutions, with the stress on transparency and accountability.

From growth to well-being

As more Asian countries progress toward high-income status, they will need to adopt policies that promote broader social well-being and better lifestyles.

Just as inclusion is critical to maintaining social cohesion and political stability in low- and middle-income countries, a greater focus on well-being, personal safety, and happiness rather than more wealth will be important as affluence increases. Such a shift is critical in view of the growing global competition for resources. It requires a dialogue in Asia to understand the implications for the region's growth model and what can be done to improve people's well-being. And it may be time to begin defining measures of well-being and incorporate them in national surveys.

Regional cooperation

Regional cooperation (including integration) is critical for Asia's march toward prosperity. It will become much more important for six reasons:

- It will cement Asia's hard-won economic gains in the face of vulnerabilities to external shocks.
- It could be an important bridge between individual Asian countries and the rest of the world, and as leverage for policy makers to push through domestic reforms that face headwinds from interest groups. To have voice and influence commensurate with its economic weight, Asian economies will need to coordinate, even harmonize, their geopolitical positions on a range of global issues. Only regular regional dialogue can achieve this.
- As Asian economies rebalance growth toward "internal" (domestic and regional) demand, transport and energy connectivity will pave the way to a single market. To sustain region-wide economic growth, they need to fully open their markets to neighbors in the region (in

the same way that US and European markets have been open to Asia since World War II). This will allow free flow of trade and investment (and greater labor mobility, particularly of skilled labor) throughout the 49 economies.
- With development assistance, it can help reduce cross-country disparities in income and opportunities, which if left unchecked could breed instability or even spark conflict in parts of Asia.
- In technological development, energy security, and disaster preparedness, it can yield significant synergies and positive spillovers.
- Through skillfully managing the regional commons, it will become increasingly important for Asia's long-term stability, peace, and harmony.

Avoiding conflict between large economies and nuclear states, and maintaining social and political stability in the region, will be paramount. Given its diversity, heterogeneity and, especially, lack of political support in the major countries, Asia will need to develop its own unique model that builds on positive experience in East Asia: a market-driven, bottom-up, and pragmatic approach that facilitates free regional trade and investment flows. This model could build on the ASEAN experience and gradually include more economies. The aim of these actions and government initiatives is to create an Asian economic community. Such an approach will require stronger—though not necessarily new—regional institutions.

The creation of an integrated Asian economic community must be based on two general principles—openness and transparency. Asia's embrace of open regionalism implies that it does not discriminate against nonmembers while it encourages regional institutions to make the most of existing global institutions and conventions. Transparency will enhance accountability and strengthen governance.

Crucial for increased regional cooperation is strong political leadership. Given the region's diversity, building Asia's regionalism will require collective leadership that recognizes a balance of power among all participants. Asia's major economic powers, like PRC, India, Indonesia, Japan, and Republic of Korea, will be important in integrating Asia and shaping its role in the global economy.

Global agenda

Asia's growth and larger global economic footprint will bring new challenges and responsibilities that have weighty implications for the region, particularly for the large economies.

Asia must take greater ownership of the global commons, including an open global trading system, a stable global financial system, climate-change mitigation measures, and peace and security.

Asia must also sustain friendly and business-like relations with countries nearby (the Gulf countries, the Russian Federation, Turkey, as well as Australia and New Zealand) as well as in

Africa and Latin America—in addition to maintaining its traditional close economic ties with North America and Europe.

Asia's stance on climate change and global warming requires a reassessment. Early action on climate change is demonstrably in Asia's self-interest—socially, economically, and politically. A change in its stance will be a concrete demonstration that Asia is willing and able to play a constructive role in preserving the global commons.

As it becomes a larger player in the global economy, Asia's self-interest and long-term prosperity will lie in ensuring well-being, peace, and security throughout the world.

Over time, Asia must gradually transform its role to that of an active participant and a thought leader in formulating the rules on the global commons. The region as a whole must play a more active role in global governance.

Finally, the region must delicately manage its rapidly rising role as a major player in global governance. It will be important that as an emerging global leader, Asia acts as—and is seen as—a responsible and collaborative global citizen, non-threatening to others, and fully aware of the global implications of its policies and actions.

This is, admittedly, an ambitious and daunting policy agenda. But its payoff will also be huge: realizing the Asian Century will make an additional 3 billion Asians affluent by 2050.

The following chapters elaborate on this agenda.

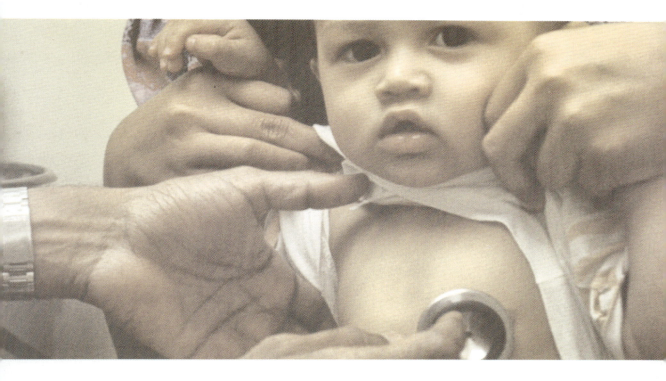

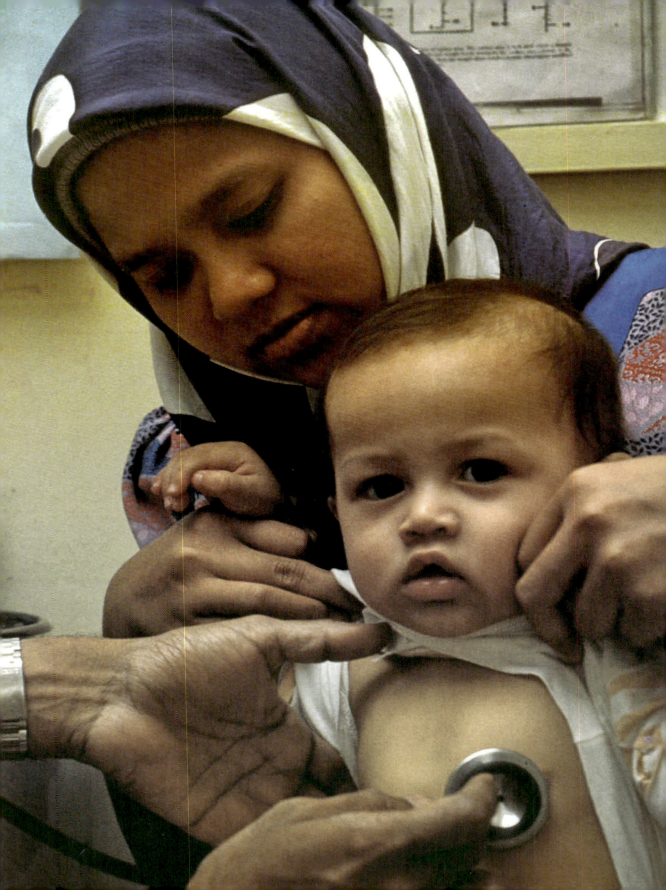

Growth and Inclusion

Chapter 7 — Jayant Menon, Sabyasachi Mitra, and Drew Arnold

Introduction[1]

Growth and equality are seen as part of a virtuous circle. While Asia has made marked progress in reducing poverty, both income and non-income inequality have remained high or even risen in a number of countries. This is most visible in the region's progress toward the Millennium Development Goals (MDGs), particularly on indicators related to health and sanitation. This has given rise to the term, "the two faces of Asia." Clearly, the fruits of Asia's potential prosperity must be shared widely by all segments of its population if this is to be the Asian Century. This chapter outlines the priorities for Asian leaders to pursue this objective. It begins by defining the concept of growth that incorporates inclusion and equity, and then makes a case for Asia's leaders to promote inclusive growth, by focusing on human development, redistribution policies, and social safety nets, together with good governance in parallel with the continued focus on economic growth.

What progress has Asia made?

While Asia's recent growth has resulted in a dramatic decrease in poverty, both income and non-income inequalities have continued to rise. Many Asian countries appear to have accepted significant increases in intracountry inequality as the necessary price for unleashing the forces of globalization. It is well known that cities and coastal areas usually benefit first from this worldwide expansion of economic activity, while interior regions lag. It is also acknowledged that skilled workers and owners of capital usually reap a large share of the gains from this trend. These lead to rising inequality in the short term.

Over the past two decades, the conversation in Asia has shifted somewhat from poverty reduction to equity. This shift is in large part due to Asia's recent growth and dramatic improvements in the lot of those at the very bottom of the pyramid.

As economies develop toward middle income, they tend to focus on poverty reduction rather than equity. As they grow beyond middle income, they tend to shift their focus to equity, since

---

1 The views expressed herein are those of the authors and do not necessarily reflect the views and policies of the Asian Development Bank, or its Board of Governors or the governments they represent.

poverty has become less of a problem. Therefore, many Asian economies are beginning to look at inequality as a significant issue.

Import substitution, export orientation, poverty, and inequality

In the 1950s and 1960s, like many developing countries elsewhere, most Asian countries began pursuing polices of import substitution, by erecting high trade barriers through both tariff and nontariff measures. They did this in an attempt to promote industrialization by limiting import competition and by generally insulating their economies from the rest of the world. At the same time, industrialized countries were reducing their trade barriers and increasing their engagement with the rest of the world (Krueger, 1995a). By the 1980s, it had become clear to Asian leaders that these policies had failed to deliver—growth had slowed, fiscal and balance-of-payments conditions had deteriorated, and the possibility of crisis loomed for many countries. The new industries that had been nurtured by these policies were highly inefficient despite large subsidies, and were highly capital intensive. They usually required massive amounts of imported capital goods, while labor was in surplus. During this era, the incidence of poverty increased in some countries, and remained stubbornly high in others (Table 7.1).

Table 7.1 | Poverty reduction in selected Asian countries, 1980–1990 (percentage of population under the poverty line)

	National Poverty Data				$2 PPP/day	
	1980	1990	2000	Latest	1990	Latest
Cambodia		47.0	36.1	30.1	77.9	56.5
Lao PDR		46.3	33.5	27.6	84.8	66.0
Malaysia	18.4	17.1	6.0	3.8	11.1	2.3
Viet Nam		>60	29.0	10.0	85.7	38.5
Indonesia	28.6	13.7	19.1	15.4	84.6	50.6
Thailand	35.5	27.2	14.2	8.8	41.0	26.5
PRC	52.8	22.2	8.5		84.6	36.3
India	44.5	38.9	26.1		83.8	75.6

Note: National poverty data is taken from national sources using national poverty lines that are unique to each country.
Source: World Bank, PovCalNet.

The switch from import substitution to export orientation as a growth strategy started in East Asia, but was quickly followed by Southeast Asia and South Asia. Tariff rates were sharply reduced and the most restrictive of nontariff barriers such as quotas were dismantled. Current account deficits narrowed as exports grew sharply and fiscal conditions improved as the private sector replaced the public sector in industry. The 1980s and 1990s also witnessed a sharp increase in the amount of foreign direct investment flowing into Southeast Asia, mostly from Japan and the US. Growth returned vigorously, was robust in most countries, and even spectacular in some, reaching or exceeding double-digit levels. One outstanding result of this period of sustained high growth was the dramatic reduction in income poverty across the region. By any measure of poverty, the reductions between the 1980s and the present have been unparalleled (Tables 7.1 and 7.2).

Table 7.2 Population living on less than $1.25 (PPP) per day (%)

	1985	1990	2000	2005	2009
Bangladesh	47.4	52.5	57.8	49.6	
India	55.5	53.6		41.6	
Indonesia	62.8	54.3	47.7	21.4	18.7
Malaysia	3.2	1.91	0.54	0.54	0.0
Pakistan	66.5	64.7	29.1	22.6	
Philippines	34.9	30.7	22.5	22.6	
PRC	69.4	60.2	35.6	15.9	
Viet Nam		63.7	40.1	21.3	13.1

Source: World Bank, PovCalNet.

A distinguishing characteristic of the economic performance of the NIEs in East Asia is the relatively equitable distribution of gains from economic growth. The rapid and sustained growth in these economies since the late 1960s has been accompanied by a reduction in poverty and across-the-board improvements in living standards. Income distribution has remained more equal than in other countries at a comparable stage of development. It is widely recognized that income inequalities remain low in Republic of Korea and Taipei,China (see, for instance, Jomo, 2006; Fei et al., 1979) while a recent OECD (2008) assessment finds that there has been only a "small increase" in income inequality in Japan. Some interpret this achievement as a natural outcome of export-led industrialization that can be replicated in other developing countries, provided the policy fundamentals are correct. Since developing countries enjoy the comparative advantage of being in relatively labor-intensive production, so the argument goes, the expansion of manufactured exports translates into higher employment. Given the fact that labor is the most widely distributed factor of production in the economy, employment expansion and the subsequent increase in real wages are expected to reduce both poverty and income inequality (Krueger, 1995b; Balassa and Williamson, 1987; Fei et al., 1979).

While this may have been the experience in the NIEs, this does not seem to have been the case in many other Asian countries. It appears that the growth with equity experience of the NIEs may have been unique, brought about largely by favorable initial conditions in these economies, and the highly accommodating world market situation at the formative stage of their economic transformation. The NIEs may have had a head start over other developing countries because they had higher educational standards, relatively even distribution of income, and broad-based wealth ownership before they embarked on their liberalization programs. Earlier they had also instituted land reforms, a critical factor that facilitated the transfer of labor from agriculture to manufacturing during the structural transition. This was not the case in many Southeast and South Asian countries. Initial conditions relating to a host of social indicators including education and health, as well as income and wealth distribution, were poor from the outset. Land reform remains an unfinished item on the policy agenda in some of these countries even today. With these initial conditions, the need for policies and institutional mechanisms that ensured inclusive growth was compelling. But it would appear that these also remain on the list of unfinished items on the policy agenda. At the same time that poverty rates were coming down sharply, income inequalities were beginning to rise. This is depicted most starkly for Thailand in Figure 7.1, where we observe a distinct negative correlation between the decrease in poverty incidence and the increase in income inequality. A similar pattern, if less pronounced, can be observed in all other countries except Malaysia.

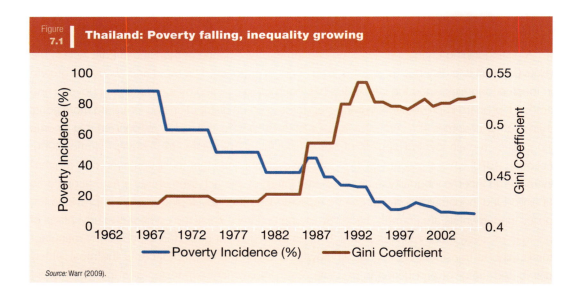

Figure 7.1 Thailand: Poverty falling, inequality growing

Source: Warr (2009).

Poverty reduction and the Millennium Development Goals (1990 to date)

Asia's progress in poverty reduction has accelerated in recent years (Table 7.2). By some estimates, the number of poor in East and South Asia was reduced by 425 million in 2005–2010

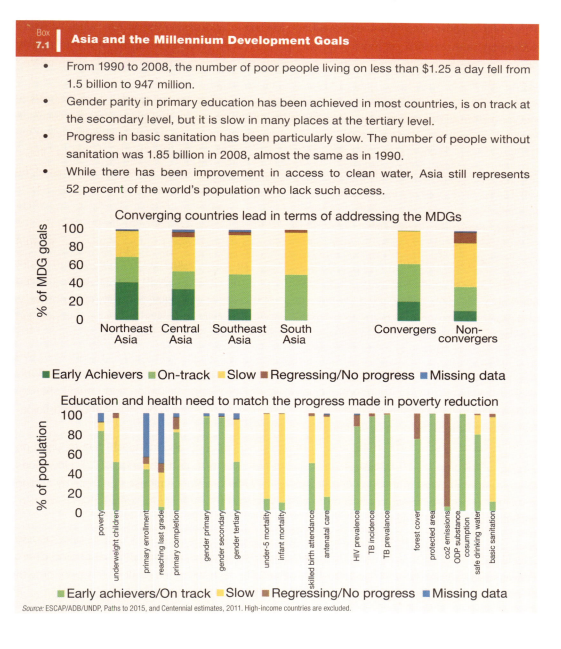

Box 7.1 — Asia and the Millennium Development Goals

- From 1990 to 2008, the number of poor people living on less than $1.25 a day fell from 1.5 billion to 947 million.
- Gender parity in primary education has been achieved in most countries, is on track at the secondary level, but it is slow in many places at the tertiary level.
- Progress in basic sanitation has been particularly slow. The number of people without sanitation was 1.85 billion in 2008, almost the same as in 1990.
- While there has been improvement in access to clean water, Asia still represents 52 percent of the world's population who lack such access.

Source: ESCAP/ADB/UNDP, Paths to 2015, and Centennial estimates, 2011. High-income countries are excluded.

(Chandy and Gertz, 2011). South Asia alone is expected to see a reduction of 430 million over 2005–2015, representing a decline in its poverty rate from about 40 percent to less than 9 percent. Progress in poverty reduction is not matched by all other indicators, as reflected in the review of Asia's performance toward achieving the MDGs in Box 7.1.

Overall, Asia's performance has been positive and has strongly influenced global progress. The region's converging countries have been leading in addressing the MDGs, while all Asia's subregions are on track on more than half the indicators. Nevertheless, the region is lagging on some crucial targets, particularly those relating to childhood and maternal health-related outcomes and sanitation.

As a general note, in contrast to the strong correlation between growth and changes in income measures of poverty, Bourguignon et al. (2006) conclude that the correlation between improvements in non-income MDGs and growth is practically nonexistent. This finding suggests that economic growth is not sufficient on its own to generate progress in the non-income MDGs. Sector policies, including targeted interventions, and other specific factors or circumstances matter as much as growth.

What is inclusive growth?

Inclusive growth recognizes that economic growth and social policy cannot be treated separately. The persistence of growing inequities and exclusion suggests that they can no longer be treated as an unavoidable residual outcome of a market-led growth process to be tackled separately. Inclusive growth must therefore encompass aspects of equity, equality of opportunity, and protection in market and employment transitions and disturbances. Inclusive growth refers to both the pace and pattern of growth, and is both an outcome and a process. On the one hand, it requires that everyone participates in the growth process, both in organizing its progression and in generating the growth itself. On the other hand, it also requires that everyone shares equitably in the benefits of growth. Therefore, inclusive growth implies participation and benefit sharing. Participation without benefit sharing makes growth unjust and sharing benefits without participation prevents it from being a desirable welfare outcome.

In the past, discussion on the impact of growth on poverty and inequality has focused on concepts such as broad-based or pro-poor growth (Tandon and Zhuang, 2007). How does inclusive growth relate to these concepts? Inclusive growth advances these concepts by adding access and opportunities, but it is more closely related to an absolute, rather than a relative, definition of pro-poor growth.

Under the absolute definition, growth is considered to be pro-poor as long as poor people benefit in absolute terms, as reflected in some agreed measure of poverty (Ravallion and Chen, 1997), regardless of the benefit achieved by others. By contrast, in the relative definition, growth is "pro-poor" only if the incomes of poor people grow faster than those of the population as a whole, so that inequality declines. However, while absolute pro-poor growth can be the result of direct income redistribution schemes, redistribution does not suffice for growth to be inclusive. Productivity must also be improved, and new employment opportunities created. In short, inclusive growth is about increasing the pace of growth and enlarging the size of the economy, while at the same time leveling the playing field for investment, expanding productive employment opportunities, and ensuring fair access to them. It allows every section of society to participate equally in and contribute to the growth process, regardless of their circumstances (Ali and Zhuang, 2007).

Why focus on inclusion and equity?

Although the rationale for focusing on inclusion and equity may appear self-evident, it is useful to clarify the multifaceted reasons for doing so, especially when tradeoffs may be involved. In addition to ethical and moral considerations, there are a number of pragmatic reasons for a focus on inclusion and equity.

Various studies, most recently the Growth Commission's (Kanbur and Spence, 2010), have confirmed that growth strategies cannot succeed without a commitment to equality of opportunity, that is, giving everyone a fair chance to participate in the growth process and to enjoy the fruits of growth that follow. For developing countries in particular, inequality appears to retard growth (Barro, 1999). More recent research indicates that inequality is also an obstacle to sustainable growth, since growth spells tend to be shorter in countries with greater inequality (Berg et al., 2008).

The persistence of inequality can trigger social and political tensions and even lead to conflict, as is currently evident in parts of Asia and in the Middle East. Political stability and social cohesion are factors that contribute to solid growth, and each of these factors can be adversely affected by income and social inequality. A deficiency in these two areas can lead to lower growth and lower effectiveness in response to economic crises (Rodrik, 1999). Rising inequalities thus pose a risk to stability and therefore to growth and economic development.

Income inequality can also lead to a misallocation of investment. Research has shown that countries with a poorly educated labor force have high income inequality. This is partly because the poor cannot finance their education, meaning that investment is essentially allocated away from the poor. A more equal income distribution promotes more efficient investment and hence stronger growth (Berg et al., 2008).

High levels of inequality can create institutions and cultures that favor those who have significant economic and political influence, thereby perpetuating the cycle of inequality. That is, income inequality entrenches discrimination in other areas such as access to healthcare and education, which reinforces and perpetuates inequality. Equity can help create influence for a larger group of people, and this can shape institutions that will promote the interests of even more members of the economy. There are different types of inequalities. "Bad" inequalities are based on an individual's circumstances, (in contrast to "good" inequalities that result from effort) and can lead to inequality traps. "Chronic" disparities in power, wealth, and status among different socioeconomic groups are perpetuated by economic, political, and sociocultural mechanisms and institutions (Bourguignon et al., 2006). The capture of political power by an elite leads to political inequality and aggravates the initial inequality in endowments and opportunities.

Even the process of addressing inequality can lead to undesirable effects in the political arena on both sides of the problem. Redistribution efforts can create disincentives for investment by raising taxes on those making the investments, dampening growth in the long run. On the other hand, economic elites may turn to corruption in the face of redistribution so as to maintain the status quo, which hurts the credibility of institutions and is also likely to decrease growth (Alesina and Rodrik, 1994).

Finally, growth and equality should not be seen as tradeoffs, but as part of a virtuous circle. More economic opportunities for the poor, when not at the expense of other groups in society, can lead to higher growth, which in turn can bring about further opportunities.

What is Asia's status?

With the success attained in reducing poverty, the focus has now shifted toward addressing inequality.

Income inequality

Although Asia's recent economic growth has been impressive, income inequality as measured by the Gini coefficient has been rising in a number of countries (Table 7.3 and Box 7.2). Income inequality has risen not because the poor are getting poorer, but because the incomes of the rich are growing faster than those of the poor. Income inequalities along spatial (rural–urban) and ethnic lines have also been increasing. Some "good inequality" can be expected during growth spells, as growth will come from different places at different times and thus create an uneven distribution of income in a natural way. However, "bad inequality" can also develop when those who do not participate in growth at the outset are not given adequate opportunity to participate in growth in the future. To distinguish between the two statistically is difficult, but it would be correct to say that increasing inequality can pose risks to future growth, and this has been observed in Asia, and is happening now in PRC. In Table 7.3, Malaysia is the only country that has seen a decrease in its Gini coefficient over the past 15 years, which represents an improvement in equality. Although the range of the increase (deterioration) in the Gini coefficient for the remaining 13 countries is broad, eight of them record increases of 10 percent or more. The smallest increases have been recorded for PRC, the Philippines, and Viet Nam.

The increase in inequality can also be seen when broken down by income deciles. For

Table 7.3 Rising inequality in Asia (Gini coefficients)

	Initial Year		Final Year		% Change
Malaysia	47.7	1992	46.2	2009	-3
PRC	40.7	1993	41.6	2005	2
Philippines	42.9	1994	44	2006	3
Viet Nam	35.7	1993	37.6	2008	5
Pakistan	30.3	1993	32.7	2006	8
Indonesia	34.4	1993	37.6	2007	9
Mongolia	33.2	1995	36.6	2008	10
India	32.9	1993	36.8	2005	12
Thailand	46.2	1992	52.5	2004	14
Sri Lanka	35.4	1996	40.3	2007	14
Cambodia	38.3	1994	44.4	2007	16
Bangladesh	28.3	1989	33.2	2005	17
Lao PDR	30.4	1992	36.7	2008	21
Nepal	37.7	1996	47.3	2004	26

Source: World Bank, PovCalNet.

example, the top decile in PRC urban income increased its share of total income from 17 percent in 1981 to 27 percent in 2005. The first through the seventh deciles declined (Figure 7.2).

Urban inequality

Urban areas—i.e., those that have seen the most economic growth—have also experienced an increase in inequality. Disparities in living conditions and in access to basic services are severe in many Asian cities. In PRC in particular but also India, urban inequality has been trending upward over the past three decades (Figure 7.3). Although urban inequality has been trending down slightly in Malaysia, the levels remain one of the highest in the region.

Inequality has been shown to have particularly undesirable effects in urban environments. Latin America, for example, urbanized at a rapid pace roughly 65 years before Asia. During those years, extreme inequality in many Latin American cities led to poorer areas becoming areas of drugs, crime, and violence. Asia must avoid the same fate.

Spatial inequality

One glaring aspect of inequality in Asia is that it is regional in nature. National averages can mask true inequality within countries, as there are cases of middle-income countries with

Box 7.2 | The two faces of Asia

The rapid growth of Developing Asia disguises rising inequalities. Rapid economic growth—and the rise of the rich alongside the millions of poor who do not have access to quality education, water, sanitation, and health services—have given birth to the two faces of Asia: one is reflected in the glittering towers of Shanghai, Mumbai, Jakarta, and Manila, while the other seen in the gloom covering the slums of these same cities.

This growing economic dualism poses a threat to Asia's sustained dynamic growth and social cohesion. The two faces need to converge if growth and social harmony are to be maintained in countries as well as within the region. There can be only one face of Asia: an Asia with opportunities open to all, an Asia where every individual can live with dignity—free of poverty and sharing in its prosperity.

Development of Asia must not only ensure that growth remains buoyant and helps lift millions out of their daily suffering; it must also ensure that growth is inclusive, so that benefits are shared equally by all.

The task of meeting this challenge should not be underestimated. Even by conservative estimates, there will be millions of poor in Asia by 2015, with incomes less than $2 a day, and millions more who still do not have access to safe drinking water, sanitation, basic education, and health services.

If Asia fails to address this challenge, the ostentatious towers will continue to share their cities with slums, threatening both the economic progress and social cohesion of one of the most dynamic regions of the world.

Figure 7.2 | PRC: Urban income deciles

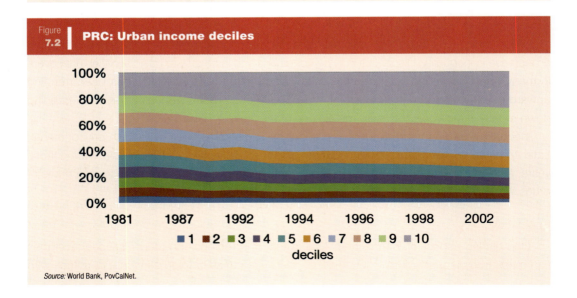

Source: World Bank, PovCalNet.

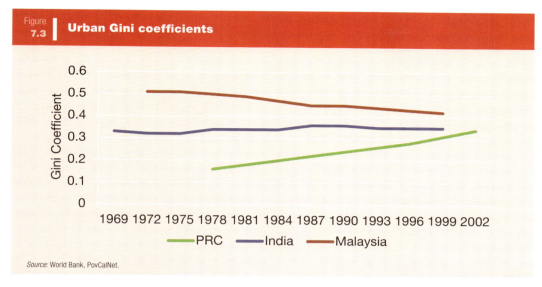

Figure 7.3 | Urban Gini coefficients

Source: World Bank, PovCalNet.

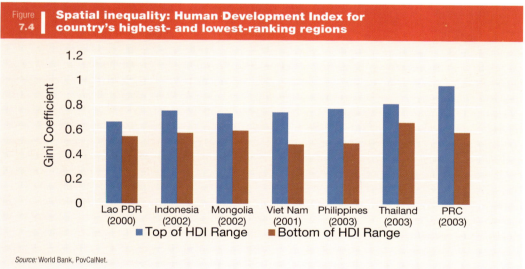

Figure 7.4 | Spatial inequality: Human Development Index for country's highest- and lowest-ranking regions

Source: World Bank, PovCalNet.

relatively high poverty rates in certain regions (Gill and Kharas, 2007). Large disparities in human development exist between regions of a country and from country to country (Figure 7.4). Coastal urban areas tend to be wealthier than inner rural areas. To be sure, part of this is an example of "good inequality," in that the coastal areas became competitive and experienced growth. At the same time, some of this difference is likely "bad inequality," in the sense that people in the inland rural areas tend to have less access to opportunities than people on the coast. The rural–urban divide is particularly stark in the least developed countries where the majority of the population are engaged in agricultural activities. In Cambodia in 2010 for instance, the rural plateau/mountain and Tonlé Sap zones had the highest poverty headcounts at 36.6 percent and 30.8 percent, respectively, while the central plains area recorded a rate of 21.3 percent (Government of Cambodia, 2011).

Non-income inequality
Education

Education is a crucial area of non-income inequality. It is a self-reinforcing type of inequality, since poor education generally leads to lower income, which in turn leads to poor education of children, and so on. Lower income is significantly associated with poorer education (Figure 7.5). In some countries, those in the highest quintile have almost twice the number of years in school than those in the lowest quintile.

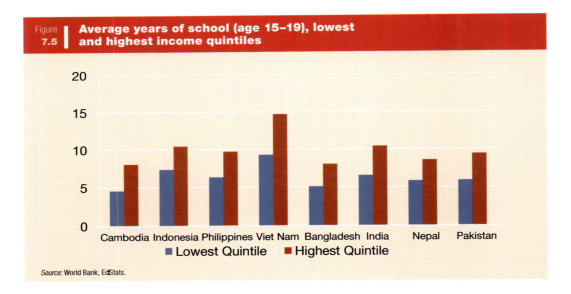

Figure 7.5 Average years of school (age 15–19), lowest and highest income quintiles

Source: World Bank, EdStats.

Another example of the effect of income on education is the level of Indian men's and women's education based on income quintiles (Figures 7.6a and 7.6b). The effect of income is clear, since nearly half the men in the lowest quintile have no education at all, while nearly half those in the highest quintile have 12 or more years of schooling. Similarly, gender has a marked effect. Nearly 80 percent of Indian women in the lowest income quintile have no education. This is a large percentage of the population that potentially cannot be fully used in the labor force because of a lack of schooling, which detracts from growth in the long run.

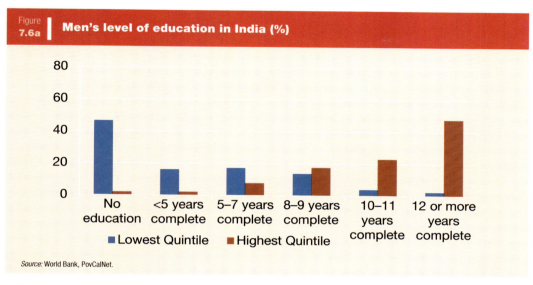

Source: World Bank, PovCalNet.

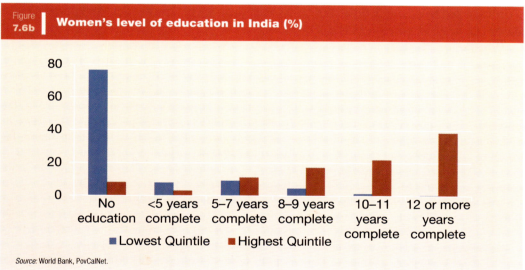

Source: World Bank, PovCalNet.

Health

Health is yet another example of self-reinforcing inequality. Impaired health hampers the ability of the poor to increase their incomes. Even though life expectancy has risen strongly in Asia over the past 30 years, the poor still lack many very basic services that would help address the inequality in health outcomes.

For instance, prenatal care is still lacking in many parts of Asia, especially among the poor. In the Philippines, 80 percent of mothers in the highest income quintile receive prenatal care from

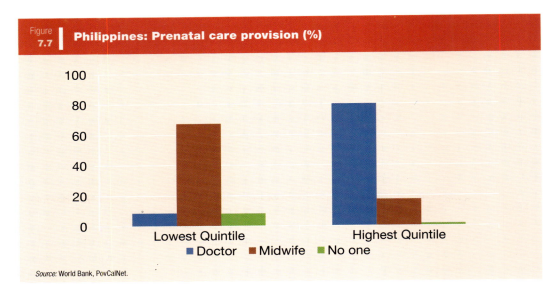

Figure 7.7 Philippines: Prenatal care provision (%)

Source: World Bank, PovCalNet.

a doctor, while fewer than 10 percent of mothers in the lowest quintile do. Eight percent in the lowest quintile receive no prenatal care at all (Figure 7.7).

Vaccination coverage is also a problem. In Indonesia, only about 60 percent of those in the lowest income quartile receive a first dose of Hepatitis B vaccination, but over 90 percent of those in the highest quartile do (Figure 7.8).

Undernourishment and food deprivation continue to be problems in a large part of Asia, despite the substantial reduction in poverty over the past two decades. One out of every six Asians is undernourished (Chatterjee et al., 2010). As one would suspect, undernourishment is worst among the poorest. In Pakistan, for example, 47 percent of children in the lowest income

Table 7.4 Nutritional status of children in Pakistan (% of children below 2 standard deviations of mean)

Quintile	Height for age	Weight for height	Weight for age
Lowest	61.6	11.5	47
Second	54.9	15.2	46
Middle	50.4	15.2	41.7
Fourth	39.8	12.8	31
Highest	30.9	7	18.8

Source: World Bank, PovCalNet.

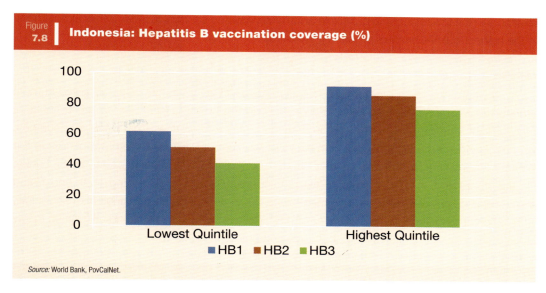

Figure 7.8 | **Indonesia: Hepatitis B vaccination coverage (%)**

Source: World Bank, PovCalNet.

quintile are more than two standard deviations below the average weight for their age (Table 7.4).

Sanitation

Poor sanitation is an issue across many parts of Asia, but particularly in South Asia where sheer scale and historical practices have slowed advances (Gosling et al., 2011). In total, 716 million people in South Asia have no sanitation. Fifty-four percent of Indians and 27 percent of Pakistanis lack sanitation facilities. Sanitation issues reflect the distribution of income. Nearly all

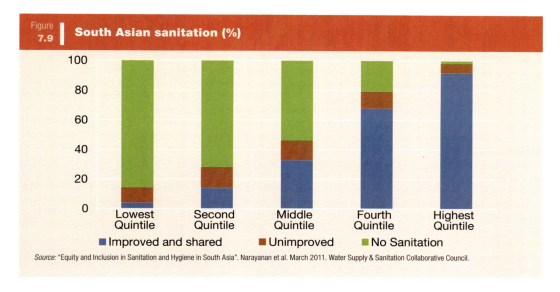

Figure 7.9 | **South Asian sanitation (%)**

Source: "Equity and Inclusion in Sanitation and Hygiene in South Asia". Narayanan et al. March 2011. Water Supply & Sanitation Collaborative Council.

residents in the lowest income quintile in South Asia have no sanitary facilities, while almost none in the highest quintile has this problem (Figure 7.9).

Gender inequality

While there has been progress in education, gender parity has not been achieved in most other areas. Women in the region experience some of the lowest rates of political representation, employment, and property ownership in the world. Major differences exist between countries, with the Philippines earning a very high score of 0.77 out of 0.85 (rank ninth out of 134) in the World Economic Forum's Global Gender Gap Report (Figure 7.10), followed closely by Sri Lanka. On the other hand, in 2010 India and Pakistan scored 0.62 and 0.55, ranking 112th and 132nd of 132 respectively, with little improvement since 2006. High-income countries also score low, with Japan at 0.65 and Republic of Korea at 0.63, ranking 94th and 104th, primarily owing to low levels of female participation in the labor force and political leadership.

Figure 7.10 Gender inequality in Asia

Source: World Economoic Forum, Gender Gap Report (2010).

Action agenda

The PRC is a strong supporter and follower of inclusive growth, a concept that is consistent with our pursuit of scientific development and social harmony. While speeding up the transformation of economic growth pattern and maintaining stable and relatively fast economic growth, the PRC is committed to integrating economic development with improvement of people's lives (Hu Jintao, 2010).

Inclusive growth is the centerpiece of our development agenda. Fast economic growth provides us with the resources and the wherewithal to address the problems of poverty, ignorance and disease. Rapid growth will have little meaning, however, unless social and economic inequalities, which still afflict our society, are not eliminated quickly and effectively. (Manmohan Singh, 2010)

Asia needs a strategy to deal with inequality if it is to maintain the social stability that has been so important for growth to this point. Inclusive growth as a development strategy is being embraced by many Asian economies, multilateral agencies, and civil societies. The 12th five-year plans of PRC and India (Box 7.3) each include a focus on addressing inequality.

Developing economies tend to have significant market failures, whether these are related to competition, credit markets, labor mobility, or land ownership. Investments are therefore allocated inefficiently leaving potential economic growth "on the table." Policies to encourage investment directed toward those with limited access can help combat inequity and help allocate investments more efficiently, thereby strengthening economic growth (World Bank, 2006).

On one level, current global trends are favorable to combat inequity. The rise in food and other commodity prices, thought to be influenced by global structural demand factors as well as supply shocks, will produce a sizable shift in the terms of trade that favor rural areas over cities. Since cities have benefited more from globalization, this shift helps balance the distribution of gains throughout the economy. More resources going to rural areas will ease overall domestic inequality, but could widen both intraurban and intrarural inequality. The gains from higher food prices will accrue disproportionately to rich farmers at the expense of landless laborers and subsistence farmers, as well as the urban poor.

More generally, Asia will have to rethink its policies toward distribution. Inequalities of opportunity can no longer be disregarded. Nor can islands of poverty coexist easily with growing affluence, whether within countries or within groups in society. The range of policy instruments is limited. Development of human capital is a good place to start, as are carefully crafted redistribution policies and good governance (Figure 7.11).

Growth and jobs

Growth is essential. But perhaps what is more important for inclusion is the pattern of growth. The most obvious method of addressing inequality is to generate employment opportunities for the poor (Thomas, 2007). Unemployment and underemployment are generally associated with inequality. So, not only will higher employment help to provide the poor with greater aggregate income, but should help mitigate the social and political stability problems that tend to accompany unemployment. Felipe (2010) argues that to achieve inclusive growth, governments must pursue full employment of the labor force, which he defines as "zero involuntary unemployment." He stresses that the most important way for a person to participate and contribute to growth is through a productive and rewarding job.

Box 7.3 | Inclusive growth in policy planning: PRC, India, and Cambodia

The benefits of rapid growth in the PRC have not been evenly distributed among individuals and regions, resulting in a skewed distribution of income in favor of coastal cities and urban citizens. The Gini coefficient has worsened from 0.16 at the beginning of the reform to 0.47 at present, one of the highest in the world. Moreover, the socioeconomic implications of population aging in the PRC threaten the sustainability of growth.

PRC's 12th five-year plan (2011–2015) seems set to increase spending on social safety nets, including the provision of low-income housing (to be made available to 20 percent of the urban population by 2015), albeit from low levels. It also has a focus on rural development, which includes more substantial investment in agriculture.

The outline of India's latest plan acknowledges that while the previous plan was successful in generating economic growth, it was not as successful in addressing inequality. Rural consumption inequality has remained relatively stable over the past 30 years, but urban consumption inequality has steadily increased, with the Gini coefficient climbing from 0.30 to 0.37. In 1983, average rural consumption was 69 percent of the average urban level, but has now decreased to 52 percent. Spatial inequality across Indian states has also increased, given that some states have participated in economic growth more than others. The gap between the lowest and highest poverty rates in Indian states was 32.8 percent in 1993, but is currently 43.1 percent.

The latest plan seeks to address inequality, while maintaining the impressive growth performance of the past several years. Particular goals include a 4 percent growth target for agriculture and a $1 trillion investment in infrastructure development by 2018, with priority to rural and backward areas.

Cambodia's income distribution is one of the most unequal in Asia, with a Gini coefficient of around 0.45 in 2007. The richest 20 percent of the population outspend the poorest 20 percent by about eight times, also one of the highest such ratios in Asia (Hill and Menon 2011b). Although great strides have been made in reducing extreme poverty, child malnutrition, child mortality and maternal mortality rates continue to be unacceptably high.

Recognizing these challenges, the Government of Cambodia (2011) has drafted a national social protection strategy to be launched in 2011. Immediate priorities of this strategy involve the expansion of targeted programs such as free health care for the poor, and the pilot testing of programs including conditional cash transfers and generating employment opportunities through labor-intensive public works.

Although the situation in only three countries is highlighted here, a number of others, such as Indonesia, the Philippines and Thailand are looking to incorporate inclusive growth strategies as part of their policy planning frameworks. It is likely that this list of countries will grow in the future.

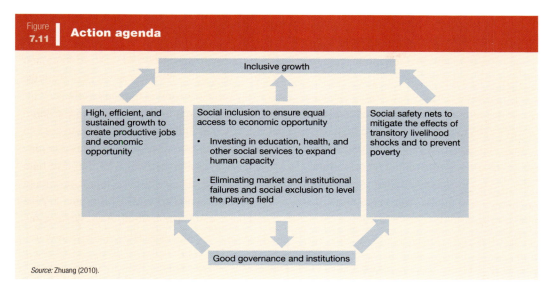

Figure 7.11 Action agenda

Source: Zhuang (2010).

The challenge in many Asian economies is to create productive jobs in the nonfarm sector, to absorb an anticipated increase in the labor force, and to absorb the excess labor that has to be shifted from the farm sector. The need to transfer labor from agriculture follows from the fact that productivity in agriculture is low. Thus the only way for agricultural productivity to rise is by facilitating labor mobility out of the sector (Ahluwalia, 2011). This will be accompanied by employment-related transitions from rural to urban, unorganized to organized activity, and subsistence self-employment giving way to employment at a livable wage (TeamLease Services, 2009).

Many job-oriented policies that focus on the economy as a whole will help the poor in particular. For example, facilitating labor mobility can help allocate labor more efficiently and expand jobs for the poor. Policies that attempt to increase productivity in the rural sector not only increase output but also strengthen incomes for these workers. Increased access to finance can benefit the poor by accelerating the hiring of unskilled labor. In addition, countries should focus on having job-rich economic recoveries. Not only does a higher rate of employment tend to reduce inequality, but recoveries with higher employment also tend to be more sustainable (Heathcote, Perri, and Violante, 2010).

Interventions and distribution policies

Meeting the non-income poverty MDG goals will require general, sectoral, and focused interventions. General interventions involve maintaining a focus on economic momentum, increased investment in infrastructure, and a scaling up of public expenditures. Sectoral interventions in areas like health care, education (Box 7.4), nutrition, and sanitation are needed so that the poor have the opportunity to obtain skills relevant to well-paid and productive jobs. Finally,

> **Box 7.4 | Vocational education and training**
>
> Access to proper education can help the poor earn higher incomes and address the inequality issue. Specifically, greater access to secondary education could help significantly. The key point is that education is essential to jobs that are in demand in the marketplace.
>
> An example is vocational education and training (VET). There is an urgent need for Asian economies to produce a workforce that can meet industry demands for relevant skills to sustain competitiveness. A VET system that is responsive to changing labor market conditions can play a crucial role. By providing an opportunity to acquire skills for employment, VET can also help the poor and disadvantaged, and those who have dropped out of school. Thus it promotes inclusion and equity. The percentage of secondary students enrolled in VET programs in Asia (13 percent) is low relative to Europe (24 percent) and particularly low in South Asia. While some Asian countries have achieved gender parity in this area, it remains a challenge elsewhere.

interventions may need to target spatial inequalities within economies.

Addressing inequality will inevitably require some form of redistribution. When designed correctly, redistribution policies have had success. Pro-poor policies have been used in Brazil, Chile, and Mexico, for example, to greatly reduce income disparity (Ravallion, 1997). These policies specifically include spending for social assistance.

Government redistribution policies and social safety nets could take the form of labor market policies and programs aimed to contain unemployment and reduce employment-related risks; social insurance programs such as pensions, health and disability insurance, and unemployment insurance; social assistance and welfare schemes, including conditional cash or in-kind transfers, and essential services for the most vulnerable groups; and child-related programs.

The last item has a major impact on developing human capabilities by providing protection to ensure the healthy and productive development of the young. Useful examples are early-child development programs, school feeding programs, scholarships, free or subsidized health services for mothers and children, and family allowances or credit.

Considering the heterogeneity of needs, social safety net programs need to be multilayered in design. For instance, although conditional cash transfers can have an immediate impact on the poor when monitored effectively, they are at best a palliative measure; the longer-term solution lies in investments to develop skills and promote sustainable livelihood programs.

Redistribution policies, however, need to be implemented carefully. Progressive taxation and enforceable labor rights can help to reduce inequality; however, policy makers should be wary of the possibility of "two" labor markets developing as a result of these policies (Walton, 2007). In addition, redistribution policies can hurt investment incentives, thereby dampening growth for the economy as a whole. "Virtually all anti-growth and anti-poor policies India has been struggling to shed for two decades had their origins in the pursuit of equity... To be sure, equity-orientated policies that improve opportunities for the poor without compromising efficiency and growth do exist. The catch, however, is that once equity becomes central to policy making, self-interested lobbies capture the policies in the name of fairness. The policies then adopted are precisely those that impede growth and poverty alleviation" (Panagariya, 2006).

Though many of the policies used to combat inequality target the poor, the middle class should not be neglected. It is not only a driver of economic growth, but also has substantial political influence, so that policy makers must find an appropriate balance between acts that focus on the poor and those that broadly improve the well-being of the majority of people.

Governance

Good governance and declining inequality are part of a virtuous circle. If governance improves, institutions are less likely to give special treatment to the wealthier portion of the population, and this will improve equality. State capture by the elite must be avoided, and if it already exists, must be addressed because it will tend to maintain or worsen inequality. Political inclusion and participation should be encouraged to avoid this problem.

Social and economic injustice that denies equal opportunity to individuals based on their status or sect or because they do not belong to certain power groups is often reflective of bad policies, weak governance mechanisms, faulty legal or institutional arrangements, and market failures. In Developing Asia, factor-market failures (land and credit) are particularly acute. The central duty of the government in promoting social and economic justice is to address all these failures. Strong institutions and good governance are fundamentally equitable and are needed to provide incentives for all citizens to have the opportunity to invent, innovate, and become entrepreneurs. These incentives can best emerge when the distribution of power and influence is not highly unequal.

The potential of excluded groups is untapped in large part because they lack access to a wide range of basic services—educational and health, as discussed above, but also financial services and security. Policies aimed at ensuring broad-based access to these services are likely to have a significant impact not only on equality but also on growth.

Climate change

Climate change will affect all countries, but its negative impacts are likely to be more severely felt by poor people and poor countries. This is because they are more vulnerable due to their high dependence on natural resources and climate-sensitive sectors, such as agriculture and fisheries, and their limited financial and institutional capacities to cope with climate variability and extremes, including the natural disasters that they induce. This will be particularly true for the least developed countries in the tropical and subtropical regions of Asia (IPCC, 2001). Climate change therefore poses a serious risk to reducing poverty and inequality, and threatens to undo decades of development efforts.

What is more concerning is that the severity of climate change impacts on the poor is likely to increase, if ignored. This is partly because the impacts themselves are likely to increase, but also because climate change is superimposed on existing vulnerabilities. Climate change will: further reduce access to poor people's livelihood assets such as drinking water; undermine the health of poor people and vulnerable groups such as children and women through increased prevalence of vector- and waterborne diseases; and threaten food security in many poor countries in Asia (Box 7.5), as well as Africa and Latin America, through increased incidence of floods, droughts, forest fires, and tropical cyclones.

Both adaptation and mitigation have roles to play. To protect the poor, however, adaptation needs greater attention, including its incorporation in development planning Adaptation measures must be represented in strategies for reducing poverty and inequality and for promoting sustainable development. They should deal with risk reduction (e.g., disaster management), strengthening adaptive capacity (e.g., diversifying livelihoods), and targeting the sources of vulnerability (economic, social, and political). Many adaptation mechanisms will be strengthened by making progress in areas such as good governance, institutional development, and natural resource management as they build the resilience of countries, communities, and households to all types of shock, including climate change.

In sum, it is now widely accepted that economic growth alone, however robust or rapid, cannot address the multidimensional nature of poverty, deprivation, or vulnerability. To address these issues, growth must also be inclusive. Inclusive growth must not only address poverty, but must also deal with aspects of equity, equality of access, and opportunity, and must provide protection to the vulnerable in the various facets of daily living.

The government, public sector, and public–private partnerships will all have roles to play in implementing of an inclusive growth strategy. An environment that provides incentives that encourage domestic philanthropy can play an important complementary role, especially in middle-income countries. While growth will be largely spearheaded by the private sector, the role of the government is to address market failures and plug the governance and institutional deficits so that everyone can participate and benefit from the region's strong growth. Much of the focus in the region so far has been on the pace of growth, but it is time for policy makers to look at the pattern of growth and make its base broader.

Finally, some forms of inequality have long-gestation, multigenerational effects. These include issues of early childhood development, health, and access to higher quality education. They merit urgent attention.

Box 7.5 Food security: Rising demands and shrinking resources

For the next few decades, high growth in Asia and Africa means that cereals imports of developing countries will rise rapidly, from about 135 to 300 million tons between 2008 and 2050 (FAO, 2008). Together with expanding bio-fuels mandated in OECD countries, this high growth in Asia and Africa has already changed the world from one of long term declining real food prices to one with much higher and possibly rising real food prices. For low income and/or slow growing Asian countries, this means that the two pillars of food security, availability of food and access by the poorer groups, are likely to become significantly more challenging. These countries can resolve the problem either through improved agricultural growth or through imports from the global market, which is expected to be able to supply the much higher demand for imports.

By 2050, for the group of 11 converging countries, especially the four emerging global players (PRC, India, Indonesia and Viet Nam), outright hunger will either have disappeared or become confined to small remaining poor populations. Quality of nutrition and combating obesity will move center stage. However, these countries have no or few land reserves, and face increasing difficulties in bringing larger areas under irrigation. They may therefore face food availability or food supply problems. The degree and nature of the problem will depend on the drivers of food demand and the countries' ability to expand agricultural production.

India's food demand will grow rapidly because its population is expected to grow by about one third over the 40 years to 2050, and its income growth is expected to be even more rapid. While per capita cereals demand is not expected to grow any further, population will expand cereals demand by about one third. In addition, livestock products, especially milk, chicken and eggs, will see a huge increase in demand from both higher incomes and a growing population. At the same time, India's agricultural growth has declined over the past two decades and is far from reaching the desired 4 percent growth rate. This is partly because its rate of agricultural productivity growth has slowed down sharply from its peak during the Green revolution. Even though India can now afford to import very large quantities of food, by 2050 it will house a fifth of the global population. Therefore it is very reluctant to become dependent on the global market for its food security, especially for its basic staples wheat and rice. In a recent analysis of agriculture in India, Parikh and Binswanger, 2011 find that under plausible assumptions about TFP growth and resource availability, the agriculture sector could constrain India's growth. The problem is likely to be even greater for Pakistan, because its population is expected to nearly double by 2050, although with its smaller population size than India it may be more willing than India to depend on imports of rice, and wheat.

The PRC is unlikely to face a similar dilemma. First of all, its population is expected to increase only slowly and its total food cereals demand per capita is already declining. It has a record of much higher agricultural growth than India and over the past two decades has

Box 7.5 — Food security: Rising demands and shrinking resources

become the global leader in agricultural TFP growth. While it is also unwilling to become heavily dependent on imports of rice and wheat, PRC is willing to import large quantities of feed grains and oilseed cakes for its very rapidly growing meat, poultry and egg sector. PRC is also pursuing a policy of exporting high valued commodities such as horticulture and fish from an expanding aquaculture.

For Indonesia and Viet Nam (which has emerged as a major global rice exporter), populations are growing only slightly less than in India, but like Southeast Asia as a whole, they have accelerated their agricultural and TFP growth. Having smaller populations also allows them to become more dependent on global markets for agriculture, both as importers and exporters.

For all Asian countries, despite the rapid decline of agriculture as a share of their economy, rising domestic food demand and higher global prices mean that they cannot afford to neglect agriculture and agricultural productivity growth; none of them can afford to be complacent about agriculture.

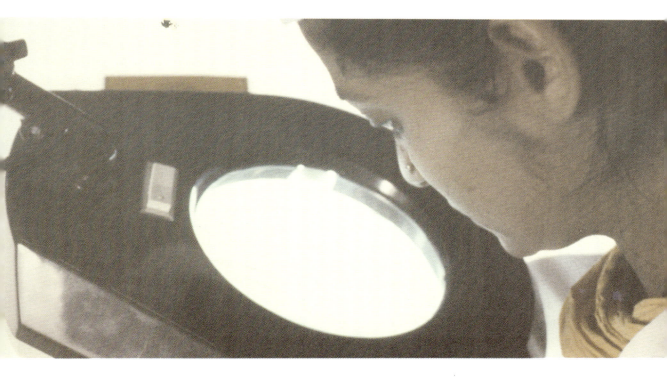

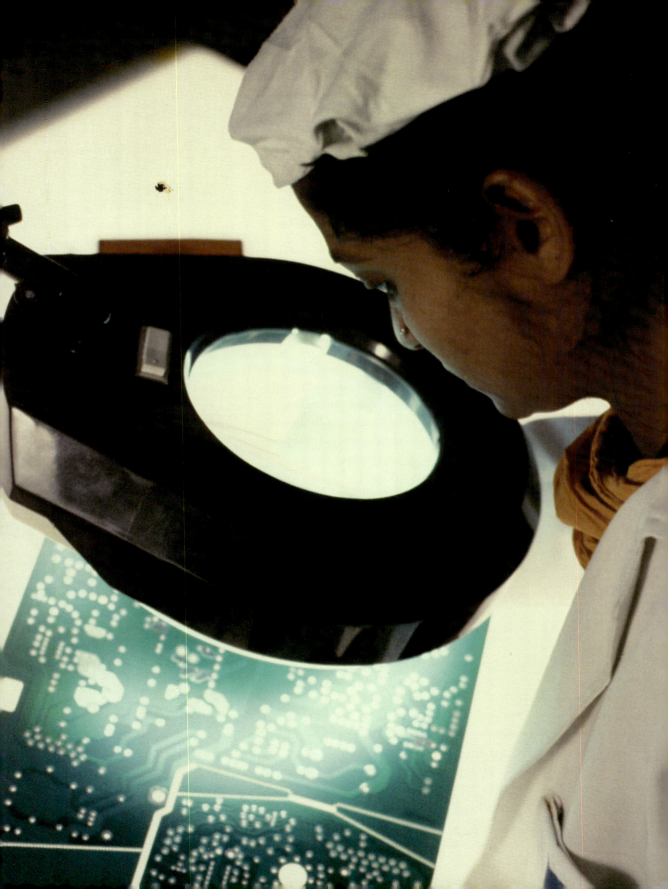

Driving Productivity and Growth

Chapter 8

Yasheng Huang and Y. Aaron Szyf

Introduction

Asia's rapid growth has been based on, and must be sustained through, continued improvements in total factor productivity (TFP). This chapter makes the case for Asian economies to promote entrepreneurship, innovation, and technology development to ensure improvement in productivity and its translation into growth and well-being.

Although entrepreneurship is not a homogeneous phenomenon or concept, this chapter attempts to make a simple distinction between two types of entrepreneurship—catch-up entrepreneurship and frontier entrepreneurship. Catch-up entrepreneurship engages in replicative activities—activities invented by others and replicated at competitive costs. Its main economic contribution is job creation and it involves relatively little new knowledge and technology. Frontier entrepreneurship is innovative and inventive, and creates breakthroughs in science and technology. It has a long left tail of failures but also a short right tail of successes that are truly transformative. Frontier entrepreneurship is an important mechanism to convert knowledge production into improvements for human welfare. This distinction is useful as a way to disaggregate the entrepreneurial landscape of emerging Asia.

Asia's high-income economies are at the frontier end while most other economies are at the catch-up end of the spectrum. PRC and India are in a special class with pockets of frontier innovation and entrepreneurship and the advantage of massive scale, coexisting with vast areas of catch-up entrepreneurship. The chapter draws on the experiences within Asia and globally to derive lessons for the converging and non-converging economies of Asia (defined in Chapter 2). Specifically, the chapter outlines the requirements for enabling and promoting productivity improvement, innovation, and entrepreneurship. A fundamental requirement for most of Asia is human capital development through high-quality education at all levels. Appendix 3 elaborates on the overall technology landscape with a special emphasis on Asia.

Why focus on productivity and entrepreneurship?

A decomposition of real GDP growth into its components of labor, capital, and TFP points to the vital role that TFP plays in the GDP growth of Asia's converging economies (Figure 8.1). Asia's

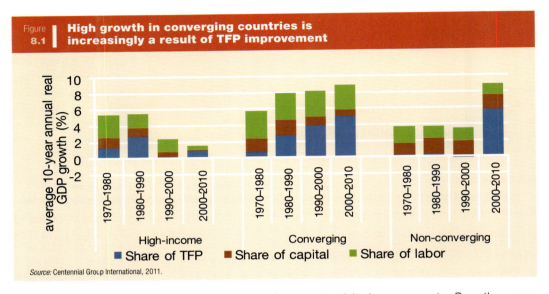

Figure 8.1 | High growth in converging countries is increasingly a result of TFP improvement

Source: Centennial Group International, 2011.

high-income countries owe much of their growth to productivity improvements. Over the years, converging countries have steadily increased their share of TFP in GDP growth from 13 percent in 1970–1980 to 56 percent in 2000–2010, a trend that shows the increasing importance of TFP growth in their path to convergence. TFP growth accounted for 59 percent of PRC's rapid growth in 2000–2010, and 42 percent in India. There is a significant difference between convergers and non-convergers not only in rates of GDP growth but also in its composition. While convergers owe much of their growth to productivity improvement, many non-convergers (such as Nepal) owe most of their growth to labor expansion. The sustained growth of Asian economies in the next 40 years must remain anchored in improvements in TFP. Appendix 4 provides additional data on GDP and TFP growth of Asian economies.

As Figure 8.2 shows, TFP levels in Asia are correlated with the level of high-growth entrepreneurial activity in the region's economies, as estimated by the Global Entrepreneurship and Development Index (GEDI).[1] Robust entrepreneurial development based on innovation and productivity will thus be central for all groups of economies in Asia in the next 40 years. For the high-income developed economies, it is the key mechanism to leverage their accumulated knowledge base. For the converging economies, fostering entrepreneurial development is the most effective strategy to avoid the Middle Income Trap. And for the non-converging economies, entrepreneurship is the most efficient catch-up strategy to help them to join the ranks of the converging economies.

Entrepreneurship contributes to economic growth through several mechanisms. First,

---

[1] The GEDI Index focuses particularly on "high-growth entrepreneurship" by not only examining outputs but the institutions and processes that drive them. It uses three subindexes and 14 variables covering both individual and institutional issues (Acs and Szerb, 2011).

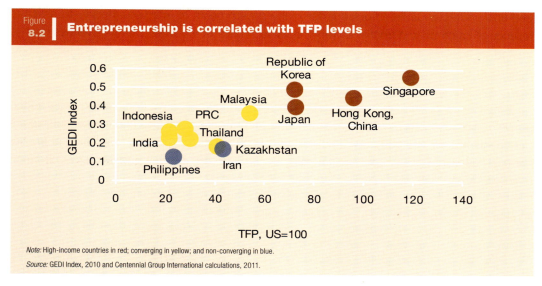

Figure 8.2 **Entrepreneurship is correlated with TFP levels**

Note: High-income countries in red; converging in yellow; and non-converging in blue.
Source: GEDI Index, 2010 and Centennial Group International calculations, 2011.

entrepreneurs create jobs. This point is brought into sharp focus by the recent experience of socialist economies as they transition to market economies. In Viet Nam, during the first seven years of reforms, net job creation in the new private sector was 10 million, whereas job creation in the state sector was negative (Johnson et al., 2002). Second, entrepreneurs challenge the status quo by competing down the rents that accrue to the established incumbents—the famous claim of "creative destruction" made by Joseph Schumpeter. This Schumpeterian view of economic growth is relevant in any economic context but particularly in developing countries where government protection and politically sanctioned monopolies have a dominant market position. The third mechanism is via innovations and technological progress. One economic analysis of important innovations in the 20th century shows that 50 percent of innovations were generated by new and small firms (Acs and Audretsch, 1988).

The broad contributions by entrepreneurs to economic growth are widely acknowledged but policy makers should guard against two common mistakes. First, governments often design policies to pick the winners, but experience suggests that this is difficult to do. One reason is that policy makers frequently lack the domain knowledge, foresight, and detailed information to forecast the growth prospects of entrepreneurial ventures accurately and their successes are often only recognized after the fact. One of the most famous cases is Alibaba.com in PRC. Today, it is the second largest business-to-business and consumer-to-consumer e-commerce platform in PRC. In 2007, its initial public offering raised $1.7 billion on NASDAQ, the second highest after Google's. Few people in the 1990s could have forecast its success.

Another common mistake many policy makers have made is to create a policy and regulatory environment to favor frontier entrepreneurship at the expense of the catch-up type. A natural, perhaps understandable, impulse is for many governments to intervene heavily to shift the balance of catch-up and frontier entrepreneurship in favor of the latter. Competitiveness often is treated as equivalent to high-tech, and innovation means advances in science and technology. According to this line of reasoning, an advanced economy is one in which products and production processes embody a high scientific content.

Both PRC and India first succeeded in catch-up entrepreneurship and subsequently added frontier entrepreneurship to their development toolkits. These two types of entrepreneurship are not substitutes for one another. In fact, catch-up entrepreneurship is the foundation of frontier entrepreneurship. Policy makers in emerging Asia will do well to avoid repeating this common mistake.

Productivity and entrepreneurship in Asia

Asia's growth in TFP between 1970 and 2010, averaging 1.6 percent per year, has been stronger than in any other region. As Figure 8.3 shows, starting from some of the lowest levels in 1970, Asia's converging countries have registered impressive TFP growth that has averaged 3 percent in the past four decades, compared to 0.2 percent for non-converging countries. Converging countries also enjoyed continuous improvement in TFP growth over each of the four decades while high-income and non-converging countries suffered from productivity losses in the 1990s. In 2000–2010, TFP growth in converging countries was most impressive at 5 percent per year, accounting for a large share of GDP growth that averaged around 9 percent per year during this time (Appendix 4).

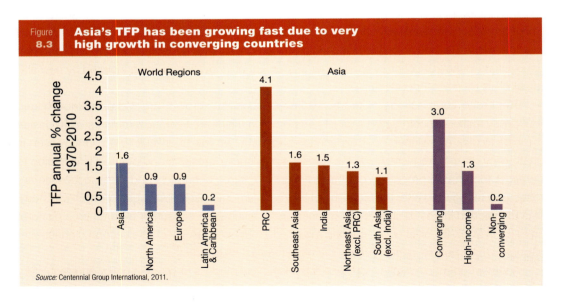

Figure 8.3 Asia's TFP has been growing fast due to very high growth in converging countries

Source: Centennial Group International, 2011.

A mapping across the dimensions of TFP levels (2010) and TFP growth (1970–2010) highlights the position of the different Asian economies on the productivity landscape (Figure 8.4). The high-income developed economies such as Hong Kong, China; Japan; Republic of Korea; Singapore; and Taipei,China are leaders with regards to TFP levels. These economies are at the frontier where entrepreneurship and innovation are concerned.

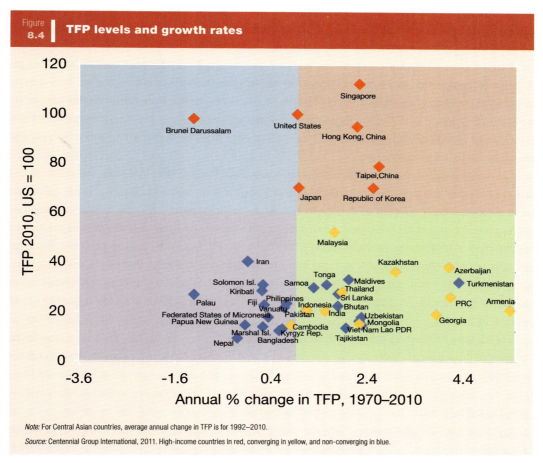

Figure 8.4 | TFP levels and growth rates

Note: For Central Asian countries, average annual change in TFP is for 1992–2010.
Source: Centennial Group International, 2011. High-income countries in red, converging in yellow, and non-converging in blue.

Japan has very high TFP but has slowed in TFP growth. Most innovations in Japan are aimed at saving energy, raw materials, time, and space to enhance global competitiveness. Thus, the central feature of innovation in Japan is continuous improvement. Innovation happens mainly in larger "corporate groups" rather than in small companies, and in a corporate culture that encourages incremental innovation, creativity, individual initiative, and radical innovation are less common.

Singapore looks most impressive for both TFP levels and growth rates. This reflects a determined commitment to scientific research, especially in life sciences. The National Science and Technology Board was established in 1991 to "raise the level of science and technology in Singapore" (Republic of Singapore, 2003). Later renamed the Agency for Science, Technology and Research (A*STAR), it built Singapore's scientific knowledge base through a series of five-year plans. The government of Singapore has funded and promoted scientific research with the goal of becoming "the Boston of the East." It pays great attention to developing its education system with a specific focus on attracting world-class education institutions to Singapore.

Since the early 1980s, Republic of Korea has gradually transformed itself from being an imitator to becoming an innovator, based on rapid growth in R&D expenditures, and greatly supported by its top universities, Seoul National University and the Republic of Korea Advanced Institute of Science and Technology, as well as its science towns (Farhoomand, 2005). The country has faced constraints similar to Japan's that arise from hierarchical limitations and seniority control in its large companies.

Converging economies such as Indonesia, Malaysia, Thailand, and Viet Nam are closer to the catch-up end of the entrepreneurship and technological innovation spectrum. These countries have experienced moderate TFP growth but have been limited by several factors. Malaysia's entrepreneurship and technological innovation is constrained by two major obstacles: education and training, and government regulation (World Bank, 2005). Malaysia, like many others, lacks an effective venture capital industry to support entrepreneurship. Thailand, Indonesia, and Viet Nam share similar problems, such as inadequate infrastructure and access to finance, an inadequately educated workforce, a relatively poor work ethic, an ineffective government bureaucracy, and political instability.

Particularly interesting are the impressive TFP growth rates (in 1992–2010) of a significant number of countries in Central Asia. Azerbaijan and Armenia stand out, possibly making up for the significant losses in GDP and productivity following the collapse of the Soviet Union, and benefiting from increases in energy production and transit. Most disappointing is the low TFP growth performance of the non-converging countries.

The continental economies—PRC and India—are in a class by themselves not just because of their size but because of the heterogeneity of their economic structures and the depth of their scientific and technological know-how. They have vast areas where catch-up entrepreneurship holds the key for growth and employment but also deep pockets of innovation clusters that contribute toward global scientific and technological leadership. The scale effect is an important source of demand and a source of supply of talent and capabilities that enable innovation. Milton Friedman famously asserted, "The conquest of the technological frontier, like the conquest of the geographical frontier, requires millions of individuals" (Friedman, 1955). The scale effect may explain why capital flocks to PRC and India. In rankings by the Boston Consulting Group of "100

BCG New Global Challengers," 38 of the challengers operate in PRC and 19 in India as against 14 in Brazil and 6 in the Russian Federation. Fortune 500 companies have 98 R&D facilities in PRC and 63 in India.

Depending on their positions along the spectrum, Asia's economies must focus on appropriate measures to enhance entrepreneurial activity. At one extreme, economies such as Japan; Republic of Korea; and Taipei,China will gain more from improvements in frontier entrepreneurship. At the other extreme, countries such as the Lao PDR and Viet Nam will gain more from improvements of catch-up entrepreneurship at this time. PRC and India fall in between.

Overall, the vast majority of entrepreneurs in emerging Asia are of the catch-up kind. Most countries there do not have in place the systems, institutions, and policy practices that satisfy the demands of frontier entrepreneurship. Although this problem has not deterred emerging Asia from rapid growth on a largely replicative model, it may very well turn out to be a stumbling block for the region to maintain its growth momentum and avoid the Middle Income Trap.

Getting entrepreneurship and innovation right: PRC and India

PRC and India merit special mention in this chapter in part because of their strong performance, size, and economic impact, but also because of their heterogeneity and the related opportunity for the rest of emerging Asia to use their experience as a source of policy ideas.

One of the important lessons emerging from these two countries is that catch-up entrepreneurship can be an important element of a strategy to achieve broad-based inclusive economic growth. More than half the poverty reduction (headcount) in PRC in 1978–2002 occurred in the first half of the 1980s when township and village enterprises grew most rapidly. The success in ramping up manufacturing in the rural areas pulled hundreds of millions of Chinese into a large-scale, globalized production supply chain. Many town and village industrial clusters were born out of these manufacturing supply chains, such as for example, the clothing and glass industries in Wenzhou city, and the electronics and furniture supply chains in Dongguan city.

In more recent years, India has made progress in catch-up entrepreneurship, with an emphasis on inclusive innovation that has built on existing social and economic platforms (Box 8.1 and Appendix 3). Concomitantly, the pace of poverty reduction has accelerated.

Models of endogenous economic growth have recognized the importance of knowledge production, and more importantly, the powerful role played by the accumulation of scientific knowledge (Romer, 1990; Grossman and Helpman, 1991; Jones, 2002) and step-by-step technical progress (Scotchmer, 1991; Gallini and Scotchmer, 2001). Knowledge production is a cumulative process rather than, as often portrayed in the media and policy discussions, one of leapfrogging. PRC and India offer some valuable lessons on the incremental process of moving from the catch-up to the frontier phase of entrepreneurship.

Shanghai missed the opportunity of supporting Alibaba.com and many other promising

> **Box 8.1 | e-Choupal—building on a traditional platform**
>
> In 1999, ITC—a business conglomerate in India—rolled out an internet platform designed to procure soybeans more effectively. The traditional method was beset with multiple problems such as price distortions, informational asymmetry, and lack of transparency. The e-Choupal initiative provided soybean farmers with weather, price, and technical information, free of charge, through access to computer equipment, internet kiosks, and training. The result— the elimination of the middlemen and price distortions—was instantaneous and substantial. Farmers' profits increased by 33 percent, and the cultivation of soybeans increased by 19 percent.
>
> One of the key features of e-Choupal is that while it was a disruption to the traditional procurement methods, it was based explicitly on a practice long accepted in Indian social norms and mores—the idea of using a public venue (*choupal*) to exchange information. The e-Choupal initiative took advantage of this traditional platform and converted it into a value proposition for farmers.

technology startups because of its strong policy approach bias toward established incumbents that equates size with innovativeness and competitiveness. Huang and Qian (2010) found that the catch-up entrepreneurial businesses in Shanghai were among the least developed in the country. This lag in catch-up entrepreneurship has actually hindered the development of frontier entrepreneurship. As measured by patent production, Shanghai has lagged substantially behind, for example, Zhejiang and Guangdong, two provinces with a large base of catch-up entrepreneurship.

Many notable success stories in the area of frontier entrepreneurship are not due to leapfrogging but to incremental progressions of catch-up entrepreneurship. India's pharmaceutical industry provides a good example. By one objective measure, India today has one of the most competitive pharmaceutical industries in the world. The World Health Organization (WHO) periodically conducts a study to prequalify drugs manufactured in developing countries as meeting its tests of quality and consistency. (WHO uses similar standards and procedures as those of the US Federal Drug Agency and European Medicines Agency.) On its most recent prequalification list, 137 drugs are manufactured in India, but only five in PRC. Indian firms, such as Ranbaxy and Biocon, have increasingly moved to an R&D profile, and are no longer limited to the manufacture of existing drugs.

These achievements did not happen overnight. The turning point for India's pharmaceutical manufacturing was the 1970 Patent Act which shortened patent protection from 16 years under the Patents and Design Act of 1911 to 3–5 years. The 1970 Patent act also removed product protection altogether and strengthened the disclosure requirements on process protection, while it substantially reduced both the scope and the extent of patent protection. With foreign exchange and price controls, the act is generally credited with the birth of India's indigenous pharmaceutical industry.

The industry, which has enjoyed double-digit growth in recent years, was a couple of years ago valued at $20 billion and is forecast to reach $40 billion by 2015 (McKinsey, 2009). It is a classic case of initial catch-up entrepreneurship transformed into frontier entrepreneurship, based on first achieving manufacturing competence and excellence, and then gaining research competitiveness. Almost all the Indian pharmaceutical firms went through a similar development trajectory by first mastering manufacturing and then venturing into more research-intensive activities. As Indian firms gained capabilities, they shifted out of the simple imitations that are a hallmark of catch-up entrepreneurship. In 2005, India formally completed its transition from catch-up to frontier entrepreneurship in the pharmaceutical industry. The milestone was the 2005 Patent Act that lengthened patent protection to 20 years.

PRC's pharmaceutical industry offers an example of a different approach, that is, an illustration of the complementary nature of catch-up and frontier entrepreneurship. While manufacturing overall is substantially stronger than in India, this is not the case in pharmaceuticals, as seen by the gap in the WHO ranking of prequalified drugs. One issue is that PRC's pharmaceutical industry is driven by top-down investments in research rather than by bottom-up developments. For example, the country has invested heavily in the upstream "supply chain" of the pharmaceutical industry, such as nanotechnology (Zhang, 2011). This is a supply-side approach that targets knowledge production rather than process improvements, which are characteristic of India's approach. But the PRC approach is expensive and few countries in emerging Asia can afford it.

Green technology offers an example of a successful transition in PRC. Though often portrayed as "leapfrogging", PRC's substantial gains in green technology are the result of a long process of accumulating and absorbing knowledge from prior practices. The plan to invest heavily in such technology was approved very early, in 1986, by Deng Xiaoping himself, according to one account.[2] PRC's success in green technology heavily leverages its manufacturing prowess. For example, one of the most successful PRC firms in solar panels, Wuxi Suntech, relies on core technology from Australia—but the firm could scale up production rapidly because the country has a well-developed cluster of sources in the supply chain of solar panels. Similarly, PRC's gains in wind-turbine technology and gasification equipment as well as grid construction can be attributed to the country's capital deepening and the scale of its equipment manufacturing. The strength of its catch-up entrepreneurship provided the foundation for the country to transition into frontier entrepreneurship.

PRC and India also offer examples of two distinct models of innovation development. Freeman (2004) divided innovative activities into: "product innovation" and "process innovation". A key

---

2 The funding vehicle was known as the "863 Program," enacted in March 1986.

distinction between the two is that product innovations tend to be non-continuous and discrete, and can often be qualitatively different from existing and prior generations. Process innovations are continuous and show quantitative improvements over past and present generations. Product innovations are more likely to happen when there are strong external specialized research organizations, such as universities and government-run research institutions.

The US provides the prototypical model of an ecosystem geared toward product innovations. It has the world's highest volume of R&D investment, and, according to one estimate, it allocates about two-thirds of its R&D to product innovations, which encourages sudden, radical technical innovation in US companies. Japan also has a very high ratio of R&D to GDP, but its allocations are at variance with the US: two-thirds of the investment in a typical Japanese company go to process innovation. The resulting Japanese innovations are more incremental and process oriented. Although Japan has a large number of patents, most revolve around incremental improvements of current technologies.

There is some evidence that the PRC environment shows a policy tilt toward product innovations, relative to the Indian approach. Our analysis offers evidence of this policy tilt, rather than an assessment of its effects. One set of crude and indirect measures of the relative importance of product vis-à-vis process innovations has to do with the state of basic scientific research, R&D, and patents. By these measures PRC is ahead of India. It is increasingly considered an essential participant in the global knowledge economy (King, 2002). Recent studies have highlighted the rising number of scientists and engineers produced in PRC institutions of higher education, and the funding allocated to producing knowledge. By 2005, PRC ranked fifth among nations in total scientific publications; in engineering it ranked second, trailing only the US in new engineering publications (NSF, 2010). PRC has also embraced major scientific projects: in genomics it was the only developing nation to participate in the Human Genome Project; in space science it was the third nation to develop a successful manned space program.

The transition to frontier entrepreneurship in PRC and India has been facilitated by a number of elements. These include foreign direct investment (FDI), R&D, political and policy focus, knowledge-production institutions, and broad policy reforms.

FDI. FDI has one feature that is relevant to a focus on entrepreneurship. Sometimes it has a spillover effect that provides the financial and human seed capital, as well as the technology, to domestic entrepreneurial ventures. In India, for example, the exit of IBM from the country in the late 1970s indirectly boosted domestic technology firms. A number of IBM employees became founders of Indian IT firms, including Infosys.

Most advanced forms of FDI in PRC and India create conditions for product innovations. India has a host of institutions that are geared toward generating new products. For example, GE–India is a very R&D-focused operation. It has the largest R&D center outside the US (with 3,500 researchers). Unlike many R&D projects in developing countries, GE–India has focused on developing India-specific technologies and applications. Microsoft's R&D center in Beijing now files the second-largest number of patents within the Microsoft system (second only to its headquarters in Seattle). Motorola developed Chinese character recognition and writing technologies in PRC that it later exported to the Middle East and Republic of Korea.

R&D. Frontier entrepreneurship and innovations are science-based and depend on the supply base of scientific knowledge. The supply base is, among many other factors, a function of the government's commitment to science and technology and its readiness to back up that commitment with resources. A commitment by the government and possible direct intervention on the supply side of innovation are especially important where the regular financing mechanisms of science-based entrepreneurship are missing. In this regard, there is a sharp difference between PRC and India. PRC has gone further and proceeded more systematically than India. Relative to PRC, India has been constrained by the fiscal resources that it can invest in science and technology.

R&D is a useful metric of a government's commitment. India invests about 0.8 percent of GDP in R&D, about half of the PRC percentage; in light of the much larger size of the PRC economy, the difference in absolute terms is even more stark. Given the low percentage of total spending in India, there is a considerable need for increased funding in both the public and private sectors.

Other measures also show India lagging. The number of persons engaged in R&D in Scandinavian countries is 7,000 per million population and 4,700 in the US; the number in India is 156. The ratio of India's "core researchers" to PRC's is 3:20. The Indian government is aware of the need to act and raised the target for R&D spending to 1.2 percent of GDP in its 11th Five-Year Plan for 2007–2012.

On the basis of the historical relationship between R&D and GDP, some economists have pronounced PRC to be on the verge of a "science and technology takeoff" (Gao and Jefferson, 2005). R&D in PRC has accelerated rapidly and it is likely that it has reached close to 2 percent of GDP, a level more common among developed countries. A more detailed analysis shows that, at least at present, PRC's spending on R&D is much less geared to applied and basic research (23 percent of total R&D) than is US R&D (42 percent) (Government of PRC, 2007). The OECD argues that the lack of basic and applied research will hamper innovation efforts (OECD, 2007).

Policy focus. An intangible measure, far harder to quantify, is the level of the political commitment to science and technology. The PRC government has demonstrated a strong commitment. One indication is the level of officials in charge of its science programs. In 1986, for example, the plan to invest in alternative energy projects was personally approved by Deng Xiaoping. A key mechanism for funding allocations, the so-called "973 Program", is said to have been personally endorsed by Zhu Rongji, the vice premier in charge of economy (later the premier during 1991–2002). Other major initiatives directing and controlling scientific research were guided after 1998 by the National Steering Group for Science, Technology and Education, chaired by Zhu

Rongji.

The Middle and Long-Term Program for Science and Technology Development 2006–2020 outlined a vision to increase the contribution to the country's development by science and technology to 60 percent, and reduce dependence on foreign technology. The plan was subsequently grounded in a specific research agenda that focused on "frontier" and breakthrough technologies in biology, information technology, and nanotechnology. More specifically, several waves of programs of substantial government funding of science and technology have controlled research resources through a strongly guided program of resource allocation. The list of the programs is long and includes The National High Tech R&D Program (or 863 Program [1986]), the Spark Program, the Torch Program, the National Key Technologies Program, Project 211 (1996), Project for Funding World-Class Universities (Project 863, 1998), and Project 111 (2006).

Knowledge production. Universities are probably the most important producer of the kind of knowledge that leads to transformative product innovations. One study of the startup businesses founded by MIT graduates, faculty, and MIT itself shows that as of 2006 the sales revenue of these businesses came to about $1 trillion, roughly equal to the size of the GDP of the Republic of Korea (Roberts and Eesley, 2009).

Both PRC and India have elite research universities. India has some world-class institutes, and a few years ago about 250 universities and engineering colleges in computer science alone (Saxenian, 2006). Data from 2001–2002 show that there were about 130,000 new IT graduates from universities and engineering colleges in India. The Indian government recognizes the importance of technological commercialization in universities and research institutes, and has completed the commercialization process for some of them, including the National Institute of Immunology, the Centre of Biomedical Technology, and the Centre for Biotechnology.

However, the collective judgment is that university technology transfer mechanisms in India are still weak. Industry and the universities remain separate spheres with limited professional or commercial interaction. As a result, learning in the Indian software industry, for example, occurs "primarily within the firm or through long-distance relationship" (Saxenian, 2006, pp. 303), rather than through interaction with local universities and research laboratories. The reasons for the paucity of collaboration between firms and universities or research institutes (as well as cooperation between firms and financial institutions, customers, and suppliers) may lie in "the export orientation of local producers, their limited differentiation, traditional secrecy, and hierarchy of older Indian businesses" (Saxenian, 2006, pp. 320–321).

Universities in PRC have yet to develop their capabilities to capitalize on and commercialize their intellectual assets. But for inventiveness measured by both publication and citation counts, universities in PRC are ahead of India. It is likely that PRC's firms can tap into a larger base of scientific knowledge than Indian firms. The number of publications in PRC has expanded dramatically and this increase coincided with the rapid escalation of investments in the country's tertiary education beginning around the mid-1990s. In 1983, the country had a scientific paper count of only 3,304; in 1998 it rose to 25,000 and in 2008 it was 110,459. This is about half the level in the US and European Union. The average level of PRC publications, as measured by a metric called the journal impact factor, is low, although in certain fields, such as medical and life sciences, PRC publications have made substantial strides (Fensterheim, et al., 2008) (Figure 8.5).

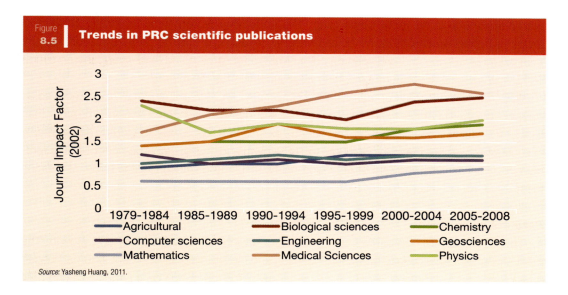

Figure 8.5 Trends in PRC scientific publications

Source: Yasheng Huang, 2011.

Broad policy reforms. In the area of frontier entrepreneurship, the two countries also differ. In India, many of the product and process innovations have come from the private sector and are market-based, not driven by government-funded programs. The demand-side dynamics have been crucial to India's innovation successes. Several market-based successes are now well known, including those in the area of "inclusive innovation"—the cheapest car, laptop, cell phone, and cataract surgery, to name a few (Appendix 3). These pioneering achievements have so far not been matched by PRC firms. The government-driven approach in PRC has offered some advantages, including the ability to target universities and R&D programs for funding and development, but has been associated with a lag of corporate development.

In India, the financial system, an important part of the policy framework, is more broadly supportive of private development, than in PRC. World Business Environment Surveys show that India's financial system lends far more to small-scale private firms than PRC. There is evidence that India's capital market appears to be better performing than PRC's (Morck, et. al., 2000). Other studies show that entry by private banks is far more substantial in India than in PRC (Banerjee, et al., 2005; Saez, 2004).

Key elements of the entrepreneurship and innovation ecosystem

The analysis of entrepreneurial dynamics, including PRC and India, shows that there are a number of conditions necessary for the development of entrepreneurship. Frontier and catch-up entrepreneurship each make substantially different demands on a country's economic and political systems. Catch-up entrepreneurship makes relatively simple demands—a sound business environment, basic infrastructure, and quality education at primary and secondary levels. Frontier entrepreneurship is far more demanding. The underlying factors include: strong intellectual property rights; infrastructure for science and knowledge; a solid tertiary education system, particularly in science and engineering; government commitment and leadership; and an overall policy framework that encourages cutting-edge innovation at the frontier.

Countries need to think of the enabling environment for entrepreneurship—even more so as they move toward frontier entrepreneurship—as a complex multifaceted ecosystem rather than simply in terms of a specific policy. This section examines Asia's landscape for the key elements of such an ecosystem that can contribute to TFP growth and enable catch-up or frontier entrepreneurship. The analysis shows that emerging Asia has a long-distance to go in terms of creating these essential conditions for successful entrepreneurial development.

Business environment

The business environment is a vital element in driving Asia's productivity and growth. The most critical elements have to do with competition and the enabling environment for broad-based private sector development. In Asia, entrepreneurship and innovation on a large scale can best be promoted by the "consolidation of competitive capitalism with the dynamism of large and small businesses depending on innovation rather than influence" (Walton, 2010). In many Asian economies, there are tendencies toward oligarchic capitalism based on state capture (as also witnessed in Latin America), which must be checked through appropriate competition policies, effective regulatory structures, procedures to check corruption and influence, a broad-based and inclusive financial system, transparency and accountability, and an independent judiciary.

Asia, on average, has a long way to go on the commonly cited Ease of Doing Business indicators (Figure 8.6). Huge regional differences exist: Northeast Asia (excluding PRC) ranks better than Europe, but South Asia ranks worse than Sub-Saharan Africa. In a positive development, some countries in Central Asia were commended in the 2010 Doing Business report for reforms to facilitate business procedures (World Bank, 2010a).

All of Asia's subregions score particularly poorly on the Entry Density indicator, which measures the number of newly registered limited liability firms in each economy (World Bank, 2010b). Generally, the data show that countries with higher levels of GDP per capita and greater financial development also have higher entry density (World Bank, 2010c). The low numbers of some high-income Asian countries, including Japan and the Republic of Korea, which score 1.3

Figure 8.6 Asia's ranking on Ease of Doing Business indicators varies by region and income/convergence level

Source: World Bank, Ease of Doing Business Indicators.

and 1.7 respectively (in contrast to 7.5 for North America and 3 for Europe) are thus noteworthy, and point to the need for greater entrepreneurship and initiative in much of Asia.

Physical and technological infrastructure

Innovative ideas can only become successful marketable products when there exists a supporting physical and technological infrastructure. The physical infrastructure in Asia is remarkably poor, with the exception of a few countries such as Japan and Singapore. The Physical Infrastructure Index, a composite index comprising six physical infrastructure indicators (roadways, railways, airports, seaports, telecommunications, and electricity) by the Asian Development Bank Institute brings out the poor state of infrastructure in most Asian countries (De, 2010). Differences across subregions are huge. While Japan and Singapore rank among the top 10 countries, Cambodia ranks among the bottom 10 countries along with nine countries in Sub-Saharan Africa (Figure 8.7). There have been significant improvements in some places, most notably PRC, over the last 10 years but other countries such as Cambodia have deteriorated. In order to benefit from regional cooperation and the cross-border sharing of ideas, physical infrastructure must be greatly improved.

Asia's technological infrastructure also needs to be enhanced. In today's globalized world, the absorption and application of ICT is critical to enhancing productivity. Total ICT spending in the region is low at 5 percent of GDP compared with the US and EU, which spend closer to 9 percent, and Latin America, which spends close to 6 percent (National Science Foundation, 2010). Asia does a little better on e-business, based on the Economist Intelligence Unit's e-business rankings: it averages a score of 6.6 relative to 7.2 in Europe and 5.2 in Latin America,

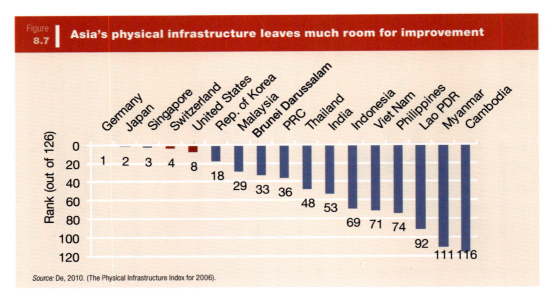

Figure 8.7 | Asia's physical infrastructure leaves much room for improvement

Source: De, 2010. (The Physical Infrastructure Index for 2006).

but many Asian countries (e.g., India at 4.1) score particularly low. E-business, of course, relies on internet connections, an area where Asia has much room for improvement. Asia's internet penetration rate of 21.5 percent remains lower than any other region except Sub-Saharan Africa. Huge differences, however, exist between countries with India at a very low 6.9 percent.

Education

Human capital requirements for the knowledge economy of tomorrow's world are different than in the past. The rapid changes in technology and the increasing importance of ICT and IT services require higher levels of education. Knowledge-driven growth requires that a greater share of the workforce master new high-level skills and, perhaps more important, internalize the skills needed for lifetime learning (World Bank, 2009a). The subject also merits attention because education shows a strong correlation with TFP (Figure 8.8). A recent ADB study concluded that all Asian countries that grew quickly possessed a workforce that was exceptionally qualified, one that was able to adopt the latest technologies. In order to avoid the Middle Income Trap, there is a need for efficient adaptation of technology and an appropriate accumulation of human capital to avoid a "technology–skills mismatch" (Kim and Terada-Hagiwara, 2010).

In the past 40 years, Asia has made strong progress in improving its educational capital. The average years of schooling in its emerging economies has increased from 2.9 years in 1970 to 7 years in 2010 (Lee and Francisco, 2010). This progress must be replicated in the 40 years

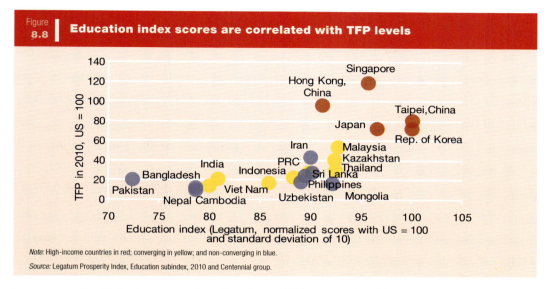

Figure 8.8 | **Education index scores are correlated with TFP levels**

Note: High-income countries in red; converging in yellow; and non-converging in blue.
Source: Legatum Prosperity Index, Education subindex, 2010 and Centennial group.

to come and sufficient progress is not a given.³ Higher growth will require much more investment in improving the quality and availability of education at all levels. Furthermore, the nature of education is particularly significant and all Asian countries need to promote greater creative thinking throughout the education process (Box 8.2).

While the coverage of basic education has improved and is reasonable throughout the region, some of Asia's non-converging countries still need to focus on this area. Even relatively high enrollment rates in most countries do not, however, necessarily translate to an equally high level in the quality of learning, particularly in South Asia.

In the education subindexes of the Legatum Prosperity Index and the World Bank Knowledge Assessment Methodology (KAM), Asia, on average, scores lower than Latin America, Europe, and North America, with significant differences between high income, converging, and non-converging countries (Figure 8.9) (Legatum Institute, 2010; World Bank, 2010d). These differences are also reflected in gross enrollment rates. High-income countries have high levels of secondary and moderate levels (above 60 percent) of tertiary education.

Secondary education is recognized more and more as the minimum level of education to succeed in an increasingly globalized economy and to guarantee a smooth transition to decent jobs (United Nations, 2010). In Asia, enrollment at the secondary level falls off sharply. Converging countries at the catch-up stage need to improve enrollment rates as well as quality of education at this level. There is a further sharp fall-off in the enrollment rates at the tertiary level as highlighted

---

3 A regression analysis (Lee and Francisco, 2010) projects that the high levels of growth in Asia's emerging economies will slow and reach only 7.6 years by 2030, putting it at 1970 levels of advanced countries. This rate of growth in education is not sufficient to keep up with rapid technological changes that will require human capital that can constantly adapt.

Box 8.2 | Asia's creative thinking deficit

The nature of education is significant. Entrepreneurship and innovation can only flourish in an ecosystem that fosters creativity, and tolerates risks, failures, and outside-the-box thinking and behavior—broad capabilities that are best addressed through a country's educational system. However, the education systems in many Asian countries, including high-income frontier economies, have come under severe criticism for their emphasis on rote memorization and test taking, leading to what is increasingly recognized as a creativity deficit by Asian leaders as well.

In the words of an education columnist who recently researched education systems in the region, Asia today exhibits a "scarcity of creative thinking" (Costello, 2010). While science is clearly important, Einstein himself is known to have said that "imagination is more important than knowledge." Some recent statements by Asian policy thinkers point to a growing recognition of this factor within Asia: "Indonesia's national education system has excelled at killing children's creativity;"[1] "teachers often hampered children's' creativity by rigidly applying the national curriculum;"[2] and "Asians have a cultural inclination to blend in rather than to stand out."[3]

---

1 Statement made by Seto Mulyadi, a well-known Indonesian child psychologist during the celebration of the 24th anniversary of the Creativity Development Foundation (YPK) in 2007.
2 Statement by member of YPK board of advisers, Conny Semiawan, 2007.
3 Statement by Professor tan Sri Dato, in Malaysia, at the District Education Officers' National Management Conference in 2009, where it was pointed out that the country needs to reinvent its education system so that it will foster creativity and challenge students to break away from conventional thinking.

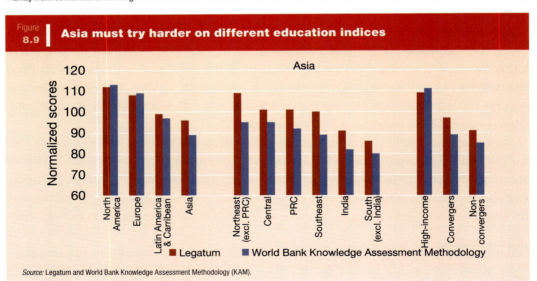

Figure 8.9 | Asia must try harder on different education indices

Source: Legatum and World Bank Knowledge Assessment Methodology (KAM).

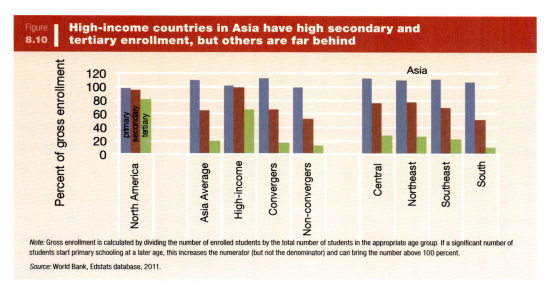

Figure 8.10 High-income countries in Asia have high secondary and tertiary enrollment, but others are far behind

Note: Gross enrollment is calculated by dividing the number of enrolled students by the total number of students in the appropriate age group. If a significant number of students start primary schooling at a later age, this increases the numerator (but not the denominator) and can bring the number above 100 percent.

Source: World Bank, Edstats database, 2011.

by PRC (21 percent) and India (only 12 percent). Non-converging economies lag even further behind (Figure 8.10).

Beyond the low enrollment rates, catch-up economies cannot ignore large gender gaps. While most countries have almost achieved gender parity at the primary level, the gap remains significant at the secondary level. With the exception of the Philippines, which has eliminated the gap, Asian countries rank poorly on the World Economic Forum's Gender Gap Report's Educational Attainment indicator (WEF, 2010). Even at the primary level, a few countries including Afghanistan and Pakistan are still far behind.

In order to produce a workforce that can meet industry demands for skilled human resources, a vocational education and training system (VET) that is responsive to changing labor market conditions can play a crucial role. Creating opportunities to acquire skills for employment, VET can also help the poor and disadvantaged, and those who have dropped out of school. The proportion of secondary students enrolled in VET programs in Asia (13 percent) is low relative to Europe (24 percent). Improving VET systems will help Asian countries reduce poverty and support growth, and can help promote inclusion and equity by providing access to vulnerable groups.

Tertiary education and R&D

Frontier entrepreneurship and innovation are based on science and knowledge. At the highest levels, particularly in science and engineering, tertiary education prepares researchers and lays the foundation for technological development and R&D. Frontier economies need to focus on this level of education.

In recent years, a number of Asian economies have greatly stepped up their investment in tertiary education, leading to far more students enrolled in tertiary programs. Between 1995 and 2008, enrollment levels have multiplied five times in PRC, between three and four times in India and Malaysia, and two times in Thailand and Indonesia. PRC now has 1.5 times as many students enrolled in tertiary programs as the US. A significantly lower "drop-out" rate in PRC than in the US translates into a much larger number of tertiary graduates who graduated in 2008 in PRC (7 million) than in the US (2.8 million) (Box 8.3). The enrollment rates of Asia's high-income economies rank highest, with the Republic of Korea at 95 percent, compared with 82 percent in the US. Low tertiary enrollment rates are the norm for the rest of the region and in the single digits in some parts of South Asia.

Improving the quality of tertiary education is vital. Universities are probably the most important producer of the kind of knowledge that leads to transformative product innovations. Despite the significant boost in the number of students, very few universities in Asia are living up to the quality that is expected of countries that aim to converge with global best practice. Asia's universities generally score very poorly on global indexes. According to the Academic Ranking of World Universities, Asia has only five universities in the top 100, all in Japan, compared with 54 in the US alone and 33 in Europe. It has 74 in the top 500 but all are in Japan, PRC, Republic of Korea, and Singapore, with the exception of two in India and one in Iran.

Many of the second-tier universities produce graduates that can memorize the subject matter but are not "industry ready". For example, in India universities produce over 3 million graduates, including 500,000 engineers; but, by some assessments, only 2 percent of them have the necessary skills for employment, compared with 68 percent in the US (Batelle, 2010). Recruiters indicate that many graduates are "non-employable" (BBC, 2010) and even among engineers, only about 25 percent "have the language skills, practical knowledge and cultural attitudes to work for international companies" (Batelle, 2010). The situation is quite different, however, in the Republic of Korea, where 96 percent of graduates have the basic vocational skills to be considered "employable."

R&D spending is a useful metric of a country's commitment to science and technology. Asia's share in global R&D has risen considerably from under 10 percent (under 2 percent if Japan is excluded) in 1970 to about one-third of the world's spending today. Its spending has recently surpassed Europe's (Figure 8.11), and is soon expected to surpass that in the US (Batelle, 2010). On R&D intensity (ratio of R&D expenditure to GDP), Asia (excluding Japan) has dramatically increased its relative spending from 0.4 percent in 1970 to over 1.2 percent today. This is particularly impressive because this increase in spending relative to GDP took place on top of extremely high overall GDP growth in many countries. Japan and Republic of Korea rank particularly high with expenditures of 3.4 percent and 3 percent of GDP, respectively. India invests a relatively low 0.8 percent of GDP in R&D.

Box 8.3 — PRC's rapid progress in tertiary education and research

PRC has made impressive progress in scaling up tertiary education. It has also greatly increased its spending on R&D, which has gone from 0.6 percent of GDP in 1995 to 1.4 percent in 2009, with a commitment to reach 2.2 percent by 2015. This has resulted in a significant increase in the number of researchers and, combined with rising R&D spending, a sharp increase in the number of patents.

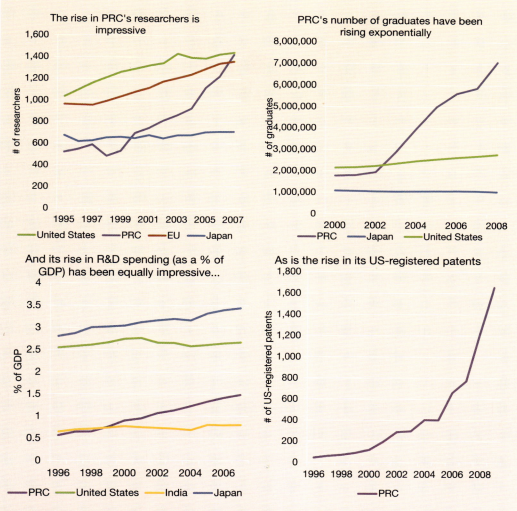

Source: National Science Foundation, Science and Engineering Indicators, 2010; World Bank, Edstats database, 2011; and US Patent Office, 2011.

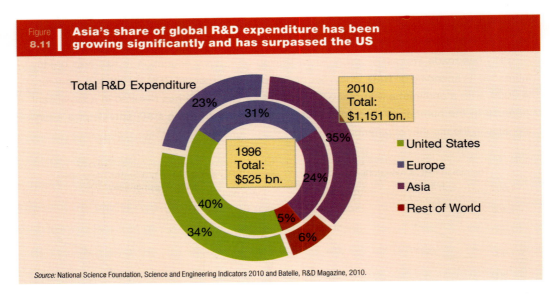

Figure 8.11 Asia's share of global R&D expenditure has been growing significantly and has surpassed the US

Source: National Science Foundation, Science and Engineering Indicators 2010 and Batelle, R&D Magazine, 2010.

Absolutes and scale—and not just the proportion of GDP—matter with research and R&D spending. In 2006, PRC spent $136 billion on R&D, overtaking the $130 billion spent by Japan and reaching about 40 percent of US spending levels ($330 billion in 2006). Today, Asia is home to about 40 percent of the world's researchers (Figure 8.12). The Great Recession of 2008–09 did not stand in the way of the impressive trends in Asia's R&D, which continued to rise. PRC stands out as the most impressive example. While most of the world slashed its spending, it increased spending by about 10 percent each year (Batelle, 2010).

About 75 percent of R&D in Asia comes from business, a share that is slightly higher than in the US. Business funds about three-quarters of the R&D expenditure in Japan and the Republic of Korea while the opposite is true in India, with the government funding three-quarters. Multinational companies are increasingly moving R&D to Asia. Many are trying to take advantage of lower labor costs and the large pool of skilled scientists and engineers as well as the opportunity to market their products to Asia's increasingly affluent consumer base. The flow of R&D from the US to Asia alone grew from $1.9 billion in 1995 to $5.6 billion in 2006 (National Science Foundation, 2010). Similarly, the share of R&D funding in the Asia–Pacific region (excluding Japan) by foreign affiliates of US multinationals has risen from 6 percent of their total foreign R&D funding in 1994 to 14 percent today. The majority of US and European Fortune 1000 companies have multiple R&D centers and manufacturing sites in Asia (Batelle, 2010).

The increased research spending in Asia is paying off. Asia's share of global innovation (measured by the share in world science and engineering articles, world citations, and share in patents) has been rising steadily over the last few years—from under 14 percent in 1998 to over 20 percent in 2008. Nevertheless, most of this innovation is centered in the high-income countries

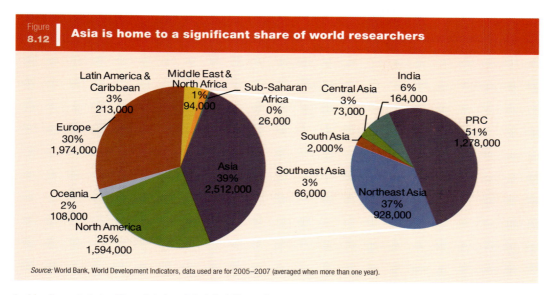

Figure 8.12 | Asia is home to a significant share of world researchers

Source: World Bank, World Development Indicators, data used are for 2005–2007 (averaged when more than one year).

in Northeast Asia. Two-thirds of Asia's US-registered patents in 2009 are from Japan and about half of the rest are from Republic of Korea. Although the absolute number of patents owned by Japanese companies is very high, most of these patents are based on improvements of current technologies, with less emphasis on breakthrough technological innovation. Despite the impressive improvements in the number of US patents noted in Box 8.2 (albeit from a very small base of 46 in 1996 to 1,655 in 2009), PRC still has only about 3 percent of Asia's US-registered patents.

India's number of patents is only about one-third of PRC's and only 1 percent of Asia's total. While this number, which relates to researchers living in India and PRC, is low, researchers of Indian and PRC heritage who live abroad have a significant share of international patents. Of all international patents filed from the US, over 30 percent of the inventors or co-inventors are of Chinese or Indian heritage, even though people of this heritage represent less than 3 percent of the US population (Wadhwa, 2009). This may point to the phenomenon of "brain drain" that has been a concern in Asia in past years. It is already showing signs of reversal as attractive opportunities appear at home, and there is reason to believe that some of these researchers may relocate to India, PRC, or other parts of Asia (Wadhwa, 2009).

A number of different indexes can be analyzed to get a better sense of Asia's global position on the various aspects of innovation. For example, INSEAD's Global Innovation Index ranks Asia just slightly below Europe with huge regional differences (Figure 8.13). The Economist Intelligence Unit index positions Asia somewhat lower (and below Latin America). In both cases, Asia's high-income countries perform extremely well overall and have a very high rank for innovation.

Some Asian countries have exemplified particularly significant leadership commitment to technology and innovation-based economic development. Some of the best "case studies" for

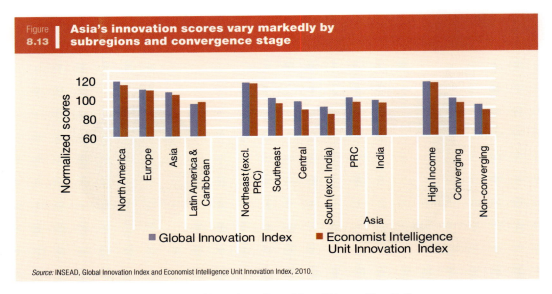

Figure 8.13 | Asia's innovation scores vary markedly by subregions and convergence stage

Source: INSEAD, Global Innovation Index and Economist Intelligence Unit Innovation Index, 2010.

Asian countries are within Asia itself, such as Republic of Korea (Box 8.4).

Overall policy framework

As critical drivers of economic growth, productivity improvement and entrepreneurship must be explicitly cultivated and given ample space for development rather than being taken for granted. One of the main challenges for all countries is finding an appropriate balance between investing heavily in the supply base of knowledge production, which inevitably calls for government backing and interventions, and relying on the flexibility and the ability of the market to innovate. PRC, for example, puts far greater emphasis on the former whereas India puts more on the latter. Both approaches entail some strengths and weaknesses, and changing economic circumstances may require further refinements and adjustments. A firm is more likely to attain competitiveness and to innovate more, as measured against the best in the world, if it operates in an environment with the right home base conditions.

A general ecosystem conducive to innovations has certain generic features, such as a depoliticized research funding process, an arms-length relationship between government and research institutions, and the spirit of free inquiry. Many Asian countries currently put too much of a premium on government controls and planning, and less on individual actions and initiative. For example, Asian countries, while in general being quite trade-driven, still retain substantial controls on FDI. One lesson from PRC and India is that FDI is an important mechanism for transferring broadly defined knowhow, such as technology, management, and ideas. An economic system closed to FDI is also one closed to best-practice management and economic ideas. To better prepare Asian countries for 2050, there is scope for more policy actions and liberalization in this

Box 8.4 — Republic of Korea's transformation into a center of science and technology

Republic of Korea is a prime example of a country that has made the transition from catch-up to frontier entrepreneurship and has exemplified a significant leadership commitment to technology and innovation-based economic development. In 1960, the country was among the poorest in the world, with a GDP of $24 billion and with unemployment rates at 22.3 percent. Today, Republic of Korea is one of the world's most modern industrial economies with a GDP of $986 billion and an unemployment rate of just 4 percent.

Like PRC and India in more recent years, the Republic of Korea built up its innovative capabilities sequentially and transitioned to frontier entrepreneurship on a solid foundation of a substantial catch-up entrepreneurship base. According to one of the best accounts of Republic of Korea's economic growth, the country in the 1960s was very entrepreneurial (Jones and Sakong, 1980). Another measure of this sequential approach—as opposed to leapfrogging—is that the Republic of Korea built up its export capabilities in equipment manufacturing on the basis of its success of labor-intensive exports. As late as 1985, textile and apparel products still accounted for 30 percent of Korean exports. Government policies and programs helped contribute to the export success but they operated on a strong foundation of the capabilities of private firms. An example is that Hyundai Motor Company got into car exports, as a condition of foreign exchange loans from the government to import body styling and designs from Italy and engines, transmission, and axle technology from Japan.

Republic of Korea's government catalyzed technology development by initiating significant R&D spending, in some instances at government institutes set up for this purpose. In 1980, the government had a share of 64 percent of R&D expenditures and government institutes performed 62 percent of R&D. Over time, the private sector has taken on the lion's share of R&D spending, and now accounts for 75 percent of expenditure and about 90 percent of R&D performance. Beginning in the 1960s and 70s with a focus on technology transfers as a means of technology acquisition, the country shifted to the development of indigenous R&D in the 1980s. The government's outward looking development strategy has encouraged investments in long-term projects, many of which have turned into impressive success stories. Gross R&D expenditures (GERD) are among the highest in the world at over 3 percent of GDP in 2011, an impressive increase from 0.77 percent in 1980.

In response to the Asian Financial Crisis of the late 1990s, Republic of Korea increased public R&D budgets and, through an overhaul of existing regulations and tax credits, created an environment that would promote the development of a technology-based SME sector and encourages venture startups. As a result, TFP levels have risen exponentially and, in PPP terms, Republic of Korea this year will bridge the gap with Japan which stood at 30 percent in 1990.

domain. A challenge, unique to PRC, is whether truly transformative innovations can occur under institutional and political conditions that put a high premium on controls rather than on discussion and debate.

One illustration of the kind of changes required to create space for frontier entrepreneurship is Japan. The country's combination of a very high TFP level but low TFP growth in part reflects the challenge of breaking out of its current mode of operations and embracing "disruptive innovation." Unlike other countries covered in this book, the Japanese system requires not so much policy and political adjustments but a change in soceital and mentality norms—in many ways, a change more fundamental than the kind of reforms being called for in other Asian countries.

First, the central feature of innovation in Japan is continuous improvement. Second, Japanese technological innovation happens mainly in larger corporate groups within a corporate culture that frequently fails to foster creativity and individual initiative. The third factor—and the one most resistant to change—has to do with the ecosystem in Japan, which is geared more toward a "catch-up" strategy. The discussion below examines the Japanese education system.

The overwhelming emphasis of the Japanese education system is on memorization and factual absorption, not on thinking and creativity. Although the teaching and learning in Japan's elementary schools are lively and thought-inspiring (Coleman, 1996), the shift toward rote learning occurs in junior high school. The fact-based education is entrenched in the entrance exam system; this is the system that many countries in Asia have emulated. The exam system has two tiers: the first taken when the student is 14 and the second at 18. There is some research that shows that the kind of human capital required for successful entrepreneurial ventures is of a "general" nature rather than specific domain knowledge. The Japanese system relies on early concentration and focus on a selected discipline.

By grade 10, students must choose whether they want to do natural science, social science, arts, or humanities in college, and their core studies will be concentrated in one of these areas (Normile, 2007). Japanese tertiary education is narrowly focused on domain knowledge, not on general knowledge. The discipline boundaries are strictly enforced. For example, a student doing electrical engineering cannot take courses in mechanical engineering within the school of engineering (Normile, 2007). Although the separation of disciplines may lead to students with a better grasp of their major, it hinders students from building interdisciplinary knowledge, which is helpful for innovation.

One huge constraint to growth in frontier entrepreneurship in Asia is the lack of early-stage financing. To some extent this is rooted in a bias that is directed toward rapid economic growth, which raises the returns of investments in those products and processes that are geared toward market size rather than technology. There is very little early-stage investment. In many Asian countries, it is easier to raise a large than small sum of money. In India, for example, Sanjay Anandaram, a private equity investor, remarked: "It is easier to raise two million dollars than it is to raise $200,000" (Anandaram, 2010). One problem in many countries is that the domestic financial institutions have yet to develop capabilities in the venture capital and private equity domains. Instead the industry is dominated by international investors who are driven more by the scale of the investment.

Finally, a government that is neither intrusive nor completely absent is vital for frontier entrepreneurship. One positive example is offered by Singapore. Of all the Asian countries, Singapore has the most systematic approach toward promoting frontier entrepreneurship and science-based innovations. It has made an impressive commitment to scientific research, especially in the life sciences. The rise of PRC and India, as formidable manufacturing powers, has nudged Singapore powerfully in this direction. The use of second-best policy instruments—direct government interventions not just in basic but also in applied research—is most extensive in Singapore. Of all the government-sponsored programs, according to an analysis by Joshua Lerner, a professor at Harvard Business School, Singapore's success is the exception that proves the rule (Lerner, 2010).

Singapore's National Innovation Policy has managed to lead the economy from "technology adoption" to one that emphasizes "indigenous innovation." To support technological innovation, especially in bioscience, the government pays much attention to developing its education system.

Priorities and action agenda

Three lessons emerge from our analysis of productivity and entrepreneurship globally, in Asia, and specifically in PRC and India.

First, entrepreneurship and technological development are heavily sequential: countries move from catch-up entrepreneurship to frontier entrepreneurship, rather than directly jumping into the latter phase. Knowledge production is a cumulative process rather than, as often portrayed in the media and policy discussions, one of leapfrogging. PRC and India first succeeded in catch-up entrepreneurship and subsequently added frontier entrepreneurship to their development toolkits. In Asia, the country that has been most successful—in terms of both the outcome and speed of this transition—is probably Republic of Korea.

Second, successes in frontier entrepreneurship have an extraordinarily long gestation period. Governments must think ahead and commit themselves to a long-term, well-planned policy course. The seeds of several innovation success stories in the PRC and India were in fact planted decades before their economic and commercial successes manifested themselves—in the early 1970s, for the Indian pharmaceutical industry, and in the mid-1980s, in the PRC green technology sector.

Third, there is a role for second-best interventions in the short run. For example, PRC and India, while quite successful in nurturing entrepreneurship and achieving some breakthroughs in innovation, still suffer from gaps in the policy and institutional environment for entrepreneurship and innovation. In the short run, it is probably only realistic to take institutional conditions as given and devise policy interventions that substitute for shortfalls. One example of such a policy intervention is targeted financing and administrative intervention by the PRC government to expand the research capabilities of its universities and to foster linkages between universities and industry. Another example is Singapore's targeted drive to become "the Boston of the East".

Entrepreneurship and innovation are vital to economic growth; they must be explicitly fostered and given ample space for development rather than being taken for granted. Some elements of the innovation and entrepreneurship ecosystem are more relevant for the converging economies since they are requirements for frontier entrepreneurship, which is much more demanding of the ecosystem than catch-up entrepreneurship. At the same time, many of the underlying measures have long gestation periods and would thus benefit from early attention. The mistake that policy makers in Asia must avoid is to create a policy and regulatory environment that favors frontier entrepreneurship at the expense of catch-up entrepreneurship.

Most Asian economies need to make significant investments in human capital development by ensuring both higher enrollment rates and higher quality at all levels of education. Some also need to address gender gaps. Improved learning with an emphasis on creativity can help foster higher productivity, innovation, and entrepreneurship. Another essential element to promote entrepreneurship is an openness to competition and a business environment that facilitates entry and entrepreneurship on a large scale.

Non-converging economies. For the non-converging Asian economies, catch-up entrepreneurship and innovation are vitally important and likely to remain the most productive strategy for some years. For countries with low TFP and slow TFP growth (such as Nepal) and for those countries that have experienced some TFP growth but from an extremely low base (such as Bangladesh, Mongolia, and the Philippines), the most urgent policy priority is to get "fundamentals" right, that is, those policies that enable catch-up entrepreneurship to grow. All non-converging economies need to focus on improving basic and vocational education, increasing gender parity at the primary and secondary levels, and simplifying business processes. For these countries, the policy priority is not high-tech development but to get the economic and business basics right. Some of the positive lessons from Taipei,China in the 1960s and 1970s are particularly relevant here. Access to finance is a huge barrier to small-scale entrepreneurs in many of these countries. Academic research shows that in Viet Nam lack of bank financing to small and medium-sized enterprises has forced entrepreneurs to curtail the geographic scope of their businesses and has limited expansion opportunities to a small, select set of customers known to them personally.

Converging economies. Converging economies are largely still in the catch-up phase, and some countries (including Cambodia, Indonesia, and Viet Nam) must still make it their priority to focus on "fundamentals." Nevertheless, to differing extents, these countries should begin to sow the field for frontier entrepreneurship. This would require considerable investment in human capital that includes a more diversified education system that cultivates creative thinking; higher enrollment levels at the tertiary level; more world-class tertiary institutions; and an increase in gender equality at the tertiary level. Converging economies should also focus on the development of capital markets, and on the growth of a multitiered financing system (including venture capital). Legal reforms and the strengthening of intellectual property rights are also crucial for countries that are ready to transition to the frontier stage but this should be undertaken with caution as a country matures from the catch-up entrepreneurship stage. Finally, there is a need for government funding of basic research, sensible and well thought-out targeting, and the creation of a platform to disseminate knowledge and information to help plant the seeds for greater levels of frontier entrepreneurship.

High-income. Asia's high-income economies need to improve the entrepreneurial spirit as reflected in their social mentality. Although these countries enjoy high-quality education as reflected by impressively high test scores, the education system must provide better opportunities for creative thinking and problem solving "outside the box". More effort should be made to strengthen peoples' initiative with regards to entrepreneurship. Gender parity is low in some of these countries, particularly for political empowerment but also in tertiary education, and women should be encouraged to participate in all levels of society. Finally, the corporate organizational structure (currently very hierarchical in many countries) should be adjusted to foster greater entrepreneurship.

A New Approach to Urbanization

Chapter 9

Anthony Pellegrini

This chapter suggests the need for a dramatically different approach to urbanization in Asia, one that will not only cope with, but also make better use of, the investments that will accompany the coming urbanization avalanche as Asia's urban population rises by nearly 1.4 billion over the next 40 years. It highlights the vital role of mega- and secondary cities for regional economic competitiveness as well as social stability; the major risks most countries face; and the accompanying management and leadership challenges. It ends by laying out a priority agenda.

Looking back 40 years at Asian cities

The past 40 years have witnessed remarkable demographic change in Asia. A predominantly rural society in 1970 with just 20 percent, or 442 million people, living in cities and towns, by 2010 Asia's urban population was 40 percent of the total—almost 1.6 billion people.

The transformation of towns and cities was as uneven as it was rapid, especially living conditions. A very small number of cities were modernizing swiftly. Tokyo, Asia's largest metropolitan area, was becoming a world-class business center. The young tiger economies of Hong Kong, China and Singapore, along with Taipei,China had rapidly developing urban-oriented economic growth models. Republic of Korea combined high levels of economic expansion with dramatic replanning in the Seoul capital region. Elsewhere in Asia however, cities suffered severe degradation in livability as better employment opportunities in urban areas stimulated an influx of migrant workers that overwhelmed city services. This was accompanied by an explosive growth of private automobile use.

Migrants poured into often illegal—and now endemic—slum and squatter settlements. In most of the larger cities of Asia (e.g., Bangkok, Bombay (now Mumbai), Calcutta (now Kolkata), Jakarta, Karachi, Manila) some 25–30 percent of the population lived in such settlements, typically in makeshift shacks without basic services of water, drainage, sanitation, or paved streets.

The expansion in motorized vehicle use—buses, trucks, taxies, but especially the private car—was changing the character of traditional urban cores. City streets built for another age were widened to meet growing demand for space by vehicles. Private automobiles, bicycles, pedi-cabs, busses, and sometimes handcarts and bullock carts, competed for street space.

Planners began warning about the consequences of unbridled increases in private automobiles as congestion increased, but this went unheeded except in a very few cities. Singapore introduced the world's first system of charging for entry into the central business district. The Singapore system—versions of which are now in London, Stockholm, and elsewhere—tamed congestion and raised revenue for infrastructure investment. The infamous traffic congestion that choked many other Asian cities in the 1980s was a consequence of ignoring projections made in the 1970s and failing to deliver demand management and public transport alternatives.

The pressure of population growth and insufficient investment led to a steady deterioration of public services. In 1970, governance was highly centralized and national authorities made most urban investments. Local governments were mostly responsible for maintenance and small investments, but had little technical capacity. Centralized control of local investment was characterized by a general underinvestment in basic urban infrastructure, neglect in local government financing capacity, insufficient attention to cost control, and low standards of professionalism among local government staff. This particularly hindered small and medium cities far from the national capital.

Kolkata is an excellent example of the changes brought by urbanization in a large South Asian city over the last four decades, demonstrating the progress made and the perils of inattention to urban policy. In 1970, the metropolitan government included two municipal corporations, 33 municipalities, 37 towns, and 544 non-municipal urban units. Yet local governments had little authority and little ability to plan or implement projects. Most urban services were provided and maintained by the state government of West Bengal.

Thirty-four percent of the metropolitan population, some 2.8 million people, lived in high-density squatter and *basti* (slum) settlements. They were often built on low-lying waterlogged land with poor drainage that frequently flooded during the monsoon. Sidewalk dwellers, vendors, and solid-waste heaps forced pedestrians on to the streets, aggravating already difficult traffic conditions. A BBC documentary, widely seen in Europe at the time, highlighted the appalling conditions facing most residents and the contrast between the "wealth and opulence" that existed in the midst of poverty and squalor.

An attempt to consolidate the many local governments into 10 municipal corporations failed. Instead, in 1970, the state government set up the Calcutta Metropolitan Development Authority (CMDA) as a single metropolitan-wide planning and development institution. The CMDA did not replace local governments, but independently undertook planning and large-scale regional investments in water supply, drainage and sanitation, housing, and a *basti* improvement program to deliver basic infrastructure (water, sanitation, paved footpaths) to a large number of slums. The *basti* improvement program dramatically improved living conditions and health for residents, but it did not deal with land titles and disputed property rights in the improved *basti* areas.

Forty years later, there have been limited changes in the structure of the city's governance.

The metropolitan development authority (now KMDA) has shifted from a focus on independent construction of large-scale infrastructure to metropolitan planning and implementation of inter-municipal projects. Since the early 1980s, elected local governments began functioning and taking limited responsibility for local services such as water and sanitation. Decentralization was strengthened in 1991 by the 74th constitutional amendment. Nevertheless, finance for projects continues to be a major problem. Tariffs and fees for services, whether provided by local bodies or by KDMA, are determined on an ad hoc basis and are generally inadequate. KMDA is dependent on grants and subsidized loans from West Bengal State and the national government. The metropolitan area continues to suffer from a long-standing tendency of KDMA to focus on projects in the central core to the detriment of rapidly growing suburban areas—leading to very high costs of retrofitting basic infrastructure in the growth corridors after they are developed. The number of local government units in the metropolitan area has grown along with the physical expansion of the metropolitan area. The area now has three municipal corporations, 38 municipalities, 72 cities, and 572 towns and villages.

Poverty and living conditions in metropolitan Kolkata have improved along with the economy, but services remain seriously deficient. Some 2.5 million people still live on the streets and in the slums, a figure virtually unchanged from 1970. Today, only 66 percent of the population is served by piped water, with service of only 10 hours per day on average. Municipal tap water must generally be boiled before use because of widespread fecal and other contamination. Only 26 percent of the metropolitan population is served by the sewerage system. Inadequate sanitation has considerable economic impact, both through lost workdays and other consequences of ill health. The land title/tenancy problems of the *bastis* (even those that have been upgraded) are still unresolved. While residents cannot be removed, they have few development rights. The lack of legal titles has prevented normal indigenous development of these areas and has led to large-scale illegal construction of very poor quality that has overwhelmed services.

Republic of Korea's capital, Seoul, tells a different story (Box 9.1). Although flooded by migrants from rural areas looking for employment during the 1960s and 1970s and faced by large-scale illegal squatter settlements, Seoul dealt with its urban settlement problems through an innovative land readjustment program, similar to those in Japan, Taipei,China, and Germany. This was a self-financing scheme under which landowners of designated readjustment areas pooled their properties under the control of local authorities. The authorities then replanned them, put in infrastructure, and returned a smaller but higher value piece of land to the original landowners. Squatters and low-income renters were offered a chance to buy very small plots or to move elsewhere in less expensive rental properties. Full legal titles were issued for all land parcels, avoiding the rights disputes that plague many low-income settlements in Asia today. Jakarta (Box 9.2) illustrates an experience between that of Kolkata and Seoul. It is a city that has made remarkable improvements since 1970, but still has a long way to go in improving basic services.

Box 9.1 | Seoul 1970 and 2010

Seoul 1970

The population of the Seoul metropolitan area was 8.9 million in 1970 and growing rapidly, after the government's successful policy of promoting the city as an export-oriented manufacturing base. Most urban transport was by bus, accounting for about 70 percent of journeys. There were fewer than 60,000 vehicles in the city and only a very small number of those were privately owned. There were more bicycles than private cars.

Despite widespread poverty, a significant program of city redevelopment was under way. A self-financing land readjustment program saw more than 50 percent of Seoul's land area redeveloped (through provision of infrastructure, changed layouts, rezoning) neighborhood by neighborhood. The goal was swift and efficient delivery of urban infrastructure that the government saw as a prerequisite for increasing the productivity of the national economy (Bertaud, 2003). Plans were underway for the first subway line, which opened in 1974.

Seoul's economic growth brought an influx of rural migrants and a wave of illegal squatter settlements. The annual number of new migrants was about 400,000 in 1970. About 30 percent of the population was estimated to live in slum and squatter settlements. Government initiatives to deal with illegal squatter areas mostly involved bulldozing shanties and busing the inhabitants to outlying areas. In reaction to civic protests over the removal of people to distant locations, new long-term plans were proposed that involved giving some voice to affected communities, allowed in situ development for certain approved locations, resolved land ownership and titling issues, and provided infrastructure through upgrading programs.

Seoul 2010

Seoul in 2010 is a major international business and financial center, ranked ninth in the world as a Global Center of Commerce by MasterCard Worldwide. Some 24.5 million people live in the Seoul National Capital Area—almost half the national population.

Heavy industry has been moved to the outskirts. The national government has adopted a green growth policy and Seoul's local government is reinventing the city to promote a better quality of life, a greener environment, and knowledge-based industries as the economic driver of the future. Sectors promoted include tourism, design and fashion, digital content, information technology, nanotechnology, biotechnology, and financial and business services.

The Seoul subway, started in 1974, is now third largest in the world, with over 200 million passengers a year. As part of its green city program, the Seoul Metropolitan Government is increasing coordination among bus, subway, and suburban rail system to maintain a 70 percent public transport share during rush hours. It has expanded dedicated bus ways, improved the convenience of public transport, and implemented toll roads, fuel taxes, and parking charges to discourage use of private cars.

Asia's urbanization avalanche

Asia is going through a historic demographic transformation from a rural to an urban society (Figure 9.1).

Asia's urban population is swelling by approximately 44 million every year (ADB, 2008a). Most people in Asia will live in towns and cities by 2025. By 2050 there will be some 3 billion urbanites—roughly twice the current 1.6 billion people (Table 9.1). This is a period of enormous challenge and opportunity for city leaders (for further data, see Appendix 5).

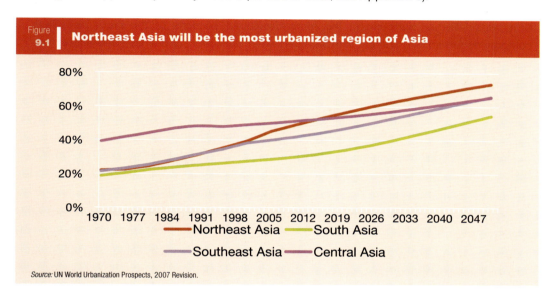

Figure 9.1 **Northeast Asia will be the most urbanized region of Asia**

Source: UN World Urbanization Prospects, 2007 Revision.

Even small, poor Asian countries will experience major change. Cambodia's urban population is forecast to be 44 percent of the national total in 2050 against today's 20 percent, an increase of 5.5 million people. The towns and cities of the Lao PDR must find space for 3.6 million more people as the urban population expands to 68 percent of the total from 33 percent.

Rural development and urban development are complementary

But while millions of people flock to the cities, many millions will stay in the countryside. Governments must address the services available to the rural poor and consider investments to improve rural productivity. Rural development is not an alternative to urban development. Both are needed. Small towns and secondary cities provide markets for rural products as well as business and social services for agricultural activities. Strengthening links between town and country will help the poor in both communities.

Most of Asia's productive rural land is already in use. It cannot increase to a level sufficient to

Box 9.2 Jakarta 1970 and 2010

Jakarta 1970

Indonesia was a rural country 40 years ago with just 13 percent of the national population living in urban areas.

Jakarta itself was a languid city of 5 million people with a few small centers of mostly low-rise commercial buildings. The majority of Jakarta's urban poor lived in a sea of undeveloped *kampongs* (villages) surrounding the more developed sections of the city. The village compounds were often swampy, without piped water, sanitation, or drainage and where most dwellings were made of bamboo matting, earth floors, and thatched roofs. Barefoot children filled the dirt roads and earthen footpaths, playing with handmade toys. Only 24 percent of the total housing stock was of permanent structures. Eighty percent of dwellings had no electricity. Paved roads were well developed in some parts of the city, but inadequate or nonexistent in low-income areas.

The average per capita income of Jakarta was about $160, twice as high as the $80 average income for Java as a whole.

Jakarta 2010

Today, Indonesia is a dynamic, developing, middle-income country with a record of economic growth.

Jakarta's population of 9.7 million is the central hub of the Jabotabek region where 26.6 million people live. Despite economic progress, less than 50 percent of Jakarta's residents have access to piped water. The city produces 6,000 tons of waste each day, but only 50 percent is collected. Clean drinking water is a luxury in many Jakarta slums. Diseases such as malaria, dengue fever, cholera, and acute respiratory infection are on the rise because of contaminated water. Where water from municipal utilities is unavailable, people can spend up to 25 percent of their income buying water from vendors. Severe flooding is becoming more frequent, perhaps caused by the increased building cover, a byproduct of urbanization. In 2007, 60 percent of the city of Jakarta was inundated (up to 7 meters deep in some areas), and 340,000 people were displaced resulting in economic costs estimated at $900 million.

A major shift in governance took place in 2001 with the decentralization of major responsibilities to local governments. Greater authority was given to local districts and cities, which now have control over their budgets. However, local authorities were given only limited additional taxing powers and local revenues still come primarily through grants from the central government.

Table 9.1 — Asia's urban population will nearly double by 2050

Asian Urbanization	1970	2010	2050
Total Urban Population (millions)	**442**	**1,587**	**2,982**
Northeast Asia	214	764	1,092
South Asia	133	480	1,221
Southeast Asia	61	249	498
Central Asia	34	94	171
Urbanization (%)	**22**	**40**	**63**
Northeast Asia	22	49	73
South Asia	19	30	55
Southeast Asia	21	42	66
Central Asia	39	51	66

Source: UN World Urbanization Prospects, 2007 Revision.

provide jobs for the larger rural population that would exist in the absence of urbanization (Bolt, 2004). On average, urban productivity is higher than rural productivity and so offers potential gains both for rural migrants and for national economies. PRC has recognized this and has adopted an urbanization strategy to absorb surplus labor from rural areas into urban areas (Webster, 2004). However, PRC's experience has also pointed to the importance of having an effective social policy for migrants.

The question for policy makers is not how to stop urban growth, but how to manage transition to ensure that both rural and urban areas develop to their potential.

Cities of the future

Asia's city-centric future implies huge increases in energy consumption and carbon emissions in the absence of a new direction. The region's long-term competitiveness—and its social stability—could depend in large part on the quality and efficiency of new urban developments.

That implies more compact, energy-efficient, safer, and livable cities. City and town planning, professional urban management, and self-financing will require much more attention.

Some countries have already achieved levels of urbanization that the rest of Asia will achieve by 2050. The economic prosperity and high living standards of Japan (67 percent urban), Republic of Korea (83 percent urban), and Malaysia (72 percent urban), along with the two economies of Hong Kong, China and Singapore, demonstrate the potential benefits of Asia's future urbanization.

Large urban mega-regions are likely to be the drivers of Asian economies in 2050. Already, cities are growing together to form contiguous urban networks. The mega region that runs from Seoul to Busan, for example, has around 46 million people and is estimated to produce about $500 billion in regional economic output (Florida et al., 2007). As Asia's urban mega regions expand, the scale economies and specializations created will amplify gains in jurisdictions that achieve the necessary cooperative planning and operation of energy, transport, and water systems. Such expansion will also require successful business promotion, licensing, and marketing.

Cross-border production networks in urban mega regions could see city-to-city ties equal to sovereign ties in importance. The growth triangle connecting Medan (Indonesia), Penang (Malaysia), and Phuket (Thailand) is one example. A triangle connects Yunnan Province, PRC with northern Lao PDR and with Viet Nam in the Mekong region (Kursten, 2004). Maximizing these international production networks requires national and local initiatives to sustain investment in transportation, power, communications, and logistics as well as trade policies necessary for efficient growth.

As Asia's wealth and technological prowess increase, it is possible to envision a few Asian cities that lead the world in technology, efficiency, and quality of life. Such an optimistic vision will not result from business as usual (Box 9.3).

Poor infrastructure and squalor are all too common in today's urban Asia. More than half the world's slum dwellers live in Asia—some 490 million people in 2005, according to UN Habitat. This number is holding steady despite rapid economic growth. Many cities have unreliable power supplies, intermittent water availability, insufficient treatment of wastewater before it is discharged into local waterways, flooding due to poor drainage, and uncollected garbage. Poor sanitation in low-income areas leads to poor health conditions. Poor systems of land registration and the lack of tradable titles for large swaths of urban slum land are disincentives to investment and renewal. Disputed land titles, the lack of a functioning land market in slum areas and unrealistic zoning are perhaps the greatest obstacles to improving slums.

The OECD estimates that cities and towns currently account for 60–80 percent of energy consumption and global carbon dioxide emissions. The pressure to reduce carbon use will only increase. Aggressive action is needed to improve the energy efficiency of buildings and appliances, to create utility systems based on reuse and recycling, and to manage land use and transportation systems to reduce costs and energy use.

Compact, higher-density cities like London, Seoul, Singapore, and Tokyo encourage a high percentage of walking and public transport trips, and have lower per capita carbon dioxide emissions than lower-density cities (Box 9.4). However, urban densities in Asia are decreasing while middle class demand for automobiles is increasing rapidly. The growth in car ownership is rising so fast that carbon emissions due to transport are expected to increase by 2.5 times over current levels in PRC and by 4 times in India by 2035, despite increased fuel efficiency (Rogers,

Box 9.3 — Vision for a successful Asian city of 2050

The successful Asian mega-city of 2050 has a density similar to Tokyo in 2010. Urban sprawl is limited because prices, incentives, and infrastructure are designed to favor infill development and compact patterns of city expansion. Mass public transport is ubiquitous, clean, and efficient. Rail dominates in the densest, richest countries; bus-based systems are the norm in others. Many journeys will be made on foot through pleasant unpolluted surroundings. Energy efficiency is integrated into building design, appliances, and systems for lighting, heating, and cooling. Utilities for water, wastewater, and solid waste rely heavily on reuse and recycling. Robots inside dwellings perform the household functions of laundry, cleaning, waste disposal, and basic cooking; other household systems monitor the health of residents, relieving the burden of care of the elderly in aging societies. New private cars entering the fleet are zero-emission vehicles, running on electricity or hydrogen fuels.

While great strides will have been made in reducing the carbon intensity of electricity generation, urban transport still accounts for 7 percent of carbon emission because of construction, maintenance, and fuel production. Cars communicate with each other and intelligent traffic management systems anticipate flows and automatically route cars to the most efficient roadways. Technology embedded in highways and some streets takes control of vehicles to reduce congestion and accidents. Most people prefer the convenience and comfort of mass transit.

Education, culture, preserved local heritage sites, parks, nearby eco-environments, and recreation opportunities are world class and vital to the city's unique brand and competitive advantage. The urban poor, defined as those below 60 percent of the city's median income, have access to high-quality health care and children's education.

Unserviced slums disappeared after a 20 year campaign of upgrading—involving land titling, regularization, replanning, and the extension of basic infrastructure services. Some of these areas still have housing units that do not conform to building codes but they are safe and affordable.

City management is autonomous under a well-defined fiscal and administrative decentralization framework that balances local responsibilities with local authority to raise resources. The local administration is business-friendly, striving to ensure that schools, universities—especially research universities—continually nurture creativity and innovation to sustain high levels of productivity for rapidly changing technology and business needs. Close cooperation exists with other cities and towns that form the local urban mega region, including those across the national border. Infrastructure and services are planned, implemented, and managed on a regional basis to ensure energy efficiency, productivity, and a minimum ecological footprint.

> **Box 9.4** | **"Compact city" concept**
>
> The concept of the "compact city" as a spatial development strategy has become popular in many OECD countries, particularly in Europe and Japan. The European Commission encourages European cities to move toward more compactness, on the basis of environmental and quality of life objectives. The British government has made urban compactness a central element of its sustainable development policy (Government of the United Kingdom, 1993) and the Netherlands government has taken similar action (National Physical Planning Agency, 1991). Most recently, the Japanese government has introduced the concept of "Eco-Compact City" as one of its top-priority urban policies (Ministry of Land, Infrastructure, Transport and Tourism, 2009).
>
> The compact city strategy aims to intensify urban land use through a combination of higher residential densities and centralization, mixed land uses, and development limits outside a designated area (Churchman, 1999).
>
> *Source:* Cohen (2004).

2006). Public transport is experiencing a significant loss of market share. Lower densities lead to sprawl and higher rates of motorization, creating more sprawl in a vicious circle. In other parts of the developing world, a doubling of the urban population is expected to result in a tripling of urbanized land area. In Asia, with declining densities, a population doubling could lead to a land area 6 times larger (Angel et al., 2005). Lower densities and greater sprawl bring higher costs for utilities and transport.

The dimensions of city building

There are three dimensions to modern city planning and building that will profoundly affect Asian cities of the future:

- *Modernizing/retrofitting old city centers.* The inefficient centers of most existing Asian cities must be modernized. Better systems of urban transport, water, sewerage and drainage, preservation of cultural heritage, and reshaped land use as well as efforts to digitize city functions are all needed to create connected populations with better IT, reduced carbon dioxide emissions and improved energy efficiency. Urban strategies should be centered on more compact land use to make mass transit feasible.
- *Using growth corridors to lead modernization.* Rapid population expansion provides opportunities to plan new corridors of "smarter" city growth. Planning land use and transport together can produce higher-density developments with integrated mass transit that incorporate IT and communications services with new urban transport facilities. Energy-saving designs in growth corridors should be explored in all fast-expanding cities.

- ***Developing purpose-built economic clusters.*** Large-scale real estate developments that cluster related economic activities to create or exploit a comparative advantage can jump-start economic output. Songdo International Business District under construction near Seoul is one example. Malaysia's Multimedia Super Corridor, launched in the 1990s and designed to take the country into the information age, had almost 3,500 small and medium-sized enterprises (SMEs) operating in it by July 2005 (Yusuf, 2007). New institutional arrangements are often employed in such developments, with companies (either private or state-owned) given comprehensive responsibilities for urban planning, design, construction, and even operations.

Managing Asia's small and medium-sized towns and cities

The management of smaller towns and cities is a particular challenge. Many of them have high rates of growth, albeit from a low base. Small towns generally have inexperienced personnel and limited systems and traditions to guide decisions, exacerbating the management problems associated with growth. The large number of small towns makes it difficult for national governments to provide support. For the same reason, small towns also typically receive little official development assistance (ODA). They particularly need support in training, systems development, and professionalization of staff.

Major risks to be managed

With 84 percent of Asian GDP generated in towns and cities, a successful national economy is intimately linked to successful urbanization. Four risks stand out: growing inequality in cities; unmet expectations of the rapidly emerging middle class; poorly planned infrastructure and land use spiraling into high-cost, high-carbon environments; and consequences of climate change and other natural hazards.

Inequality, growth of slums, and breakdown of social cohesion

Disparities in living conditions and access to basic services of shelter, water, and sanitation are severe in many Asian cities. Levels of inequality in income are also high in many countries, with Gini coefficients above the alert level of 0.4 (Figure 9.2). Income inequality within cities has been increasing rapidly in PRC and has been trending upward in India (Figure 9.3). Social cohesion can break down when levels of inequality grow too high.

Most Asian cities have not yet faced severe problems of crime, drugs, and violence. However, the combination of rapidly growing cities, growing slum populations, disputed land tenure, corruption, and high unemployment can lead to an explosive situation. Latin America presents a cautionary tale. Urbanization there is roughly 65 years ahead of Asia. Argentina, Brazil, Mexico, and Venezuela were unable to manage rapid growth of illegal, unserviced settlements and failed

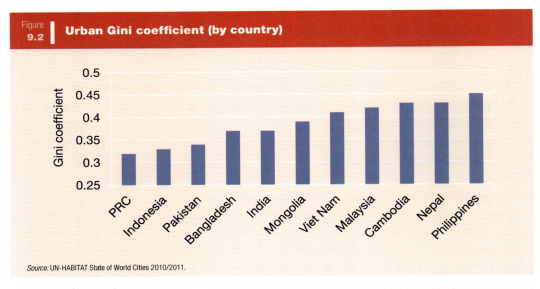

Figure 9.2 Urban Gini coefficient (by country)

Source: UN-HABITAT State of World Cities 2010/2011.

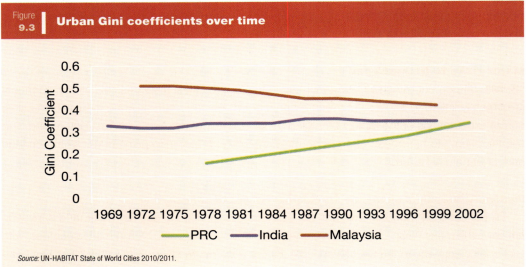

Figure 9.3 Urban Gini coefficients over time

Source: UN-HABITAT State of World Cities 2010/2011.

to provide adequate services. Slums and low-income urban peripheries are hotbeds of assault, aggression, drug trafficking, and violence of all kinds. In many cases urban gangs filled a gap left by underperforming local governments. Delayed action to improve living conditions for the poor in Asian cities could lead to Latin American–style development—with zones of modernity co-existing with zones of misery and violence.

Unmet expectations of the expanding middle class

Asia's rapidly growing middle class is largely urban. It is better educated and more in touch with global standards for services than ever before. Improved infrastructure, services, modern shopping, cultural and recreational facilities, and more green areas are in high demand—and can be part of a virtuous circle leading to further growth. Most innovation, which is the heart of a competitive global economy, occurs in urban centers. Talented people, so-called knowledge workers, are attracted by places where they can enjoy life. Urban areas that accommodate these new aspirations will have a better chance of succeeding and innovating over the longer term. This is vital to recognize if Asia's larger and medium-sized cities are to successfully shift from manufacturing to services. Cities that are unable to manage the increased expectations for better services and governance face increased potential for instability.

Poorly planned infrastructure and land use

Unplanned urban sprawl is driven by both the demands of middle class citizens for more space and private transport, as well as migration from rural areas. Some national and local governments are responding. Japan's "eco-compact city" concept is a priority for urban policy. Shanghai, which now has the longest metro system in the world, plans to double the length of metro lines by 2020 in a bid to cut dependence on car commutes as its population becomes wealthier. Singapore has long been an innovator in automobile demand management. Higher-density, more compact cities are less expensive, per capita, than low-density cities. Higher-density cities can also be vibrant places to live, as exemplified by Berlin; Hong Kong, China; London; New York; Paris; San Francisco; Singapore; Tokyo.

But while a few Asian cities have adopted a formal vision for a sustainable future, most are moving in the wrong direction and risk being locked into a high-cost, high-energy land-use and infrastructure pattern.

Environmental risks

Many Asian cities face unpredictable risks from volcanoes, earthquakes, tornadoes, and the effects of climate change.

Climate change risks are particularly profound. These include severe water shortages from a drier climate and reduced fresh water flows from Himalayan glaciers, seawater intrusions into aquifers, more severe weather patterns leading to possibly more intense typhoons, amplified storm surges, increased flooding of coastal mega-cities, and increases in vectorborne and diarrheal diseases. Among the more vulnerable larger cities are Bangkok, Dhaka, Guangzhou, Hai Phong, Ho Chi Minh City, Kolkata, Manila, Mumbai, Shanghai, and Yangon. Flooding risks are exacerbated by subsidence from groundwater extraction: subsidence in Bangkok has been measured at 4 cm per year and in parts of Jakarta at 6 cm per year. It is estimated that a 30-year storm event in Ho Chi Minh City by 2050 could affect 12.5 million people and create 2 million refugees (Fuchs, 2010).

Improving collaboration and cooperation across countries in research, standards, planning, and investment to mitigate these risks can yield large payoffs.

Priority agenda for moving to a better urban future

Urbanization is a complex phenomenon. But experiences in different regions point to a set of approaches that have broad applicability in Asia. National and local governments must be part of the action plan. Strong leadership is required to deal with entrenched interests and political inertia.

Recommendations for national government

National government policy sets the framework within which cities operate.

Effective decentralization

Experience indicates that local knowledge, as well as autonomy and accountability are needed to manage complex urban economies. Decentralization away from central government is always difficult. It can take decades until the details of the legal and regulatory measures that guide local governments are fully implemented and the skills and management systems needed for effective local governance are improved. Asia has experienced significant decentralization over the past 20 years. But this, so far uneven process, should be accelerated and refined.

Local revenue-raising powers, clear prudential national rules to prevent excessive borrowing, transparency in budgeting, accounting, and procurement, and local government accountability via the political process are all required for successful decentralization (Alm, 2010).

National capacity-building programs and professional training institutes for local government officials (which can be public or private) need to be created or strengthened. Programs should cover senior policy and administrative staff as well as technical staff. Cross-country regional sharing of curricula, teaching staff, and even joint programs in specialized topics (such as wastewater treatment technology, traffic management, and use of public-private partnerships (P-PPs) would be beneficial. Research and policy institutes have been set up in many countries and should also be strengthened. Links should be established with other institutes in the region and elsewhere.

Regulations governing pay and allowances must also be reviewed to ensure local governments can attract staff with the necessary skills.

National rules requiring full public disclosure and transparency in budgeting and financial transactions and publication of results in achieving service levels at the local level can help create a competitive incentive to improve performance. A growing, well-educated middle class will increase popular demand for more transparency, better governance, and improved service delivery at the local level.

New national frameworks for financing urban infrastructure

ADB has estimated the "urban infrastructure deficit" in Asia and the Pacific at $60 billion per year (ADB, 2008a) after recurrent revenues from local governments, national subsidies, and ODA. It is imperative to enable local government borrowing from private domestic banks and domestic capital markets if that funding gap is to be bridged.

A formal system of public-private partnerships (P-PPs) for revenue-earning projects like toll roads and bridges would be helpful. This is being done in Republic of Korea, India, and increasingly elsewhere in Asia, often with the help of multilateral development banks. The majority of urban investment though will be for non-revenue-earning infrastructure (such as city streets and storm drainage) that has limited P-PP prospects. Local governments will therefore need the capacity to borrow for such capital investments.

A framework for local government access to commercial credit could involve the following:
- Financial and management reform by local governments, where needed, as a condition for access, such as stronger financial management, modern accounting systems, improved planning, implementation and operation of projects, expenditure control, and greater attention to own-source revenues;
- Legal frameworks specifically applying to local government debt whether from banks or capital markets. These would cover borrowing authority, rules for issuance, disclosure and transparency; tax treatment, allowable credit structures, record keeping, and requirement for credit ratings if any, etc.
- Clear and firm prudential regulatory rules that determine the conditions under which borrowing can take place. Such rules exist in many countries.[1] The Philippines, for example, has a reasonable system. However, many local governments in Asia are prevented or discouraged by national authorities from making use of private domestic finance even when they have the financial capability to be responsible borrowers. As a result, most local governments borrow almost exclusively from government-owned banks, often supported by ODA, instead of beginning the process of tapping commercial financing sources;
- Market-based intermediaries that can facilitate market access by small and medium-sized local governments. Direct bond issues are not feasible except for the larger local governments (this is also true in the West). The high fixed cost of bond issuance

---

1 There are many ways to specify such rules, which may include measures such as limitations on borrowing in foreign currency, absolute borrowing limits, such as total debt service not to exceed a specific percentage of recurring revenues, restriction of borrowing for capital investment purposes only, limits on guarantees, requirement for independently audited accounts, disclosure of existing debts and debt service, contingent liabilities.

(documentation, credit rating, marketing) relative to the size of their borrowing, makes direct bond issues by small and medium-sized local governments prohibitively expensive. Market-based financial intermediaries that specialize in local government lending can help fill this gap.

- The Tamil Nadu Urban Fund in India has adopted this approach and periodically aggregates the needs of multiple local governments and issues domestic bonds on their behalf. This model has local variants in many developed countries.[2]
- Some Asian countries have established municipal development funds (MDFs) to lend to local governments using government and ODA funding. The MDF in the Philippines lends to a wide range of local governments and has done so with negligible rates of nonperforming loans. MDFs can be useful as transition mechanisms, but sustainability requires that such institutions move away from exclusive reliance on government and ODA funding (as the above fund in India has partly done) and provide market-based access to commercial funds.
- Transparent legal frameworks for P-PPs that apply to the local government level and that P-PP legal frameworks that meet international standards (such as the well-designed Republic of Korea P-PP system) have been instrumental in increasing private investment in countries that have adopted them. Such frameworks should be prepared at national level for adoption at local government level.

Market incentives for better urban design, conservation, and green energy development

National government can eliminate or drastically reduce subsidies that in many countries increase demand for gasoline, coal powered energy and water. A charge for environmental damage (negative externalities) would reduce uneconomic use and raise revenues that can be used for environmental repair. Such an approach would increase interest in mass transport and city designs that use space more efficiently. It would also encourage a shift in demand to low-carbon energy sources.

Cross border, city-to-city mega regions

Sustaining city-to-city logistics chains in urban mega regions that extend across national borders requires cooperation between national and local leaders on regional transport, power, communications, and logistics investments. Equally important are trade policies that promote efficient growth.

---

2 In Canada, there are six provincial municipal finance corporations, including the Municipal Finance Authority of British Columbia. In Norway, there is Kommunal Bankan; in Sweden, Kommuninvest; in Netherlands, Bank of Netherlands Municipalities; in Denmark there is KommuneKredit; in Finland, Municipality Finance Plc.; in the US, there are state revolving funds in every state for water investments, and 17 states have state bond banks.

Recommendations for local governments
Attractiveness to private investment

National economic and social policies exert a strong influence on corporate decisions to locate facilities in a particular country. But policies made at the city level are often crucial in overall competitiveness. Property rights, land use regulations, business registration, and permitting procedures and the level and fairness of local taxes should be regularly assessed for their impact on city productivity and competitiveness. Reviewing the availability of key infrastructure—including IT and city services such as police and emergency services—with business leaders can be helpful.

One study of 23 PRC cities estimated that productivity of firms in a city could be increased by about 45 percent depending on local policy decisions that affected the city investment climate (Dollar, 2004). Another study estimated that if a city in Pakistan adopted all existing best practices (in starting a business, dealing with construction permits, registering property, paying taxes, trading across borders, and enforcing contracts) that were found among the Pakistan cities reviewed, that city would rank 69th out of 183 world economies in attractiveness to business—16 places ahead of Pakistan's own position in the ranking (World Bank, 2010e). In Indonesia, Yogyakarta and Bandung have taken steps to improve their cities' attractiveness to business by establishing one-stop shops for licensing, reducing time for property registration, etc. (World Bank, 2010f). Ahmedabad, India also made significant efforts to improve its business climate. In recent years Ahmedabad has witnessed a major construction boom and many foreign companies have set up units there.

City management

Many Asian cities have a long way to go in improving the functioning of their administrations. A well-functioning city administration needs professional staff with clear incentives to perform at a high level. It needs institutions and policies to improve property rights, land registration and titling, land use regulations, business registration and permitting procedures, and taxation and resource mobilization policies, among others. The professionalization of financial management is another key priority.

Large cities may need to create their own training academies or work with local universities to supplement the training by national programs. Cities and towns also need to accept that contracting out and using consultants can be the most efficient way to obtain specific skills. Small cities and towns may have an especially strong need to contract out for services and consider joint operations with nearby jurisdictions.

In addition to skills and training, institutional and regulatory reform is needed to reduce bureaucracy and create incentives for more nimble decision making. The use of periodic independent evaluations of municipal performance can also be very useful.

Infrastructure planning and land use

Expenditures on urban infrastructure per capita vary widely from country to country. India spends about $17 per capita compared with $116 per capita in PRC (Kohli and Sood, 2010).

When urban areas are growing rapidly, infrastructure investments cannot be considered in isolation. Transport, especially, greatly affects future city shape and land use. The investment choices made on technology and location through road, rail, bus, even port and airport facilities will have long-term effects on land use, the city's efficiency, and its environmental footprint.

Severe congestion can be a disincentive to investment and a deterrent to location for knowledge workers. The relatively high densities of Asian cities mean that rail mass transit will have a significant place in the future of Asian cities. McKinsey estimates that 170 new mass transit systems could be built in PRC alone by 2025. But rail mass transit is expensive and not the only solution, especially for medium and smaller cities. Curitiba, Brazil and Bogota, Columbia through its TransMilenio system have been examples of innovation in bus-based urban transport technology and land use. Jakarta has successfully adapted these models in its TransJakarta express bus lane system. Seoul has removed over 7 km of elevated highway in the city center while building an extensive bus rapid transit system and promoting nonmotorized transport solutions (ADB, 2008a).

Understanding space and its cost is key to successful city development. Accommodating Asia's large projected growth in urban population is much more expensive at low densities than at those of, for example, Hong Kong, China; Seoul; Singapore; or Tokyo of today. The additional greenhouse gas emissions and energy costs of lower density development are also very significant. Cities, especially larger ones, should consider compact strategies while freeing zoning restrictions and floor area ratios to allow densification on a market basis and to provide mass transit options that will encourage nonautomobile travel (Bertaud, 2010).

Land markets and the resolution of land title disputes

The persistent problems of disputed or unclear title, restrictive covenants on property sale, arbitrary building codes that specify unaffordable standards, and outdated master-plans that distort land markets of many Asian cities need to be dealt with. Slum and squatter areas often persist because of disputes over land titles or restrictions on titles that discourage legal investment and development by residents. Functioning land markets, and land management and property registration systems that clarify property rights, can affect economic growth as well as social equity. For example, in the Philippines, the value of land with unclear title has been estimated at over $100 billion (De Soto, 2000). Potential commercial land use is affected by lengthy and costly land transfer mechanisms. Incomplete land registration causes local governments enormous losses in forgone property taxes. Hong Kong, China has highly developed and efficient systems for land registration and administration.

Development of inclusive policies

Reducing inequalities, increasing access to basic services, and developing adequate social safety nets are critical components of the quality of life. Provision of services to the poor is a necessary ingredient of good urban management that can have an impact on the ability of a city to market itself as a good place to live and work. Low-income and slum areas of cities need to be dealt with systematically through upgrading programs that provide basic infrastructure (drainage, local roads, water and sanitation, electricity) and through resolution of land tenure issues. The absolute numbers of urban poor are highest in the middle-income countries, which have the greatest need for sustainable strategies.

Human capital development is key to sustainable growth. The knowledge economy, based on innovation, is largely centered on cities. Cities are where innovation and new ideas are incubated, developed, and exchanged. Improving education as part of a long-term strategy to improve innovation and the skills of a workforce is an obvious need. The existence of research universities is associated with innovation. While it is not always possible to create such institutions, city leaders need to be aware of their importance. In the absence of large world-class research universities, networking among second tier-universities can be a means of building technological capabilities. Such networking can build spheres of excellence and critical masses of complementary skills (Yusuf, 2007).

Talented people are often termed footloose, because they can choose where they work. As incomes and expectations increase, talented people give greater consideration to working in cities where they can enjoy life (Castells, 2000). Edward Glaeser, Richard Florida, and others have found that cultural activities and amenities are central determinants of urban competitiveness. These can involve well-preserved city centers and other cultural heritage sites, parks, museums, art galleries, movie houses, theaters, restaurants, and sports and reaction facilities.

Targeted programs of health and education need to be available to the poor.

Environmental sustainability and risk management

The management of resources to reduce the ecological footprint of cities needs to involve new approaches to planning for cities that incorporate energy efficiency in building regulations, land use and transport planning, as well as the management of water, air, and solid waste to promote recycling and reuse.

Contamination of air and water, as well as poor sanitation facilities in Asian cities have made environmental management a severe challenge. Few developing Asian cities have been successful. Shanghai has invested heavily in environmental infrastructure as part of an explicit strategy to become known as a good place to live. The city authorities believe that this will enhance its ability to attract foreign direct investment and high-level workers, both foreign and local. At a smaller scale, the Songdo business district in Republic of Korea is a planned business neighborhood based on LEED[3] green building standards.

Mitigation measures are needed to protect cities from rising sea levels and changing temperatures due to climate change. Recommended measures include (Fuchs, 2010): better identification and mapping of flood and other risks at a sub-city scale; flood protection works; warning systems; integrating climate risk into land use planning to channel future growth to less flood-prone zones; control of land subsidence; and setting up needed institutional mechanisms for planning, mitigation, and disaster response.

Disaster mitigation is also necessary to lessen the consequences from other more sudden natural risks including those from volcanoes, earthquakes, and tornadoes.

Not all of these measures can be adopted in the same way by every city. Each Asian city needs a realistic vision for its future. Then it can start to build a strategy to get there based on its physical and human endowments and its competitive advantage.

Visionary leadership

Action is needed now. Delays only contribute to further distortions that will have to be undone later. Asia needs city and national leaders who are visionary, who can create new ideas for what modern cities should be, and who take advantage of the current wave of urban growth to implement that vision.

---

3 According to its website, LEED is an internationally recognized green building certification system, providing third-party verification that a building or community was designed and built using strategies aimed at improving performance across all the metrics: energy savings, water efficiency, carbon dioxide emissions reduction, improved indoor environmental quality, and stewardship of resources and sensitivity to their impacts.

Transforming Finance

Chapter 10 — Andrew Sheng

This chapter discusses the transformation of the Asian financial system necessary to underpin the advent of the Asian Century. It starts with a short history of Asia's financial rise in the past few decades and compares its structure and size to the West's. It then outlines the likely growth of finance in the two scenarios portrayed in the book: the Asian Century and the Middle Income Trap. It makes the case why Asia should move beyond conventional wisdom and evolve its own financial system to better serve the needs of the real sector. The heart of the chapter is a description of the financial transformation necessary. The chapter goes on to discuss Asia's role in the governance of global monetary and financial systems. It concludes with the priority action agenda, including priorities for regional cooperation.

Asia's financial rise: Past and present

When looking forward 40 years to 2050, it is useful to look back at the past. In the 1970s, Japan was the only Asian country to be counted as developed, but its GDP was only 20 percent that of the US. The Asian financial landscape was largely a highly regulated bank-dominated system, with small equity markets and nascent debt markets. Even the foreign exchange markets were small, since exchange controls existed for most Asian currencies. It was only in the 1980s that financial deregulation began in earnest and Asia's financial landscape changed significantly.

In 1980, the size of the traditional finance sector of the global economy (banking assets, stock market capitalization, and debt market outstanding, excluding derivatives) was roughly 100 percent of GDP. By 2009, the gross assets of the financial markets (excluding derivatives) reached $232 trillion or four times global GDP (Tables 10.1 and 10.2). The notional size of the financial derivatives markets at the end of 2009 was $615 trillion or 10.6 times global GDP.

In contrast, emerging Asia's gross financial asset/GDP ratio was only 245 percent, indicating financial depth half that of the European Union (EU) (409 percent), while Japan's level (477 percent) was slightly higher than that of the US (431 percent). The NIEs, however, have a financial asset/GDP ratio of 603 percent, dominated by the two financial centers of Hong Kong, China and Singapore.

Emerging Asia's finance sector is still largely bank-dominated, with bank assets at 126 percent

Table 10.1 Global finance sector indicators, 2009 (% of GDP)

	GDP (US$ trillion)	Bank assets/ GDP (%)	Stock market capitalization/ GDP (%)	Debt securities*/GDP (%)
World	57.8	161	82	159
Asia	12.9	145	68	123
US	14.1	100	107	224
EU	15.3	189	43	177
North America	15.4	109	108	217
Emerging Asia	7.9	126	69	50

Note: *Excluding derivatives.
Source: IMF, 2010, Statistical Appendix, Table 3.

Table 10.2 Global finance sector indicators, 2009 (% of assets)

	Bank assets, stock market capitalization, and debt securities* ($ trillion)	Share of bank assets (%)	Share of stock market capitalization (%)	Share of debt securities* (%)
World	232.2	40	20	40
Asia	43.5	43	20	36
US	60.9	23	25	52
EU	62.9	46	10	43
North America	67.1	25	25	50
Emerging Asia	19.3	51	28	20

Note: *Excluding derivatives.
Source: IMF, 2010, Statistical Appendix, Table 3.

of GDP, compared with stock market capitalization 69 percent and debt market capitalization 50 percent. In the debt market, public debt far outweighed private debt issuance, indicating heavy private reliance on banking finance. In contrast, the debt market size of the EU was 177 percent of GDP, of which private debt was over double the size of public debt.

Asia intermediates a large part of its savings through markets in the US and Europe, which are generally deeper and still more efficient, robust, and liquid in spite of the Great Recession. Asia's foreign exchange reserves are largely invested in American and European markets. Asian economies held more than $6.1 trillion or 71.5 percent of the world's foreign exchange reserves (excluding gold) at the end of 2009 (by the end of 2010 they exceeded 75 percent), but a relatively small proportion was invested in Asian paper.

Institutional development in Asia's nonbank sector is weaker than that in Europe and the US. Innovative capital market and insurance skills are still tapped from London or New York. Although fund management skills are improving, the largest contractual savings institutions tend to be led by a public sector with conservative and domestic-oriented investment strategies. For example, the assets of contractual savings institutions in Malaysia and Singapore, two of the most developed sectors in Asia, amount to only 60–80 percent of GDP, compared with 160–180 percent in most of Europe and 100 percent in the US.

Despite Asia's high savings, its financial system has been volatile and vulnerable to huge wealth losses, partly because of structural flaws. Before the Asian crisis, stock market price-earnings ratios tended to exceed developed market ratios because of small public floats and the tight control that families or closely knit companies had over the markets, which prevented takeovers by outsiders or foreigners. The Asian stock markets also tended to be speculative and were used more to "double leverage" holdings of equity as collateral against bank loans to concentrate control than they were to raise funds directly from the public or to spread equity ownership.

Alternative scenarios of Asian finance in 2050

In 2009, Asia accounted for 28 percent of global GDP and 23 percent of global financial assets (Figure 10.1). By 2050, in the Asian Century scenario, Asia's share of global GDP almost doubles to 52 percent at market exchange rates (Figure 10.2). Based on current configurations

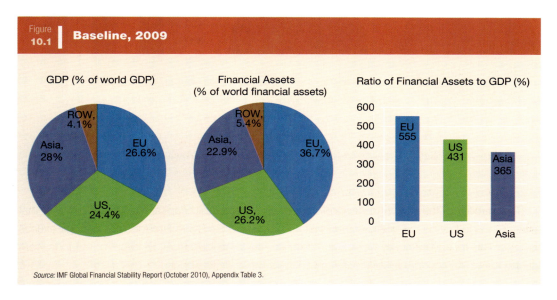

Figure 10.1 Baseline, 2009

Source: IMF Global Financial Stability Report (October 2010), Appendix Table 3.

of advanced-country financial deepening, Asia's share of global financial assets could rise to as much as 45 percent of the total, with the financial deepening ratio (total financial assets excluding derivatives as a percentage of GDP) rising to 549 percent by 2050, comparable to current levels in the EU and the US. On the other hand, in the Middle Income Trap scenario, where Asia's share of global GDP remains at only 31 percent (as a number of Asian economies fail to break out of the trap) financial deepening is lower at 470 percent of GDP (Figure 10.3).

In either scenario, Asia will be host to some of the largest global equity, debt, and banking markets, with the region increasingly shaping the global financial architecture, the monetary system, and global financial intermediation (Figures 10.4–10.6).

Such scenarios of Asian economic or financial leadership are neither preordained nor inevitable. Indeed, the Asian financial crisis and the Great Recession remind us that poorly managed finance can be highly disruptive of trade, investment, and growth. Long-term projections of Asia in 2050 cannot rule out the possibility of a "perfect storm" scenario where the combination of bad macro policies, exuberance combined with lax finance sector supervision, natural disaster/climate change risks, demographic changes, and weak governance can bring about a major setback to Asian growth.

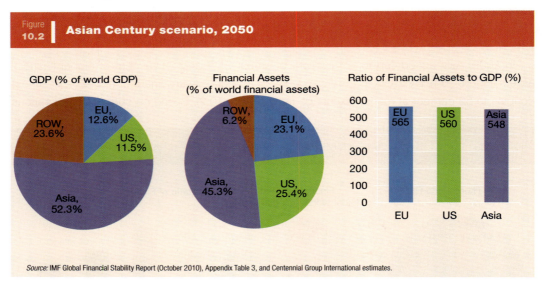

Figure 10.2 Asian Century scenario, 2050

Source: IMF Global Financial Stability Report (October 2010), Appendix Table 3, and Centennial Group International estimates.

The inability of the region to develop deeper and more liquid capital markets has meant that Asia still has to rely on the financial markets of Europe and the US to intermediate its huge excess savings. This reliance actually increased after the Asian financial crisis, as even more funds were placed in the advanced markets to self-insure against financial shocks.

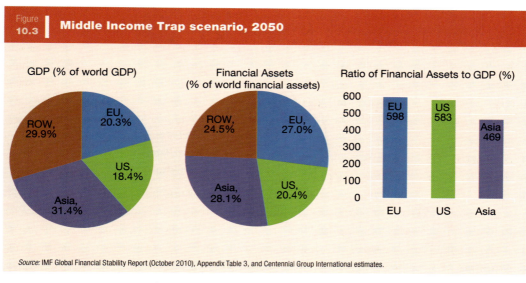

Figure 10.3 | Middle Income Trap scenario, 2050

Source: IMF Global Financial Stability Report (October 2010), Appendix Table 3, and Centennial Group International estimates.

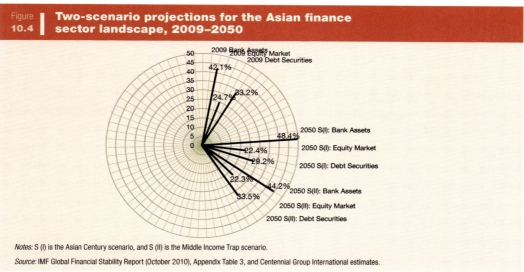

Figure 10.4 | Two-scenario projections for the Asian finance sector landscape, 2009–2050

Notes: S (I) is the Asian Century scenario, and S (II) is the Middle Income Trap scenario.
Source: IMF Global Financial Stability Report (October 2010), Appendix Table 3, and Centennial Group International estimates.

Implications of the Asian Century for Asian finance

The realization of the Asian Century means that Asia should no longer be a price taker or a rule taker. Increasingly it must become a price maker and rule maker in partnership with the other major economies. What is true of the real sector on a geopolitical basis should also be true of the finance sector. But to be a globally responsible citizen, Asia must also be a thought leader on all global commons, including finance.

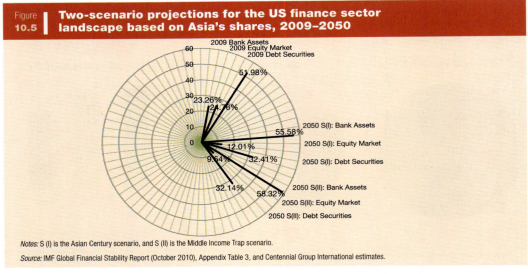

Figure 10.5 Two-scenario projections for the US finance sector landscape based on Asia's shares, 2009–2050

Notes: S (I) is the Asian Century scenario, and S (II) is the Middle Income Trap scenario.
Source: IMF Global Financial Stability Report (October 2010), Appendix Table 3, and Centennial Group International estimates.

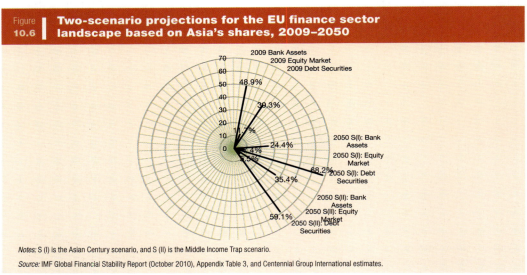

Figure 10.6 Two-scenario projections for the EU finance sector landscape based on Asia's shares, 2009–2050

Notes: S (I) is the Asian Century scenario, and S (II) is the Middle Income Trap scenario.
Source: IMF Global Financial Stability Report (October 2010), Appendix Table 3, and Centennial Group International estimates.

As demonstrated by the recent spectacular rise of global finance and its sudden collapse, the modern finance sector increasingly has a life of its own and can be either a facilitator or disruptor of real sector activities. Recent official diagnoses of the global financial crisis have attributed it to human error and systemic failure (US Financial Crisis Inquiry Commission, 2010), of which four factors are heavily debated—the failure of conventional wisdom in economics and finance theory to predict the crisis, the flawed global financial architecture, the "too big to fail" scale of finance, and the need to transform finance so that it once again serves the real sector.

To date, Asia has been far less ideological and more pragmatic in its approach toward the role of finance in economic development. This approach has served Asia well in the past, and should continue in the future. As a rising economic power, and with the highest level of savings, Asia can build a different financial system to better serve its needs by learning from past financial crises. This requires a radical departure from the current mind-set in the developed economies.

Thus far, Asia's success in the real sector has been based on the fundamental premise that finance serves the real sector, not the other way around. Asia's future approach to finance should be based on this same premise.

Asia needs a financial system that will efficiently intermediate its huge savings to finance its massive investment needs in infrastructure, urbanization, climate change mitigation, and adaptation, as well as in technological development and business creation. Inclusive finance will be a particular priority.

Conventional wisdom in finance: The Great Recession of 2007–2009

The conventional wisdom of current economic and financial theory is based on assumptions of rational expectations and efficient markets. The belief in unfettered finance and free markets has allowed global finance to expand exponentially since the 1990s. However, financial regulation and risk management of financial derivatives in developed economies were seriously flawed, causing an unsustainable conundrum whereby finance was allowed to grow without limits, with its systemic risks underwritten by the public sector. The unintended consequence was unprecedented state intervention to stem the global financial crisis, with OECD governments almost doubling their fiscal debt to 100 percent of GDP after the crisis.

The underdevelopment of the Asian finance sector and its lack of preparation for globalization was the main reason that the earlier Asian financial crisis proved to be such a shock. The crisis economies paid severely for the failure to strengthen their domestic financial systems against large and volatile capital flows and for inattention to the dangers of the double mismatch—borrowing short-term funds to invest or lend in long-term assets and borrowing foreign currencies to invest in long-term domestic currency assets. Memory of the painful lessons of this crisis—mostly the overleverage of the corporate sector, undersupervision of the banking system, and lack of appreciation of the dangers of volatile capital flows—caused Asian policy makers and financial regulators to be extra cautious and prudent, thus helping to cushion Asia against the Great Recession.

The Asian crisis was a harbinger of the Great Recession, although the latter's scale was considerably larger and its origins were different. The Great Recession was a crisis of the overleveraged banking wholesale market, where bank funding collapsed in the asset securitization market when the property bubble deflated (US Financial Crisis Inquiry Commission, 2010). The Asian crisis was largely one of traditional banking, due to bad loans to the overleveraged corporate sector, caused by overexposure to real estate and stock market bubbles.

The "free market knows best" dictum caused complacency in financial oversight and surveillance. The Independent Evaluation Office of the IMF concluded that the IMF and the advanced countries paid little attention to the risks of contagion and spillovers, due to "a high degree of groupthink, intellectual capture, a general mindset that a major financial crisis in large advanced economies was unlikely, and inadequate analytical approaches" (IMF, 2011).

The Great Recession has highlighted the weaknesses of looking at monetary, fiscal, and financial regulatory policies as relatively mutually exclusive tools to deal with emerging asset or credit bubbles. Under this thinking, policy tools were delegated to segmented bureaucracies to implement. This technocratic approach did not recognize that the problem was systemic, coming in from all fronts with cross-institutional, cross-national, and cross-border ramifications.

While Asia has not been hurt directly due to the late development of its financial derivatives markets, the region was hurt indirectly through the shock to global trade and investments, transmitted through financial contagion (Azis, 2011; Boorman et al., 2010).

Current reform proposals and Asia

The current reforms already call for greater state intervention in finance through more stringent regulation, lower leverage, and disincentives against excessive risk taking. As the world reexamines conventional wisdom and financial theory, the Asian approach should remain pragmatic, based on the premise that finance should not grow at the expense of the real sector. Instead, it must complement and support real sector activities.

As Asia has learned from past crises, there is no magic nor free lunch in finance. Systemically, finance cannot grow indefinitely faster than the real sector without higher inflation or asset bubbles (Azis, 2011). Financial innovation cannot be useful if it is based only on leverage. Finance sector compensation should have a reasonable relation to real sector compensation. And, finance cannot be seen to help only the rich.

In short, finance must support development of the real sector, be stable, inclusive, and sustainable in the long term.

Asia in the international financial architecture

Finance is global and therefore national reforms are necessary but not sufficient. Domestic financial stability cannot be maintained without a reexamination of the role of the global reserve currency and the shape of the global monetary and regulatory system in sustaining worldwide financial stability.

As the world moves away from a single dominant economy, it is only natural that there should be a more representative, multipolar global monetary and financial architecture. As Asian finance becomes more sophisticated and larger in relative size, it will be inevitable that leading Asian policy makers and regulators will get more actively involved in the global forums that will set the future international financial structure and rules.

Having learned costly lessons in the 1990s, the reserve buildup by Asian economies and subsequent liquidity support arrangements (in the form of the Chiang Mai Initiative and Asian Bond Fund Initiative based on the ASEAN+3 frameworks) offered a higher level of self-insurance against volatile capital flows and balance-of-payments deficits. But without reform of the global financial architecture, such self-insurance has high opportunity costs and spillover effects through global imbalances.

The unraveling caused by the Great Recession has afforded Asia a timely opportunity to launch further measures to shield the region from the impact of future crises. Asian governments in general recognize the imperative to reform the existing system, through active participation and representation in international financial institutions and forums. They also support the G20 decision to intensify cooperation among regulators and strengthen global financial surveillance (Asia Policy Forum, 2009).

Global reserve currency

One of the roots of the Great Recession was a flawed global financial architecture, centered on the dominant role of a single national global reserve currency. The cumulative current account deficits arising from the Triffin dilemma have resulted in large global imbalances, including an unsustainable US international balance sheet and large current account deficits.[1]

There are four possible paths to the future global reserve currency system. The first is the status quo, if Asia is to flounder and be non-convergent, fragmented, and subject to economic setbacks and internal conflict. The second is a single dominant Asian currency that then contends for the dominant position in the global reserve currency system. This is unlikely because it would be quite difficult for a single Asian economy to achieve both Asian and global dominance on its own. The third path is an intermediate Asian Monetary System (before joining the global reserve currency system). This is likely to be a choice if negotiations with the current global reserve currency issuers fail. The fourth path is direct or phased migration from the status quo to a new global reserve currency system through renegotiations of the status quo. This is the objective of the set of proposals put forward by the French presidency of the G20 in early 2011.

There are two related current topics that deserve some comment, namely, the issue of currency revaluation and importance of a stable international monetary system.

First, over the long term of 40 years to 2050, it would be almost impossible to predict whether any single or group of regional currencies would be overvalued or undervalued. It is assumed in this book that over the long term, regional disparities in real effective exchange rates will correct

---

1 The Triffin dilemma states that the reserve currency issuer has to run looser monetary policy (and by definition larger current account deficits) to meet global liquidity needs.

themselves. Thus, the scenarios presented here are fundamentally exchange rate neutral.

Although there may be national differences in approach, an "ideal" international monetary system over the long term is one that is more representative and legitimate, that supports the freedom of global trade and payments, and improves financial intermediation without systemic instability. There is growing recognition that global problems cannot be solved at the level of individual nations. Policy makers need to recognize that individual national behavior has global spillovers. To prevent global instability, the international monetary system has to enforce financial and fiscal discipline on all global players, if necessary through legal, fiscal, and other means.

If Asia is to be a global leader, it will have a legitimate stake, with national and regional responsibilities, in contributing to global stability. Accordingly, the new international monetary system is likely to evolve from negotiations where Asian economies play a leading role, either individually or through a regional platform.

Future Asian financial system: Taming finance to serve the real sector

All financial systems have three important functions: to efficiently allocate resources; to improve the payment system by reducing transaction costs; and to manage risk through better transparency and corporate governance.

For Asia to succeed, the Asian financial system must evolve in ways that will perform the above functions well while managing the major risks highlighted by the Great Recession, such as shadow banking, highly toxic derivatives, the inequities and systemic externalities, and issues of moral hazard.

The Great Recession has interrupted but not changed the following broad trends in finance. First, the postcrisis world is converging with slower growth in rich countries, and in the rapid growth in emerging markets led by Asia, alongside substantial wealth accumulation. However, all signs point toward intra-economy widening of income and wealth inequities. Finance appears to help the concentration of wealth because the rich are able to access finance and obtain investment returns superior to those available to the poor.

Second, market turnover and liquidity in almost all financial markets have increased as transaction costs have come down through deregulation, reduction in stamp duty and taxes, and shifts toward highly computerized trading, clearing, and settlement systems. By definition, volatility has also increased.

Third, financial markets demonstrate the network effects of "winner takes all," as the largest financial institutions survive and concentrate through mergers with smaller institutions and widen their footprint across borders.

Fourth, capital market activities are gaining ground relative to traditional retail banking as households age and seek higher returns on their savings for retirement.

Fifth, tighter financial supervision post crisis will greatly affect the growth of the finance sector, its incentives, profitability, and the pace of innovation.

Broadly, the key contours of the future sustainable Asian financial system should:
- Efficiently meet the resource allocation needs of the real sector, particularly in providing credit, liquidity, and payments functions, as well as risk capital;
- Improve the price-discovery process and trading so that liquidity and transparent markets are maintained;
- Improve risk management, including insurance in the new volatile environment;
- Enforce credit and financial discipline on all finance sector stakeholders by strengthening governance and self-restraint, and by preventing conflicts of interest with the real sector;
- Protect long-term risk-adjusted real returns to pension and social security needs; and
- Be inclusive and responsive to all segments of society, particularly those with less access to finance.

Asia has a less developed financial system where the state plays a larger role in finance and economic life. To show leadership, Asian finance must provide long-term risk capital and funds for real sector development without the state having to underwrite huge losses. This is likely to come from major reforms in policies and institutions and greater use of technology and innovation.

Specifically, there will have to be a radical transformation of financial and structural policies in tandem, in order to shift the bias that favors low-risk activities and proprietary trading toward the funding of small and medium enterprises (SME) and micro-financing, large-scale infrastructure financing, housing, and environmental protection. Fortunately Asia has successful examples of large micro finance (Grameen Bank) and of Islamic finance, which has become the fastest growing segment of the global financial system (Kohli and Ahmed, 2011). Such innovations and successes need to be replicated.

Transformational changes to serve the real sector

The transformation of Asian finance will be multifaceted and continue over several decades.

Reform of Asia's financial markets is now urgent for both internal and external reasons. Within Asia, policy makers recognize that the lack of deep, liquid capital markets is retarding domestic efficiency and growth. Strong equity markets can help improve the corporate governance of companies, particularly state-owned ones, by subjecting them to the market test and discipline. Deep and liquid bond and derivatives markets are needed both to finance long-term social infrastructure and to improve monetary and exchange rate management.

Externally, the advanced markets are exerting pressure on Asian economies to revalue and adopt more flexible exchange rate regimes to correct the global imbalances. Asia has built up huge official reserves as self-insurance against volatile capital flows and speculative attacks against domestic exchange rates. Nevertheless, these high foreign exchange reserves have large opportunity costs. No one wants the potential withdrawal of these huge foreign exchange reserves to destabilize global markets. No one disputes that weak Asian capital markets would pose global systemic risks.

Almost all the conditions are in place for Asia to move quickly on the necessary reforms. There is no shortage of savings, and technology is readily available to quickly upgrade the hardware or software for modern financial markets. Even the sequencing of reforms is broadly understood. It should begin with the money market as the prerequisite for foreign exchange and government debt markets, followed by corporate debt, equity and asset-based securities, and complex derivatives markets (Karacadag et al., 2003).

What is needed is the political will to import the skills, to allow competition (to drive innovation), and to work on a regional cooperative basis (to transform finance).

Transforming business models for Asia's financial institutional structure

Asia's needs in infrastructure, urbanization, improving energy efficiency and mitigating climate change, and innovation and entrepreneurship will require the finance sector to support structural and macroeconomic policies that address these massive challenges.

Finance acts as a crucial hard budget constraint on real sector behavior. If Asia is to develop with higher income, greater equality, and environmental sustainability and realize the Asian Century. Asian finance must act as a key disciplinarian on resource consumption and the credit culture. This suggests that finance will need to change radically, as will the business models for different finance subsectors.

Retail and commercial banking[2]

In the period to 2050, retail and commercial banking will become bipolar, comprising a few very large complex banks with global span and many smaller banks that serve their local communities. Financial innovation will most likely come from massive improvements in ICT, which will allow direct customer services through phone or internet banking, using web-based and mobile phone platforms, real-time monitoring of risks, and social interactivity. Indeed, technology will be one of the key drivers of change in banking.

Technology will transform the delivery of services to the masses, as it distributes knowledge and transfers information and payments to people previously constrained by geography and bad communications. The rapid decline in costs of mobile communications has meant that the widest network to the poor has been through mobile technology. This is particularly true in Asia, where there is considerable experimentation in mobile banking in PRC, India, and Southeast Asia.

Commercial bank services and finance for everyone will change as mobile technology incorporates payment and credit services within social networking platforms. Collaborative

---

2 Included in this category are micro-finance and postal savings type activities, which provide funding to the household and enterprise sector, in addition to payment services, such as credit and debit cards.

communities are cutting down the barriers erected by traditional functional and institutional silos that inhibit cooperation, learning and progress. Mass collaborative information sharing will also improve the enforcement of credit culture and blow the whistle on systemic weaknesses such as corruption and bad behavior. Wiki-type nongovernment and nonprofit organizations will coexist with profit-oriented banks to provide micro-finance and financial services to the masses in ways that never existed before.

Local and foreign banks in Asia have to serve the following financial needs of a richer, increasingly urban middle class and provide for an aging Asian population, by:

- Providing simple, convenient and trustworthy consumer banking, with easy-to-understand simple wealth management products that yield long-term risk-adjusted positive returns, at reasonable intermediation costs;
- Helping Asian investors—private and institutional—diversify their portfolios. Asian outward portfolio and direct investment will be the major capital outflow that the world has not yet begun to appreciate. As PRC, India, and other middle-income Asian economies begin to open up their capital accounts and internationalize their currencies, global asset management portfolios will experience a quantitative and qualitative shake-up;
- Going back to the basics of their long-term ethical values, by maintaining their fiduciary responsibilities and trust in customer service and financial inclusiveness. In particular, banks should reduce the "taxation" of depositors and investors through high net interest margins and fees;
- Providing more finance and advice to SMEs, as well as assist Asian corporations to merge, consolidate, and restructure a more globalized and competitive Asia;
- Meeting huge infrastructure and urban finance needs in Developing Asia;
- Improving payment systems and domestic operations to international standards;
- Taking risk management, regulatory quality, and operational efficiency to global standards;
- Localizing and regionalizing financial innovation to customer needs; and
- Improving human resource skills.

As indicated in Chapter 9, urbanization will be a driving force for social change in Asia. The urban population will almost double to 3 billion people by 2050, 63 percent of the population in Asia will be urban. Urbanization will require substantial investments in social infrastructure, including residential and commercial housing, transport systems, utilities, and basic health and education.

This will necessitate a huge amount of financing, from simple residential and commercial real estate to large-scale infrastructure projects. As cities become more sophisticated, insurance will also play a role in managing the risks of population concentration.

Specifically, commercial banking will have to tackle the complex issue of inclusive finance, which cannot be solved without changes in financial and nonfinancial policies and the institutional delivery framework. The World Bank has estimated that 70 percent of SMEs in low-income countries do not have access to basic financial services. In East Asia, an estimated 39 percent of the population has access to banking services, whereas in South Asia, the proportion is 24 percent (Shapiro, 2010). Large parts of underdeveloped Asia still depend on "gray" and possibly illicit payment services.

The financing of SMEs faces many obstacles and challenges. In most countries, the conventional financial system pays little attention to funding SMEs because of the perception of higher risks and costs of delivery. Banks prefer lending to larger enterprises because they have collateral and economies of scale that lower transaction costs. SMEs also do not have access to traditional equity markets for capital. The record of government intervention in direct lending to SMEs, or imposition of interest rate ceilings or government-backed credit guarantee schemes, has not been very successful. There is the need to rethink means to support SMEs.

Experiences in PRC, India, Japan and Republic of Korea suggest that funding programs can be successful if they are linked with an overall policy to nurture SMEs (Garcia Fontes, 2005):

- Funding should be part of a total package of a consistent long-term development strategy for SMEs, aimed at creating a competitive business environment that fosters strong links between large firms and SMEs. SMEs should be part of a supply chain that encourages efficiency and competitiveness. Direct subsidies should be avoided.
- The credit programs should be channeled by well-capitalized and professionally managed institutions, which are autonomous and adopt market-based criteria in assessing loan applications.
- Assistance should be given to SMEs to build up clear business plans with transparent accounting information to raise their eligibility for loans.
- Where possible, ICT technology, as well as accounting and disclosure information, should be standardized and adopted so that SMEs can access global markets through the latest web technology. Service delivery to support SMEs and regulatory functions should be web-based or mobile phone–based to reduce SME transaction costs.

To accomplish the above and absorb the risks of higher real sector volatility, the capital adequacy ratios of the banking system will need to be much higher than at present, probably at 10–15 percent of risk assets, compared with the current 7–8 percent. Financial regulation must be tighter, specifically to address the problems of systemic risk.

Asia needs to upgrade its bank-dominated financial system and deepen its capital markets to absorb the greater uncertainties of the coming decades. While the region has many commercial banks, service quality and financial inclusiveness leave much to be desired. Since financial systems are still largely government-led, with varying degrees of financial repression, there is insufficient risk management, and compliance with global standards varies.

Investment banking

Investment banking in Asia is still nascent and reliant on non-Asian players. The reason is obvious—Asian finance sectors are less open to competition and depth of financial knowledge is inadequate. Operationally, most Asian economies practice variants of the US Glass–Steagal legislation (now repealed), which mandated the separation of commercial and investment banking. But capital market activities and the role of investment banks are growing in importance due to the need for the corporate sector to restructure, merge, consolidate or seek greater capital.

The aftermath of the Great Recession suggests conditions that there will be calls for a radical restructuring of both demand and supply within Asia. The first is that exports to advanced economies can no longer be the primary engine of growth and countries will need to shift toward greater emphasis on stimulating domestic consumption and exports to emerging markets to maintain a rapid pace of economic expansion. The second is that evolving lifestyles required by climate change and growing resource constraints will require higher energy efficiency, lower carbon footprints and savings on water and other natural resources—in short, a green economy. Moreover, there will need to be a shift out of industries based on cheap labor costs toward higher knowledge-intensity and green-technology industries.

All these call for investment banking to act as catalysts and facilitators for industrial change. In 2009, McKinsey estimated that Asia accounted for 36 percent of global corporate banking revenue and 21 percent of global equity capital market revenue. It estimated that 45 percent of all new growth in global wholesale banking up to 2014 will be in Asia. Global investment banks are ramping up their presence in Asia and already dominate in some ASEAN corporate banking businesses.

At the heart of the capital market debate is the question: To what extent should proprietary trading of financial institutions be supported by an implicit or explicit public guarantee of their financial stability? Asset trading may be individually profitable; however, in the long run it is a zero sum game, sustainable only if the real economy generates new resources that support the rising debt burden. The point is that speculative trading initially has a social value of providing liquidity and price discovery. But beyond a certain point, the accumulation of speculative profits going to the trading class directs incentives in the real economy from productive investments and into speculation and gambling, which ultimately fuels bubbles.

The challenge in Asia therefore is to separate proprietary trading by investment banks and its advisory role from any public safety net for financial institutions. Asian governments should indeed be more relaxed and allow greater private initiative in the high-risk areas of finance, where such activity is compensated by high rewards, but it should be clear that such activity is done without any implicit or explicit public guarantee in order to avoid moral hazard.

Asset management and capital markets

The asset management industry forms one of the cores of global capital markets and has grown rapidly in the last 30 years during a period of unprecedented financial innovation and deregulation (McKinsey Global Institute, 2010).

In 2001–2008, total global capital market assets (excluding the insurance industry) grew from $107.3 trillion to $252.9 trillion, with commercial bank assets increasing marginally from 35.3 percent to 38.1 percent of total (Table 10.3). The securities industry accounted for 61.9 percent of the total in 2008, but there was a substantial change in relative strength within the industry. In 2001, equity market capitalization accounted for 26 percent of total capital market size, but by 2008 had declined to 14.1 percent. The debt market remained at roughly one-third market share, whereas the derivatives market value was eight times as large and its relative market share jumped from 4.3 percent of the total to 14.9 percent.

Table 10.3 | Global capital markets, 2001 and 2008

	2001 $ trillions	2001 % of total	2008 $ trillions	2008 % of total
Equity market capitalization	27.9	26.0	35.8	14.2
Debt securities outstanding	36.9	34.3	82.9	32.8
Derivatives market value	4.6	4.3	37.8	14.9
Securities market total	69.4	64.7	156.5	61.9
Commercial bank assets	37.9	35.3	96.4	38.1
Financial markets total (excluding insurance)	107.3	100.0	252.9	100.0

Source: SIFMA, 2009, p. 78.

If the financial derivatives market value is calculated at the notional principal value of derivatives, the market was estimated at $649.8 trillion, 17 times its gross market value at the end of 2008, larger than equity market capitalization, by absolute or relative values (Securities Industry and Financial Markets Association, 2009, p. 103).

The dominant role of the advanced markets' share in financial assets reflected in part their wealth and their aging population, and the resulting increases in pension and retirement funds. For example, at the end of 2008, total retirement assets of US households reached $13.9 trillion, roughly 100 percent of GDP. Total global pension fund assets under management were around $21.6 trillion (McKinsey Global Institute, 2010).

The long-term prospects for the fund management industry in Asia are bright due to changing demographics and long-term economic prospects for the region. The rise of Asia and its emergent middle class has meant that the number of high net worth Individuals is increasing rapidly.

In the last 30 years, Asia has benefited from the demographic dividend of a growing, young, and mobile workforce. In 1970, 40 percent of the Asian population was below 15, but by 2007 that level had fallen to 24 percent, meaning that a larger proportion of the young had entered the work force. From 1970 to 2007, the proportion of the population aged 65 and over grew only modestly from 4.1 percent to 6.6 percent (United Nations, 2005). The dependency ratio was still modest, but with an aging population in North Asia and the one-child policy in PRC, population growth will slow and the demographic dividend will rapidly switch to a burden, similar to that in the advanced countries. For example, by 2050, it is estimated that the working population will rise by about 99 percent in Pakistan and fall by 33 percent in Japan.

The demand for financial services has changed rapidly with the demographic profile, as a younger population requires better payment services and loans for residential mortgages and educational finance. As the population becomes middle aged and approaches retirement, the demand for finance will switch toward better wealth management products, retirement funds, and insurance products, including health and medical insurance.

The biggest lesson drawn from aging societies is that it is important to ensure that financial savings have returns that preserve their real value over the whole demographic cycle. This implies having positive real interest rates and relatively stable exchange rates. Moreover, the investment asset allocation policies of long-term pension and asset management funds should not be regulated in such a way that constrains them from seeking total returns in line with their demographic objectives.

For example, rural–urban migration will accelerate the need for a social security network to provide some sort of safety net for the growing numbers of workers that have uprooted themselves to live and work in urban areas.

Asia remains weak in its long-term wealth management capabilities. Its fund management, insurance, and pension schemes lack institutional depth, they are constrained by overly inward-looking portfolios, and some are bound by capital controls. Well-funded pension schemes must be put in place to meet the needs of the aging population in some societies. Stronger pension and insurance schemes will in turn require well-developed domestic capital markets in many Asian economies. Otherwise, capital could flow out of these markets and the cost of intermediation could rise. Such market-based instruments to provide a safety net during old age are also necessary to allow Asians to reduce savings rates and thus help reduce global imbalances.

Despite the high savings accrued from the high demographic endowment, Asia has yet to fully invest in itself. One of the top priorities is therefore for Asia to develop a strong asset management and pension fund industry, by allowing greater private participation and by liberalizing portfolio restrictions on the pension fund industry, so as to allow for a larger field of alternative and foreign investments.

Development finance and policy-based financial institutions

The move toward market-based financial systems in the last 30 years has seen development finance institutions and policy-based lending largely lose their roles at the national level. Postal savings banks have been commercialized and gradually privatized. Some development banks have moved into funding large-scale public infrastructure or micro-financing.

The Great Recession has revealed serious flaws in the assumption that commercial banking can solve all financial needs, particularly those of SMEs. At the municipal government level, there is a shortage of funding for urbanization, local infrastructure, and climate change projects, and this is not met by the commercial debt market or the commercial banks.

The nature of urbanization funding will become different from the current approach. Because urbanization is at base a governance challenge, resources will have to be shared and allocated very differently from the manner of past, centralized fiscal systems. At the heart of the urbanization problem is the funding of local governments, particularly municipal and county-level financing, either through central government grants, sharing of tax revenue, or the creation of a municipal debt market. Private–public sector partnerships will have to be initiated to invest in technically innovative, green, and commercially viable urban infrastructure projects. Funding such long-term high-risk projects from short-term bank loans would expose the financial system to unnecessary risk.

Furthermore, infrastructure needs will grow significantly at national and regional levels to improve Asian connectivity. The region is being connected through a grid of Asian highways, maritime routes and air transport networks, as well as telecommunications link. Most of Asia still lacks the transport facilities and the water, electricity, and other basic utilities expected of moderately developed nations.

Long-term infrastructure projects are constrained by the limited availability of long-term funding and the governance capacity to implement and fund these projects sustainably. The irony is that the governance mechanisms, technology and excess savings are all available within Asia, but the financial architecture and institutions have not yet been built and the political will to make things happen has not been established.

There is therefore a great opportunity for Asian financial institutions and centers to work together to create the long-term financial market for infrastructure that could be one of the engines of growth in both the Asian real sector and financial market (Box 10.1).

Another challenge is to mobilize the requisite finance for adaptation to climate change and global warming. This will have to be done in conjunction with major structural and fiscal policies to change incentives toward a green and resource-efficient economy.

Box 10.1 | Infrastructure finance

The Asian Development Bank has estimated the "urban infrastructure deficit" in Asia and the Pacific at $60 billion a year. In the next 40 years, including rural and interregional infrastructure, the investments needed are likely to be multiples of that estimate. Even though there is no shortage of savings within Asia and outside the region, what is lacking is the mechanism to finance the infrastructure development in a viable and sustainable manner. There are substantial capacity constraints at national and local government levels to design, finance, and implement projects. Inevitably, a large proportion of the infrastructure projects in Asia will have to be supported by private sector participation and public–private partnership. However, there are many impediments to putting in place an effective infrastructure finance framework that is necessary to achieve the goals of Asia 2050.

Impediments to private sector financing of infrastructure

Because returns from investments in infrastructure materialize over the long term, stretching to over 20 years, there are inevitable project implementation delays, cost escalations, and legal/policy risks that jeopardize projected cash flows, and these add to project financing costs and viability.

Low income countries in the most need of basic infrastructure are trapped in a situation where low levels of affordability mean that tariffs recovered from users may not generate sufficient revenue to cover the investment costs.

High-risk premiums to cover these uncertainties greatly reduce the number of commercially viable projects that can be undertaken by the private sector, unless there is government cofunding or guarantees. These are complex to negotiate and involve intricate central/local government revenue and expenditure sharing issues. As has been said; "… the core issues are not public versus private, but how they share the risk and rewards in a way that works for both sides, and how the public sector harnesses the efficiency gains that the private sector can bring. The sources of funding and ownership are secondary." ADB, World Bank, and IBIC, 2005).

At the same time, private initiatives should also involve public financial markets, so that ultimately, public financial markets can assist the completion of successful projects and generate the confidence for investors in newer infrastructure projects.

Creating an enabling environment for infrastructure financing, public–private partnerships and public financial markets

The first step is to properly allocate roles and responsibilities among stakeholders.

> **Box 10.1 | Infrastructure finance**
>
> The design framework would involve:
>
> - Financial and management reform by local governments, particularly to have stronger financial management; modern accounting systems; improved planning, implementation, and operation of projects; tighter expenditure control; and stronger transparency and auditing;
> - Legal and regulatory frameworks for local government debt whether from banks or capital markets, which would cover borrowing authority, rules for issuance, disclosure and transparency, tax treatment, allowable credit structures, record keeping, reporting, and requirement for credit ratings if any;
> - Clear and firm prudential rules that determine the conditions under which borrowing can take place, including disclosure and public issue rules; and
> - Creation of specialized infrastructure and market-based intermediaries or central funds that will help to develop the municipal/infrastructure financing market.

Given the unpredictability and risks associated with climate change, it is unlikely that short-term profit-oriented commercial and investment banks will be willing to absorb the high risks in these long-term low-return areas. Given the need to develop specialist expertise in highly knowledge-intensive sectors, such as climate change, reforestation, and ecological sustainability projects, Asian governments may need to selectively revive and reform the roles of policy-based financial institutions and point them in new directions.

Insurance

Asia is grossly underinsured.

The insurance industry comprises the property and casualty business, life and health insurance, and reinsurance. Gross premiums of the insurance business globally reached $4.1 trillion in 2009, of which reinsurance premiums were around $200 billion. At the end of 2007, total asset size of the insurance industry amounted to $18.5 trillion.

In recent years, however, the difference between insurance products and capital market products has blurred, through the securitization of insurance products. These insurance-linked securities are a growing field and the outstanding amount was recently somewhere around $50 billion (World Economic Forum, 2008).

The insurance industry has been growing rapidly but has been hurt by low return on investments, a large number of catastrophes, and the Great Recession. Following some company failures, insurance regulation has been tightened globally.

In both life and nonlife products, the potential for insurance penetration in Asia is enormous.

In 2008, gross insurance premiums accounted for 6 percent of GDP in Asia and 3.6 percent in Africa, but 7.3 percent in the US and 7.5 percent in Europe. In recent years, the growth of Islamic insurance has been 25 percent a year.

Given the rising incidence of natural disasters from global warming, there is also considerable potential for the insurance and reinsurance of climate change–related risks. For example, in 2008, the total economic loss from man-made and natural catastrophes around the world was $269 billion.

The insurance sector will benefit most by providing risk protection, loss prevention, and amelioration from climate change. Worldwide insured losses from weather-related disasters have jumped from $5.1 billion a year in 1970–1989 to $27 billion annually over the past two decades (Swiss Reinsurance, 2010, p. 3). According to estimates of the Economics of Climate Adaptation Working group (2009), current climate risks cost emerging markets between 1–12 percent of GDP. By 2030, high climate change scenarios could increase the cost to 19 percent of GDP. The United Nations has estimated that by 2030, the world should be spending an additional $36 billion–$135 billion annually to address the effects of climate change.

Innovative forms of insurance can make communities more resilient to disaster by forcing them to model, price, and manage the risks of climate change. For example, the working group estimated that in Maharashtra, India, a drought-prone area, an extreme event such as a 1-in-25-year drought might affect up to 30 million people (or 30 percent of the population) and reduce foodgrain production by as much as 30 percent.

The insurance market is probably the most knowledge-intensive area of the finance sector, as its primary role is risk transformation. To cover specific risks, it must invest its premium income, generate a return, and provide reserves that are sufficient to cover payouts. The knowledge-based skills for the insurance industry, particularly its risk-management and actuarial expertise, currently reside mainly in the advanced markets. This needs to change. Hence radical transformation of Asian insurance deserves greater policy priority.

Exchanges and clearing systems

Stock exchanges and clearing houses form the most important hub for equities and financial product trading. In recent years, demutualization and the move toward markets with higher liquidity and quality have led to more mergers and cross-holdings of stock exchanges on a global basis. Stock exchanges are also consolidating the trading of equities, warrants, financial derivatives, and commodities into single clearing platforms. In emerging markets, debt issues are also traded on many stock exchanges.

The financial derivatives and foreign exchange markets, however, remain largely over the counter. In 2008, of the total notional value of financial derivatives of $649.8 trillion, 91.1 percent was traded over the counter, and the balance on exchanges. Most of these are in the advanced markets (SIFMA, 2009, p. 103).

The Great Recession has prompted financial regulators to rethink a system that allows financial derivatives to be entirely traded over the counter with little transparency. There is now greater awareness that some over the counter activities are subject to fraud and market manipulation, hence the movement to shift the trading of financial derivatives toward exchanges and centralized clearing (where possible) to make markets more transparent.

Competition and consolidation in Asia are creating mergers as well as upgrades to exchange and clearing businesses. The latest example was the attempt of the Singapore Exchange to take over the Australian Stock Exchange. The pooling of technology, trading processes, and convergence of standards will improve the liquidity and transparency of financial markets in Asia.

Regional cooperation and Asia's global financial leadership

The finance sector will need to be substantially reformed if Asia is to assume a leading role in the global financial system. Much of this reform will be national, but much will also depend on cooperation regionally and with non-Asian partners.

Individually, Asian financial systems lack the critical mass of research, experience, and skill to become leaders in finance. However, national borders no longer bind knowledge and talent. To achieve scale and leadership, Asia should confront the issue of lack of regional financial cooperation, including currency arrangements.

Intraregional financial service trade is constrained by regulatory and institutional barriers. It is understandable that each Asian economy is wary of allowing premature financial liberalization to weaken its financial stability, but individually, many of the smaller markets are too insignificant to attain global competitiveness.

From a macro perspective, the key initiatives for regional financial reform should include the following:

- Reduce global imbalances to sustainable levels to allow market forces to work and to allow for more flexible exchange rate regimes and phased liberalization of the capital account;
- Improve domestic financial efficiency through greater market competition and by achieving global regulatory standards;
- Ensure that interest rates, exchange rates, tax rates, and regulatory costs/policies do not distort long-term sustainable returns to depositors and investors (consistent with risks);
- Deepen capital markets and manage "too big to fail" issues in the banking and finance sector for long-term financial stability, including creating mechanisms for resolution of failed institutions;
- Liberalize and deepen risk management mechanisms and venture and hedge-fund structures to improve long-term returns to investors;

- Deepen long-term social security and pension fund institutional capacity to deliver positive risk-adjusted returns to investors over the demographic cycle, as Asians live longer, and retire earlier.

To ensure that policies are consistent with open regionalization and with global standards of openness, transparency and fairness will require the following measures:

- Open capital markets to greater private competition and participation, especially regionally and internationally. This will deepen financial innovation, and raise institutional capacity.
- Foster greater regional cooperation on financial market infrastructure, especially among the leading Asian markets in the region, such as PRC, India, Indonesia, and Japan.
- Improve risk management standards. With more standardization of operations across the board—involving banks, financial institutions, insurance agencies, even central banks—the problem posed by financial repression would abate.
- Create open regional networks in stock, debt, commodity, and derivatives markets. They should meet global standards of scale, transparency, efficiency, and robustness. This implies accelerating the integration of regional stock markets and clearing infrastructure, as well as the upgrading to international standards.
- Adopt multitrack approaches to liberalize and complete structural, institutional, and governance reforms.
- Open wealth management capacity to a greater number of private pension and social security fund managements. Allow pension, insurance, and long-term funds to invest in higher-risk financial products that yield long-term adjusted returns to long-term savers.
- Push insurance companies to improve their risk management products in agriculture and climate change areas.
- Increase the Asian voice in the international arena through regional subsets of the Financial Stability Board, the central bank grouping in the Bank for International Settlements, and the International Organization of Securities Commissions to ensure regional input into global policy decisions as well as implementation and enforcement of global standards in Asia.

The time has come to institutionalize Asian regional cooperation, particularly for financial safety nets. During the Asian financial crisis, the advanced countries objected strongly to the creation of an Asian Monetary Fund (AMF). But with the creation of the European Financial Stability Fund, global objections to regional financial safety nets (which can coexist with the global financial safety net, the IMF, at its apex) have been removed (Gros, 2010). In other words, it may be timely to consider expanding the Chiang Mai Initiative Multilateralization as an Asian financial safety net that can coexist with European Financial Stability Fund and the IMF. The secretariat for the Initiative, the ASEAN+3 Macroeconomic Research Office (AMRO), can then act as the research center on policy options for Asian financial cooperation, complementing the regional surveillance and cooperation roles of other forums, such as the Executive Meeting of the East Asia and Pacific Central Banks (EMEAP) and other bodies.

There is also considerable scope to institutionalize regional cooperation efforts in building long-term infrastructure funding frameworks, working closely with the Asian Development Bank to tackle sector issues of demographic change, urbanization, municipal finance, infrastructure, industrial restructuring, and climate change.

There is scope to make progress on two tracks, by involving the political leadership (ASEAN and ASEAN+3 ministers) and technocrats (notably the trade and central banking communities).

At the political level, the progress in the Chiang Mai Initiative Multilateralization, ASEAN+3 Macroeconomic Research Office, and the ASEAN Bond Market Initiative represent the most visible proof of the region's desire to move forward on regional financial stability. Other initiatives include the Leaders' Vision on an ASEAN Economic Community Blueprint to transform ASEAN into a competitive single market and production base that is fully integrated into the global community by 2015. The Roadmap on Monetary and Financial Integration of ASEAN attempts to accelerate cooperation in the areas of capital market development, capital account liberalization, financial services liberalization, and ASEAN currency cooperation.

Encouraging progress has been made among the regional central banks, notably the development of the EMEAP Roadmap on Regional Financial Cooperation in Asia in 2006. An early outcome of this roadmap was the establishment of the EMEAP Monetary and Financial Stability Committee in 2007. It serves as an early warning system for crisis management and resolution in the region, including real-time sharing of information of financial market developments as they unfold, and joint intervention where appropriate. It complements the regional surveillance of the ASEAN and ASEAN+3 processes and could serve as a forerunner to an Asian financial stability forum or board.

While progress continues in strengthening regional financial cooperation in Asia, its pace will be determined by the level of political will and commitment to push ahead. Once can hope that the baptism of fire of two crises in 10 years has galvanized the Asian financial community and strengthened its commitment to move forward.

To sum up, the process of Asian financial integration must depend primarily on the degree of deepening in Asian financial institutions, first at the national level, but with an eye on regional and global convergence/cooperation. This can only be done through exposure to more global and regional competition.

Priority action plan for Asian finance in 2050

For finance to complement and support real sector activities, the entire Asian financial infrastructure to 2050 must focus on ways to mobilize the large amounts of capital in the region for productive investment. Current consumer finance needs are easily developed by private initiatives. However, the four areas of immediate priority are inclusive finance; financing for SMEs; large-scale infrastructure financing; and long-term pension, insurance, and social security reforms.

In the short run, non-Asian global financial institutions will be preoccupied with short-term capital replenishment to meet the Basel III requirements, but growth opportunities in Asia will intensify Asian financial market competition. As Asian institutions have reasonable capital cushions and capacity to lend, there is an opportunity created by the global financial crisis for Asia to advance as a major financial hub.

A radical transformation of Asian capital markets is critical—strong equity markets would promote competitiveness and enhance corporate governance; investment banking and venture capital would help consolidate and restructure many industries with overcapacity and reengineer them to green market needs; and deep and liquid bond and derivatives markets would provide the channel for infrastructure financing. Further strengthening of the insurance and pension/social security funds would ensure that risk management and retirement funds are enhanced.

Since size, scale, and clustering matter in finance, the regional integration of capital markets in Asia must deepen if Asia is to become a market maker on the same footing as the EU and the US, both of which have head starts in their market infrastructure, institutional development, technology and trading practices, international standards, and regulatory frameworks—mechanisms that readily support cross-border alliances.

Development of Asian capital markets should be considered at two levels. At the country level, priority is contextual, depending on local conditions. But the reform focus must be on creating conditions that facilitate regional (and global) integration at the right time.

To develop equity markets, domestic exchanges need to demutualize and be listed in order to compete with other major exchanges in Asia. Vertical and horizontal integration of clearing and the settlement of equities, debt, and derivatives in each domestic exchange is a part of the consolidation process prior to demutualizing it.

On the regulatory front, national capital market reforms include compliance with international standards for the protection of investors, in particular by harmonizing laws or regulations on market abuse; issuance of prospectuses; mergers and takeovers; settlement finality arrangements; secondary market transparency; adequate trading and market surveillance systems; regulations to detect and deter unfair trading practices; and financial disclosure standards.

Regulators and policy makers should be more open to institutional innovation, by allowing more entry of capital market intermediaries, such as private equity funds that bring risk capital and market knowledge into industry consolidation and reengineering. Instead of protecting the financial industry, regulators should allow entry from other sectors, such as electronic trading platforms and mobile telephone operators that can bring new social network technology into the delivery of financial services and monitoring of credit risks.

Traditionally, banks have relied more on collateral-based lending, but new trading platforms such as Alibaba and eBay use trading and cash-flow information to manage credit risks. Widespread availability of cash-flow and collateral information to lenders and SMEs would enforce a credit culture and discipline. Other examples of new institutional forms include higher-disclosure trading and exchange platforms for SMEs using social network engines that facilitate lower-cost listing and trading of SME financial products, including fund raising.

There is also a need for higher-quality and more consistent enforcement of market practices and ethical standards by financial regulators and a shift from a positive vetting regulatory regime (i.e., what is not specifically allowed is forbidden) to a negative vetting regime (i.e., what is not specifically forbidden is allowed). This will foster innovation and accelerate market development.

A phased reduction or removal of capital controls or portfolio restrictions (since they fragment liquidity between onshore and offshore markets and increase transaction costs) will be an essential requirement for more cross-border trading. Other measures to support domestic capital markets are given in Box 10.2.

The speed of regional market integration will depend on agreement and commitment at the political and organizational level, supported by continuous infrastructure improvements:

- National capital market development plans should specifically provide for future regional market integration, with common regulatory and operating standards.
- Within formal "coordinating and implementing" structures, strategies for regional financial market integration should be promulgated, including strategic options and implementation approaches, market consultation, policy-making processes, harmonization of securities market regulation in line with international standards and best practice, and an agreed set of core principles.
- Phased open access to national markets by any exchange within the region, should be negotiated at the political level.
- Listed exchanges to merge with or acquire other exchanges.
- Regional and foreign entities should be permitted to issue in domestic markets, starting with multilateral financial institutions (e.g., regional development banks and infrastructure finance institutions). The priority is to provide a new range of high-quality assets in local currency for domestic investors; it also enhances the credibility of market regulators and intermediaries.

The importance of using global best practice

The biggest challenge in Asia is not the lack of rules, but the lack of effective implementation of the global best practice that best fits local conditions. Like the proposed set of simpler International Accounting Standards SMEs, one of the issues will be whether there should be a

> **Box 10.2 — Supporting domestic capital markets**
>
> Developing the Institutional investor base will support the growth of domestic capital markets. Measures include:
> - Development of new tradable fund holdings for retail (ETFs, REITs, etc.);
> - Improvement of market liquidity and float through reduction of tightly held family and government shareholdings;
> - Opening up entry, through appropriate legislation and regulations to private mutual funds and fund management;
> - Development of private pension and social security funds; and
> - Diversification of investment options for insurance companies and pension funds.
>
> Deepening of the domestic bond market is through:
> - Enhanced diversity and supply of debt instruments to allow corporate and municipal issuance, subject to appropriate rules;
> - Development of benchmark securities and a yield curve;
> - Development of central trading platforms of unified rules and regulations for over-the-counter bond and derivatives markets;
> - Removal of tax distortions;
> - Improvements in liquidity through repos and liquidity facilities;
> - Improvements in information sharing and cooperation with domestic and foreign counterparts;
> - Increases in high-quality issues;
> - A move to disclosure-based regulation; and
> - A strengthening and enforcement of corporate governance standards.

simpler version of the core regulatory standards where there is some guidance on priorities for emerging markets.

Next, infrastructure and enforcement capacity need to be enhanced so that there is greater compliance and more concern over systemic stability and sustainability. Asia needs a system-wide view of financial stability, at national and regional levels. A domestic financial stability forum will help engage multi-stakeholder ownership and enhance implementation of risk management capacity. In other words, a strong global network must begin with strong and resilient domestic networks. Regionally active institutions along the lines of the Financial Stability Board, the Bank for International Settlements, and the International Organization of Securities Commissions, will act as building blocks for a stronger global architecture. Specifically, regional arrangements will strengthen regional cooperation, support deliberations of the Financial Stability Forum at the global level, and motivate training and implementation locally.

Institutionalizing Asian regional and global cooperation will be challenging, given that it is a geographically vast, culturally diverse, economically disparate, and politically complex region. Nevertheless, there is increasing awareness that many of the problems that Asia and individual economies face cannot be solved by national action alone. The interdependence and interconnectivity are such that there must be greater dialogue and policy research. Given the varying levels of financial development and understanding of the issues, convergence toward global standards will inevitably take time.

Asian finance as a global leader

In conclusion, if the Asian Century scenario is to be realized, Asia needs to become a global leader in finance. This will require the sector to play its monetary and credit disciplinary role.

Asia has a unique opportunity to build a leaner and more focused, responsible, and efficient finance sector that serves its real sector objectives. Instead of being a source of instability (as in the Great Recession), an important role of the financial sector should be to help domestic economies become even more resilient to external shocks (Kohli and Sharma, 2010). Finance must first therefore discipline itself.

None of these outcomes are inevitable. They can only be achieved with strong value systems, hard work, political will, and self-discipline. Above all, they require Asian policy makers, regulators, and market players to work with each other and with the rest of the world.

Reducing Energy Intensity and Ensuring Energy Security

Chapter 11

Hossein Razavi

Introduction

Asia accounted for about 20 percent of the world's energy consumption in 2000, 27 percent in 2007, and the share is projected to rise above 40 percent by 2050. PRC surpassed the US in 2010 to become the largest energy consumer, and Asia is expected to surpass the OECD before 2030 to become the foremost energy consuming bloc according to the International Energy Agency (IEA) (Figure 11.1).

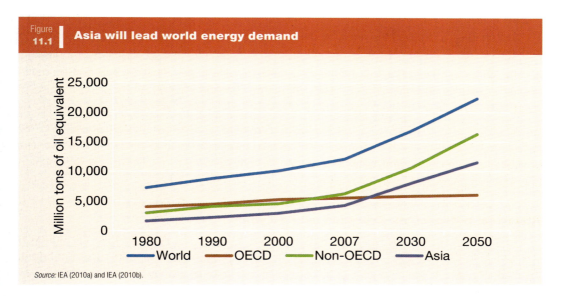

Figure 11.1 Asia will lead world energy demand

Source: IEA (2010a) and IEA (2010b).

The rapid growth of Asia's energy use has created two major concerns for both the region and the world. First, it implies an increasingly larger claim on global energy resources and greater dependence on imports, triggering worries about the security of energy supplies, particularly oil and gas. Second, it generates a rapid increase in carbon emissions. The IEA has projected that by 2030, PRC alone will have higher carbon emissions than all OECD countries combined

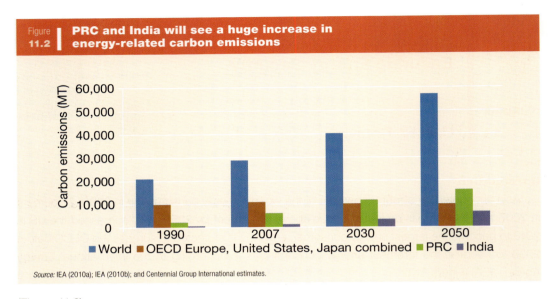

Figure 11.2 | PRC and India will see a huge increase in energy-related carbon emissions

Source: IEA (2010a); IEA (2010b); and Centennial Group International estimates.

(Figure 11.2).

This chapter addresses the need for many Asian economies to reduce energy intensity and manage energy security concerns through programs to improve energy efficiency and diversify energy sources. It suggests that future national energy strategies must be built first on much greater emphasis on improving efficiency of energy use and second on reducing the use of fossil fuels. The chapter also explores the scope of energy security that could be enhanced through regional collaboration. It suggests forms of regional cooperation that can provide win-win outcomes for the entire region. These forms will help governments to increase the effectiveness of their energy security strategies, and enable the private sector to seize the unprecedented opportunities and better serve the huge investment requirements of the new energy technologies.

Historical perspective: Evolution over 40 years

A brief look at Asia's energy consumption over the past 40 years reveals the dramatic changes in both geographic usage and fuel composition of energy use, and, more important, the means by which Asian countries have dealt with emerging challenges (Table 11.1). Its experience of more advanced economies in resolving energy security concerns has helped others to develop their own policies. Japan's energy use had already reached maturity by the 1970s. This triggered a determined effort toward energy efficiency and diversification. Its experience proved useful for Republic of Korea, whose energy consumption doubled each decade between 1970 and 1990. Republic of Korea's approach has now been recognized as the best practice in implementing energy efficiency and diversification. Although Japan, Republic of Korea, and other high-income Asian economies will still have to struggle with energy security concerns, the

Table 11.1 Past and projected energy demand and supply in Asia (base case)

	1971	1980	1990	2000	2007	2030	2050
Asian energy demand (Mtoe)	1,189	1,585	2,220	2,910	4,242	7,980	11,480
High-income Asia	311	421	591	674	806	901	996
PRC	391	603	872	1,105	1,970	3,637	5,011
India	156	207	318	457	622	1,341	2,389
ASEAN	86	149	243	389	513	903	1,177
Central Asia	61	95	198	128	159	256	385
Iran	17	38	68	120	194	373	565
Asian energy supply mix (%)							
Coal		36	40	42	47	48	50
Oil		25	16	17	20	21	20
Gas		4	9	10	11	12	11
Nuclear		3	6	5	4	5	7
Hydro		4	3	2	2	2	1
Biomass		28	26	24	15	10	7
Other			0	0	1	2	4
Asian electricity consumption (TWh)	765	1,346	2,327	3,294	5,511	14,161	22,318
High-income Asia	408	742	976	1,012	1,128	1,411	1,746
PRC	127	259	586	1,081	2,717	7,513	10,630
India	55	90	197	369	544	1,966	3,440
ASEAN	29	55	167	321	497	1,383	1,956
Central Asia	38	63	162	124	152	443	715
Iran	8	21	53	101	145	332	544
Reference energy consumption (Mtoe)							
World	5,533	7,228	8,761	10,018	12,013	16,790	22,288
OECD	3,357	4,050	4,476	5,249	5,496	5,811	6,011
US	1,587	1,802	1,913	2,280	2,337	2,396	2,412
Non-OECD	2,176	3,178	4,285	4,769	6,517	10,979	16,277

Source: EIA (2010), IEA (2008), IEA (2009), IEA (2010a), IEA (2010b), World Bank (2010) and Centennial Group International estimates.

discussion of various aspects of energy consumption and supply is at present dominated by the growth patterns in PRC and India. For them, as well as most ASEAN countries, energy security concerns have emerged in the last decade, exacerbated by the projections of rapid expansion in energy demand over the next 40 years.

High-income Asia

This group comprises Hong Kong, China; Japan; Macao, China; Republic of Korea; and Taipei,China.[1] Japan and Republic of Korea account for more than 90 percent of energy consumption in this group. Japan has very limited domestic energy resources and depends heavily on energy imports. It is the third-largest oil importer in the world behind the US and PRC and the world's largest importer of both liquefied natural gas (LNG) and coal. Japan, concerned about energy security longer than any other country, has a stringent strategy for energy diversification, energy efficiency, and securing import sources. It is widely recognized as a pioneer in experiments to ensure energy security through various instruments.

Japan's energy mix depends heavily on oil. Oil's role in total energy consumption has, however, declined from about 80 percent in the 1970s to 46 percent in 2007. Coal continues to account for a significant share of total energy consumption (21 percent) while natural gas represents 17 percent of total energy supply. Nuclear energy provides 11 percent of energy supply. Japan is the third-largest consumer of nuclear power following the US and France. The nuclear option had been viewed as an important instrument in decarbonizing the energy sector. However, the earthquake/tsunami-triggered nuclear accident of March 2011 could have a significant impact on the country's future energy development strategy. Energy efficiency improvement has been a cornerstone of the Japanese energy strategy, such that Japan is viewed as the most energy-efficient economy in the world, given its energy intensity and state of industrialization.

Japan's energy strategy has been to encourage Japanese companies to increase energy exploration and development projects around the world to secure a stable supply of oil and natural gas for the country. The government's goal is to import 40 percent of the country's total crude oil imports from Japanese-owned concessions by 2030, up from the currently estimated 19 percent. The Japan Bank for International Cooperation supports upstream companies by offering loans at favorable rates. Japan's overseas oil projects are primarily located in the Middle East and Southeast Asia. Its current oil imports are about 80 percent dependent on the Middle East (Saudi Arabia, Kuwait, the United Arab Emirates, Qatar, and Iran).

Republic of Korea, like Japan, lacks domestic energy resources, and has also pursued a similar energy security strategy, but with some time lag in line with its development and growth in income. It is the fifth-largest importer of crude oil and the second-largest importer of both coal and LNG. Its energy mix comprises 45 percent oil, 27 percent coal, 14 percent gas, and

---

1 Singapore and Brunei Darussalam are not included in the ASEAN group for data availability reasons.

14 percent nuclear. Its oil imports are 75 percent dependent on the Middle East. In an effort to improve the nation's energy security, state-owned oil, gas, and electricity companies are aggressively seeking exploration and production opportunities overseas. The government has also helped to encourage this private sector exploration and production through tax benefits and by extending credit lines to oil companies through the Korea Export–Import Bank, as well as by providing diplomatic aid in overseas negotiations. The country has oil interests in production fields in the Gulf of Mexico and Viet Nam, acquisitions in Canada's oil sands, and ventures with other oil companies in, for example, Peru and Kazakhstan.

Republic of Korea is recognized for its best practices in improving energy efficiency. It has also pursued an aggressive diversification strategy. It has the sixth-largest nuclear generation capacity in the world. Its first nuclear plant was completed in 1978 and over the ensuing three decades it allocated large resources to developing the nuclear industry. The country now has four nuclear power stations, with 20 individual reactors; 12 more reactors are scheduled to be completed by 2022. The share of nuclear power in total electricity generation was expected to increase from 35 percent in 2007 to about 50 percent by 2020. However, this goal is likely to be reassessed in light of the earthquake/tsunami-triggered nuclear accident of March 2011 in Japan.

Since its emergence as an international leader in nuclear technology, the country has pursued opportunities to export it. In December 2009, Korea Electric Power Corporation won a $20 billion contract to build four 1,400 megawatt nuclear reactors in the United Arab Emirates, the first of which is expected to be operational by 2017.

PRC

PRC's large population and rapid economic growth constitute the main factors in its substantial energy requirements. The growth in energy consumption has accelerated sharply since 2000. Average annual growth in energy demand was 8.7 percent in this period, compared with 2.2 percent in the 1990s.

The energy demand structure in PRC is unique in that industry accounts for the largest share of energy use (60 percent). It used 727 million tons of oil equivalent (Mtoe) in 2007, making PRC by far the largest industrial user of energy in the world; the second-largest is the US with industrial consumption of about 292 Mtoe in 2007.

PRC industry—mainly cement, iron and steel, and aluminum—grew very rapidly in 2000–2007, when its energy consumption doubled. Energy use in the transport sector amounted to 158 Mtoe in 2007, 11 percent of the total, significantly lower than the transport share in industrial countries. This share is expected to increase as the number of passenger vehicles rises. Government policy is aimed at investing in sustainability by building high-quality public transport and encouraging more efficient vehicle technologies.

Power supply capacity expanded at 14 percent in 2000–2007, reaching 718 gigawatts

(GW) and comprised 556 GW coal-based, 148 GW hydro, 8.8 GW nuclear, and 4.2 GW wind power. Electricity generated by coal now stands at 81 percent, for an average carbon dioxide intensity of 777 grams per kilowatt hour (g/kWh), compared with the world average of 507 g/kWh. Hydropower represents 15 percent and nuclear energy 2 percent of electricity generation. In 2006, the government adopted a policy of closing smaller and less efficient power plants. It also implemented a policy that all new plants must be large (600 MW and above) and use new supercritical and ultra-supercritical technologies. Wind power capacity, remains small but progress has received attention because PRC's wind capacity was almost nonexistent in the mid-1990s, and now, despite its small relative size in the country, is the largest in the world. PRC now builds almost all its wind equipment domestically.

India

India's energy consumption increased at 9 percent annually in 2000–2007. The residential and service sectors account for 50 percent of energy demand, met largely by oil, electricity, and biomass. Industry accounted for 38 percent of total energy consumption in 2007. Electricity represents only 15 percent of industry's energy consumption but accounts for 45 percent of total energy consumption. The transport sector is a relatively small consumer of energy, representing 11 percent of final energy demand in 2007.

India's energy consumption projections indicate steep growth for all primary sources. The share of coal is expected to increase from 40 percent in 2007 to 48 percent in 2050. The share of oil remains stable at 24–25 percent, and the share of natural gas increases from 5 percent to 7.5 percent. Domestic supply of all fossil fuels will be less than corresponding demand, increasing import dependency, which is already a serious concern. In particular, oil imports are expected to grow from about 2.3 million barrels per day (mb/d) in 2007 to 6 mb/d in 2030, and 15 mb/d in 2050.

India had a power supply capacity of 143 GW in 2008, consisting of 53 percent coal, 25 percent hydro, 10 percent natural gas, 8 percent renewable energy sources, 3 percent nuclear, and 1 percent diesel. A significant amount (27 GW) was added between 2000 and 2007 but was insufficient to meet the growing demand. The growth of wind power capacity, though still relatively small, has been impressive because it demonstrates the country's success in adopting new technologies at a rapid pace. Electricity supply will have to climb fast to meet the economy's requirements. However, if the country relies more on advanced and renewable energy it has strong potential to lower its energy and carbon intensity.

ASEAN countries

The ASEAN countries were major exporters of oil and gas 40 years ago. They are now, as a group, a net oil importer, and are likely to become a net importer of gas in the next three decades.

Oil production in ASEAN countries peaked at 2.9 mb/d in 1996. Since then, the oil producing countries have launched major exploration and development activities in an attempt to sustain output. Overall production stood at 2.7 mb/d in 2008, with Indonesia still the largest producer at 1.0 mb/d followed by Malaysia at 0.8, Viet Nam at 0.4, Thailand at 0.3, and Brunei Darussalam at 0.1 mb/d. Total imports amounted to 0.9 mb/d, most of which came from the Middle East.

The oil import requirement is expected to reach 3.9 mb/d by 2030 and 5.4 mb/d by 2050, while oil import dependency increases from 25 percent in 2008 to 73 percent in 2030 and 88 percent in 2050. Except for Brunei Darussalam, all ASEAN countries are net importers of oil.

Historically, ASEAN countries have been a major source of world LNG exports. Gas production in the region grew at about 7 percent a year in the last two decades, reaching 200 billion cubic meters (bcm) in 2008. The bulk of gas resources and production are in Indonesia, Malaysia, and Brunei Darussalam, which are also major LNG exporters. However, both Indonesia and Malaysia are reassessing their export commitments due to the rapid growth of domestic gas demand.

ASEAN electricity demand has grown at 8 percent a year in the last three decades. In 2007, electricity generating capacity reached 138 GW, and total generation about 568 TWh. Generation was heavily dependent on fossil fuels (46 percent natural gas, 27 percent coal and 11 percent oil). Hydropower accounts for about 12 percent of electricity generation but is mostly concentrated in the Lao PDR, Myanmar, and Viet Nam. Electricity generation is expected to grow at 4.5 percent annually in 2007–2030 and 3.5 percent in 2030–2050. The share of fossil fuels is expected to remain at around 84 percent. The share of gas will decline slightly from 46 percent to 43 percent while the share of coal will increase from 27 percent to 38 percent.

The region is expected to be comparable with worldwide efficiency improvements in thermal power generation, particularly in its coal plants, where efficiency is expected to rise from 35 percent in 2007 to 42 percent in 2030 and 48 percent in 2050. There are no nuclear plants in the ASEAN countries and no firm plans for embarking on nuclear generation. There is general interest in exploring nuclear potential in Malaysia, the Philippines, Thailand, and Viet Nam.

Central Asia

Energy demand in Central Asia declined in the first half of the 1990s. Largely reflecting tumult following the breakup of the former Soviet Union. It then resumed modest growth in the second half. Growth in energy consumption accelerated from 2000 to 2007 as consumption increased from 128 Mtoe to 159 Mtoe. Current projections indicate that energy consumption will increase by about 61 percent in 2007–2030 and by about 50 percent more in 2030–2050.

Energy production amounted to about 320 Mtoe in 2007, of which 159 Mtoe was consumed (the rest was exported). The major energy producers are Kazakhstan, Turkmenistan, Uzbekistan, and Azerbaijan. Kazakhstan is by far the largest oil producer with production of 1.6 mb/d in 2010.

Azerbaijan produces 1 mb/d. Total production in the subregion was 2.7 mb/d and is expected to reach 5.4 mb/d in 2030. The main driver behind the increase is Kazakhstan, where oil production will rise from 1.6 mb/d in 2010 to 4.2 mb/d in 2030. Although these four countries produce and export natural gas, only Turkmenistan has gas resources substantial enough to sustain a considerable level of export in the long term. Turkmenistan's reserves are estimated at 220 bcm; the gas reserves of Kazakhstan, Uzbekistan, and Azerbaijan are estimated at 50 bcm, 50 bcm, and 30 bcm, respectively.

Iran

Iran is richly endowed with oil and gas. Its proven oil reserves at the end of 2008 were estimated at 18.9 billion tonnes (10.9 percent of the world total and thus second in the world after Saudi Arabia); its proven gas reserves were estimated at 29.6 trillion cubic meters (16 percent of the world total and the second only to the Russian Federation). Its primary energy consumption in 2008 was estimated at 194 Mtoe—55 percent gas, 43 percent oil, and the rest hydro. Iran's electricity consumption reached 153 TWh in 2008. Peak demand of the system is forecast to grow 8 percent annually, tapering off to 5 percent in 2008–2020.

Iran is interconnected with the power systems of Afghanistan, Armenia, Azerbaijan, Iraq, Pakistan, Turkey, and Turkmenistan. Several new interconnections are either under construction or in the planning and negotiation stage. Interconnection with the Russian Federation (presumably via Azerbaijan), interconnection with Tajikistan via Afghanistan, a submarine high-voltage direct current (HVDC) link to the United Arab Emirates, and an HVDC link to Turkey are under discussion and study.

Gas production has grown rapidly at 8.6 percent annually, reaching about 131 bcm in 2008. Iran has developed an extensive domestic gas supply system. In addition, a significant percentage of the gas produced is used for reinjection in oil fields for enhanced oil recovery. It is reported that about 30 bcm of gas was reinjected into oil wells in 2008. This could reach a peak of 100 bcm a year within the next decade. Iran has a long list of existing and potential gas trade schemes. The existing schemes carry rather small volumes of gas. Potential schemes are aimed at exporting large volumes but have shown little progress. At present, Iran imports gas from Turkmenistan to meet the gas requirements of the northern parts of the country, and exports gas to Turkey.

Implications for energy security

The focus of energy security planning varies over time and across countries. The key factors are the diversity of a country's fuel mix, its dependence on imports, the concentration of import sources, and political stability.

The overarching concern relates to the sources of oil supply, particularly when there will be fewer oil exporting countries in the future, and a greater geographic concentration (mostly in a potentially vulnerable region of the Persian Gulf). A similar concern is emerging over the sources of gas supply. Until a few years ago, dependence on imported natural gas was considered less risky than dependence on imported oil. This perception is changing as sources of gas exports are dwindling. From at least 10 countries that could be considered potential exporters of substantial volumes of natural gas to Asia, the list is shrinking to only a few.

Concerns about oil security in Asia are expected to heighten over the forthcoming decades for three main reasons: further concentration of oil consumption in the transport sector, where the possibilities for fuel switching are limited (based on currently available technologies); increased import dependency, as a result of which, Asia will become 90 percent dependent on imported oil by 2050; and concentration of sources of imports in fewer countries. Asia's dependence on oil imports, 55 percent in 2008, is projected to increase to 72 percent in 2030 and 85 percent in 2050 (Table 11.2). PRC started to import oil only in the late 1990s and passed the milestone of relying on imports for more than 50 percent of its oil consumption in 2008. The trend is expected to continue despite solid push toward energy diversification. PRC's oil dependency is projected to be 80 percent in 2030 and 87 percent in 2050. India's import dependency is already at 75 percent and expected to increase to 95 percent by 2030 and almost 100 percent by 2050.

The role of natural gas in Asia's energy security has become more complex in recent years. Historically, Asian countries viewed the gas option as an avenue for improving energy security. They made a radical switch from oil to gas believing that gas was inexpensive and abundantly available. The push to developing domestic gas resources accelerated in the 1990s, when many

Table 11.2 | Past and projected oil demand and import dependency (million barrels per day)

	1980	2000	2008	2030	2050
Asian oil consumption	10.2	17.9	21.9	36.8	55.1
High-income Asia	5.8	6.3	5.7	5.8	6.1
PRC	1.9	4.6	7.7	16.3	22.6
India	0.7	2.3	3	6.9	14.7
ASEAN	1.1	3	3.5	5.3	6.8
Central Asia and Caucasus	0.5	1.1	1.3	2.8	3.2
Asian oil imports	4.6	9.4	12.1	26.4	46.7
High-income Asia	5.7	6.2	5.6	5.9	6.1
PRC	-0.2	1.4	3.9	12.1	19.8
India	-0.4	1.5	2.2	6.3	14.1
ASEAN	-0.7	0.6	1.3	2.8	5.4
Central Asia	0.1	-0.7	-1.2	-2.6	-1.9

Source: OPEC (2009), IEA (2010b), BP (2010) and author's estimates.

initiatives were undertaken to import gas through cross-border pipelines and in the form of LNG.

The security of gas supply is now less certain as a larger number of countries depend on imported gas, and a fewer countries offer substantial export potential. Asian gas imports are growing very strongly, largely due to the increased requirements of PRC and India. Gas import dependency of PRC is expected to increase from 1 percent in 2007 to 48 percent in 2030 and 53 percent in 2050. India's import dependency is projected to rise from 25 percent in 2007 to 39 percent in 2030 and 78 percent in 2050 (Table 11.3).

Table 11.3 | Gas demand and import dependency

	1980	2000	2007	2030	2050
Asian gas consumption	118		475	965	1,228
High-income Asia	27	112.3	152	181	212
PRC	14		73	242	327
India	1		39	132	180
ASEAN	32	96	140	240	320
Central Asia	41	66	93	190	275
Asian gas imports					
High-income Asia	23	104	142	175	199
PRC	0		4	117	174
India	0		10	82	140
ASEAN	12		-60	-40	40
Central Asia	-55		-103	-113	-120

Source: OPEC (2009), IEA (2010b), BP (2010) and author's estimates.

The prospect for Asia's gas security is heavily influenced by the gas import requirements of the EU. The EU is expected to have the biggest increase in its import requirements in the projection period because of the decline in gas-production capacities of the UK and the Netherlands. Gas import dependency is expected to increase from about 60 percent in 2007 to more than 80 percent in 2030 and more than 90 percent in 2050. In volume terms, the EU's gas imports will increase from 250 bcm in 2007 to 429 bcm in 2030. Currently some 55 percent of the EU's gas imports come from the Russian Federation. However, for the first time, the EU is developing a regional import strategy aimed at mitigating the risks of gas supply. The strategy, which requires further diversification of import sources, has turned into various initiatives to secure gas from the Middle East and the Caspian region. These initiatives are in direct competition with the import efforts of Asian countries.

The number of potential gas exporters is projected to shrink. The only countries that have the resource potential for large long-term exports are the Russian Federation, Qatar, and Iran. Other countries in the Middle East and the Caspian region are also considered significant gas producers but only for the next two decades. Turkmenistan may, however, have potential for long-term gas export.

Long-term sustainability is critical but is also complex. A notable example is Indonesia, which in the 1980s became the world's largest LNG exporter. At the time, it was considered a reliable long-term supplier of gas. Today it is struggling to fulfill its old contracts that stipulate supply of LNG to Japan, Republic of Korea, and others.

As in Indonesia, gas supply in several current LNG exporters could become very tight due to increased domestic demand. This is a concern even for long-term supplies from Iran (with the second largest gas reserves in the world). Iran's domestic gas consumption quadrupled in the last 20 years and reached 131 bcm in 2009. The country has become the world's third-largest gas consumer after the US and the Russian Federation. The sharp increase in domestic gas use is happening at the time that Iran is also in need of greater volumes of gas to inject into wells to enhance oil recovery. The combination of these needs has resulted in recent serious gas shortages. Therefore, as said, assessing gas availability for export purposes is complex, even though the size of the gas resource may suggest substantial export potential in the form of LNG and piped gas.

Implications for climate change

A very important aspect of Asia's energy trends is their impact on environment and climate change (Masud et al., 2007).

Worldwide, energy-related carbon dioxide emissions were about 30 giga tonnes (GT) in 2009. Current projections indicate that these emissions will soar to 41 GT by 2030 and to 57 GT by 2050. This level would lead to a concentration of greenhouse gases in the atmosphere that could raise global temperatures by about 6°C above pre-industrial levels, thereby causing irreversible changes in the global climate. To limit the average increase in global temperatures to a maximum of 2°C, considered essential to ensure climate stability, the concentration of greenhouse gases in the atmosphere would have to be stabilized. This would require energy-related carbon dioxide emissions to be reduced by about 80 percent by 2050.

This ambitious reversal target has been translated by the IEA into a new roadmap that advocates a "global revolution" in energy supply and use, and requires far greater energy efficiency, large-scale use of renewable and nuclear energy, and deployment of carbon capture and storage technologies (Energy Technology Perspectives, 2010). The IEA analysis makes a distinction between two scenarios. The reference (or base-case) scenario portrays an energy world in which energy efficiency improvement and energy diversification are pursued as currently envisaged by various stakeholders. The energy trends that result are likely to be within the limits of resource availability but are still considered unsustainable because of the unacceptability of carbon emission levels.

Therefore, the IEA has developed a "decarbonization" scenario that reduces carbon emissions drastically by using a new set of technologies. The decarbonization scenario results in significant changes in the level and composition of energy supply. As expected, the use of coal will be seriously affected to the point that coal consumption in 2050 will be 36 percent less than in 2007. The impact on oil demand is also significant. In the reference scenario, oil demand rises from 85 mb/d in 2007 to 122 mb/d in 2050, while the decarbonization scenario results in an oil demand of 66 mb/d for 2050, which is 23 percent lower than oil consumption in 2007. The climate change agenda thus offers significant collateral benefit for energy security.

The IEA's decarbonization scenario focuses on global rather than country-specific energy trends, but is has two important implications for any analysis of Asia's future energy needs. First, Asia's energy-related carbon emissions are significantly above the allowable targets. In a business-as-usual scenario, the carbon emissions of PRC alone (about 15 GT in 2050) exceed the allowable global target (14 GT in 2050). Second, the underlying assumptions of the IEA's decarbonization scenario for future technologies, including changes in lifestyle and consumer behavior, provide a framework for devising Asia's energy supply and demand scenarios, presented below (Table 11.4).

Improving energy security through efficiency and diversification

Policy makers in Asia are gradually developing the conviction that there is close synergy between energy security and the climate change agenda. Asian countries need to pursue energy efficiency and diversification (EED) in order to improve their energy security. Linking these efforts to the climate change agenda will offer Asian countries a bright opportunity to increase the effectiveness of their EED initiatives by using the most advanced emerging technologies. The climate change agenda and its corresponding roadmap provide the most practical framework for addressing EED.

The present energy demand projections, which could be labeled the "business as usual" (BAU) scenario, incorporate ambitious measures for EED. Nevertheless, this section presents an alternative scenario that reflects more stringent measures of EED, and more ambitious development of renewable and nuclear energy than envisaged by the IEA's technology roadmap (IEA, 2010a).

Table 11.4 contains a summary comparison of the BAU and the EED scenarios of Asia's energy demand and supply mix. It indicates that the region can achieve further savings of about 14 percent in its annual energy consumption if it adopts more stringent methods of energy efficiency. However, a much more significant aspect of the EED scenario is the radical shift in the energy mix where reliance on fossil fuels is reduced by the increasing shares of renewable energy and nuclear power.

The power sector's generation mix shows the most noticeable change where renewable energy and nuclear options assert their influence. The collective share of renewable energy and nuclear power could exceed 40 percent in the EED scenario, compared with 19 percent in the BAU scenario. The division between renewable energy and nuclear is subject to considerable uncertainty. However, renewable energy should have priority over nuclear and be developed to its maximum extent.

Yet growth in renewable energy is from a very small base and it is hard to foresee renewables replacing fossil fuels in a significant way by 2050. Based on the current state of technological development, only nuclear energy can offer a large-scale substitute for fossil fuels. Countries will therefore face a difficult dilemma between the use of fossil fuels versus nuclear power.

It is also clear that all of the current plans and the long-term vision of nuclear power will need to be reexamined in the wake of Japan's nuclear accident. Major lessons of the accident are: the need for much more careful selection of plant sites, better design of plant and equipment, even greater safety measures, and a search for better technologies. But, the exact nature and costs of these measures are not known, increasing the uncertainties about future costs of building and

Table 11.4 Asia's energy demand and supply scenarios

	Historical		BAU Scenario		EED Scenario	
Year	1990	2007	2030	2050	2030	2050
Total energy (Mtoe)	2,220	4,242	7,980	11,480	4,242	9,947
Energy mix (%):						
Coal	40	46	48	50	42–46	35–39
Oil	16	20	21	20	19	12
Gas	9	11	12	11	11	10
Nuclear and renewable energy	35	24	19	19	24–28	39–43
Electricity consumption (TWh)	2,327	5,511	14,161	22,318	15,726–19,649	38,775–45,583
Generation mix (%):						
Coal	52	56	64	63	53–57	37–41
Oil	13	5	1	1	1	1
Gas	5	11	12	12	11	11
Nuclear and renewable energy	30	28	23	24	31–35	47–51

Source: IEA (2010b).

operating nuclear power plants. Public opinion against nuclear power may also make it harder to build new plants, particularly in democracies. It is therefore not possible to anticipate the role of nuclear power in the future energy mix of Asian economies. The fundamental implications for Asia are that countries must put an even heavier emphasis on energy efficiency and renewable energy.

The renewable energy option may have much greater potential than currently envisaged. Globally, the geography of the renewable energy industry is changing greatly. For example, renewable energy power plants existed in just a handful of countries in the 1990s but are now being operated or built in over 82 countries, including PRC and India. Indeed, these two countries became world leaders in the wind industry in a span of less than a decade (Figure 11.3).

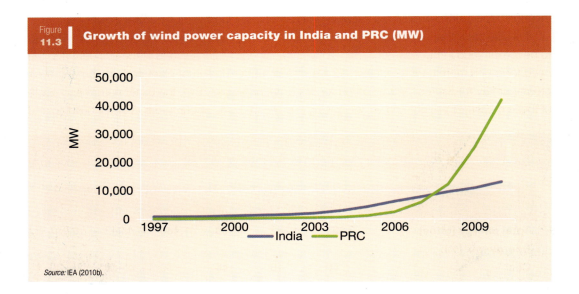

Figure 11.3 Growth of wind power capacity in India and PRC (MW)

Source: IEA (2010b).

Should a similar pattern develop in the solar energy industry, Asia could become heavily reliant on solar power. Asia's potential solar resources are very large, but most Asian countries are at an early stage of using them. Worldwide, India seems to be taking the most ambitious position in developing a solar energy industry. It has announced the goal of making India a global leader in solar manufacturing while constructing 20 GW of solar power capacity by 2022. Realizing this vision would scale up the prospects for the role of solar energy in Asia's fuel mix.

Enhanced emphasis on energy efficiency

Energy efficiency offers the greatest and most economical potential for improving energy security and reducing carbon emissions of most Asian economies. Although some Asian countries have already taken many steps, they have substantial room to reduce the energy intensity and thus delink energy use from economic growth. The large-scale efficiency improvement potential is most prevalent in power, industry and transport.

PRC has made much progress in improving the energy intensity of its economy. Energy policy is often devised and implemented in the form of setting explicit and specific targets. The most recently finished development plan (2006–2010) set an explicit goal of reducing the country's energy intensity by 20 percent. Current estimates indicate that PRC has attained this target. A major avenue for achieving such efficiency improvement quickly was closing old (and often small) power plants and industrial facilities. Another important initiative focused on enforcing top-down energy performance targets for local authorities from governorates to the county level.

PRC's energy efficiency successes have been internationally reviewed by numerous authors (for example Levine et al., 2010; Taylor, 2008), who rate PRC experience in improving the energy efficiency of appliances, lighting, buildings, vehicles, and industrial equipment as best practice.

The next development plan (2011–2015) is also very ambitious. It aims to reduce the country's carbon emissions by 40–45 percent by 2020 compared with 2005. The main components of the carbon reduction strategy have already been announced and include the installation of 80 GW of nuclear capacity, 100 GW of wind generation, 300 GW of hydropower, and 1.8 GW of solar plants by 2020. Adopting such targets would have been inconceivable in PRC 10 years ago.

India could obtain substantial efficiencies by pursuing a similarly aggressive strategy. The power sector is an important case in point. India's electricity transmission and distribution loss stands at 25 percent—6.7 percent in PRC. India would need to use the best available existing (and future) technologies and rely heavily on other countries' experience.

India's industries have wide room for efficiency improvement. The iron and steel sector is expected to continue its rapid expansion to supply the surging demand for steel-based goods for the domestic market. The cement industry is also expected to grow in response to the extraordinary expansions in infrastructure and building construction. These sectors will be the major users of coking coal.

The energy mix in India will continue to rely on coal in every conceivable scenario. However, under the EED scenario, a combination of energy savings and renewable and nuclear energy results in 50 percent less coal-based generation than in the reference scenario, and the total energy supply in 2050 is about 30 percent lower than the reference scenario. This stems mainly from efficiency improvements in power, industry, and transport. The shares of coal and oil in 2050 is 21 percent and 20 percent, respectively. As a result, the share of nuclear, biomass, and renewable energies increases substantially to compensate for the drop in the share of coal and oil.

In ASEAN countries, the EED scenario lowers the growth in energy demand to 2.1 percent annually, compared with 2.5 percent in the reference scenario, mainly because of the fall in energy intensity in industry and transport. The EED scenario also leads to a change in the fuel mix of the power sector, where the use of coal declines because of the increase in the share of renewable energy and nuclear power. This scenario leads to decreased oil demand as well. Oil consumption in 2030 reaches only 4.4 mb/d, compared with 5.3 mb/d in the reference scenario.

There is also potential to improve the efficiency of energy consumption and production in Central Asia. In the past, these countries have shown little interest in adopting the efficiency practices of industrial countries; however, they might be receptive to learning from other Asian countries, particularly PRC. With its deep involvement in the oil and gas sector of Central Asia, PRC could also assist in reducing waste in gas flaring by constructing the infrastructure needed to gather and market the gas.

Minimizing damage from sudden supply disruptions

As discussed, energy security policies attempt to manage supply risks through reducing energy intensities and the diversification of the energy mix. Two additional instruments—strategic petroleum stockpiling and electricity and gas interconnections—are normally used to minimize damage from sudden supply interruptions.

Strategic petroleum stocks

Strategic and mandatory stocks have emerged since the 1970s as the governments of major consuming countries recognized the economic damage of an oil supply disruption and became aware of the necessity of government intervention to preserve some degree of stability. Government involvement can occur in one or a combination of the following forms: establishment of strategic petroleum reserves; imposition of mandatory minimum stock levels for private oil companies; and the formation of public corporations to finance and manage emergency reserve programs.

Asian countries have shown varying levels of concern about energy security depending on their endowment of domestic energy resources. Japan and Republic of Korea, both of which have limited domestic energy resources, have long been concerned about energy security and have thus undertaken various emergency measures, such as stockpiling. Japan has also pioneered the idea that energy security should be assured at the regional rather than the national level.

ASEAN countries as a group have been conscious of the vulnerability of their economies to possible oil supply disruptions. They have therefore systematically reviewed various options for emergency response, but they have yet to reach a consensus on whether to commit themselves to holding strategic stocks. Instead, most ASEAN countries impose some mandatory floor on the operational stocks of private refiners and distributors. This arrangement is inadequate to deal with potential supply disruptions. Consequently, discussions continue regarding the means to coordinate an emergency response time for allowing ASEAN countries to mitigate the impact of sudden disruptions. It is also clear that this initiative must be developed with other major countries in the region and with the international community. The current deliberations involve ASEAN+3 (Japan, PRC, Republic of Korea) and the IEA.

Regional energy integration

Regional interconnections of gas and electricity networks provide economic and security benefits to the participating countries. Besides enabling energy imports, interconnected networks—particularly power grids—impart other benefits, such as peak sharing, improved system reliability, reduced reserve margin, reactive power support and economy energy exchanges, daily and seasonal demand diversity, and generation-capacity dispatch management. Despite these benefits, cross-border projects face numerous technical, institutional, and implementation challenges. A distinct feature of regional integration projects is the protracted preparation time. Most of these projects have taken many years (even several decades) to start implementation. Each project has been restructured multiple times. On occasion, deficiencies in the initial formulation have resulted in further revisions. Yet another factor is the difficulty of working out cross-border issues and coordinating solutions among participating countries.

South Asia, Central Asia, and ASEAN countries have made many attempts to integrate their energy systems (Bhattacharyay, 2010; ESMAP, 2008). However, the landscape for energy integration is changing, largely due to the increased role of PRC in the energy scene of most Asian countries. This new landscape needs to be analyzed and projected into the future to arrive at an optimum pattern of energy integration.

The most systematic effort to integrate power and gas grids has been launched by the ASEAN countries. In the 1980s, these nations decided to establish a regionwide energy market, which led to the creation of the framework for the ASEAN Power Grid and Trans-ASEAN Gas Pipeline, which emphasizes the fact that creating a regional market is a step-wise process. There should be a continuation of reform to expose the energy sector to open competition. More specifically, national regulators and transmission system operators should cooperate to adopt a model energy pool, which would enable participants to make optimum use of their energy grids.

Elsewhere, PRC developed a strong position in the oil and gas sector of Central Asia. It entered Kazakhstan's oil sector in 1997, when the national oil company, CNPC, bought a 60 percent share of Aktobe Munaigaz (later increased to 85 percent) that would supply oil to a 2,900 km pipeline from Atyrau to Alashankou on the Kazakh–PRC border. The completion of this project has established a world record for the speed of implementing such projects, and has further convinced industry observers that partnership with PRC can result in exceptionally rapid construction of cross-border pipelines.

Subsequently, recognizing the significance of Turkmenistan's gas resources, PRC established a strong presence in this sector in 2006 by signing a framework agreement that included the development of upstream gas resources and the construction of a new pipeline that would carry 30 bcm of Turkmen natural gas annually across Uzbekistan and Kazakhstan to PRC. The first phase of the pipeline system, including the Uzbek and the Kazakh sections, was completed in mid-2010. The entire pipeline is scheduled for commissioning by 2012. With its impressive implementation capacity and abundant financing capability, PRC seems to have established an advantageous position in the Turkmen gas sector, compared with Western and Russian Federation oil companies. This position is expected to become even stronger when the gas pipeline becomes fully operational.

Other gas pipelines are under consideration to take gas from Central Asia to the Russian Federation, Europe, and South Asia. The most notable proposals include the Caspian gas pipeline, with a capacity of up to 20 bcm per year, that would run parallel to the existing pipeline system to transport gas from Turkmenistan through Kazakhstan to the Russian Federation; the Iran–Pakistan–India pipeline—a 22 bcm per year project to be increased to 55 bcm per year at a later stage, and costing $7.5 billion—which was conceptualized in 1989 and has gone through many cycles of negotiations; and the Turkmenistan–Afghanistan–Pakistan–India pipeline, which has been under review and preparation for more than 10 years.

Finally, energy exports from Iran becomes complicated when one tries to separate the real prospects from the numerous ideas that have been proposed for cross-border energy trade. Iran's substantial gas reserves give it a competitive advantage in electricity and gas exports to Turkey and possibly to the European systems via Turkey. Iran will also be a key transit country for electricity exports from Turkmenistan to Turkey and beyond. In the short term, a 180 km submarine HVDC link between Iran and the United Arab Emirates is imminent. The link will have a transfer capacity of 1,500 MW and will connect Iran to the Gulf Cooperation Council Grid.

Priorities for domestic action
Energy efficiency and diversification

Climate change concerns are having an impact on the policy mind-set in most Asian countries, leading to greater recognition of the significant synergy between the agenda of climate change mitigation and energy security. The shift is particularly noticeable in: the adoption of advanced methods of energy efficiency; the push toward developing renewable energy; and the openness to other sources that follows from the recognition that the objectives of energy security and the climate change agenda cannot be achieved through energy efficiency alone.[2]

Achieving energy security would also require a fresh set of policy measures that provide clear incentives for unprecedented improvements in efficiency, for private investments, and for advanced technologies.

---

2 It is still too early to assess how the March 2011 nuclear incident in Japan will affect the future role and prospects of nuclear energy.

For most Asian countries, energy pricing is an important, though sensitive, issue due in part to the prevailing energy subsidies, and to the need to move to more advanced pricing regimes. For example, improving energy efficiency would require an aggressive time-of-day tariff design. At the same time, encouraging renewable energy development would require various subsidies. Such subsidies must be kept transparent, well-targeted, and confined to a limited timeframe. Desirable subsidies include R&D support, feed-in tariffs, tax incentives, and access to soft sources of finance. The predominant instrument is the feed-in tariff—the price at which utilities are obligated to buy the electricity generated by renewable energy. It has increased investments in new renewable energy technologies, particularly in developed economies. This type of tariff should be considered an option and must be tailored to the renewable energy available in each country.

Emerging energy technologies

Technology transfer has always been an embedded characteristic of energy sector development. However, the present circumstances differ in that technology is being developed on a fast track and intended for rapid diffusion. There is strong momentum behind the "energy technology revolution" that stems from strict targets set by the EU and other industrial-country groupings to cut their carbon emissions. The new targeted technologies are mostly proven but not yet fully commercialized. The most notable of them are: renewable energy, especially wind and solar technologies; carbon capture and storage (CCS); and transport technologies such as electric and plug-in hybrid vehicles, as well as advanced biofuels.

Wind power technology has greatly improved and is now widespread around the world. Although the cost of wind power depends on site characteristics, its average cost has declined from over 20 US cents per kilowatt hour in the early 1990s to 6–7 cents today. Advances in wind power technology were initiated in Denmark, when the country decided to develop a competitive advantage in this industry. Since then, the industry has spread to many other industrial countries including Germany, Spain, and the US, as well as PRC, India, and Republic of Korea.

Solar technology is at a much earlier stage of development, though several new technologies are expected to emerge. Most solar energy produced today is based on photovoltaic cells, which are expected to be improved by thin-film technology. This will result in a decrease of the generation cost of solar photovoltaic systems to around 5–7 cents per kilowatt hour by 2050. A promising new technology is concentrated solar power, which intensifies direct sunlight several times to reach higher energy densities and thus higher temperatures. It is expected to play an important role in the decarbonization of the power sector, where it would account for over 10 percent of worldwide electricity supply by 2050. Asian countries, such as India, are expected to be producers; large-scale development is likely to require substantial financial support for at least 20 years.

CCS will play a critical role in decarbonization as it becomes the fallback technology to reduce carbon emissions to an acceptable level. On average, they are expected to add 3–4 cents per kWh to the cost of electricity generated in a new coal-fueled plant. Worldwide, their capabilities are forecast to emerge after 2030 and reach a total capacity of 5 GT a year by 2050.

The expansion of nuclear capacity faces serious challenges. Though the technology is proven, there is a need to demonstrate the industry's capacity to build plants within a specified timeframe and budget. The events of March 2011 in Japan are likely to prompt a reevaluation of nuclear energy, as discussed earlier.

The transport sector is a focus for new technologies because of its importance in climate change and energy security. The most promising option as an alternative to fossil fuels is electric cars using electricity generated by alternative energy sources. Improving transport technologies requires an effective partnership between the public and private sectors. The IEA estimates that with such an effective partnership, electric vehicle sales could reach 100 million a year by 2050, and account for approximately half the new light-vehicle market. The overall objective should be to develop sustainable transport strategies based on an "avoid-shift-improve" approach (ADB Sustainable Transport Initiative, 2009). Within Asia, Japan and PRC are likely to be pioneers.

These new technologies offer major market opportunities for Asia. The global market for low-carbon technologies in 2050 is estimated to be about $3 trillion. Several Asian countries, especially PRC and India, are well positioned to gain a solid share of this market.

Public and private sector roles

A sustainable energy sector should rely on private investors to build new supply capacities and manage the operation of various facilities, while the government takes charge of developing the energy diversification strategy and devises incentives to encourage participants to serve the overall objective of improving energy security. There is a strong synergy between energy security and low-carbon energy options. Some new technologies, such as wind and nuclear power, are already economically viable when based on an appropriate price for carbon. Others require government support to move to large-scale production in order to lower the average cost of supply.

In either case, widespread diffusion of new technologies requires a government push and a market pull, with close public–private cooperation. Such cooperation would enable technologies to be transferred more efficiently while available sources of international support are used.

Finally, regulatory bodies are important role in ensuring that the energy sector functions properly. Independent and specialized regulators are needed to encourage competitive market behavior. Regulators need financial autonomy and clear authority to set tariffs. Still regulation has limits and should be confined to segments of the industry with significant economies of scale (i.e., natural monopolies).

Priorities for regional cooperation

Asia's energy security agenda can be substantially enhanced through regional cooperation, notably in three areas:

- Asia's regional cooperation agenda should address the transfer and sharing of several important energy technologies including: renewable energy, such as wind and solar technologies; CCS; and transport technologies, particularly electric and plug-in hybrid vehicles. Many countries in the region are planning to devote substantial effort and resources to these technologies. Regional cooperation will enable them to maximize the effectiveness of their efforts. These countries can also benefit from the experience of Japan, a world leader in developing new energy technologies; the advances from Republic of Korea; and from the experiences of PRC and India in indigenous R&D and the adaptation of technologies.
- Some Asian countries have considered the creation of joint petroleum stockpiles, yet have not reached workable agreements. Today, almost every Asian country is in the process of reviewing its own emergency response mechanism, and ASEAN+3 has begun discussions. An initiative should be launched to support and expand deliberations to develop an Asia-wide energy emergency response system based on: a long-term vision of the system; a transitional path to move from the present status to the ultimate model; mechanisms which are at present viable for a coordinated response; and an institutional arrangement that could serve as a vehicle to implement short-term mechanisms and move toward the long-term vision.
- The integration of electricity and gas networks is the objective of numerous initiatives in Asia, and a regional energy market will be increasingly appealing as Asia becomes the largest energy-consuming region in the world. The ASEAN approach of stepwise integration may provide a good start. While the full integration of energy markets can only be considered a long-term goal, it is feasible to design an interim plan for creating subregional energy pools that are also in harmony at the regional level. The process might include three phases: expand bilateral trade (additional volumes, additional numbers of countries); move to a multilateral trade arrangement; and move to a power-pool organization.

Regional cooperation in these areas would address Asia's two distinct energy security risks: the sudden interruption of energy flows, and the risks in the long-term energy resource availability. Building strategic petroleum reserves and integrating gas and electricity networks are effective means of addressing the risk of sudden interruption of energy flows. The above recommendations for lowering an economy's energy intensity and diversifying from fossil fuels address the risk of long-term energy resource availability.

Action on Climate Change in Asia's Self-Interest

Chapter 12

Cameron Hepburn and John Ward

This chapter discusses the growing role of emerging markets in global carbon emissions and then assesses the economic and social impacts of climate change on emerging market economies to provide a fresh perspective for Asian policy makers.[1]

Specifically, the analysis looks at the economic self-interest of emerging markets in three scenarios: a do-nothing scenario—also called the business-as-usual approach—in which the current trends in climate change go unchecked for the next 40 years; a scenario in which the developed countries listed in Annex 1 of the Kyoto Protocol take steps to reduce their emissions by 80 percent from 1995 levels[2] by the end of 2050; and a third scenario in which the major Asian emerging market economies (plus Brazil and Mexico) take parallel actions to restrain their emissions by 2050 to the same levels as their 2005 emissions, as proposed by the PRC in Copenhagen.

The chapter provides an overview of the likely rise in global temperatures by 2100 under each scenario.[3] It goes on to estimate the economic implications of each scenario for emerging market economies in Asia, including the impact on agriculture production, with specific references to the impact on the region's two largest developing countries: PRC and India. It makes the case for early action by large developing Asian economies—particularly PRC, India, and Indonesia—to mitigate the threat of dangerous levels of global warming and climate change by joining the efforts of Japan, Republic of Korea, and other developed countries around the world. It concludes with a description of adaptation and risk management efforts that also align with Asian countries' self-interest.

Emerging economies' contributions to global emissions

The nine largest emerging economies that are members of G20—Argentina, Brazil, PRC, India, Indonesia, Republic of Korea, Mexico, South Africa, and Turkey—already account for just

---

[1] This chapter is based on a detailed study prepared by Vivid Economics for Centennial Group International (forthcoming).
[2] In all work of the Intergovernmental Panel on Climate Change and global discussions on climate change, 2005 is used as the base reference year.
[3] The book uses the year 2100 to be consistent with UN-sponsored negotiations on a new global treaty on climate change that uses 2100 as the benchmark year to estimate changes in average global temperature.

under half global emissions. And 90 percent of these emissions are from Asian economies. Commensurate with their rising economic status, they have become large emitters. These developing economies currently account for a greater proportion of global greenhouse gas emissions than the developed countries: US, Japan, Germany, France, UK, Canada, Italy, and Australia (Figure 12.1). Symbolically, PRC has recently surpassed the US as the world's largest emitter of carbon dioxide and largest energy consumer (IEA, 2010).

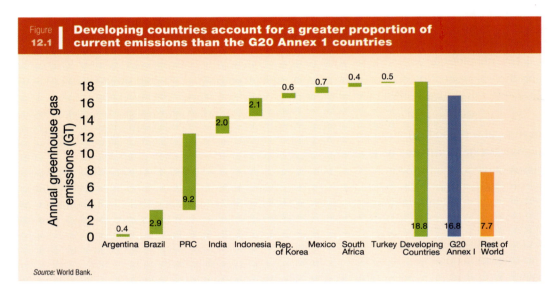

Figure 12.1 Developing countries account for a greater proportion of current emissions than the G20 Annex 1 countries

Source: World Bank.

Unsurprisingly given their recent rapid economic growth, the nine largest emerging countries have accounted for the bulk of global growth in combustion-related carbon dioxide (CO_2) emissions over recent years. Nearly three-quarters of global growth in fossil fuel–related CO_2 over the period 2002–2007 was driven by these countries, with PRC alone contributing over half (Figure 12.2). More recent data are expected to confirm this trend. Just over half PRC's increase was attributable to the power sector, with the growth in industrial emissions also accounting for a significant proportion, although much of this was associated with the manufacture of goods exported to developed countries.

Impact of climate change: Business-as-usual scenario

The business-as-usual scenario is based on the historical relationship between gross domestic product (GDP) and emissions for each country between 1990 and 2005, taking into account any improvements in the ratio over this period. The model uses forecasts for economic growth through 2050 under the high-growth Asian Century scenario.

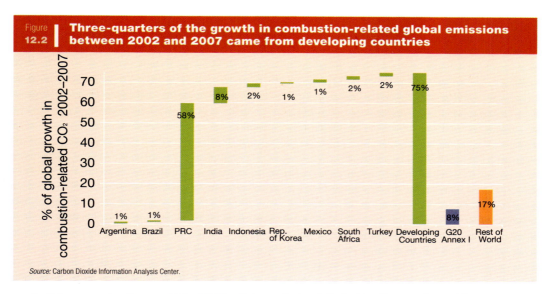

Figure 12.2 | Three-quarters of the growth in combustion-related global emissions between 2002 and 2007 came from developing countries

Source: Carbon Dioxide Information Analysis Center.

In this scenario, the world in 2100 will be substantially hotter than today, with an average temperature increase of 4.4°C above 1990 levels and 4.8°C above preindustrial levels. These temperature increases are associated with carbon dioxide atmospheric concentration levels of more than 900 parts per million (ppm).

Physical impact

Temperature increases of 5°C represent dangerous climate change. Although the exact nature of the physical and social impacts in a world that is 5°C warmer is not known, it is commonly believed that the last time temperatures were this high—the Eocene period, 35 million–55 million years ago—swampy forests covered much of the world and alligators lived near the North Pole (Stern, 2007).

In such a coming world, the global water cycle would be significantly altered, with billions of people experiencing significantly altered water supplies (Warren et al., 2006). The flow of rivers from the Himalayas, which serve a number of Asian countries that account for around half of the world's population, would likely be disrupted (ADB, 2009a). In addition, ocean acidity would significantly disrupt marine ecosystems and commercial fisheries worldwide (Royal Society, 2005).

Sea-level rise

A global temperature increase of 4.4°C would lead to sea levels rising by as much as 46 centimeters (cm) by 2100. Such a rise would threaten a large number of Asian cities.

Measured by the size of the population that would be exposed to such a rise in sea levels,

Table 12.1 | GEM cities feature prominently in the list of cities most exposed to a half-meter sea-level rise

City	Exposed population (2070) (thousands)	City	Exposed assets (2070) ($ billion, 2001)
Kolkata	14,014	Miami	3,513
Mumbai	11,418	Guangzhou	3,357
Dhaka	11,135	New York–Newark	2,147
Guangzhou	10,333	Kolkata	1,961
Ho Chi Minh City	9,216	Shanghai	1,771
Shanghai	5,451	Mumbai	1,698
Bangkok	5,138	Tianjin	1,231
Rangoon	4,965	Tokyo	1,207
Miami, US	4,795	Hong Kong, China	1,163
Hai Phong	4,711	Bangkok	1,117
Alexandria, Egypt	4,375	Ningbo	1,073
Tianjin	3,790	New Orleans	1,013
Khulna	3,641	Osaka–Kobe	968
Ningbo	3,305	Amsterdam	843
Lagos, Nigeria	3,229	Rotterdam	825
Abidjan	3,110	Ho Chi Minh City	652
New York–Newark	2,931	Nagoya	623
Chittagong	2,866	Qingdao	602
Tokyo	2,521	Virginia Beach	582
Jakarta	2,248	Alexandria, Egypt	562

Source: Nicholls et al. (2007).

15 of the 20 most exposed cities (and 9 out of the top 10) are in Asia (Table 12.1). The number of exposed people in Asian cities in 2070 is expected to be almost 95 million. In terms of expected asset exposure, 13 of the 20 (and 8 of the top 10) most exposed cities are in Asia, with a combined asset exposure of $17.4 trillion.

Finally, climate change (and subsidence) under the business-as-usual scenario would increase the number of people exposed to coastal flooding in Bangladesh, India, and PRC by some 30 million.

Economic impact

Developing Asian economies would suffer significantly in this world. In this scenario, climate change's drag on annual GDP growth in the Asia region in 2100 would range from 3.1 percent to 10.6 percent.

Agriculture is one of the sectors most affected by climate change, as well as being an important sector in most Asian countries. Agriculture currently accounts for about 10 percent of the region's GDP. Significant reductions in crop yields are expected in most countries in the business-as-usual scenario.

Analysis from the Asian Development Bank (2009b), World Bank, and Müller et al. (2009) shows that dangerous climate change would lead to declining agricultural yields in the vast majority of developing countries. In the cases of India, Indonesia, and Republic of Korea, the decline in yields would range between 14 percent and 20 percent. On the other hand, PRC is expected to experience higher yields because of more favorable climatic conditions.

Health impact

The health of Asians is also expected to suffer significantly from such dramatic temperature increases. Studies that estimate future health impacts on specific developing Asian countries are rare, but an example of the impact on developing countries in Africa is provided by Tanser et al. (Tanser et al., 2003), which estimates changes in malaria exposure in Africa by 2100. Results suggest that in a business-as-usual scenario, by 2100 parts of Africa could see nearly a fivefold increase in malaria exposure. Such studies should be regarded as a wake-up call by Asian policy makers.

In summary, climate change and global warming will have major adverse economic and social impacts on Asia. Earth is a resource shared by all human beings. It is not possible for Asia to carve out and isolate its part of the planet. Any deterioration in its quality will affect all human beings, albeit to different degrees. With more than half the world's population today and likely more than half global GDP by 2050, Asia has the most at stake in preserving a healthy and vibrant planet. The analysis summarized above shows that the region as a whole will suffer from global warming, and in some areas it will suffer disproportionately. It is therefore in the long-term self-interest of Asia to join global efforts to mitigate and adapt to climate change.

Impact of climate change: Mitigation by developed countries only scenario

If only developed countries were to take action, global warming would still be substantial. Even if Kyoto Protocol Annex 1 countries reduced their emissions by 80 percent by 2050, the average global temperature in 2100 would still increase by 3.9°C above 1990 levels (4.3°C above preindustrial levels). This would be associated with carbon dioxide atmospheric concentrations of 780 ppm.

A world that is 3.9°C warmer in 2100 still implies a radical disruption to the physical and economic geography of the earth. It is estimated there would be a 40–45 percent decrease in annual water runoff in South Africa and South America, and a 20 percent increase in South Asia (Arnell, 2006). The most affected regions of the world would become too hot and dry to grow crops. It is estimated that 1.5 billion more people would be exposed to dengue fever than in a world with no climate change (Hales et al., 2002). Unsurprisingly, therefore, Asia would still experience hefty material economic losses. Aggregate annual losses for all of Asia would range between 2.6 percent and 8.1 percent of GDP in 2100.

Of course, these losses are lower than in the business-as-usual scenario, but—strikingly—only by a small amount. Relying exclusively on action by the developed countries only reduces Asian annual economic losses by just 20 percent.

With the global temperature increases still substantial, potential losses from agricultural yields remain substantial in many Asian countries. India would face a yield decline of over 10 percent, and Indonesia and Republic of Korea of more than 15 percent. Sea levels would still rise substantially by 41 cm, compared with 46 cm in the worst-case scenario, and threaten many coastal cities in Asia.

In summary, even if developed countries undertake the climate change mitigation measures that were proposed at the Copenhagen and Cancun negotiations, the adverse impacts of climate change would still be very significant for Asian economies. Without a proactive approach, most Asian economies will suffer major negative consequences. Therefore, Asia cannot afford to remain outside global climate change mitigation efforts.

Impact of climate change: Complementary mitigation actions by developing Asian economies scenario

Only if the large Asian economies (plus Brazil and Mexico) act together with the developed economy signatories to the Kyoto Protocol would there be an opportunity for meaningful mitigation of climate change. Furthermore, Asian economies have a much greater incentive to act, since the damages they would suffer in the other two scenarios are the highest of any region (Figure 12.3).

Consistent with their high and growing levels of emissions, large Asian economies can play a decisive role in slowing global temperature increases. In a situation in which action by Kyoto Protocol Annex 1 countries to reduce emissions by 80 percent from 1990 levels is matched by a commitment from developing Asian countries to ensure that their emissions in 2050 are no higher than they were in 2005 (and emissions from land use change are 50 percent lower in 2050 than in 2005), projected temperature increases would be greatly reduced.

Compared with the business-as-usual average global temperature increase of 4.4°C between 1990 and 2050—and an increase of 3.9°C when Annex 1 countries alone take action—the rise of global temperature falls to 2.7°C under the complementary-mitigation-efforts scenario. As a result, the economic damages in developing Asian countries associated with these temperature

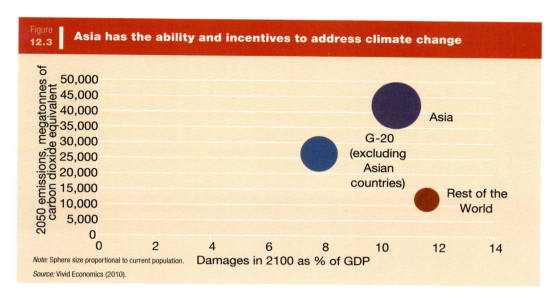

Figure 12.3 — Asia has the ability and incentives to address climate change

Note: Sphere size proportional to current population.
Source: Vivid Economics (2010).

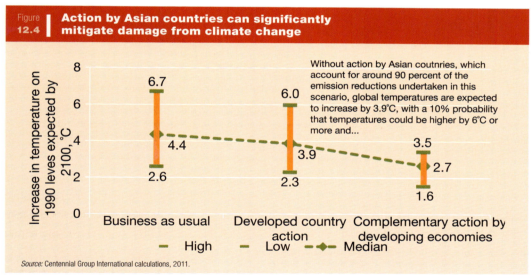

Figure 12.4 — Action by Asian countries can significantly mitigate damage from climate change

Without action by Asian coutnries, which account for around 90 percent of the emission reductions undertaken in this scenario, global temperatures are expected to increase by 3.9°C, with a 10% probability that temperatures could be higher by 6°C or more and...

Source: Centennial Group International calculations, 2011.

increases are significantly lower, although they are still not negligible. Annual economic losses in 2100 fall to between 1.7 percent and 3.6 percent of GDP. At the high end, this would be a reduction of more than 50 percent compared with the scenario where only Annex 1 countries take action. Figure 12.4 compares the increase in temperature depending on the action taken. They illustrate the importance of Asian action to diminish potentially serious economic damages.

The resulting lower temperature increases of complementary Asian action are expected to have a beneficial impact on agricultural yields for most Asian economies. In the case of India, Indonesia, and Republic of Korea, the potential decline in agricultural yields would be reduced significantly—by more than 5 percentage points in the latter two countries.

The rise in sea levels is also much lower in this scenario. Compared with a sea-level rise of 46 cm in the business-as-usual scenario and 41 cm when only developed countries take action, the increase when Asian countries also take concerted action is 32 cm. Thus, while action by developed countries alone only generates a reduction in rising sea levels of about 10 percent, when coupled with action by developing Asian countries a reduction of more than 30 percent is possible (Figure 12.5).

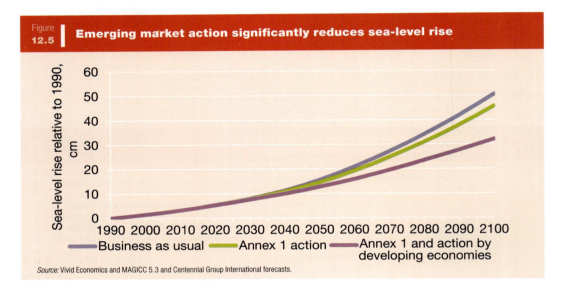

Figure 12.5 | Emerging market action significantly reduces sea-level rise

Source: Vivid Economics and MAGICC 5.3 and Centennial Group International forecasts.

In summary, the ability to mitigate the adverse effects of climate change—including economic damages and social disruption—is essentially in Asia's own hands. Asian economies should take aggressive steps to mitigate climate change not because the global community is asking them to do so but because it is in their own self-interest.

Transition to low-carbon economies

By making the transition to low-carbon economies, Asian countries can move toward a new technological paradigm. Such a transition offers greater energy security, healthier and more productive citizens, cleaner cities, more productive agriculture, and more efficient and competitive industry. Overall, it will make Asian economies more globally competitive and thus sustain the region's high growth rates over the long-term.

Fortunately, the larger Asian economies—Japan, Republic of Korea, and (more recently) PRC and India—are already pursuing the technological development and innovations necessary to promote green economies. Over the last 2–3 years, major Asian economies have accelerated their action on climate change and clean energy. PRC, for instance, is now one of the leading countries in the world in solar and wind, electric car, and even high-speed rail technologies. It is also the leading producer of solar photovoltaic cells, having gained market share from the US.

During the recent global financial and economic crisis, several developing countries in Asia led the world in terms of the percentage of economic stimulus devoted to green measures. The economic stimulus plans of Republic of Korea and PRC allocated 80 percent and 38 percent of their respective totals to investments consistent with stabilizing and then cutting emissions of greenhouse gases, a significantly greater share than either the US or individual European countries (HSBC, 2009).

In November 2009, Republic of Korea pledged to reduce its emissions by 4 percent below 2005 levels by 2020. In July 2010, it was reported that PRC would begin a domestic carbon trading program during its 12th Five-Year Plan (2011–2015) to help meet its target of reducing carbon intensity by 40–45 percent by 2020. Furthermore, in the same month, India imposed a domestic carbon tax in the form of a levy on coal producers, which is expected to raise approximately $535 million annually (Bloomberg Business Week, 2010). Despite their expressed reservations about a binding treaty at global negotiations in Copenhagen and Cancun, the major Asian economies—particularly PRC, India, Japan, and Republic of Korea—are moving ahead with improvements on their own.

Asia has a strong incentive to accelerate the race to a low-carbon global economy as it has the most to lose from a slow transition and the most to gain from a fast one. Waiting to take action will only increase the costs, especially if current capital investments are inconsistent with the requirements of a low-carbon world and have to be scrapped prematurely. Delays now will necessitate steeper annual reductions later in order to reach the same goal. For instance, if developing Asian economies started taking action in 2012 to bring emissions back to 2005 levels by 2050, they would have to achieve annual reductions in emissions of 0.4 percent per year. If they wait until 2030 before taking action, with the intention of reaching the same target by 2070, then average reductions of 1.5 percent per year would be required. Reductions of more than 1.0 percent per year are expected to be associated with prolonged economic recessions.

Developing economies in Asia and elsewhere are increasingly becoming locations for low-carbon innovation. Since 2000, low-carbon energy patenting activity has accelerated rapidly in the developing world (Figure 12.6).

Accelerating action could trigger a low-carbon race that Asia should win

In the EU, countries and firms are seeking leadership in a "race to compete" in the low-carbon

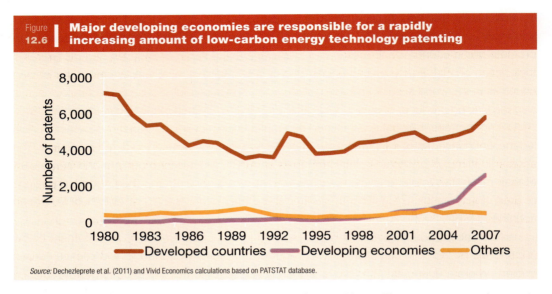

Figure 12.6 | Major developing economies are responsible for a rapidly increasing amount of low-carbon energy technology patenting

Source: Dechezleprete et al. (2011) and Vivid Economics calculations based on PATSTAT database.

world. In July 2010, a coalition of chief executive officers of large European companies wrote to support the ministers of the UK, Germany, and France in pushing for a 30 percent reduction in emissions by 2020. They argued that without such a target "Europe might lose the race to compete in the low carbon world to countries such as PRC, Japan, and the US."

In the US, the president has stated that the country must "win the clean energy race." And that "the nation that leads the clean energy economy will be the nation that leads the global economy. And America must be that nation" (White House, 2010). Yet to the disappointment of many, the US has not yet pass significant clean energy legislation. A large number of jobs are at stake as well. In the US alone, it is estimated that investments of $80 billion in clean energy under the Recovery Act will generate over 800,000 jobs.

As well as reducing the damage of climate change, the coordinated actions of developing countries in Asia could trigger Annex 1 countries to ramp up their emission reductions, providing larger markets for Asian low-carbon products. For instance, a recent HSBC report predicted that if governments went beyond the commitments they made during the runup to Copenhagen, by 2020 the low-carbon market could be worth as much as $2.7 trillion. The market would be 30 percent larger than it would be if governments simply kept to their Copenhagen commitments, and an impressive 100 percent larger than the low-carbon market in the business-as-usual scenario (HSBC, 2010).

In the past, eras of rapid technological progress in core industries such as energy generation have often driven major changes in the relative economic rankings of countries. For example, Great Britain leapfrogged the Netherlands as an economic power in the 18th century due to being a first mover in the industrial revolution. In the late 19th century, the US overtook it through the adoption of mass-market production technologies. Major Asian economies already have a strong base from which to seize clean energy opportunities as evident by the rapid increase in their low-carbon energy-system patenting activities. It is not surprising that US and EU firms are increasingly fearful of the consequences of their Asian counterparts winning the clean energy race.

Delaying action increases costs

A recent survey of the literature on cost estimates derived from a wide range of integrated assessment models concluded that the costs of meeting the goal of only a 2°C increase in average global temperatures between 1990 and 2100 (versus 4.4°C) are likely to be 1–5 percent of annual global GDP (Bowen and Ranger, 2009). There has been little research done on the specific costs for Asian economies. The goal of a 2°C increase is more ambitious than the scenarios that have been examined in this chapter, which implies that the costs associated with realizing the benefits discussed in this book might be toward the lower end of the 1–5 percent range. These cost estimates should be seen in the context of the possibility that the damages might be much worse than suggested by most modeling assessments. In this light, the costs can be seen as an insurance policy against the much more catastrophic damages.

Failure to accelerate transition for low-carbon innovation would also slow the rate of technical progress in green technologies and make the eventual switch to these technologies more costly (Acemoglu et al., 2010). Two recent studies suggest that if the countries were to begin taking rational steps today for a low-carbon economy they could save between 25 percent and 33 percent of the eventual costs of that transition (Bosetti et al., 2009; Blanford et al., 2009). Finally, as mentioned above, delayed action would also require steeper and potentially more disruptive annual reductions to reach the same goal.

Greater energy security

Many Asian economies are currently reliant on significant imports of fossil fuels to meet their energy needs. Six of the world's nine large developing countries[4] import more than 20 percent of their total energy needs and import more energy than they export. A dependency on imports for energy resources leads to concerns that energy supplies and prices may be vulnerable to uncontrollable events or political pressures in the exporting country (or both).

Exploiting low-carbon energy sources offers the opportunity to reduce reliance on imported energy. The uneven geographic distribution of fossil fuel resources provides a relatively small number of countries with control of much of the world's current energy supply. By contrast, the wide variety of low-carbon energy technologies—solar, wind, hydro, nuclear, biomass, geothermal—can provide much greater scope for domestic energy supply, depending of course on the

---
4 Argentina, Brazil, PRC, India, Republic of Korea, and Turkey.

conditions in each country.

Healthier, more productive, and more efficient societies

The investments needed to achieve a low-carbon transition will help make Asian societies cleaner, healthier, and more productive.

Improved air quality. As well as carbon dioxide, fossil fuel combustion releases air pollutants—such as particulate matter, sulphur dioxide, and nitrogen dioxide—that are damaging to human health. These contribute to a range of cardiovascular and respiratory diseases, including lung cancer, bronchitis, and asthma. Particulate matter—small inhalable particles that can penetrate deep into the lungs—is particularly problematic.

Asia is home to nine out of 10 of the world's cities with the worst air pollution (Table 12.2). These Asian cities, with a combined population of over 50 million, have annual mean concentrations of PM_{10} that are five to eight times the WHO guideline level of 20 micrograms per cubic meter.[5]

Table 12.2 | Nine of the ten cities with the worst air pollution (particulate matter) are in Asia

City	PM_{10} concentration (micrograms per m³)	Population (thousands)
Cairo, Egypt	169	7,764,000
Delhi, India	150	12,100,000
Kolkata, India	128	5,100,000
Tianjin, PRC	125	7,500,000
Chongqing, PRC	123	5,087,000
Kanpur, India	109	3,100,000
Lucknow, India	109	2,342,000
Jakarta, Indonesia	104	10,100,000
Shenyang, PRC	101	5,090,000
Zhengzhou, PRC	97	2,600,000

Source: World Bank (2007) World Development Indicators (Table 3.13), City Mayors statistics. Bold indicates cities in G20 Emerging Markets (GEM) countries.

Over half the PRC's urban population lives in cities with PM_{10} concentrations over five times the WHO guideline level. According to World Bank (2007) estimates, this level of exposure to PM_{10} and other pollutants leads to approximately 270,000 cases of chronic bronchitis and 400,000 hospital admissions from respiratory or cardiovascular disease each year in PRC, as well the

---

5 PM_{10} refers to particulate matter of 10 microns or less in size.

premature deaths of 13 percent of PRC's urban population. The total cost of air pollution in PRC is estimated to be 1.2–3.8 percent of GDP.[6]

The health benefits of reducing greenhouse gas emissions are considerable, substantially offsetting the costs of abatement. In the most polluted cities, including the health benefits of pollution reduction in the cost–benefit analysis of many carbon emission–reduction projects would make them cost beneficial. In PRC, O'Connor et al. (2003) estimate that a tax that reduced emissions by 15 percent would yield health benefits of 0.14 percent of GDP, offsetting two-thirds of the loss in consumption from the tax.[7] Combined with further benefits from increased agricultural productivity, these benefits have the potential to completely offset losses in consumption resulting from mitigation policies.

Increased agricultural productivity. Fossil fuel combustion leads to the formation of low-level ozone that damages crop yields by reducing photosynthesis activity and growth in plants. This is already affecting yields worldwide. On the basis of current air quality and trends in air pollution, an additional $6 billion–$10 billion in crop yield losses per year is expected in India and PRC by 2030 (Van Dingenen et al., 2009). Some of these losses could be avoided through mitigation action.

In PRC, it is estimated that a 15 percent reduction in carbon dioxide emissions would increase the national output of rice by 0.29 percent and wheat by 0.68 percent (O'Connor et al., 2003). In monetary terms, the overall benefit of increased crop productivity in PRC is placed at 0.1 percent of GDP. In conjunction with the health benefits reported above, this would more than offset the consumption losses caused by the tax needed to reduce emissions. Further, this analysis does not include damage to crops through acid rain, which can also be significant. The World Bank (2007) estimated the economic cost of reduced crop yields due to acid rain in PRC at $3.6 billion (2003 prices) per year.

Increased efficiency. Mitigation action can improve overall economic efficiency and save money over time, boosting GDP. Energy efficiency improves competitiveness, and the use of waste methane to generate electricity can also lower costs. Such opportunities have not always been exploited because of market failures, including information gaps, savings accruing to parties other than those who bear the cost (as can be the case with property development) and improperly functioning capital markets.

Annual savings through such low-cost mitigation measures could be greater than $100 billion (2008 prices) per year by 2030. Table 12.3 shows the estimates of potential savings in PRC and Indonesia.

Although these opportunities are unlikely by themselves to completely offset the overall costs of undertaking a low-carbon transition, they are another beneficial side effect and illustrate

---

6 Depending on whether measured in terms of adjusted forgone earnings (the lower measure) or willingness to pay to avoid (the higher measure).
7 Assuming that the tax revenues are recycled.

Table 12.3 | **Substantial abatement opportunities that reduce costs are available**

Country	Metric	Value of savings ($ billion)	% of current GDP	Annual emissions savings in year shown, megatonnes of carbon dioxide equivalent
PRC	Annual benefit in 2030	53.5	1.2	~1900
Indonesia	Annual benefit in 2020	1.9	0.4	~180

Source: PRC, McKinsey (2009) and (2009); Indonesia, ADB (2009). All figures are in $2008.

the value of a sensible policy of extracting short-term benefits in the transition to low carbon economies.

Adaptation and risk management

In addition to mitigating measures, Asian economies must also take urgent steps to adapt to climate change and manage its risks. It is hoped that the mitigation measures will prevent dangerous increases in the average global temperature, but a rise still appears inevitable because of the past buildup of carbon emissions and the time needed for proposed measures to have an impact. Climate change policies must consider mitigation and adaptation measures as complementary. To the extent possible, they should seek to create synergies between them (ADB, 2009a and 2010a).

Adaptation to reduce vulnerability. Many Asian countries are particularly vulnerable to climate-related natural disasters, having long experienced a disproportionate share of global floods with high fatalities and economic damage. Large segments of the populations of South Asia, Southeast Asia, East Asia, and the Pacific live in low-lying coastal areas, river deltas, or floodplains. These areas are particularly prone to frequent and severe floods. Future climate change will cause more intense typhoons, coastal floods, droughts, heat waves, desert (dust) storms, and landslides. It will also enhance the risks from a variety of geophysical hazards such as volcanic eruptions, earthquakes, fires, landslides, and tsunamis. Countries must find ways to reduce the vulnerability of people and economic assets to such risks.

Adaptation in development planning. Policy makers need to dramatically increase efforts to adapt their development strategies and programs to the impacts of climate change. They should apply precautionary principles and invest in climate proofing of both hard and soft infrastructure. Policy makers should also consider introducing cost-saving, climate-proofing measures to minimize the adverse impacts on people and economic assets.

High priority should be given to investments in adaptation measures through sustained land

and water management; reduced risks of land degradation; and improved infrastructure to prevent damage from, for example, increased flooding, drought, and dust storms (Table 12.4).

Disaster risk reduction and management. Countries can reduce climate-related risks by developing and periodically updating systematic risk management plans to minimize the economic impact of and vulnerability to climate change disasters. Disaster risk reduction and management programs should be given the highest priority in all national climate change adaptation plans.

Increasing resilience of sector strategies and projects. The sectors most vulnerable to the impact of climate change are agriculture and natural resources; urban development; water supply and sanitation; transport, particularly coastal roads, interisland ferries, and ports; and energy, including hydro. Sector plans, key projects, and other country-specific activities must be reviewed carefully and adjusted to incorporate climate change disaster risk assessment and management considerations.

Climate change resilience in agriculture. Climate change will necessitate shifts in crop production and land management techniques in many Asian countries, and will require major changes in water use. There is an urgent need to develop both country-level and regional knowledge on the links between climate change, water availability and management, the impact on crop yields, and dry land management. In many countries efforts need to be initiated to search for more climate-resistant seeds and cropping patterns. Agricultural research needs to be disseminated to farmers (particularly small farmers) quickly through effective extension services and other means of education.

Disaster risk finance. Countries can reduce climate-related risks by developing systematic disaster risk management plans that incorporate innovative risk financing instruments and techniques. Experience in developed countries has shown that disaster risk finance can play a pivotal role in developing active risk management capacity to reduce the economic impact of and vulnerability to climate-related disasters. Financing instruments can provide disaster risk reduction capability, emergency credit or liquidity, and access to external risk transfer markets, including reinsurance.

Global burden sharing

By taking proactive actions to mitigate climate change, major Asian countries can also demonstrate that they are willing and able to play a constructive role in tackling this pressing common global challenge. And they would be doing so even though some emerging markets' opinion makers believe that their economic growth may suffer in the short term. At the same time, it is important that developed economies participate in equitable global burden sharing in addressing the current stock of carbon emissions that was generated mainly by them, in reducing future emissions, and in providing technological and financial assistance to developing nations.

Table 12.4 Climate change adaptation types and examples by sector

Sector	Type and category of adaptation	Example of adaptation options
Agriculture	Share the loss	Crop insurance
	Prevent the loss (structural, technological)	Investment in new capital
	Prevent the loss (market-based)	Removal of market distortions (e.g., water pricing) Liberalization of agricultural trade to buffer regionalized losses
	Change use	Change crops, promote crop diversification After planting dates
	Research	Development of heat- and drought-resistant crops
Coastal zones	Prevent the loss (structural, technological)	Coastal defenses and sea walls Surge barriers Upgrade drainage systems, salt-water intrusion barriers
	Prevent the loss (on-site operations)	Sediment management Beach nourishment Habitat protection (e.g., wetlands, mangroves)
	Prevent the loss (institutional, administrative)	Land use planning
Water	Prevent the loss (structural, technological)	Loss reduction (leakage, control, conservation, plumbing Capacity increase (new reservoirs, desalination facilities)
	Prevent the loss (institutional, administrative)	Water allocation (e.g., municipal versus agricultural) Risk management to deal with rainfall variability
	Prevent the loss (market-based)	Water permits Water pricing
	Education and behavioral	Rational water use Rainwater collection
Health	Prevent the loss (structural, technological)	Air-conditioning Building standards
	Prevent the loss (institutional, administrative)	Improvement in public health Vector-control programs Disease eradication programs
	Research	Research and development on vector control Vaccines Disease eradication

Source: OECD (2009).

Transforming Governance and Institutions

Chapter 13

Shigeo Katsu

This chapter discusses the greatest challenge Asia faces in its endeavors to realize the Asian Century: the transformation of governance and institutions.[1] The chapter presents an analytic framework to assess the current state of governance and institutions and the changes within them over time. It compares various governance indicators of Asian economies with other emerging countries and outlines the key drivers for change (demographics, urbanization, and an expanding middle class combined with the communications revolution). It concludes by identifying key actions of institutional change and discusses principles and priorities for transforming governance throughout Asia.

Analytic framework

It is essential for all Asian countries to focus on improving governance and to transform institutions in order to meet the challenges of the coming decades. There is a clear message from the research on governance for development: bad governance has a disproportionately high negative impact on the poor and institutions matter for growth and poverty reduction (Box 13.1).

The recent deterioration in the quality and credibility of national political and economic institutions in many Asian countries is a source of concern and a reason why Asia's rise should not be seen as preordained.

Transparency, predictability, and accountability are elements that establish the long-term domestic legitimacy of authorities. They make governance and institutional dimensions, even over a 40-year time horizon, a good foundation to discuss the broad direction of Asia. The wide range of issues and their multifaceted aspects require that one should look for a wide variety of indicators in measuring governance—even if there are obvious uncertainties associated with a 40-year

---

[1] For this book, governance is defined as the exercise of power/authority in the management of a country's economic and social resources. This exercise is reflected in incentive structures, legal and regulatory frameworks, policy, political, and institutional frameworks, institutional capacity, and transparency and accountability dimensions. Governance is embedded in the political culture and collective perceptions of the citizenry. Institutions are defined as sets of "rules of the game" (laws, formal processes, systems), including the locus of exercising those rules. Regulations, in turn, are defined as expressions of formal processes ("rules") meant to guide the implementation of authorities' intent. Although regulations can be changed quickly (e.g., 1 to 3 years), institutional changes and development need to be assessed over a 10 to 15-year span at least. Governance evolves incrementally over a long time horizon (decades) unless exposed to sudden and fundamental disruptions such as revolutions and armed conflict.

Box 13.1 | Evidence of the impact of governance on development outcomes

An overview of governance for development presents a mixed picture, and shows that governance reforms have not always resulted in the improvements expected in development outcomes and poverty reduction. It is often argued that this is because the success of governance reforms depends on political factors. Other clear messages from the research are that bad governance impacts negatively on the poor and that institutions matter for growth and poverty reduction (Earle and Scott, 2010).

Democratization: Democratic states are neither the best nor the worst performers when it comes to economic performance and poverty reduction, and there is evidence that shows that democratic systems prevent the worst humanitarian crises from occurring. Over long timeframes, it would seem that consolidated democratic regimes enjoy higher quality governance, are able to promote greater levels of economic growth, and institute social policies to help the poor.

Justice and rule of law: The literature widely acknowledges the negative impact on the poor when the rule of law is weak, in particular regarding inadequate property rights and dispute resolution mechanisms. There are some positive case studies of attempts to improve poor peoples' access to justice that may suggest that this approach can be a means of reducing poverty.

Corruption: To date, very little empirical evidence has been generated on the impact of anti-corruption initiatives on poverty levels, or on development in general. The main focus in the literature is on the link between corruption and economic growth, where the impact on poverty reduction is implicit or indirect.

Decentralization: There is a wealth of material that argues that decentralization can have a very positive effect on development by improving state efficiency, responsiveness, accountability and citizen voice. However, little robust empirical research supports these claims and many academic studies consider the overall developmental impact of decentralization to be negative.

Public administration reform: There is general consensus in the donor and academic literature that there is a strong link between improvements in the efficiency and accountability of public institutions and development outcomes. However, the potential of reform has not always been realized because of contextual factors and poor design of interventions.

Public financial management (PFM): Improved public financial management is important if countries are to reach their developmental goals. However, the impact of PFM on poverty ultimately depends on the quality and focus of government objectives and the policies themselves. The link between PFM and development is therefore often posited intuitively, rather than on the basis of empirical evidence.

period. The conceptual complexities require that the use of different indicators to measure the transformation of institutions.

Table 13.1 provides a framework to identify entry points to stimulate governance and institutional changes, together with related principles. The framework combined with the drivers for governance changes (see below) point to likely directions for Asia over the coming decades. However, Asian policy makers cannot rely on "international best practice" but rather have to seek

Table 13.1 Analytic framework for governance and institutions

The issue	Actors and instruments	Good principles	Bad principles
Who leads the public sector?	Government through economic and social policies	• Growth-oriented • Inclusive • Oriented toward sustainable development • Accountable	• Lack of clarity of direction • Exclusive • Rent-seeking oriented • Not accountable
How are policies applied?	Through a clear legal, institutional, and regulatory framework and related agencies	• Rule-based • Equitable (law applies equally to everybody) • Accountable	• Ad hoc • Selective, captured • Not accountable
How are policies implemented?	Through/by the civil service and other service providers	• Competent • Merit-based, competitive • Efficient • Accountable	• Incompetent • Nepotism-based and/or captured • Inefficient • Not accountable
How are resources allocated?	Through the budget process	• Transparent • Competitive • Accountable	• Nontransparent • Arbitrary and/or interest-group oriented • Captured
How are public oversight functions carried out?	Through multiple actors: • Parliament • Media • Civil society • NGOs	• Accountable • Demand for public accountability • Access to information	• Ineffective • Laden with conflict of interest • Captured
Are there redress mechanisms?	Through sundry appeals and conflict-resolution systems (e.g. ombudsmen)	Yes	No

the "best fit" for their specific national circumstances. They must ultimately decide on a model, or combination of models, for those institutional changes that are most likely to lead to improved performance in the specific context of each country.

The past 40 years

Over the last 40 years Asia has generated many headlines involving international development.

From the 1960s through the 1980s Japan led Asia in the quest for prosperity. Then it hit a huge pothole when the asset bubble burst in the 1990s. Japan grew to become the second-largest national economy in the world, a position it held until early 2011. Japan invested wisely in its institutions, and created a blueprint that was followed with some adjustments by the cohort of the NIEs of Hong Kong, China; Republic of Korea; Singapore; and Taipei,China. Some of the more important institutional reforms Japan introduced were to switch from growth at all costs to sustainable growth by giving attention to the environment, prompted by several high-profile cases of industrial pollution; to focus on industrial innovation accompanied by establishing clear intellectual property rights; and to ensure more stringent competition policies for the tradable sector. The finance sector was geared to support export-oriented manufacturing, to finance energy and raw material imports, and to strengthen infrastructure. While very efficient in the development phase, the structure of the finance sector was late in adjusting to structural changes in a rapidly maturing economy, and facilitated the buildup of the asset bubble. The 1990s saw substantial changes in corporate governance—unbundling of the "related-company" (*keiretsu*) system. The Japanese government skillfully used external pressure (mainly from the US) to induce domestic reforms in areas it considered in need of change. Furthermore, Japan developed a structured approach to official development assistance, for a part of the 1990s, and became the largest donor in the world. The post-bubble 1990s and first decade of this century have seen Japan struggling to escape a deflationary cycle and institutional and political stagnation in the public sector.

The NIEs rapidly followed Japan's footsteps: they climbed the technology ladder, developed knowledge economies, and sustained a broad range of institutional reforms that allowed them to avoid the Middle Income Trap. Notable institutional reforms were as follows:

- Hong Kong, China's path-breaking anticorruption initiative in the mid-1980s succeeded in tackling police and other civil service corruption. This helped cement it as a preferred destination for foreign investment in Asia and confirmed the economy's foundation as the most liberal in Asia;
- Republic of Korea's relentless drive to catch up with Japan helped develop world-class brands in car manufacturing, electronics, and engineering, and create the most "wired" society in the world while establishing a strong democratic tradition;
- Singapore's unique brand of meritocracy-based public and economic management structure and its open-economy stance, coupled with visionary and disciplined decision

making and political authoritarianism, allowed the country to take full advantage of its geographic location; and
- Taipei, China's fostering of entrepreneurship and innovation facilitated the economy's transformation into a technological powerhouse.

Initially, some 40 years ago ASEAN was formed by five countries; today it has grown to encompass 10. Motivated by a shared desire for economic development, peace, and stability in a turbulent environment, the members cultivated what is commonly referred to as the "ASEAN way". It is characterized by principles of non-interference, informality, consultation and consensus, minimal institutionalization, and non-use of force and confrontation. These principles have served the organization well in establishing the ASEAN Free Trade Area in the 1990s and in designing the next step toward an ASEAN Economic Community. However, in reaching outside ASEAN to establish structured economic, financial, and political relations with the "Plus Three" (PRC, Japan, and Republic of Korea), these principles will likely be put to the test when many of the formal arrangements need to be implemented. With a view toward avoiding the Middle Income Trap, it will be important to avoid implementation arrangements that are characterized by the lowest common denominator. Among the five founding members of ASEAN, two, namely Indonesia and Malaysia, for the most part modernized economic governance and institutions and overcame the crisis of the late 1990s.

Twenty years ago, on the dissolution of the Soviet Union, Central Asia started its reintegration with the rest of the world. The newly independent countries opted for a variety of economic regimes. These ranged from early reformers that introduced market-oriented economic practices—such as Kazakhstan, and the Kyrgyz Republic, as well as Mongolia (although it was not part of the former Soviet Union)—to late reformers such as Turkmenistan and Uzbekistan, which resisted fundamental reforms in the 1990s and thus largely avoided the so-called transition recession, though they still exhibit features typical of command economies. A common feature of most Central Asian economies is that they are largely resource driven, creating additional governance and institutional challenges to diversify the economy and to assure balanced development. Governance surveys have consistently placed them in the lowest ranks in Asia.

In contrast, parts of Asia moved in the direction opposite from prosperity, peace, and stability: some fell into the category of fragile or postconflict states (or both). While circumstances differ among countries, most of the fragile states have experienced long debilitating internal conflict and strife. Afghanistan may be the most prominent case. Myanmar and the Democratic People's Republic of Korea come to mind as well. Indeed, an "arc of instability" stretches from West, Central, and South Asia all through parts of Southeast Asia.

The most compelling development in recent decades has been the rise of the two Asian giants, PRC and India. Since launching its first rural reforms in 1978, PRC has recorded average annual growth of almost 10 percent over the last three decades and reduced absolute poverty (using the $1-a-day threshold) from 75 percent in the 1970s to 15 percent. PRC's gradualist approach of building a "socialist market economy with Chinese characteristics," centered on experimentation, learning, and scaling up, and avoiding overly risky initiatives. And once a decision was taken, implementation was swift. Above all, PRC's leadership has exhibited unremitting commitment, recognizing that development is a long-term process of dynamic and continuous change. Today PRC has become the largest industrial producer and the second-largest economy in the world. Along the way, it has developed and refined its economic and social institutions, nurtured a rapidly expanding middle class that demands increased personal liberties and greater trust between the state and its citizens. The resolution of this emerging tension will shape the future direction of the country. Internationally, PRC heads the phalanx of emerging economies that will drive the future global economy and it is increasingly moving from being a price taker to a price setter.

India embarked on full-fledged economic reforms in the early 1990s having followed decades of import-substitution strategies characterized by what the Commission on Growth and Development termed "an economy where the existing institutions of a capitalist society were put to the service of the goals of a planned economy" (El-Arian and Spence, 2008). Since then India has recorded average annual growth of over 7 percent and appears poised to follow PRC's growth path with a lag of some 10 years. India's demographic, linguistic, and ethnic diversity and its complexity as a democracy, demanded different approaches to foster societal consensus and to develop workable decision making, but the core aspects of experimentation and learning are similar to those in PRC.[2]

Therein lies perhaps the most significant lesson from the rise of these two Asian giants— namely the importance of adapting development and growth models to country circumstances, of experimenting under uncertainties, and learning from both those outcomes and from experiences elsewhere—not a "best practice" but "best fit" approach—and the essential role of a visionary and committed leadership.

Asia's diversity is striking, as we have seen in the sketches. This diversity is also confirmed in studies such as Transparency International's annual surveys over the last decade. The 2010 Corruption Perceptions Index places three Asian countries or territories in the top 20 as in the past, plus an additional four in the top quarter of all countries surveyed (a total of 178), eight more in the next quartile, 13 in the third quartile, and 13 in the bottom quartile. If one accepts corruption perceptions as a derivative of good or weak governance, most of the economies placed in the top half have seen a rapid expansion of the middle class (discussed later in this chapter).

Governance challenges in Asia today

There is no shortage of published indicators that track the governance and institutional

---

2 For a more thorough discussion on PRC and India's growth performance see M. A. El-Arian. and M. Spence (2008).

evolution of countries over time. Although survey methodologies, sources, and scope differ, the overall picture points in one direction. The 2009 Worldwide Governance Indicators published by the World Bank Institute consist of a composite of six core dimensions: voice (of people) and accountability (of government); political stability/absence of violence; government effectiveness; regulatory quality; rule of law; and control of corruption. Simply averaging the scores of Asian economies does not indicate any major changes between 1998 and 2009; there was slight deterioration in the voice and accountability component, but a slight improvement in political stability. Weighting the country scores by GDP reveals quite a different picture: the overall scores improve dramatically, reflecting the weight of the Asia-7, especially in areas of government effectiveness, regulatory quality, and rule of law; however, they are also accompanied by a drop in the scores for voice and accountability and political stability (Figure 13.1).

A comparison of the 2009 results between Asia-7 and the rest of Asia, weighted by GDP, shows that Asia-7 outscores the rest of Asia consistently, with once again the best scores for

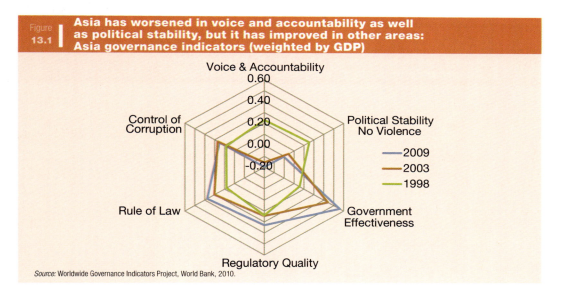

Figure 13.1 | Asia has worsened in voice and accountability as well as political stability, but it has improved in other areas: Asia governance indicators (weighted by GDP)

Source: Worldwide Governance Indicators Project, World Bank, 2010.

government effectiveness, followed by regulatory quality and rule of law. The scores themselves are also strong, especially when compared to the indicators weighted by population (Figures 13.2 and 13.3). They point to remaining differences between the advanced economies of Asia (which have large GDPs but modest population size) and the two emerging giants.

The same Asia-7 group over time, however, shows a mixed picture: while government effectiveness and regulatory quality have improved substantially, the other dimensions show little progress. It is disappointing that even the Asia-7 do not fare well vis-à-vis the rest of the world in

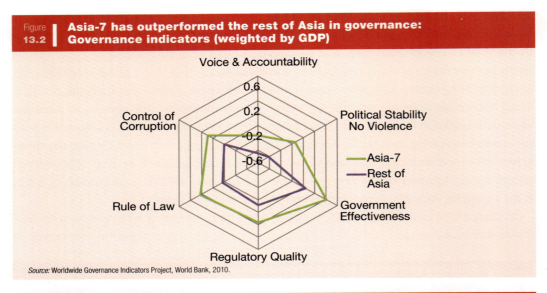

Figure 13.2 Asia-7 has outperformed the rest of Asia in governance: Governance indicators (weighted by GDP)

Source: Worldwide Governance Indicators Project, World Bank, 2010.

Figure 13.3 Asia-7 has outperformed the rest of Asia in governance: Governance indicators (weighted by population)

Source: Worldwide Governance Indicators Project, World Bank, 2010.

any of the dimensions (Figure 13.4). The remaining economies—mainly non-converging low and lower-middle-income—are worse than both Asia-7 and developing countries in other regions. In other words, the governance performance of countries parallels the three tiers of countries used in this book in discussing economic performance.

Specifically on the dimension of controlling corruption, the regional differences within Asia are informative, particularly when weighted by GDP. The correlation between economic development

Figure 13.4 | Asia-7 has lagged behind the rest of the world in governance: Governance indicators (weighted by GDP)

Source: Worldwide Governance Indicators Project, World Bank, 2010.

and control over corruption clearly emerges (Kaufmann et al., 2006).[3] Yet again when compared with the rest of the world, even weighted by GDP, Asia and the Asia-7 lag by a significant margin, although the gap is slowly closing (Figures 13.5 and 13.6).

Figure 13.5 | Northeast Asia outperforms other subregions in control of corruption

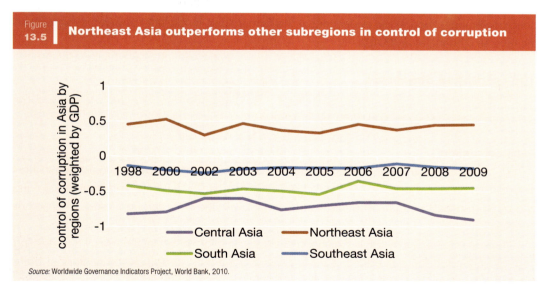

Source: Worldwide Governance Indicators Project, World Bank, 2010.

---

3 The authors state that "Studies have shown that a one standard-deviation increase in corruption lowers investment rates by three percentage points and lowers average annual growth by about one percentage point." (p. 5).

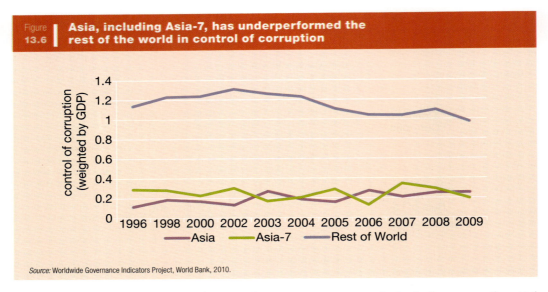

Figure 13.6 | Asia, including Asia-7, has underperformed the rest of the world in control of corruption

Source: Worldwide Governance Indicators Project, World Bank, 2010.

The quest to understand the impact of governance on growth, including corruption and institutional quality, has spawned many theoretical and empirical studies as well as numerous surveys (Zhuang et al., 2010; ADB, 2010; Acemoglu et al., 2001).[4] The correlation between governance and institutions on the one hand, and growth and income over time on the other, has been confirmed, although the evidence that the former flows to the latter appears stronger than the reverse (Zhuang et al., 2010).

The corruption dimension

While establishing a universally accepted definition of corruption has proven difficult, broad agreement exists on basic features and forms (Box 13.2).

Petty corruption

In Asia as anywhere else one encounters what is referred to as petty, mostly administrative, corruption where bribery is expected and paid in order to "facilitate" registration, permits, and other transactions that bring citizens in contact with the state through the civil service or bureaucracy.

While one has to be mindful of differing cultural and informal societal norms when defining corrupt behaviour, there is evidence that rising incomes tend to reduce the sectors of petty corruption, concentrating them in specific areas such as law enforcement and tax administration. There is evidence that a combination of more competitive recruitment and retention of civil

---

[4] Acemoglu et al. conclude that if Nigeria were to improve its institutional quality to match Chile, it would attain a sevenfold increase in per capita incomes.

> **Box 13.2 | What is corruption?**
>
> "Corruption is abuse of public office for personal gain or actions causing transfer of public money to private hands, in violation of rules. It entails acts of omission, commission or illegality. Some kinds of corruption go on even within the framework of laws appearing as lawful acts. Procedural correctness in administration does not preclude the possibility of corruption. Similarly the deficiencies in procedures or lapses in formalities alone cannot be inferred as actions falling within the ambit of corruption. Corruption occurs even as part of policy formulation aimed at benefiting some interest groups without violating any statue, rule or regulation" (K. Rajasekharan, 2011, p. 1).

servants, more attractive public sector remuneration, a culture of meritocracy, a reduction in the arbitrary authority of bureaucrats, and stricter penalties serve as effective measures to mitigate petty corruption. To be sure, the issue is that toleration of petty corruption as a cultural phenomenon is a slippery slope that may lead to grand corruption.

Grand corruption

What raises the stakes significantly is what is often referred to as "grand corruption", where the value of transactions and rents grows and more sophisticated and prearranged acts of graft are demanded. Traditionally, grand corruption generally took the form of bribery to influence implementation of government policies and decisions related to high-value procurement or industry regulations.[5] Typical mitigation measures include bureaucratic accountability and transparency (e.g., publication of procurement decisions), regulatory oversight that is predictable and enforceable, and avoidance of conflict of interest.

State Capture

In recent decades, the spotlight has been shone more intently on a different type of grand corruption, namely state capture. This term became more popular in the context of the reform process of transition economies. It refers to oligarchic interests that manipulate policy formulation for their own substantial but narrow interests, i.e., when firms try to put their imprint on laws, and regulations to the exclusion of others through bribes. This form of corruption connects not only bureaucrats with the captor firms seeking illicit gains, but politicians. It is quite telling that in recent surveys, such as AsiaBarometer, in most countries politicians and political parties are seen as the most corrupt actors.

State capture leads to countries being stuck with partial reforms as subsequent reform

---

[5] Not all corruption is illegal but may reflect a time-honored "way of doing business" that often goes unquestioned until a crisis erupts. A good example is regulatory collusion between oversight agencies and firms they regulate facilitated by the exchange of senior officials.

efforts are blocked by the collusion of anticompetitive forces. This particularly corrosive form of rent seeking entices talent to engage in state capture activities, by rewarding connections not competence and influence not innovation. State capture is not only a symptom of a weak state, but also becomes the root cause of bad governance (Hellman and Kaufman, 2001).[6]

> **Box 13.3 | Corruption and impact on the poor**
>
> Empirical studies have shown that those hit hardest by corruption are the poorest, whether because they have to pay more in relative terms or because they cannot afford to buy protection from law enforcement. Often they are priced out from education and health providers, as they cannot afford the additional under-the-table payments demanded, or they are disenfranchised in the political deliberation process. Chapter 7 warned of growing inequality, the lack of inclusive growth strategies, and persistence of poverty in Asia. Add to this mix poor governance and weak institutions, and the challenges that Asian policy makers face as they aspire to lead their countries to prosperity come into even starker relief.

Militating state capture is particularly difficult as a corrupt alignment of powerful politicians and firms amounts to a formidable barrier for change. General mitigation recipes are well known, but national circumstances dictate how true reformers can push for improvements, for example by aligning themselves with stakeholders such as firms that seek entry, but are currently shut out, by giving voice to the disenfranchised poor and civil society organizations, and by making use of international pressure (Box 13.3). An expanding middle class with its increasing demands and will be a powerful factor for reforms.

The Worldwide Governance Indicators and similar surveys provide the following observations:
- In Asia as a whole, progress in governance indicators from 1998 to 2009 has been disappointing with the exception of government effectiveness, and more modestly, regulatory quality and rule of law, but there has been a clear retreat in voice and accountability as well as political stability.
- The Asia-7 fare better, but even so, they perform worse than the rest of the world in all dimensions. Unless these shortcomings are addressed, Asia can hardly call itself the leading region of the world.
- Particularly for controlling corruption, the "governance deficit" relative to the rest of the world is worrisome. Together with the shortfall in rule of law and in voice and accountability, this key institutional deficit may hinder many Asian countries from overcoming the Middle Income Trap.
- Yet in today's Asia the "C" word is now acknowledged by virtually all governments as a

---

6 The authors provide a succinct analysis of state capture.

societal cancer and serious constraint to improving institutional quality. This is a welcome development, since addressing it begins with acknowledging it through discussion by all stakeholders.

The point of the above is that the quality of institutions will be decisive in enabling fast-growing countries to avoid the Middle Income Trap, and slower-growing countries to establish the basic conditions to move toward sustained rapid growth, social inclusion, the Millennium Development Goals, and political maturity.

Managing the challenges common to Asia, be they rapid urbanization, building a fundamentally sound finance sector, or fostering entrepreneurship and innovation, requires effective governance that reflects principles of accountability and subsidiarity at both central and local government levels.

Drivers for change in governance and institutions

As elsewhere, the pressure to change governance and institutions in Asia comes from the domestic rather than the external front. Three drivers—demographics, urbanization, and the demands stemming from an expanding middle class combined with the communications revolution—will undoubtedly become the game changers over the next 40 years.

Demographics

The first driver for change derives from the demographic outlook for the region (see Appendix 1 for more detail). Broadly, Asia can be divided into three groups:

- Countries with rapidly aging societies, mainly in Northeast Asia where the demographic window has already closed or is about to close: Japan; Republic of Korea; PRC (with a slight lag); and Taipei,China; Singapore; and Thailand. By 2050, more than 40 percent of Japanese and Koreans will be over 65—already 20 percent of Japanese are over 60, as are some 12 to 15 percent of the populations of PRC and Republic of Korea. By 2050, Japan's population will have shrunk by 30 percent. Republic of Korea's population is projected to decline by almost 9 percent; however, the working age population is likely to drop by 36 percent while the population over 60 years old is to grow by 150 percent. PRC's working age population will start to decline starting in 2015, trailing Japan's demographic decline by roughly 20 years.
- Countries (several in ASEAN) with a robust demographic balance between working age populations, elders and minors. These can still benefit from their demographic window for another decade or two.
- Countries with a very large proportion of young people, whose demographic windows will remain wide open for several decades. This group includes some of the poorest and most fragile countries, many of them in South Asia and Central Asia.

Table 13.2 provides an overview of these demographic trends, using working age population as an important indicator of demographic windows and potential dividends. The crucial question is how these contrasts will play out in the decades to come.

Table 13.2 **Working age population (%)**

	2010	2020	2030	2040	2050
Aging Asia	64	63	60	57	55
"Robust" Asia	58	60	60	59	58
"Young" Asia	54	57	60	62	61

Source: UN Statistics Division, 2011.

Aging societies

Countries with aging populations will carry a growing constituency which is inherently conservative on substantive economic and political reform issues and feels strongly about having earned the right to be looked after, in terms of health care and pensions.[7]

These demographic trends will not only translate into new, more modest economic realities, but also into different intergenerational expectations and relations. Older people are more conservative and more resistant to change. They prefer stability and certainty. These factors, in turn, will impact all aspects of governance and require wide-ranging institutional adjustments. Yet the demands of an aging population will raise fiscal affordability and sustainability issues, and thus their demands are not automatically certain to be met.

Aging societies will have to adjust economic structures, institutions, and policies to take account of the increasing number of elderly. Labor-intensive industries will disappear as the labor force shrinks.

Technology and innovation will have to be relied on more and more to replace labor (in manufacturing as well as in services). Health care (including long-term care) and related regulations will have to be adjusted to the special needs of the elderly, and the looming shortfall in health care workers will have to be covered by opening labor markets (Japan is a noteworthy example). Pension and social security payments will increasingly crowd out whatever fiscal space exists. Local administrations will have to develop "elderly" oriented service windows, and the adoption of more active population policies is likely.

A particular challenge for the aging countries in Northeast Asia (PRC, Japan, and Republic of

---

[7] The current and forthcoming aging generation in Japan pride themselves on having rebuilt the country from the ashes of WW II. The same age cohorts in Republic of Korea; Singapore; and Taipei,China designed, implemented, or supervised the transformation into the "Asian tigers," and similar age groups in PRC have been at the center of the most massive transformation in history from a backward, centrally planned, largely rural nation, to the second largest economy in the world.

Korea) is that there are no historical precedents. This shared challenge may yet open opportunities for cooperation such as peer learning from one another and from aging societies in Europe.

"Young and robust" societies

"Young" countries in a positive scenario will increase the size of their economic pie, and over time will improve public services, in a manner similar to today's OECD and other advanced Asian economies. On the governance front, the pressure will be on the authorities to deliver economic growth, to raise living standards, to create jobs, and to ensure the public's desire for legitimacy.

These pressures take on contrasting dimensions across different groups of countries:

- For the converging economies (e.g., India, many ASEAN countries), it means ensuring the smooth expansion of the middle class, remaining competitive and moving up the innovation and technology ladder, and focusing on productivity gains in order to avoid the Middle Income Trap. Investments in people through quality education at all levels will play an important role.
- For the fragile states (notably Afghanistan, but also some Central Asian and Pacific island states), it means rebuilding the authority of the state, coping with the threat of religious extremism and the radicalization of the young, and managing the risk of social unrest. Furthermore, these countries are also undergoing rapid urbanization—at low income levels—which represents additional challenges for urban management.

When economic development is fostered, the implications for economic structures, institutions, and policies are well known. They represent more traditional development challenges and relate to improving the investment climate, competition policies, and job creation; to education and skills development; to innovation and moving up the value chain; to infrastructure and urban redesign; to water, energy, agriculture, and the environment; and to citizens' demands for voice and participation. Young countries are likely to sustain a greater appetite for reforms than aging countries.

Urbanization

The second driver for change emerges from the inescapable trend toward urbanization. Where today about 40 percent of the PRC's population is urban, by 2050 city dwellers will account for over 70 percent; the shift in India will be from about 30 percent to over 50 percent (see Chapter 9).

Well-run cities with quality amenities (education, health, finance, infrastructure, sanitation, air quality, recreational facilities, etc.) will have a decisive edge over other, less well-run urban agglomerations. Cities will house the knowledge workers, serve as the locus of innovation, and forge enabling institutions. Citizens will demand competent mayors and city managers, and more frequently turn to their local government leaders to get results. In turn, powerful mayors will exert greater and greater influence over national politics, with significant changes in national vs. local fiscal relations and decision-making authority. The citizenry will demand more predictable, transparent and accountable governance, possibly via scorecards and similar instruments.

The push for decentralization under increasingly federated structures is inevitable. Mayors of principal cities will have broader sway over national politics, but this will also contribute to tensions between national and local governments. Well-designed and implemented decentralization will make a huge difference. The global experience has actually been quite sobering, pointing to the difficulty of achieving the right balance in center vs. local relations and the importance of institution building.

The challenge lies in identifying the form of governance and institutions best suited to the Asian context.[8] This has significant implications for the relationship and distance between the state and its citizens, including the forms of competitive politics at the local level. It emphasizes the need for safeguards against capture and corruption. In particular, land registration and management will constitute the core of governance issues.

Asia's expanding middle class and the communications revolution

Easterly (2001) and others have developed the argument of a "middle-class consensus" that facilitates economic growth by allowing the emergence of a societal consensus on public goods believed to be critical to economic development. The middle class is regardless essential for the accumulation of human capital and savings, and through its increasing purchasing power as well as its willingness to pay for higher-quality products, a major driver for firms' willingness to invest and move up the value chain.

Throughout Asia, an expanding middle class—a desirable product of rapid socioeconomic growth in and of itself—will also exert new demands for a stronger voice and increased participation, for a transparent allocation of (budget) resources, for accountability for results, for enhanced personal space, and equality under the rule of law.[9]

Although a daunting challenge, combating corruption is critical for all countries to ensure essential social and political stability and retain the legitimacy of governments. Here, the quality of communication between those who govern and those who are governed will be of paramount importance because new social media and other new tools as yet unknown, but guaranteed to emerge, will not be denied, as recent events in the Middle East and North Africa have amply illustrated.

As noted, with increasing incomes and an expanding middle class in Asia, demands for better

---

8 Emerging Asia's "behind-the-border" responses will not be fundamentally different from those societies that have gone through such transformations historically; thus overall, the evolutionary path will broadly resemble that of the OECD countries, in terms of institutional development, regulations, national vs. local fiscal relations, and decentralization.
9 This is not to say that law and legal institutions did not play a role in Asian economic development, especially of the Asia-7. See also Pistor and Wellons (1999).

services and quality of life will become a powerful driver for institutional change. The accumulation of assets by the middle class will create demands for more efficient financial intermediation, institutions, and instruments (chapter 10). Over time, a substantial transfer of wealth from the state to its citizens will occur. This shift will spur further innovation (e.g., in the finance sector), but also have an impact on national vs. local fiscal relations, affect public finance management (including debt management—now increasingly needed), and give further impetus to concerns about income differentials.

More money in the pockets of citizens, combined with the demographic profile of major Asian countries, will facilitate the shift from an export-oriented model of economic growth to a domestic demand-led model, with an impact on investments, consumption, and savings. Asia overall is fortunate to be in a position to address this new challenge in a gradual, cautious manner, a luxury that most other regions did not have.

Yet the emergence of a newly emboldened citizenry should not be equated with a transition into a Western democratic model. Fundamental determinants of governance will not change so soon. The relationship, distance and social contract between the state and its citizens, and the forms of citizens' participation in the state's decision-making process will, for the most part, continue to differ from Western parliamentary democracies. This is not to buy into the overly simplistic view of "Asian values", but rather the recognition that governance will have some "Asian characteristics". Traditional hierarchical relationships embedded in Asian societies will not be set aside over such a short period, nor would it be desirable, as the capacity for collective action is a substantial asset.

However, a wild card in this setting is the future of communications. This is not the place to speculate about future technological scenarios, but what seems rather likely is that the world will experience hitherto unimagined new communications technologies and tools that may either dramatically accelerate the push for more participation and voice by citizens, or conversely, allow for even tighter surveillance by authorities. Recent events in the Middle East have again illustrated the power of such technologies.

The pressures arising from these domestic drivers, required actions, and related risks are summarized in Table 13.3. The priorities and related principles are elaborated further below.

Key actors of institutional change

Asian governments will have to be the key actors to realize the Asian Century, but they cannot do it alone. Governments have to design and implement the sound growth-oriented and inclusive economic and social policies that have been discussed throughout this book. To do so they must devise enabling institutional and regulatory frameworks that are rule-based, thus predictable, equitable, and accountable to the citizen. Governments must keep an eye on corruption and cronyism. Governments also have to be able to rely on a capable civil service and honest

Table 13.3 | Pressures for governance and institutional transformation—domestic

The Issue	Developments	Actions	Risks
Demographics	Northeast Asia is aging, South and Southeast Asia are young	• Aging countries should adjust institutions • Young countries should improve public services	• No precedent in Asia for adjusting institutions in response to aging • No delivery of public services can lead to unrest
Urbanization	Urban population growth will be significant through 2050	• Governance and institutional reforms should account for the urban population growth • Decentralization policies	• Urban growth could lead to tensions between national and local governments • Urban–rural income gap will likely grow wider
Expanding middle class	Expanding middle class will lead to demands for higher quality of life	• Government must keep up with growing expectations and demands for governance and institutional reforms	• Could lead to demand for more voice • The distance between state and citizen will be affected

judicial institutions to ensure the sustained implementation of intended policy directions and the exercise of state authority. But developing such capacity is a time-consuming undertaking; wise governments will use the key drivers cited in this book to their advantage, especially the three featured in this chapter (demographics, urbanization, and the expanding middle class) to accelerate institutional change.

As economies and contractual relations grow more complex, reflecting Asia's growth performance, governments will gradually respond to these pressures by accepting both a stronger voice and expanded role for both civil society and the private sector. By accepting as rule of law institutions that reduce the state's discretion and create more space for individuals and social groups alike, the authorities will secure legitimacy. While politics will increasingly be contested, civil society and media outside of the formal political system will demand accountability, monitor government performance (both at the national and local level), and thus exercise public oversight. The ultimate challenge for Asia will be to maintain this positive momentum for institutional change over a generation. Failing to do so will stunt the dream of the Asian Century.

Principles and priorities

Analysis of the drivers of change, the entry points for governance and institutional change, and the results of surveys such as the Worldwide Governance Indicators will provide the direction that Asian governments should consider, and map how they should attain their goals of stability and prosperity. This chapter argues that three domestic factors are likely to put pressure on governments to introduce reforms. These are stronger than external pressures up to a certain point: when it would be solely up to the authorities' judgment, reactions to pressures are only launched when a tipping point comes, i.e., when the domestic costs of failing to reform are higher than external pressures. Legitimacy as well as stability concerns will drive the central decision makers, and this process cannot be rushed.

How then can attainment of the tipping point be accelerated? One answer might be to emphasize welfare gains for the middle class through reforms. The three domestic drivers for change are not isolated; on the contrary, they tend to reinforce one another, thereby accelerating demands for reforms. However, it is also important to understand that governance outcomes are not likely to follow the examples of Western democracy (Chu and Huang, 2007; Nathan, 2007).

The following eight principles and priorities deserve special attention:

1. **Focus on building strong transparent institutions—they define success.** The most important factor that will determine whether Asian countries will escape the Middle Income Trap, make a successful transition from postconflict, poor countries to converging economies, and allow the developed economies to meet the pressing challenge of aging, is the quality of institutions. Institutions are the means by which the intangibles of governance are translated into structure and form. They allow intergenerational exchanges and societal learning. In broad terms, priorities for institutional investment should be:
    - For the converging economies: foster world-class skills and innovation systems, and attract knowledge workers to avoid the Middle Income Trap.
    - For fragile states: built or rebuild basic institutions of the state. There is much international experience to draw on, but the political will has to exist and a societal consensus for change must be established.
    - For aging societies: adjust institutions to account for the demographic transition by enacting transparent and welcoming immigration laws and systems to attract foreign skills and labor; and ensuring fiscally sustainable pension and social security systems.
    - For emerging Asia: escape the Middle Income Trap by developing world-class institutions (including a legal system with clearly articulated and enforced property rights, educational and health systems, a civil service, and a financial system) and create opportunities and incentives for citizens to invest in themselves. In particular, both the rule of law and skill development, including entrepreneurial

and scientific skills, should be top priorities.

The focus on institutions and human development are the primary elements that enabled Singapore to escape the Middle Income Trap: in recent years it has ranked third in the world PPP per capita income. Yet it is these areas where emerging Asia has struggled the most. Many countries understand this, but none has focused on institutions and people to the same extent as Singapore. The contrast between Singapore, and, for example, Malaysia or Brazil (ranked in the 50s and 70s in PPP per capita, respectively) is not because of the recipe; rather it is the thorough and relentless manner by which the recipe was followed. Even with its extraordinary focus, it took Singapore many decades to get where it is today. Emerging Asia has to set its sights very high and do so now.

2. **Corruption cannot be left unchecked; failing this, it will eventually suffocate rule-of-law institutions.** The 2010 Global Corruption Barometer, mirroring a global trend, reports that citizens in almost all Asian countries, regardless of income level, feel that corruption has worsened over the past three years. Georgia is one notable exception.

Corruption has featured centrally in a number of recent high-profile scandals in India. This raises concerns that these scandals will have a negative effect on inward foreign investment. In PRC the central authorities have been worrying about the corrosive effect of corruption on the system's legitimacy.

The continued rise of the middle class will be a force to bring about more transparency and accountability. Success or failure in dealing with corruption and other governance issues will go a long way in determining where Asian countries will find themselves on the path toward prosperity in 2050.

3. **Devise participatory approaches to policy making and build accountability mechanisms.** Demands for new forms of accountability will rise. In the emergent stage, the citizenry's demands are focused on growth; later, expanding demands, mostly urban and middle class, relate to noneconomic factors like quality of life and (political) participation. The role of the state will be debated; the relationship and distance between the state and citizens will see far-reaching changes related to different forms of civic activism, such as green movements, taxpayer associations, and initiatives involving such things as culture, heritage, and charity. Citizens will demand from the state more transparency and a different treatment of corruption. Managing expectations of an increasingly vocal citizenry will pose complex challenges to governments.

4. **Designing policies is only a start; implementation is what matters.** Investment or business climate–related surveys such as the World Economic Forum rankings or the World Bank's Doing Business surveys have had a positive effect on the regulatory quality of Asian countries by stimulating competition among nations eager to attract both domestic and foreign investors. Similarly, countries have become used to being in the

spotlight for various dimensions of governance (e.g., Worldwide Governance Indicators by the World Bank Institute or Transparency International's Corruption Perceptions Index), and started to adjust policies in response. Yet feedback from nongovernment actors such as private sector groups or civil society organizations often paints a different picture, one that indicates that policy reforms all too often remain on paper rather than being enforced. Where the gap between paper and reality is too great, the ensuing disconnect threatens to compromise the credibility of governments. Governments must increasingly work with the business community to ensure genuine implementation and they must follow up where it matters. The role of nongovernment actors that monitor implementation and provide feedback and public oversight should be actively sought, not merely tolerated.

5. **Ensure that the rule of law applies equally to everyone.** If the events in North Africa and the Middle East and the other popular uprisings in recent years are any guide, selective application of the rule of law, which is evident in the arbitrariness of the state and the lack of personal security, is the fulcrum of citizen anger. It is against the background of an expanding Asian middle class with growing demands for public and personal space that an emphatic premium must be put on building a judiciary and police force that are seen as honest, fair, and acting with integrity. Throughout emerging Asia, the fruits of economic growth have translated into a transfer of assets from the state to its citizens, most commonly in the form of land and housing. However, the greater that scarce land in primary locations is seen as a source of economic rent, the more frictions have come to the fore. These have pitted citizens against local authorities (as in PRC) or against private land developers who often have close links to those in positions of power (as in Cambodia). So far, the outcome has gone decidedly against citizens. Similarly, in many countries members of the elite have been flouting the law, counting on permissive informal arrangements, and acting oblivious to the growing anger of ordinary citizens. The elite must understand that the rule of law applies to everyone, and the public must be convinced that the ways of working have changed. These will be vital elements to ensure long-term stability.

6. **Build a civil service based on merit.** The civil service is relied on to implement government policies. It follows that the quality of the civil service has a significant impact on the outcomes of government actions. Yet in most Asian countries the quality of the civil service is wanting and often it is identified as a constraint to economic development. A common feature of the economies that have joined the ranks of the developed countries is that their civil service is perceived as honest and highly competent. They have been able to attract the best and the brightest, and successfully institutionalized a meritocracy. Singapore's political commitment to invest in its merit-based civil service to perpetuate

a performance-oriented public sector has translated into a competitive advantage. But Singapore's civil service was not built overnight; countries aspiring to realize the Asian Century by 2050 must start now.

7. **Realize that a healthy relationship between authorities and citizens is a function of trust.** Trust is built through consistent, transparent, accountable, and verifiable results, together with built-in mechanisms of recourse. The more the relationship between government and citizen is equitable, the more likely it is that stability will be achieved. This requires that governments recognize citizens as the country's real sovereigns and put in place effective oversight and accountability mechanisms. It also follows that mechanisms need to be established to replace governments through contestable elections anchored in constitutional rights.

8. **Realize that best practice approaches will not suffice. Countries have to adapt for "best fit".** Efforts to address these principles and priorities and other governance-related tasks have tended to focus more on the form of the institutions than the functions performed by them, and even less on the context of individual nations. Countries and donors alike have looked at state-of-the-art practices to provide the blueprint to create formal, rules-based institutions modeled after those in OECD countries. In most cases these reforms have yet to yield the desired results. The reason is that not enough attention has been paid to the country-specific informal institutions, relationships, and interests that underpin formal arrangements. Looking forward, countries must select institutional models that are likely to yield an improved performance within their own national context—that is, seek models that best fit their circumstances. This realization, though fundamental, will not make it easier for emerging Asia. It means that rather than importing ready-made models that can then also be blamed for any failures, a new national consensus must be established. It must be based on rigorous analysis, combined with soul-searching, to identify models that best fit. In some countries this means addressing uncomfortable or inconvenient truths, yet it is an essential requirement if appropriate and adaptable high-performance institutions are to be developed.

Regional Cooperation and Integration

Chapter 14 | Johannes F. Linn

Asia is on the rise. It is undergoing a renaissance of great intensity and significance, returning to a relative standing and influence in the world economy that it has not seen for centuries. Asia is part of a global economy and polity that is interconnected as never before, and one that is marked by a rapidly evolving system of global governance. A key question is whether and how Asia will continue its rapid ascent: as a collection of individual states and economies, increasingly connected by market forces within and without, but lacking in strong regional institutions? Or will Asia develop regional institutional solutions that can help support and steer Asia's market-driven integration process; reinforce its growth momentum through active cooperation across borders; establish trust between neighbors and prevent regional conflicts; and enable it to react as a regional entity to major internal or external shocks, thereby giving it a strong voice in global affairs?

The purpose of this chapter is to contribute to an understanding of the recent history and significance of regional economic integration and institutional cooperation in Asia,[1] and to explore the opportunities and challenges for Asia in expanding and deepening regional integration and cooperation over the next 40 years.[2] It draws on a large number of studies,[3] with the aim of presenting a high-level composite picture of the key trends and issues, and of the opportunities and challenges that lie ahead.

This chapter discusses the five reasons for the growing importance of regional cooperation in

---

* The author gratefully acknowledges the many comments received from Asian Development Bank (ADB) colleagues, Richard Pomfret, and members of the Asia 2050 team.

1 In this chapter, "regional economic integration" refers to the economic links formed between economic agents in different countries of a particular geographic region through trade, transport and communications, financial flows, and migration. "Regional institutional cooperation" refers to the coordination of efforts by governments to provide the necessary public infrastructure that supports regional economic integration and to remove barriers to regional integration that may arise from national policy regimes.

2 The chapter complements other chapters in this volume, some of which cover specific aspects of regional integration and cooperation, including financial development and integration, and energy. These areas are therefore not treated in detail here.

3 Most significant among these is an ADB trilogy of studies on Asian regionalism (ADB, 2008a), Asian regional infrastructure (ADB, 2009), and Asian regional institutions (ADB, 2010a). Also of direct relevance for pan-Asian integration is the study by Centennial Group International (2006) on the lessons for Asia of European and Latin American integration and cooperation. On East Asia, Gill and Kharas (2007), Nehru (2010), and Pomfret (2010) provide valuable insights, as do Ahmed et al. (2010), Baru (2010), Chandra and Kumar (2008), and Das et al. (2011) for South Asia. For Central Asia, UNDP (2005) provides a comprehensive assessment of regional integration and cooperation. For a fuller version of the paper and the literature on which it draws, see Linn (2011).

Asia's future growth and prosperity; presents a framework for understanding relations between countries on the spectrum from conflict to cooperation; assesses the progress of regional integration and cooperation against the baseline conditions prevailing in 1970; identifies priority areas to facilitate future regional cooperation; and, finally, discusses institutions for regional cooperation.

The importance of regional cooperation for Asia's future

Greater regional cooperation and integration within Asia will become significantly more important for the region's overall development for a number of reasons:

First, in order to sustain regionwide economic growth, Asian countries will need to increasingly rely on internal (domestic and regional) demand and ensure open markets with neighboring countries and the rest of the world in the same way that US and European markets have been open to Asia since the end of World War II. At a minimum, this will require the creation of an integrated market for goods, services, and finance to permit the free flow of trade and investment across the region, with low barriers to entry for the rest of the world.

Second, there are many areas in which increased regional cooperation will help respond better to global challenges and yield significant synergies and positive spillovers, such as technological development, energy security, and disaster preparedness. The key is to reap scale economies that are critical to sustained growth, as Gill and Kharas (2007) have stressed in analyzing the East Asian growth experience. Regional integration and cooperation allow the creation of larger markets, specialization in production, cross-border investments, scale economies in public infrastructure service provision, and replication of successful innovations and development interventions by sharing knowledge and experience across borders. This, in turn, will allow businesses and governments to generate enhanced growth.

Third, the skillful and joint management of several regional commons will become increasingly important for Asia's long-term stability and prosperity. The management of the regional commons will involve diffusing and mitigating internal political and social risks associated with drugs and terrorism; avoiding conflicts among the mega-economies and nuclear states; and maintaining social and political stability in the region, especially to support the economic and security concerns of fragile states.

Fourth, regional cooperation can be a stepping stone for poorer countries to move up the value chain and maximize their growth potential.

Fifth, regional cooperation has the potential to be an important bridge between the interactions of individual Asian countries and the rest of the world. In order to have the voice and influence in the global agenda that is commensurate with its economic weight, Asia will need to formulate a unified geopolitical position on a range of global issues. This can only be achieved through regional dialogue and cooperation.

Cooperation instead of conflict

Cooperation is not the only mode of interaction among neighbors. They may also compete or be in conflict. In fact, regional cooperation, competition, and conflict are part of a continuum of relations among neighboring states. Conflict involves the attempt to resolve differences of interest among neighbors through hostile and mutually damaging means; competition engages countries in the pursuit of resources or benefits to each other's exclusion, but through peaceful means and in ways regulated by international law, intergovernmental agreements, or accepted norms; and cooperation means working together as partners in maximizing common or shared benefits. Of course, neighboring countries should aim to reduce or eliminate conflict because of the great human and economic damage that it causes.

Depending on the specifics of the situation, competition may provide incentives for improved performance through a "race to the top" (e.g., competing for foreign direct investment (FDI) through general reform to the business climate); or it may involve costly duplication of investments and loss of resources, leading to a "race to the bottom" (e.g., competing selective and distortionary tax incentives for foreign investors). Cooperation usually will be the most desirable approach, provided it is not achieved at the expense of third parties.

Figure 14.1 shows the typical range of relations between countries in areas of regional significance along the spectrum from conflict through competition to cooperation. For example, development assistance for the poorer countries is a clear area for cooperation. Trade policy traditionally can involve measures to gain national benefits from protection in a competitive mode, but also can be pursued through cooperative solutions based on coordinated reductions in protection and improvements in border and transit management. However, if these reduced barriers apply only to participants in the regional agreement, other countries not included may incur actual costs from trade diversion.

In other examples, transport involves regional cooperation in instances where national transport links connect across borders, especially as a part of agreed regional transport corridors. However, nations can also compete through transport investments by developing competing port or airport capacity, or by building competing regional road or railroad lines. In the case of water (as well as maritime resources), interstate relations can run the gamut from conflict to competition to cooperation. For disaster preparedness, there is no obvious room for conflict and competition, but plenty of opportunity for cooperation. Conflict prevention is in principle a cooperative activity, but in practice it gets wrapped up in interstate and geopolitical conflict and competition, as the current situation on the Korean Peninsula demonstrates. Of course, a history of painful and bloody conflict can also be a driver for cooperation, as was the case with the creation of the European Union (EU) (Box 14.1).

A key element in moving from regional conflict to constructive competition and cooperation is the establishment of trust among neighbors. One of the benefits of looking at the full range

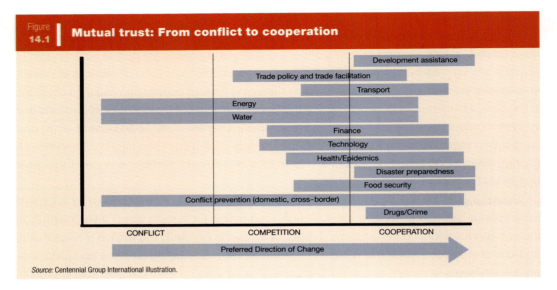

Figure 14.1 Mutual trust: From conflict to cooperation

Source: Centennial Group International illustration.

of regional integration and cooperation efforts across the spectrum of cooperation–competition–conflict is that it allows priorities, tradeoffs, and risks to be better identified. For example, by focusing regional relationship building on those areas where there is little room for conflict and competition, trust can be established among neighbors; on the other hand, neglecting areas that are prone to conflict will interfere with cooperation in other areas, if and when conflict breaks out.

> **Box 14.1 Moving toward cooperation without conflict: Learning the lessons of history**
>
> The opportunity exists for Asian regional relations to build on the successes of past integration and cooperation initiatives; in effect, Asia can learn from history. Perhaps the most important lesson is to avoid the mistake that Europe made during the first half of the 20th century. After a golden era of rapid industrialization, growth, and integration during the second half of the 19th century, Europe entered the 20th century with great expectations for continued growth and prosperity. However, Europe repeated its errors of previous centuries and fell into 30 years of intense conflict marked by two world wars that caused unfathomable human losses and economic dislocation. Born out of this experience, Europe managed during the second half of the 20th century to create the regional cooperative institutions that have allowed it to overcome a history of harmful conflict and unproductive competition, and to attain peace. Asia can learn both from European history as well as from its own experiences of moving successfully from conflict to cooperation, as in the case of the Association of Southeast Asian Nations (ASEAN) and the Greater Mekong Subregion (GMS) Program. Asia now has an opportunity to enhance mutual trust and strengthen the regional institutions that will allow the region to avoid the ravages of conflict and continue its high-growth performance.

Cooperative outcomes, once achieved, need to be worked on if they are to be sustained however. Unless continuous efforts are made to keep the cooperation momentum moving forward, there is a risk that countries could slide back towards competition or even conflict.

The state of play 40 years ago: Asia in disarray in 1970

Anyone in 1970 who predicted the subsequent spectacular rise in Asia's economic fortune would likely have been dismissed as a hopeless optimist. PRC was just beginning to emerge from its Cultural Revolution and remained largely shut off from the rest of the world economically and politically. A long-term war was raging in Viet Nam, with massive spillover effects on its neighbors. Indonesia remained poverty stricken and was only beginning to recover under the new order after the transition from the Sukarno to the Suharto regime. India and Pakistan were in the midst of an uneasy truce following the Indo–Pakistan wars of 1965 and 1971. Indian economic policy was inward-looking and focused on import substitution. Finally, the Soviet republics of Central Asia were largely sealed off from the rest of Asia economically and politically, and oriented entirely toward Moscow in their infrastructure and economic relations.

The growth rates of PRC, ASEAN–5 (Indonesia, the Philippines, Malaysia, Thailand, and Viet Nam), and South Asia hovered around 2–3 percent per annum during the 1960s. The only exceptions to this dismal story were Japan, which had experienced its great postwar resurgence with an average annual growth rate of over 9 percent between 1958 and 1970; and the Newly Industrialized Economies (NIEs) of East Asia (Hong Kong, China; Republic of Korea; Singapore; and Taipei,China), which grew at an average of 5 percent during the same period (Figure 14.2).

Although Asia's regional integration, as measured by the share of intraregional trade in total trade, grew quite rapidly in the 1960s, it remained in 1970 substantially below that of Europe and North America (Figure 14.3a). Much of the intraregional trade was concentrated within East Asia, a pattern that persisted until the early 1980s (Figure 14.3b). Asian regional institutions were virtually nonexistent in 1970. ASEAN, which is now Asia's flagship regional organization, was still in its infancy, having been founded in 1967 by Indonesia, Malaysia, the Philippines, Singapore, and Thailand.

Forty years of progress with regional economic integration: 1970–2010

Some of the patterns that would mark the region's future dynamism were already emerging in Asia in the 1970s, including Japan's post-World War II economic miracle and the beginning of the sustained economic boom among the NIEs based on export orientation, rapid industrialization, and FDI. After 1970, significant changes in the political and economic landscape brought about very dramatic shifts in the economic growth performances of PRC, the ASEAN-5 countries, India, and eventually even among the former Soviet republics of Central Asia.[4] Key factors explaining

---

[4] Japan's growth decline mirrored the performance of the rest of Asia, but in reverse.

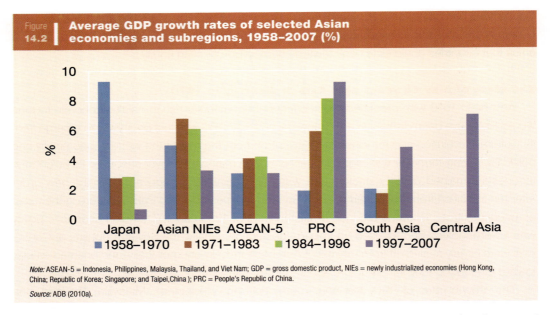

Figure 14.2 | Average GDP growth rates of selected Asian economies and subregions, 1958–2007 (%)

Note: ASEAN-5 = Indonesia, Philippines, Malaysia, Thailand, and Viet Nam; GDP = gross domestic product; NIEs = newly industrialized economies (Hong Kong, China; Republic of Korea; Singapore; and Taipei,China); PRC = People's Republic of China.

Source: ADB (2010a).

high and sustained growth performances in developing Asia included the economic reforms and opening up of PRC in the late 1970s; the integration of the NIEs and ASEAN-5 through the rapid expansion of East Asian and trans-Pacific trade during the 1980s and 1990s, driven in part by the policies of open regionalism espoused by ASEAN (Box 14.2); the liberalization of domestic and external economic policies in India starting in the early 1990s; and the recovery of the Central Asian economies after the disintegration of the Soviet Union and fall of the Iron Curtain in the early 1990s.

As a result, Asia as a whole has been increasingly open to trade. Its ratio of trade to gross domestic product (GDP) reached 62 percent in 2008, only 3 percentage points lower than the EU's, and much higher than either Latin America's or Africa's. While historically Asia has relied mostly on trans-Pacific trade, its trade and nontrade economic links with Europe have been expanding rapidly since the dissolution of the Soviet Union, offering new opportunities for the cross-continental integration of Eurasia (Linn and Tiomkin, 2007).

Concerning intraregional trade, Figure 14.3a shows how Asia has been integrating rapidly over the last four decades, with its intraregional trade share rising from about 30 percent in 1970 to over 50 percent in 2008. Largely driven by market forces and complemented by national policies, economic interdependence in East and Southeast Asia has grown rapidly in recent decades. Intricate regional production networks and supply chains have been established in industries such as electronics and cars. This process has resulted in the fragmentation of production—the scattering of portions of the production process across different economies as part of the development of far-flung international production chains and deepened trade in intermediate

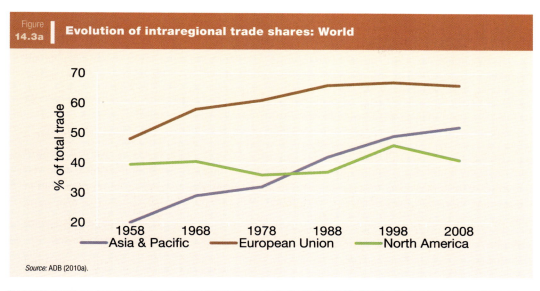

Figure 14.3a Evolution of intraregional trade shares: World

Source: ADB (2010a).

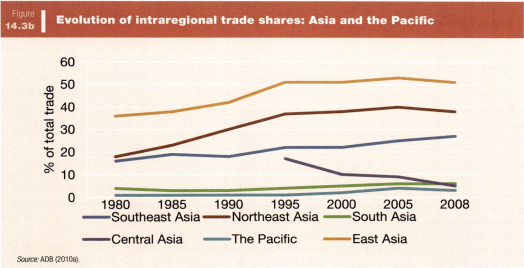

Figure 14.3b Evolution of intraregional trade shares: Asia and the Pacific

Source: ADB (2010a).

goods—and led the process of regional and global integration. FDI played an important role in this process and increased interdependency among Asian countries, which, in turn, helped attract further foreign investment. This virtuous circle created great scope for economies of scale and technology, and boosted growth in the region. FDI flows have gravitated increasingly to PRC, especially after the 1997–1998 Asian financial crisis, as PRC became the main assembly plant for "factory Asia" and emerged as a significant export market for other East and Southeast Asian economies, as well as a base for final goods exports to the rest of the world.

Box 14.2 | ASEAN: An example of constructive regional cooperation

The Association of Southeast Asian Nations (ASEAN) is the most ambitious and significant Asian regional institution. Founded in 1967 by Indonesia, Malaysia, the Philippines, Singapore, and Thailand, ASEAN has since expanded to include Brunei Darussalam, Cambodia, the Lao People's Democratic Republic, Singapore, and Viet Nam.

For the first decade of its existence, ASEAN was a weak grouping with little impact in terms of regional cooperation initiatives. Beginning in 1976, ASEAN engaged in successive phases of increasingly ambitious economic integration efforts, starting with merchandise trade, followed in the 1990s by services, investment, and labor. ASEAN also expanded its membership in the 1980s and 1990s. A key aspect of its approach to regional trade cooperation was trade liberalization initiatives; while regionally negotiated and agreed, these initiatives also were generally extended to other non-ASEAN trading partners on a non-discriminatory basis.

During the Asian financial crisis, the limitations of ASEAN in assisting members affected by the crisis became apparent. ASEAN reinforced its commitment to regional economic cooperation by setting the goals of establishing an ASEAN economic community by 2015 and entering into free trade agreements with other countries, including PRC. ASEAN members also agreed to an ASEAN charter with binding legal obligations; engaged ASEAN finance ministers; took functional initiatives in energy, biodiversity, environment, and human rights; and supported subregional growth areas. The ASEAN Charter sets out a framework for dispute settlement, but this has so far not been called upon. Perhaps most important, ASEAN has been the platform on which other regional initiatives have been based, particularly ASEAN+3 (PRC, Japan, and the Republic of Korea), the ASEAN Regional Forum, and the East Asia Summit.

ASEAN is a successful regional initiative of long standing, but has limitations in terms of organizational structure and impact. ASEAN has a small secretariat with limited capacity and authority, decisions are made by consensus, and its financial resources are constrained by the fact that its budget is funded with equal contributions from all its members.

Perhaps one of ASEAN's greatest achievements, despite these limitations, has been its ability to bring together a very disparate group of countries, including some previously engaged in long-lasting conflicts or a difficult transition from communist central planning to a market-based economy. ASEAN's ability to build trust and engender a spirit of peaceful cooperation among neighbors has been one of its strengths.

Source: ADB (2010a); Hill and Menon (2011a).

As a result of this integration process, trade integration in Asia of over 50 percent now exceeds that of North America (about 40 percent), but falls short of that of the EU (about 65 percent).

However, as Figure 14.3b demonstrates, the degree of integration of different Asian subregions still varies tremendously, with East Asia by far the most integrated, while South Asia, Central Asia, and the Pacific lag far behind.

At the subregional level, East Asia leads the way in openness. The East Asian integration story has been studied in detail (Gill and Kharas, 2007; ADB, 2008b; ADB, 2010b) and is closely related to its exceptional growth performance in the virtuous circle of the creation of economies of scale through a combination of growth-oriented policies stressing domestic and foreign integration. East Asia accounts for almost one-third of world trade in manufacturing, with the intermediate goods trade accounting for more than half all intraregional trade in East Asia (ADB, 2010a). Led initially by Japan, and subsequently by the NIEs and now PRC, the Asian story is one of growth in sectors with increasing returns to scale (Figure 14.4) and an expanding intermediate goods trade (Figure 14.5). Relatively low trade barriers, open capital markets, and high levels of investment in infrastructure have helped support this integration process in East Asia (Gill and Kharas, 2007; ADB, 2010a; Pomfret, 2010).

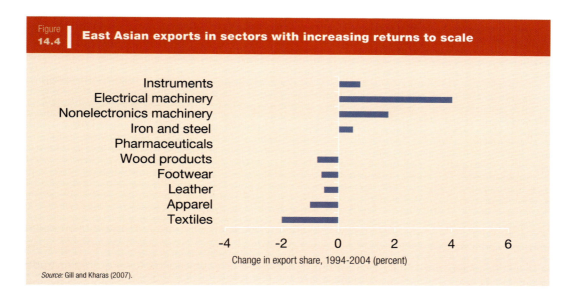

Figure 14.4 | East Asian exports in sectors with increasing returns to scale

Change in export share, 1994-2004 (percent)

Source: Gill and Kharas (2007).

South Asia lags far behind East Asia in regional integration. It has a much lower degree of trade openness and a lower share of intraregional trade (Table 14.1). Its share of world manufacturing trade remains very small, as does its intraregional trade share in parts and components (ADB, 2010a). High trade barriers (especially with neighbors), limited access to capital markets, and low-quality infrastructure and services have constrained regional integration in South Asia (Chandra and Kumar, 2008). Indeed, many of South Asia's important land borders are effectively

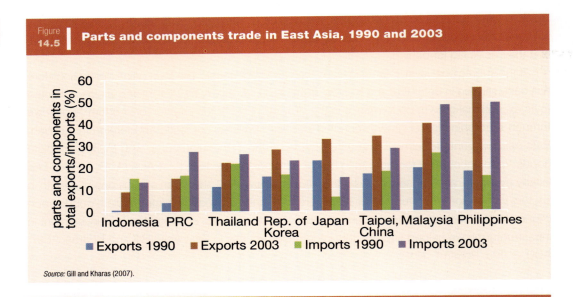

Figure 14.5 **Parts and components trade in East Asia, 1990 and 2003**

Source: Gill and Kharas (2007).

Table 14.1 **Uneven economic integration in Asia and the Pacific to date**

	Production integration	Final goods integration	Services integration	Labor integration	Monetary and financial integration
East Asia	High	Moderate	Moderate	Low	Low
Central Asia	Low	Low	Low	Moderate	Low
South Asia	Low	Low	Low	Low	Low
Pacific	Low	Low	Low	Low	Low

Source: ADB (2010a).

blocked to trade, such as that between India and Pakistan, although there have been some improvements recently including Bangladesh, which now allows access to ports for shipments originating in Northeast India (Baru, 2009). More generally, the trends toward greater trade openness and integration, while starting from a low base, are also notable in South Asia, as the major countries, particularly India, have liberalized their economic regimes and reduced barriers to trade. The trade share in South Asia's economy more than doubled between 1990 and 2008, and there has been rapid growth in South Asia's trade links with the rest of the world in parts and components (Figure 14.6).

The economic links between India and PRC are noteworthy. For example, PRC's share of Indian imports of manufactured goods increased from about 2 percent to 12 percent between 2000 and 2007, while PRC's share of parts and components in Indian imports rose from about

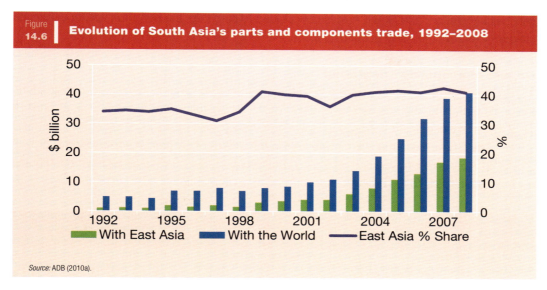

Figure 14.6 | Evolution of South Asia's parts and components trade, 1992–2008

Source: ADB (2010a).

4 percent to 21 percent over the same period (Figure 14.7).

Table 14.1 looks at the extent of current integration across various dimensions beyond trade, including production, final goods, services, labor, and monetary and financial integration. It shows that for most dimensions and in most subregions integration remains low. Hence, although East Asia is far advanced in production integration and moderately advanced in final goods and

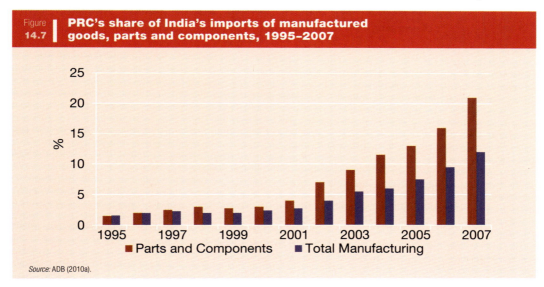

Figure 14.7 | PRC's share of India's imports of manufactured goods, parts and components, 1995–2007

Source: ADB (2010a).

services integration, and South Asia is now poised to catch up, the opportunities for continued integration across the Asian economic space, even for East Asia, remain substantial.

Drivers of economic integration

The key drivers of—and obstacles to—regional economic integration relate to infrastructure, the costs of trading, the competitiveness and quality of institutions, and in some cases conflict. An analysis of these determinants leads to the following conclusions:

- There have been many improvements in the drivers of integration and economic growth in Asia in recent years, especially in East Asia. These improvements have contributed substantially to the region's superior growth performance.

Figure 14.8 Intra subregional trade costs in Asia and other regions

Note: In this study, the category of North and Central Asia includes the Russian Federation. Estimation of trading costs is subject to considerable technical difficulties and academic debates. Pomfret (2010) provides a review of alternative methods and their constraints. He also refers to his own estimates for ASEAN countries, which showed ad valorem trading costs falling after 1990 and generally converging on the low levels of Singapore.

Source: Duval and Utokthum (2010). ASEAN = Association of Southeast Asian Nations, EU5 = European Union Five (France, Germany, Italy, Spain, United Kingdom), NAFTA = North American Free Trade Association, SAARC = South Asian Association for Regional Cooperation.

- However, Asia generally still lags the performances of the EU and North America in key areas that relate to trading costs, transport and logistics, the quantity and quality of infrastructure, competitiveness, and institutional quality (Figure 14.8).
- Trade tariffs are generally not a significant barrier anymore, but other border barriers—such as quantitative restrictions, border administration, and even closures—and behind-the-border constraints related to logistics, transport, infrastructure problems, and weak institutions remain significant barriers to integration (Figure 14.9).
- East Asia does much better than South Asia and Central Asia on most drivers. ASEAN performs especially well where overall trading costs are concerned.
- South Asian countries have generally improved their economic performance in recent

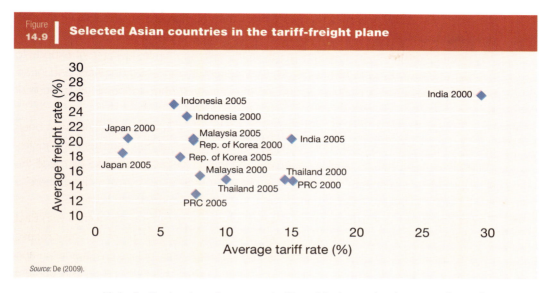

Figure 14.9 | Selected Asian countries in the tariff-freight plane

Source: De (2009).

years, with India the best performer and still rapidly improving in many dimensions.
- There are great differences in country performance within the subregions. Political tensions and conflicts within and among countries present serious obstacle to integration in parts of Central Asia, Northeast Asia, and South Asia.

Prospects for further economic integration

If Asia wants to continue on a path of rapid integration and growth to 2050 it will have to:
- improve the effectiveness of integration drivers to levels that are either as good as or better than those of the EU and North America;
- ensure that subregions, and countries within subregions, that are lagging behind eventually catch up with the rest of Asia;
- in addition to reducing and harmonizing tariff barriers, focus on nontariff trade facilitation measures, both at and behind borders;
- improve the quantity and quality of infrastructure, the quality of logistics, the quality of institutions, and the competitiveness of all economies to address behind-the-border issues; and
- reduce or eliminate barriers to integration including distrust and conflicts within and among countries.

If supported by the appropriate policies, the scope for further Asian economic integration is large. Deepened integration will be the result of continued high growth and investment, which, in turn, will be a driver of further high growth. A number of factors argue for this prognosis:
- In all likely growth scenarios, Asia's economy will continue to grow relative to the rest of

the world. By 2050, Asia may represent more than 50 percent of global GDP, offering great opportunities for intraregional trade, investment, and economies of scale.[5]

- The need for some Asian countries to rebalance their economies away from exports to the rest of the world, particularly the US, and reorient them toward domestic and intraregional consumption provides a strong impetus for the further economic integration of Asia.
- Recent trends in Asia's integration drivers show that barriers to integration have been reduced not only in East Asia but also in South Asia. India has been successful in fostering bilateral trade with its smaller neighbors and PRC. Central Asia has so far made the least progress. Given Asia's pragmatic approach to economic policy making, there is every reason to believe that the trend toward increased integration will continue.
- One of the drivers of integration within Asia (in particular of Central Asia's links with East and South Asia) will be the trans-Eurasian continental integration process. This process places the land-locked countries and regions of Central Asia (including Afghanistan and the western PRC) at the hub of growing economic links between the growth centers of East and South Asia, and the economies of Europe and the Russian Federation (Box 14.3).

Two significant risks could derail this continued integration process:

- Asian economies cease reducing barriers to integration, fail to build the necessary cross-border infrastructure, and do not improve the behind-the-border conditions that support domestic growth and cross-border integration.
- International conflicts, failing states, and internal unrest hinder continued integration.

These risks call for collaboration and a regional dialogue among the countries of Asia and with the international community to ensure that the necessary conditions are present for intra- and interregional economic integration. It will be necessary for policy makers to avoid conflicts that disrupt the integration process and to support the continued rapid growth of the Asian economies.

Contours of future cooperation and integration

Regional cooperation and integration will have its role to play in Asia's march toward prosperity. Asia will need to develop its own unique model that builds on the positive experience of development, cooperation, and integration in East Asia: a market-driven, bottom-up, and pragmatic approach supported by an evolving institutional framework that facilitates unhindered regional trade, services, and investment flows, as well as a degree of labor mobility throughout the region. As the European and East Asian experiences have demonstrated, production

---

[5] The World Bank's *World Development Report 2009* characterized Asia as "far from world markets". It is debatable whether this statement was correct in 2009 since Asia already represented a significant share of world markets. It will definitely not apply in 2050.

> **Box 14.3** | **Central Asia's triple integration opportunity**
>
> Central Asian countries have traditionally seen themselves—and have been seen from the outside—as isolated economies that are land-locked and distant from world markets. While this has been true in the past, Central Asia now faces huge opportunities due to its proximity to the buoyant markets of Asia, its location at the hub of a rapidly integrating Eurasian super-continental economic space, and the potential for greater intraregional integration.
>
> To take advantage of this triple opportunity, Central Asian countries can build on relatively well-developed infrastructure and human capital, and on the fact that they have relatively open trade regimes. However, they also need to overcome severe handicaps imposed mostly by their own weak policy regimes and failure to cooperate with each other. Their infrastructure is deteriorating rapidly in the absence of effective management and maintenance, the access to and quality of education and health services have been eroding since Soviet times, their borders have become serious obstacles to transit and trade within the subregion, their behind-the-border business conditions are stifling private investment and trade, and failure to cooperate in the management of regional water and energy resources has created severe economic, social, and environmental losses, and increased the risk of serious interstate conflicts.
>
> Central Asian countries need to overcome these obstacles with aggressive improvements to their domestic business climates and social and physical infrastructures, and strengthened border management. Central Asian integration would also get a strong boost if every country in the subregion were to promptly join the World Trade Organization. Estimates show that the cost of trade could be halved through appropriate trade-facilitation measures. With cooperation across a wide range of potentially beneficial areas, Central Asian GDP could double (UNDP, 2005). Overall, the key to benefiting from these opportunities will be to build stronger economic links with East and South Asia, complementing Central Asia's existing strong ties with the economies of the former Soviet Union.
>
> The Central Asia Regional Economic Cooperation (CAREC) is a regional economic forum that in its first 10 years has contributed to improved trust among neighbors, investments in regional transport and energy infrastructure, and facilitation of regional trade. With a membership of 10 countries, and with support from six multilateral institutions, led by ADB, the capacity of CAREC to intensify its efforts to support integration within the region and beyond is significant. However, it requires the engagement of all member countries at the highest level and the willingness of participants to overcome what are still high barriers to integration and to reduce the risk of conflict.

networks facilitated by the free flow of goods and services help both the lower-wage economies, by bringing new investments and technical know-how, and the higher-wage income economies, by allowing them to preserve their core manufacturing capacity through outsourcing lower value-added activities to lower-wage areas.

This bottom-up, market-driven model could use ASEAN+3 as the initial building block and gradually include more economies, ultimately developing into a regionwide market that permits not only uninhibited trade and investment, but also more labor mobility. In the process, Asian countries will develop stronger mutual trust that will be necessary for any subsequent, more ambitious initiatives such as the creation of a genuine single market, which would require supranational institutions. The sooner such a pan–Asian common economic space is created, the sooner all countries can share in the benefits of Asia's economic growth and integration. Such an approach will require stronger—though not necessarily new—regional institutions.

Unfortunately, the impact of regional cooperation on growth is difficult to quantify accurately because of the multitude of potential areas of cooperation and the difficulty in assessing the indirect (dynamic) benefits beyond the more easily estimable direct (static) welfare benefits.[6] Estimates of the benefits of cooperation in reducing trade tariffs under free trade arrangements generally find modest benefits (Ando, 2009; Hertel et al., 2004). Infrastructure investments and quality improvements have been estimated to have growth impacts of about 1–2 percentage points a year, which translates into improvements of GDP of around 10–20 percent over 10 years (Fay et al., 2011).

Estimates of the benefits of comprehensive regional cooperation across the whole spectrum of regional interactions have shown much larger potential benefits. For example, a scenario of economic cooperation in the Maghreb (western North Africa) that combines the creation of a trading bloc with the EU, the liberalization of services, and investment climate reforms shows benefits of some 40–60 percent of GDP over 10 years (World Bank, 2010g). An estimate for Central Asia that combines the benefits of cooperation on trade and trade facilitation, investment climate, transport, energy, as well as disaster and conflict mitigation, yields benefits of a GDP increase of 100 percent or more over 10 years (UNDP, 2005).

Quantitative evidence on the costs and benefits of regional cooperation arrangements is limited, and what is available is mixed (Barro and Lee, 2011). While there is some evidence to suggest that poorer regions can benefit disproportionately from regional projects (Menon and Warr, 2008; Warr et al., 2010), benefits are not evenly distributed among countries. Some countries, and some people within countries, may lose from regional integration and cooperation. When this happens, ways will have to be found to minimize their losses or to provide offsetting

---

6 Even for the EU, estimates of the benefits of cooperation and integration are hard to ascertain. According to Centennial Group International (2006, p. 44) "[i]t is virtually impossible reliably to estimate the impact of European integration on growth..." The study summarizes isolated estimates of benefits, including the direct benefits from monetary union amounting to 0.5 percent of GDP, benefits from financial integration amounting to 1.1 percent, and benefits from the internal market program of about 1.8 percent of GDP.

benefits to help create support for regional programs and provide for fair outcomes. The proliferation of often overlapping FTAs also raises concerns relating to spaghetti bowl effects, which threaten the benefits expected to accrue to members (Pangestu and Goopta, 2004; Menon, 2009).

In order to enhance the prospects of realizing benefits, regional cooperation initiatives should extend beyond simple tariff reduction to include the many other important areas of cooperation in pursuit of shared interests and the mitigation of shared threats.

Priority areas to facilitate regional cooperation

Regional cooperation can pursue shared interests among neighboring states in many different areas. These include efforts to maximize potential benefits for growth from coordination in trade integration through trade policy and facilitation, development of transport infrastructure, cooperation in macroeconomic management, and shared access to natural resources such as energy, water, and maritime resources. They also involve common responses to shared threats to growth from financial contagion and instability, natural disasters, epidemics, drugs, and regional conflicts. Ultimately, countries need to set priorities among these manifold areas of potential cooperation.

Trade policy and the role of free trade agreements

Trade policy has traditionally received the lion's share of attention in regional cooperation efforts, with free trade agreements (FTAs) becoming in recent years the principal instrument of regional trade policy in Asia. Until the mid-1990s, there were relatively few FTAs in place as Asian, and especially East Asian, countries liberalized their economies mostly unilaterally or as part of global trade agreements. However, since the mid-1990s and especially in the 2000s, bilateral FTAs multiplied, most likely as a response to the stalled WTO negotiations under the Doha Round and in a competitive response to the proliferation of bilateral FTAs elsewhere in the world (ADB, 2010a).

The most successful FTA among developing countries anywhere grew out of the ASEAN Free Trade Agreement (AFTA), which was signed in 1992 and led to the establishment of an ASEAN free-trade area by 2005. AFTA serves as a hub for FTAs with other neighbors (ASEAN+1 FTAs), including PRC, Japan, and the Republic of Korea. Other regional FTAs are also in place, most notably the South Asian FTA (SAFTA) under the umbrella of SAARC. It was adopted in 2004 and its implementation started in 2006 for completion by 2013 for non–least developed countries and by 2016 for least developed countries. However, SAFTA suffers from significant weaknesses because it does not cover services trade or large segments of goods categories, and does not address nontariff barriers (Weerakoon, 2010).[7]

Transport and trade facilitation

As previously noted, the coverage and quality of domestic and regional transport systems is a major determinant of the total cost of trading. Hence improvements in the overall system are important for effective regional integration. Plans for the development of an integrated regional transport network have been in existence since at least 1992 under the leadership of ESCAP. The Asian Highway and Trans-Asian Railway networks form the backbone of the ESCAP initiative. However, according to ADB (2009c, p. 28), "[a]t present regional infrastructure cooperation in Asia is relatively underdeveloped. Little progress has been made on various pan-Asian initiatives, such as the Asian Highway and the Trans-Asian Railway…" More promising have been two subregional transport cooperation initiatives, under the auspices of the Greater Mekong Subregion (GMS) Program and CAREC, both of which have received strong support from ADB. For each of these programs, regional transport corridors have been designed and approved by the ministers and are under implementation. The hardware part of these plans is being implemented according to recent reviews (CAREC, 2010a). It is expected that continued implementation of these plans will lead to significant improvements in transport along these key inland corridors.

Beyond the physical transport infrastructure, the "software" aspects of trade and transport need to be addressed, including all aspects of the physical movement of consignments; import and export procedures, such as visas, payments, and insurance modalities; inspections and legal and extra-legal payment requirements along inland roadways; logistics facilities and the computerized tracking of cargo; and the movement of people across borders (Bin, 2009).

The importance of these software aspects of trade and transport systems is now well recognized, and ASEAN, CAREC, and GMS, as well as the Asia-Pacific Economic Cooperation (APEC), all have initiatives to help facilitate trade and transport.[8] The CAREC initiative is noteworthy since it includes a sophisticated system of monitoring the time and costs required to transit along principal CAREC corridors. This makes it possible to assess the impact of the facilitation measures and determine where remaining bottlenecks need to be addressed. Progress reviews for both CAREC and GMS show that the implementation of software improvements tends to lag behind physical improvements (CAREC, 2010; ADB, 2010b). Sustained intensive efforts on the part of all governments concerned are needed for this area of regional engagement to bear fruit.

Macroeconomic cooperation on integration and financial stability

Financial integration usually follows on the heels of trade integration, and the combination of

---

7 Weerakoon (2010) also points out that SAFTA is losing steam because of the importance of India as the key market for most South Asian countries and the prevalence of bilateral agreements between India and many of its smaller neighbors, granting them virtually free access to India's markets.
8 For APEC, see Bin (2009); for ASEAN, see Alburo (2009); for CAREC, see CAREC (2010a); and for GMS, see ADB (2010b).

trade and financial integration tends to lead to macroeconomic convergence and exposure to external financial shocks, and hence instability. According to ADB (2010a), financial integration, while still low, has been on the rise in Asia and macroeconomic convergence has progressed as "the business cycles of the region's economies have narrowed sharply [and] the gap between the richest and poorest countries, although still very high, has decreased much faster than in other regions of the world" (ADB 2010a, p. 22). This means that economic shocks from within and outside Asia tend to be passed on quickly and intensively across the region. To counter this, the region needs to establish effective coordination and regulatory mechanisms to mitigate the spillovers of regional or global contagion (Azis, 2009).

This process was already on full display during the Asian financial crisis and played itself out again, albeit in less severe ways for Asia, during the recent global financial crisis. In response to the earlier crisis, Asian economies followed two important approaches: they increased the resilience of their national economies by assuring sound macroeconomic fundamentals and accumulating high levels of foreign reserves; and they began to develop cooperative regional mechanisms, initially among the members of ASEAN and ASEAN+3.

Three main steps have been taken on regional macroeconomic cooperation. First, ASEAN+3 ministers of finance established a mechanism for macroeconomic cooperation by initiating the Economic Review and Policy Dialogue in 2000. While still at a nascent stage and limited mostly to information exchange on global, regional, and national economic trends, it represents a first step toward policy harmonization.

Second, ASEAN+3 finance ministers set up the Asian Bond Market Initiative in 2002 as a way to deepen domestic financial markets, help create greater regional resilience to economic crises, and enable regional funding for infrastructure investments. In 2009, ASEAN+3 ministers followed up by setting up an ADB trust fund—the Credit Guarantee and Investment Facility—which is designed to deepen East Asia's bond markets by providing guarantees for local currency bond issues.

Third, ASEAN+3 launched the Chiang Mai Initiative (CMI) in 2000 as a direct response to the Asian financial crisis. Initially, CMI was a bilateral swap facility for its members to draw on to meet emergency liquidity needs. Following the recent global crisis, during which Republic of Korea and Singapore activated bilateral swap arrangements with the US Federal Reserve instead of drawing on CMI, ASEAN+3 finance ministers moved forward in 2009 turning CMI into a multilateralized facility, known as CMIM, which came into effect in March 2010. The fund now amounts to $120 billion, involves an explicit burden-sharing agreement (Japan and PRC each contributes 32 percent, Republic of Korea 16 percent, and ASEAN countries make up the remaining 20 percent), and thus represents a genuine multilateral facility. The finance ministers also agreed to set up an ASEAN+3 Macroeconomic Research Office, which will provide analytical and surveillance support. Some observers remain skeptical that CMIM is a strong regional mechanism

(Yuan and Murphy, 2010), but CMIM embodies critical elements of serious regional multilateral monetary and financial cooperation. A key question for the future is how it can be deepened and its regional coverage expanded beyond ASEAN+3.

Access to natural resources

Securing mutual access to natural resources—particularly energy, water, and maritime and seabed resources—is a key area of cooperation, competition, or potential conflict in Asia. Starting with energy, an increasing portion of Asia's energy needs is met by imports from the rest of the world.[9] Much of the oil is shipped from the Middle East through pirate-infested sea lanes in the Indian Ocean and the Straits of Malacca. Cooperative solutions to keep these sea lanes secure should ideally be found on a regionwide and global basis.

In addition, transcontinental oil and gas pipelines are being planned and built from Central Asia to East and South Asia, and from Iran to South Asia. Many of these involve passage across third-country territory, which requires cooperative solutions among the neighbors concerned. At the same time, major energy-consuming countries in Eurasia such as PRC, India, and EU members, are competing with each other to secure access to the energy resources of Central Asia. However, aside from a proposal sponsored by the UN Economic and Social Commission on Asia and the Pacific for a Trans-Asian Energy System, no Asia-wide energy cooperation mechanisms have been established or planned.[10] Chapter 11, which discusses energy, proposes a number of regional cooperative initiatives for energy security, including regional collaboration in the transfer and deployment of technologies, management of strategic petroleum stocks, and integration of electricity and gas networks.

Access to water resources is closely linked to the need for energy since countries can exploit their rivers for hydropower. In addition, water is a critical resource for agricultural production and human consumption. Asia has many large rivers, but the most important ones are in the 10 river basins of the Hindu Kush–Himalaya region, which lies at the center of Asia's continental space. These river basins span multiple countries and subregions. Interstate competition for these water resources has long historic roots, whether in the Indus Valley, Brahmaputra River Basin, Mekong River Basin, or Aral Sea Basin of Central Asia. It reveals the mixed record of efforts to cooperate regionally and bilaterally in sharing these resources, and the many plans to develop the river beds in major projects for electricity generation, irrigation, and use in rapidly growing urban centers (especially by PRC and India). The countries competing for these scarce water resources have thus far managed to do so peacefully, guided by international conventions and regional or bilateral

---

9 For details, see Chapter 11.
10 A subregional energy sector strategy has been developed under CAREC, which envisages long-term electricity interconnectivity in Central Asia and South Asia. Similarly, GMS has developed plans and projects to support regional interconnectivity.

agreements.[11]

While the impact of climate change on the water flows of Asia's major rivers cannot be predicted with certainty, judging from past glacier losses it is likely that long-term river flows will decline (Aon et al., 2010), further exacerbating regional water scarcities and increasing the potential for interstate conflict. Hence early attention to seek optimal solutions for the management and fair distribution of scarce water resources will be a critical factor in maintaining peace and permitting an effective adaptation to changing environmental conditions.

East Asian countries also compete with each other and at times have appeared on the verge of conflict over control of the maritime and seabed resources in the East China Sea (Guo, 2010) and South China Sea (Energy Information Administration, 2002). ASEAN agreed on a Declaration on the South China Sea in 1992 and agreed with PRC on a Declaration on the Conduct of Parties in the South China Sea in 2002. Both declarations envisage "peaceful dispute settlement and the mutual exercise of restraint" (ADB, 2010a). Continued interstate tensions over seabed resources show that competition for these resources does not need to result in conflict. Rather, collaboration for optimal resource exploitation is one of the key challenges of regional cooperation in Asia.

Responding to common regional threats: Natural disasters, epidemics, and the drug trade

A number of regional threats, some natural in origin, others man-made, can seriously affect the long-term prospects for growth and human security in Asia. Increasingly, the response can be on a regional or subregional basis.

Asia is subject to a wide range of potentially dramatic natural disasters. As a region, Asia is home to many areas with high levels of seismic activity, making major earthquakes very likely. Over the last century, major earthquakes have struck large cities and densely populated areas in Asia with disastrous consequences.[12] In addition, substantial parts of Asia's agricultural lands are threatened by recurring droughts, while low-lying areas of major river basins and coastal regions are subject to repeated flooding. The risk from both drought and flooding may dramatically increase with continued climate change.

In addition, parts of Asia are subject to tsunamis and cyclones. As the recent Japanese earthquake and tsunami demonstrated, many of these disasters have subregional and regional impacts, and therefore require subregional, regional, as well as global responses. Moreover, regional preparedness and risk pooling for insurance purposes may in many cases be the optimal

---

11 However, these agreements can easily come under stress, as the recent strains in PRC–India–Pakistan relations over use of the waters of the Indus River have shown. Tajikistan and Uzbekistan have also engaged in a war of words over Tajikistan's plans to build a large dam that would allow it to export power to South Asia, with Uzbekistan disrupting transit trade with Tajikistan (Linn, 2010).

12 The earthquake that struck Japan on 11 March 2011 is only the most recent reminder of the great seismic risks many parts of Asia face and the damage that major earthquakes can cause. Japan's extraordinary measures to prepare for such events are an example that other countries in the region need to emulate.

response.¹³ Asia has a regional disaster preparedness organization based in Bangkok, the Asia Disaster Preparedness Center, which supports national initiatives for disaster preparedness and response. However, not all Asian countries are involved in its activities and a review of national and international responses to recent natural disasters in Asia shows that many countries have a long way to go to achieve effective preparedness (Cohen, 2008). Disaster preparedness and response need to be given a much higher level of attention and funding from national, regional, and international agencies.

In health, with the exception of Central Asia, overall HIV/AIDS prevalence rates remain relatively low and stable in Asia.¹⁴ However, the absolute numbers are large and in some countries prevalence is rapidly increasing and the potential for long-term expansion of the epidemic, especially when coupled with expanded drug use (see below), is significant. National and international agencies have been engaged to varying extents in addressing the HIV/AIDS problem in Asia. However, regional dimensions of the problem deserve more attention. Other epidemics, including tuberculosis, malaria, SARS, and avian influenza, also involve cross-border and regional transmissions through the migration of people, animals, and insects, which calls for regional approaches to detection, information sharing, control, and response.

An epidemic of a special kind is the production and spread of illicit drugs. Asia is the principal source of opium, the primary ingredient in the production of heroin. Heroin and opium are mainly consumed in Eurasia. About 90 percent of the world's opium production takes place in Afghanistan, with another 4 percent originating in Myanmar (UNODC, 2010). About three-quarters of all heroin distribution takes place on the Eurasian continent, with about a quarter each in Asia, the Russian Federation, and Europe. Transit routes traverse all Eurasia, with particularly negative impacts on the health and governance of countries neighboring Afghanistan (UNDP, 2005).

Asian countries, along with their Eurasian neighbors, have an overriding interest in seeing Afghanistan's opium production curtailed, the cross-border trade of heroin and opium intercepted, and domestic consumption controlled. Asia has several subregional initiatives to control cross-border drug trafficking (UNDP, 2005). Whether these initiatives, combined with production controls in Afghanistan and Myanmar, will suffice to limit the flow of drugs to the major centers of consumption is uncertain and indeed unlikely. More will have to be done on a national, regional, and international basis for this epidemic to be halted and reversed.

Conflict prevention

Asia is, as said, a continent with many conflicts, both active and latent. Some interstate conflicts seem to be purely politically motivated, built on decades of distrust and antagonism,

---

13 For a good regional program of disaster preparedness, including insurance provision and risk pooling for Southeast Europe, see World Bank and ISDR (2008).
14 See http://www.avert.org/aids-asia.htm for further information.

disagreements over border alignment, or fears of aggression at the hands of a neighbor. Some intrastate conflicts are grounded in ideology, religion, or clan enmity. But most conflicts have two aspects in common: at the heart of the conflict is an economic reason, either as a major cause or as a facilitating factor (UNDP, 2005); and the effects of the conflict include substantial economic losses, especially if it involves widespread and sustained violence or warfare.[15] The preceding analysis has given examples of where economic reasons may lead to interstate conflict in Asia, especially over access to energy, water, and maritime and seabed resources. Control of drug production or transit can be another economic cause. Economic disruptions on top of long-standing economic grievances, such as the utility tariff increases in the Kyrgyz Republic in the spring of 2010, can trigger domestic violence and civil war.

Regional cooperation and regional institution building can be key factors in limiting conflict by settling disputes, building trust, and creating economic benefits for all parties. Fortunately, there are a number of success stories in Asia. ASEAN and GMS brought together countries that had previously fought bitter wars. The Shanghai Cooperation Organization was established to buttress regional security in Central Asia and succeeded in peaceful border delimitation of a previously unsettled border. SAARC has been credited with providing opportunities for the leaders of India and Pakistan to meet and establish exchanges at the highest level (Ahmed and Bhatnagar, 2008). Regional organizations and forums have been credited with the socialization of the neighboring countries of Asia through the building of mutual understanding and trust (see, for example, Acharya 2005).

One way to make regional institutions more effective in helping to prevent conflict is to call in a third party for mediation or to agree on conflict resolution mechanisms. In the case of India and Pakistan, the World Bank president played this role in 1960 in helping to forge a lasting agreement on the sharing the waters of the Indus River (Linn and Pidufala, 2008). Very few Asian regional organizations have conflict resolution mechanisms and those that do, such as ASEAN, have never used them (ADB, 2010a). Over time, formal regional conflict-resolution mechanisms need to be created; in the meantime, Asia will have to rely on informal diplomatic channels to help ensure that latent—and in some cases growing—tensions do not spill over into armed conflict.

Setting priorities

With a long list of cooperative opportunities and challenges, the question for Asia is which priorities regional leaders should focus on the following:
- reduce barriers to integration at and behind borders;
- invest in regional transport and communications infrastructure;
- assure regional energy security;

---

15 United Nations Development Programme (UNDP) (2005, p. 133) cites estimates that typically "30% to 50% of GDP [is] lost for a major civil war (Bosnia, Georgia, Tajikistan, etc.)."

- address the regional challenges of climate change adaptation and disaster preparedness;
- provide bilateral and multilateral assistance to countries that lag behind to facilitate their integration;
- support people-to-people exchanges, such as professional networks and cross-country volunteer programs, to foster personal contacts and build mutual understanding, goodwill, and trust; and
- create a high-level political forum to help resolve, when possible within the region, actual and latent conflicts (e.g., river basin issues) before seeking help and intervention of extraregional parties (whether bilateral or multilateral).

Increased integration will mostly be driven by market forces. Institutional efforts should be aimed at removing any remaining barriers to the free flow of goods, finance and, eventually, skilled labor.

Institutions for regional cooperation

From the virtual absence of any significant regional institutional structures in 1970, Asia has developed a multitude of regional, transregional, and subregional organizations, forums, and programs over the last 40 years.[16] However, Asia's regional institutional system remains informal, flexible, and consensus-based, with either weak or nonexistent secretariats. Arbitration and enforcement are also either absent, inoperative, or nonbinding; there is either limited or no monitoring and evaluation of country and institutional performances. This weak institutional regional system is the logical outcome of the strong sense of national identity and sovereignty of Asian governments and people.

A review of the structure of regional cooperation initiatives worldwide and Asia's regional opportunities and challenges concludes with these 10 lessons for Asian policy makers:[17]

1. Regional cooperation is not easy to achieve and the implementation of stated intentions is frequently weak. The experience of the EU, with its strong supranational regional institutions—including the European Commission, President, Parliament, and Court—is an exception and difficult to emulate.
2. Effective regional cooperation and integration efforts take time to develop and require incremental, gradual, and flexible implementation with visible payoffs.
3. It is preferable to keep the number of members in subregional and regional organizations manageable. Membership should be based on shared geography and common regional interests.
4. Adequate funding mechanisms for regional investments are essential.
5. Successful cooperation requires leadership at the country, institutional, and individual

---

[16] ADB (2010a) inventoried 40 regional, transregional, and subregional organizations, programs, and forums.
[17] This list is based on Linn and Pidufala (2008), and Haggard (2009).

levels.
6. External assistance can be helpful in setting up and sustaining subregional institutions, and was critical in the case of CAREC and GMS.
7. Open regionalism—the creation of institutions that are open to extraregional participation and do not discriminate against nonregional economies in the long term—is the most successful strategy.
8. Regional economic cooperation organizations that involve ministries of finance or economy and central banks tend to be more effective than those that rely on the leadership of line ministries or foreign affairs.
9. The engagement of the business community and civil society strengthens the mechanisms for regional cooperation.
10. Monitoring and evaluating the performance of countries under regional agreements is important, as are incentives for better compliance.

Among the existing subregional programs and institutions in Asia, ASEAN, CAREC, and GMS have each internalized many of these lessons. In fact, they have been identified as the more successful of the non-EU regional institutions worldwide. In the rest of the world there are few initiatives—outside the EU—that can match their performance. South Asian regional organizations have traditionally been weak and ineffective, but there are signs that subregional cooperation and institution building is on the rise in South Asia (Box 14.4). Nonetheless, Asia cannot be complacent. There are many more opportunities to be reaped from further integration and cooperation, especially in those subregions that lag behind. But significant threats also exist that require regional interventions for maximum effect.

Prospects and institutional options

In recent years, Asian leaders have called for an Asian community with shared interests and cooperation. Such support should open the door for a more cohesive, cooperative, and integrated Asia. Consistent with these statements, in 2008 ADB set out an ambitious vision for Asian regional integration and cooperation by 2020 (ADB, 2008a). This vision remains appropriate provided that expectations are kept realistic. An Asian community, based on shared interests and increased cooperation, is unlikely to be achieved in the next 10 years, but it could be achieved over the next 40.

It will be necessary to show more institutional innovation to ensure that existing institutions are increasingly cohesive and effective. This could take place at four levels: subregional, Asia-wide, interregional (with Europe and the Americas especially), and worldwide.

- At the subregional level, the examples of GMS and CAREC can serve as models for other Asian subregions.
- At the Asia-wide level, a gradual expansion and deepening of the "ASEAN+" approach

Box 14.4 | Regional cooperation and integration in South Asia

South Asia is a relative latecomer to regional cooperation and integration. The South Asian Association of Regional Cooperation (SAARC), established in 1985, was the first regional cooperation initiative in South Asia. The heads of state of Bangladesh, Bhutan, India, the Maldives, Nepal, Pakistan, and Sri Lanka participated at the first SAARC Summit in Dhaka in 1985.

SAARC was once described as "act of faith" given the absence of a shared security threat and the low level of formal intraregional trade and investment. The need to accelerate the SAARC integration process spurred Bangladesh, Bhutan, India, and Nepal to form the South Asia Growth Quadrangle (SAGQ). The South Asia Subregional Economic Cooperation (SASEC) program was launched in 2001 as the first formal and comprehensive subregional cooperation initiative in South Asia. The SASEC program provided a forum for the four countries to discuss, identify, and prioritize cooperation projects in transport, energy, environment, trade, investment, private sector development, tourism, and information and communication technology (ICT). The project-based approach of SASEC complements the policy and dialogue driven mechanism of SAARC.

SASEC has resulted in two important regional projects: the Information Highway Project and South Asia Tourism Infrastructure Development Project. The latter seeks to improve connectivity, providing a higher quality tourist environment and visitor services, and enhance natural and cultural heritage sites. Discussions are ongoing to expedite the service connection agreements for the regional information highway network, formation of community e-centers, and the conduct of ICT research and training.

In January 2010, Bangladesh and India signed a wide-ranging economic cooperation agreement that provides a comprehensive framework for cooperation in water resources, power, transportation, tourism, and education. The agreement allows the use of the Mongla and Chittagong sea ports for the movement of goods to and from India through road and rail. Bangladesh also conveyed its intention to give Nepal and Bhutan access to the Mongla and Chittagong ports. The agreement envisages energy trade between the two countries.

South Asia's interest in developing closer collaboration with other regional groupings has also grown. Countries in South and Southeast Asia have started inter-regional cooperation initiatives such as the Bay of Bengal Initiative for Multi-Sectoral Technical and Economic Cooperation (BIMSTEC) to pursue inter-regional cooperation. BIMSTEC is an important vehicle to facilitate integration between South Asia and Southeast Asia, the realization of which is critical for the achievement of Pan–Asian regional cooperation and integration.

provides the best institutional prospects.
- At the interregional level, APEC and the Asia–Europe Meeting (ASEM) are good starting points for greater engagement with neighboring regions, with a focus on improvements in physical connectivity, trade facilitation, and behind-the-border policy reforms for greater integration.
- At the global level, Asia could pursue a stronger regional stance within global international institutions and forums. ADB, in its recent publication, *Institutions for Regional Integration: Toward and Asian Economic Community*, proposed specific institutional innovations that deserve consideration (Box 14.5).

Box 14.5 | Proposals for new regional institutions

Key recent proposals put forward by ADB and other stakeholders include:
- Establishing an Asian Financial Stability Dialogue;
- Setting up a Pan-Asia Infrastructure Forum;
- Creating an Asian Infrastructure Fund;
- Addressing the impacts of overlapping FTAs, such as through the creation of a regional FTA and multilateralizing regionalism in the WTO context;
- Working toward an Asian Monetary Fund to conduct regional macroeconomic surveillance and establish crisis-prevention mechanisms;
- Setting up a cooperative framework for dealing with capital flows and regional exchange rates;
- Broadening the Asian Bond Market Initiative to Asian Capital Market Initiative;
- Setting up regional public goods forums to promote cooperation in dealing with natural disasters, climate change, and health concerns; and
- Setting up a Council of Asian Cooperation—an umbrella organization governed at the highest political level to address a range of pan-regional issues.

Source: ADB (2010a).

A crucial prerequisite to achieve increased regional cooperation is strong political support and leadership. Collaboration between the three mega-economies—PRC, Japan, and India—remains crucial. These three economies will have to establish cooperative leadership in the region by supporting the creation of open, well-connected markets among each other and with their smaller neighbors. They could shoulder the responsibility for fostering stable political conditions and the convergence of economic development in Asia. It will be particularly important for them to settle their distrust and work together—if necessary, with partners outside the region including the US and EU—to assure that other conflicts in the region are either prevented or terminated promptly. In this context, one or more medium-sized countries, such as Indonesia, Republic of Korea, and Malaysia could play a useful role in facilitating regional cooperation and collaboration.

The major challenge for Asian regional relations is to build on the successes of the past and find ways to maintain or establish mutual trust. Without a minimum degree of trust, little can be achieved in regional cooperation, institution building, or conflict prevention.

Realizing the Asian Century: Asia's Role in the World

Chapter 15

Harinder S. Kohli

Dramatic change in Asia's global footprint

Asia's role in the global economy is already dramatically different than after World War II when the current global governance, financial, and trading systems were conceived. It will be further transformed in the Asian Century scenario.

Asia's global economic footprint has expanded significantly since it hit the low point in the mid-1950s. Asia now accounts for 28 percent of the world economy, almost double its share in the mid-1950s. In the Asian Century scenario, the region's global footprint will continue to steadily expand and Asia will generate over half global GDP by 2050 (Figure 15.1).

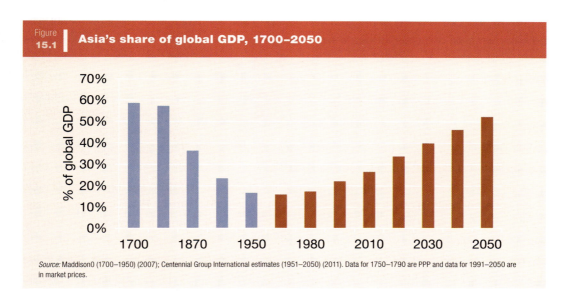

Figure 15.1 Asia's share of global GDP, 1700–2050

Source: Maddison0 (1700–1950) (2007); Centennial Group International estimates (1951–2050) (2011). Data for 1750–1790 are PPP and data for 1991–2050 are in market prices.

This transformation is not limited to share of global GDP. Sixty years ago, Asia was the poorest region in the world with per capita income a small fraction of the global average. It had meager savings and investment rates, and was a net importer of capital. It had negligible foreign exchange reserves and weak currencies. It was the largest recipient of international (Western) development assistance and very little FDI. It was heavily dependent on imported technologies.

Today, it is the first developing region to have achieved the income-related MDG, well ahead of 2015. Seven Asian economies are now classified as developed. PRC, India, Japan, and Republic of Korea now rank among the world's leading economies. Asia is now the largest saver and exporter of capital. It has over 75 percent of global reserves. Its domestic savings and investment rates have risen and absolute poverty has fallen. Indeed, PRC, India, and Republic of Korea have now joined Japan in providing technical and financial support to other parts of the world (mainly Africa). And, PRC and India have joined Japan, Republic of Korea, Singapore, and Taipei,China in providing sophisticated manufactured products and information services to the rest of the world.

This book postulates that in the Asian Century these trends will continue and Asia will assume a leading position in most aspects of the global economy. Not only will it account for over half global GDP, savings, investment, and financial assets, but its per capita income will exceed the global average perhaps for the first time in history. Some 3 billion more Asians will become affluent and expect to enjoy living standards of an average European today.

Implications of Asia's global role

Perhaps because of the unprecedented speed of Asia's reemergence (Chapter 4), but also perhaps because of its low-key approach to geopolitics until recently, few—within and outside Asia—appreciate how small Asia's role is in global governance relative to its share of global GDP, trade, savings, and investment.

Indeed, until the creation of G20, global governance was based on the architecture agreed after World War II, which assigned leadership to the G-7 countries. The current system is already inconsistent with the new economic realities, and will become more and more untenable as Asia continues its march toward the Asian Century. All parties, including Asia itself, must grapple with the fundamental implications of these new realities.

Asia's growth and the rapid expansion of its economic footprint will bring with it new challenges and obligations for the region and its largest economies: PRC, India, Indonesia, Japan, and Republic of Korea. This will have far-reaching implications for the region's role in the world, how it sees its long-term self-interest, and how it interacts with other parts of the world.

Asia needs to rethink its role in a very wide range of issues and institutions: its stake in the global commons, its relation to other regions, the implications of domestic and regional policies for others, and so on. Instead of being an outsider looking into an insiders' club, Asia will become the insider looking out at the rest of the world.

They also see that global peace and security are a prerequisite for Asia's economic and social well-being. So the region's self-interest will extend well beyond economics and encompass global political governance and security arrangements. The region will therefore need to transform its role in global governance, economic and political.

Global commons

The central implication of Asia accounting for half or more of global GDP and population by 2050 is that the center of gravity of the global economy will shift gradually from the Atlantic Ocean to mainland Asia.

As Asia becomes half of the global economy, it will be crucial for its own well-being that the global commons, on which the global economy depends, continue to function. As a result, Asia will become the biggest stakeholder in the global commons, taken to include an open trading system, a stable financial system, the international rule of law, and, of course, peace and security. So far, the Western powers have been the prime stakeholders since World War II. But Asia will no longer be able to afford not to share that responsibility. It must start to play a co-leadership role. Otherwise, it will be unable to grow and prosper over the longer term.

Asia must therefore take greater ownership of the global commons. Indeed, in its own self-interest, it should become a forceful advocate and defender of the commons. But its efforts to enhance regional cooperation must not be at the cost of its traditional openness to the rest of the world. Asia must adhere to its long-standing strategy of open regionalism from which it has benefited handsomely since the 1950s.

Global trading system

East Asia's growth since the 1950s was greatly facilitated by an increasingly open global trading system. As discussed in Chapter 2, Asia has done very well from the system. Today, its ratio of trade to GDP is the highest among the major regions.

In the future, even as domestic and intraregional markets account for a larger share of Asian economies, the region will need to continue trading heavily with the rest of world to supply ultimate consumers in North America and Europe, to acquire the latest technologies and know-how wherever they exist in the world, and to import the natural resources needed by domestic economies.

In short, it is of vital interest to Asia that the world continues to have an open and free trading system.

Global shipping lanes, trading routes, and communications channels

Open shipping lanes and other trading routes are the arteries of Asia's economic health. As the region most reliant on global trade, Asia will have a vital interest in keeping them open, and free of conflict or piracy. For example, open sea-lanes in the Persian Gulf and the Malacca Straits are essential for Asia's imports and exports. Similarly, safe air space lanes accessible to all are essential. And channels for digital communications will become equally important.

Asia must become an advocate in this area.

Global financial system

Finance is global, and so although national reforms are necessary and regional cooperation desirable, they are not sufficient—Asia must pay much more attention to the robustness of the global financial system.

With its enormous savings and investment rates, Asia should host some of the largest global equity, debt, and banking markets well before 2050. It is already the biggest holder of global reserves. Heavily reliant on trade, Asia would therefore have a huge stake in a well-functioning and fair international monetary system and the associated institutions. It will be in Asia's interest that the global financial system (as well as its own) is sound and efficient. This is necessary for the region's savers to have acceptable risk-adjusted returns and for its economies to have access to investment funds at rates competitive with those elsewhere.

Given its rising weight in global reserves, savings, and investment, the region will have an opportunity to increasingly shape the global financial architecture, the monetary system, and global financial intermediation. Asia needs to play an active and constructive role in the governance of the global monetary and financial system.

Asia must also transform its role from being a rule taker to being a rule maker (or rule co-maker) in policy forums and from being a price taker to a price maker in the marketplace.

Climate change

Chapter 12 argued that Developing Asia's stance on climate change requires a reassessment. Analysis carried out for this book demonstrates that early and forceful action on climate change is in Asia's own self-interest—socially, economically, and politically.

A change in the current stance of large Asian economies in the global climate change negotiations will be an early demonstration to the world community that Asia is able to play a constructive role in protecting the global commons, even in areas where its short-term interests may be at odds with others.

Global peace and prosperity

As Asia becomes the center of the global economy, it will be in its own interest that the rest of the world is also doing well economically and politically. Peace and security throughout the world will be essential for its own long-term prosperity just the way during the past 50 years the currently developed countries have supported peace and security efforts throughout the world.

Since the end of World War II, Asian countries have not felt the need to play an active role in sustaining global peace and security and have relied on the Western countries. In line with the rise in its share of the global economy and thus its rising stake in the well-being of the rest of the world, Asia needs to devote greater intellectual and material resources—jointly with Europe and North America—to the economic, social, and political stability of the world as whole.

Asia also needs to recognize that it cannot rely forever on outside powers to help preserve peace and security within Asia. It will soon need to consider regional security arrangements. The change in Asia's role is neither urgent nor will it come immediately. But Asia needs to start preparing for it soon.

Relations with other parts of world

Asia already has, and will continue to have, close economic, political, and security relations with other countries and regions, near and far. For example, various Asian economies have strong economic relations with countries nearby: the Gulf countries and the Russian Federation for petroleum supplies; with Australia and New Zealand for food, coal, and other minerals; and with Turkey as a conduit for trade with the Middle East and Europe. More recently, Asia's twin giants have followed Japan in seeking closer economic ties with Africa and Latin America, to secure access to mineral resources and export markets. Many countries, such as the ASEAN countries, have close political and security ties with the US and Australia.

Such relations will become even more important in the future. They must not be allowed to suffer even as Asian economies redouble their efforts at regional cooperation and integration. Indeed, these efforts must keep in view the longer-term perspective of Asia playing a central role in global trade, finance, and investment. The region must keep its borders open to others in order to have equal access to markets worldwide.

Indeed, Asia's approach to realizing the Asian Century should be based on the concept of shared global prosperity.

Development assistance

In the past, Asia has benefited greatly from development assistance and private capital flows from the West. This was necessary when Asia was a relatively poor region and home to billions of absolute poor. In broader financial terms, too, these flows were justified as the region was capital deficit and the developed countries were capital surplus.

This position is changing fast. The incidence of absolute poverty in Asia has already dropped hugely. Under the Asian Century scenario, by 2050 there will no poor countries in Asia and the average per capita incomes of Asia will exceed the global average. Asia has already become a net exporter of capital and has accumulated massive reserves. This comfortable financial situation is likely to continue through 2050, if not improve further.

Asia should not therefore expect external development assistance for long from non-Asian sources. Asia needs to seriously consider formulating its own regional development assistance strategy under which the better-off Asian economies provide technical and financial assistance to the less well-off in a systematic manner and take over the role traditionally played by the OECD countries.

Japan has long provided large-scale development assistance to the less developed countries in Asia and elsewhere. Other developed economies in Asia (including Brunei Darussalam; Republic of Korea; Singapore; and Taipei,China) should consider joining such efforts soon. And over time, as they develop further, PRC, India, and Indonesia will need to consider greatly increasing their development assistance programs, within and outside Asia, that meet the guidelines of the Development Assistance Committee of the OECD.

Impact of national and regional policies on others

As demonstrated during the Great Recession, in today's globalized economy major developments or crises in the largest economies can lead to contagion elsewhere. Transmission is not limited to crises. Indeed, changes in the major policies of large economies, including monetary, exchange rate, fiscal, and immigration policies, can have substantial effects on others.

As the relative size of individual Asian economies and the region's global footprint expand, the larger economies especially, as well as the region as whole, will need to pay greater attention to these effects when formulating their domestic or regional policy agendas.

Global governance

If it succeeds in realizing the Asian Century, the region will need to greatly change its role in global governance and rule making. While working on the national and regional agenda discussed in Chapters 6–14, Asia must begin to assume greater global responsibilities. With six members in G20, Asia can and must show leadership on critical global issues.

It will need to gradually transform itself from a passive onlooker in the debate on global rule making and a reticent follower of the rules, to an active debater and constructive rule maker. How these global rules are formulated, supervised, and implemented—WTO protocols, rules of the Bank for International Settlements, IMF guidelines, and so on—can have an enormous impact on the costs and competitiveness of countries and regions.

To play a proactive role in global rule making and enforcement, Asia must pursue a stronger stance in global international institutions, such as the Financial Stability Forum, the Bank for International Settlements, and WTO, as well as political forums, such as G20, Asia-Pacific Economic Cooperation, and the United Nations Security Council.

To perform a leading role in the above apex bodies, Asian leaders must be capable of putting forward their own ideas, beyond responding to proposals from the traditional global powers. They must also groom and nurture a strong cadre of well-trained individuals who can play lead roles in these institutions, just as the G-7 countries have done since World War II.

Given the complexity of the issues discussed in such bodies, Asian leaders will also need to be supported by world-class institutions and by professional experts in related government bodies and in local think-tanks and academic institutions (though some will have to be regional, as not all countries in the region can develop such capacity).

Managing Asia's rise

Finally, Asia must delicately manage its rapidly rising role as a major player in global governance non-assertively and constructively. As an emerging global leader, Asia should act—and be seen to act—as a responsible global citizen.

Conclusion: Cost of Missing the Asian Century

Chapter 16 — Harinder S. Kohli, Ashok Sharma, and Anil Sood

Tackling transformation

Achieving a potentially historic transformation in a region that encompasses half of humanity (over 4 billion people) depends primarily—though not exclusively—on tackling the intergenerational challenges and managing the risks discussed in this book. Many economies in the region face the challenge of rising inequality that could undermine social cohesion. The converging economies face the risk of falling into the Middle Income Trap and stagnating. Rapid growth and rising expectations could result in intense competition for finite natural resources. Rising income disparities across countries could destabilize the region. Climate change could threaten agricultural production, coastal populations, and urban areas alike. Importantly, inadequate governance and institutional capacity could become a binding constraint to growth.

These challenges and risks are not independent. They could affect one another, lead to conflict, and create new pressure points within Asia that could jeopardize regional growth, stability, and security.

Mitigating actions span three dimensions: national action; regional cooperation; and a global agenda. National action would vary by country given the wide disparities of individual country conditions. Although prescribing country specific actions is beyond the scope of this book, the agenda discussed in Part II provides policy and implementation direction that individual countries could consider in their pursuit of the plausible, but by no means preordained, Asian Century.

National action agenda

Success at a national level depends on meeting seven core challenges: achieving growth with inclusion and equity; enhancing productivity, entrepreneurship, and innovation; managing mass urbanization; making a financial transformation; radically reducing energy intensity and natural resource use; mitigating and adapting to climate change; and dramatically improving governance and the quality of institutions.

Achieving growth with inclusion

To sustain growth over the long term and maintain social cohesion, Asian countries must give much greater priority to inclusion and elimination of inequalities—rural/urban, educated/uneducated, or along ethnic lines. Inclusive growth must not only address poverty, but must also deal with aspects of equity, equality of access and opportunity, and provide protection to the vulnerable.

Rural development, including agriculture, will remain important in all low- and middle-income economies. Ensuring food security will reduce the vulnerability of the poor. Urban inequity—rising in parts of Asia—will need to be addressed, and slums will need to be eliminated.

A sharper focus on education and development of human capital, with a particular focus on women, will be essential to fully realize the demographic dividend. Governments must also increase access to high-quality infrastructure services and promote innovation that meets, affordably, the needs of those at the bottom of the pyramid. Adaptation measures need to be incorporated into development strategies to mitigate the impacts of climate change on the poor and vulnerable. Supportive environments for domestic philanthropy can also play a significant mitigating role, as can various forms of insurance against risks, such as unemployment, disability, illness, or death of a family wage earner. Generating employment for the poor and ensuring minimum wage through active labor-market policies, such as guaranteed employment schemes, can make a difference (though there can be leakages).

Productivity, entrepreneurship, and technological development

The continuing rapid growth of Asian economies over the next 40 years will require the full potential of technological change, innovation and, critically, entrepreneurship to be harnessed.

The model in Asia, with a few exceptions, has been that of catching up with the more advanced economies and adapting the technologies developed there to produce for Western markets. This was appropriate when Asian countries were far from global best practice and on the lower rungs of the convergence ladder. But as more Asian countries emulate Japan, the Republic of Korea, and Singapore and come closer to Western best practice, catching up will be inadequate.

The fast-growing converging economies, particularly PRC and India, must move to frontier entrepreneurship and innovation, and create breakthroughs in science and technology, if they are to become high-income countries. A particularly fruitful area, where India has already demonstrated notable success, will be inclusive innovation to meet the needs of millions of people on modest incomes.

The core requirement—where many Asian economies fall short—is high-quality education at all levels. Education systems in much of Asia need to be reformed to promote creativity, innovation, and entrepreneurship. The most critical element will be an overall policy framework that promotes competition and enables private development.

Managing massive urbanization

Urbanization is an unparalleled opportunity to increase productivity and improve the quality of life of citizens. Asia must adopt a new approach to urbanization by promoting compact, energy-efficient, green, safe, and livable cities, which will be more reliant on mass transit than on cars. It must also manage some significant risks, particularly those associated with inequality, slums, and a breakdown of social cohesion.

Better financing and management of cities will require governments to further decentralize responsibility to local levels, offer more local accountability, and move toward market financing of urban capital investment with particular emphasis on public–private partnerships. Urban development takes many decades. Timely action will require visionary leadership.

Making a financial transformation

In growing and transforming their financial systems to serve their real-sector and financial-inclusion objectives, Asian economies must heed the lessons of the Asian financial crisis and the recent global recession. Above all, they must avoid falling prey to another bubble of excessively exuberant expectations. Asia needs to put in place a financial system that efficiently intermediates its savings to support real sector activities, particularly infrastructure, urbanization, and entrepreneurship.

Asia will need to formulate its own financial model, avoiding both an overreliance on self-regulation by markets as well as the excessive government control of bank-dominated financial systems present in many parts of the region. It should become more open to institutional innovation. It must also, immediately, develop instruments and create an enabling environment to finance its massive infrastructure and urban development needs through public–private partnerships. Asia, especially Northeast Asia, has to pay greater attention to the special needs of its aging societies through well-developed pension and insurance markets. Asia's finance sector must also provide affordable access to the millions at the bottom of the pyramid.

National reforms must aim to create conditions to facilitate regional (and global) integration. Asia should become home to one or more global financial centers and several global financial houses, and assume a larger role in the international financial architecture.

Reducing energy intensity and natural resource use

The key policy implication for all Asian countries is that their future competitiveness and well-being depend heavily on improving the efficiency of natural resource use and winning the global race to a low-carbon future. Out of self-interest, Asia will need to take the lead in securing and decarbonizing energy through radical energy efficiency and diversification programs, especially switching from fossil fuels to renewables. There are similar issues related to most other natural resources, including water and fertile land. The only way out is a combination of price increases (hence removal of subsidies), technological breakthroughs, and adjustments in consumption patterns supplemented by more stringent standards (for buildings and transport).

Remedial actions will be required nationally, regionally, and globally. There is a strong synergy between energy efficiency and total factor productivity growth, which is needed for sustained convergence and global competitiveness.

Mitigating and adapting to climate change

By taking early action to mitigate climate change and by making the transition to a low-carbon future, Asian countries can transform their economies toward a new technological paradigm. This will bring greater energy security, healthier and more productive citizens, cleaner cities, more productive agricultural societies, and more competitive industries. Overall, it will make Asian economies globally more competitive and thus sustain the region's high growth over the long term.

"Grow now and pay later" would only add to the cost. Poor suffer disproportionately from adverse impacts of climate change. It is in Asia's own interest to act now.

Transforming governance and quality of institutions

The recent deterioration in the quality and credibility of national political and economic institutions (illustrated by rising corruption) is a key concern. High-quality institutions will help the fast-growing converging economies avoid the Middle Income Trap, and the slow- or modest-growth or aspiring economies establish the basic conditions for moving toward sustained economic growth. Managing the common challenges requires effective central and local governance.

Throughout Asia, an expanding middle class—itself a desirable product of rapid socioeconomic growth—will demand increased voice and participation, transparent allocation of resources, accountability for results, and enhanced personal space.

Although daunting, eradicating corruption is critical for all countries to maintain social and political stability and retain the legitimacy of governments. As recent events in the Middle East illustrate, the quality of communication between the governing and the governed will be crucial as new social media and other tools as yet unknown (but certain to emerge) become available. Asia will need to substantially improve governance and its institutions, with an emphasis on transparency and accountability.

Regional cooperation agenda

Cooperation and integration are critical for Asia's prosperity, and they will become more important. In addition, avoiding conflict between mega-economies and nuclear states while maintaining domestic social and political stability will be fundamental.

Given its diversity and heterogeneity, Asia will need to develop its own unique model that builds on the positive experience in East Asia: a market-driven, bottom-up, and pragmatic approach supported by an evolving institutional framework that facilitates free regional trade and investment flows across all 49 Asian economies. This model could build on the ASEAN experience and gradually include more economies. The aim of these actions and government initiatives is to create an Asian economic community. Such an approach will require stronger—though not necessarily new—regional institutions.

An Asian economic community must be based on two general principles—openness and transparency. Asia's embrace of open regionalism implies that it is open to new members and does not discriminate against nonmembers while it encourages regional institutions to make the most of existing global institutions and conventions. Transparency will enhance accountability and strengthen governance.

Crucial for increased regional cooperation is strong political leadership. Given the region's diversity, building Asia's regionalism will require collective leadership that recognizes a balance of power among all participants. Asia's major economic powers, such as PRC, India, Indonesia, Japan, and Republic of Korea, will be important in integrating Asia and shaping its role in the global economy.

Changing Asia's role in the world

One of the most important messages of this book is that Asia's growing importance to the global economy will bring new challenges and obligations. Asia must take greater ownership of the global commons, including an open global trading system, a stable global financial system, climate-change mitigation measures, and peace and security.

As it becomes a larger player in the global economy, Asia's self-interest and long-term prosperity will lie in ensuring well-being, peace, and security throughout the world.

The region as a whole, and particularly the larger economies of PRC, India, Indonesia, Japan, and Republic of Korea, will have to take into account the regional and global implications of domestic policy agendas. Delicate management of this ascendancy in a non-assertive and constructive way is vital. Asia should act—and be seen—as a responsible global citizen.

Asia must gradually transform its role to that of an active participant and a thought leader in formulating the rules on the global commons. Early action by Asia will be a concrete demonstration that it is willing and able to play a constructive role in preserving the global commons. The region as a whole must play a more active role in global governance.

Priorities across countries

The intergenerational challenges exist in most Asian economies, but their priority depends on which of three groups each economy belongs to: the seven that have grown rapidly since the

1950s, avoiding the Middle Income Trap to become high-income, developed economies in one generation; the 11—including PRC and India—that have grown fast since 1990 to reach middle-income status and now face the biggest risk of falling into the Middle Income Trap; or the 31 that have grown slowly and whose shift to rapid growth would help to spread affluence to all Asians.

The first group—especially Japan, Republic of Korea, and Singapore—must lead the way in scientific and technological developments that are of special importance to Asia, such as biotechnology, medical care for the aged, and the mitigation of climate change. This group is also expected to move beyond the promotion of high economic growth into delivering broader social well-being. Asia's high-income economies—and middle income nations such as PRC—face the singular challenge of the aging of the very generation that created the Asian miracle. This demographic and economic reality affects all aspects of governance, demanding wide-ranging institutional adjustments that raise issues of fiscal affordability and sustainability.

Avoiding the Middle Income Trap is the paramount objective of the second group (Box 16.1). Reducing inequality is the biggest single challenge here, but it is also vital to develop modern and more agile institutions for property rights and competition, as well as a critical mass of highly skilled people, in order to grow through innovation, as affluent countries do. Avoiding the middle income trap also requires financial system transformation to foster development in the real economy and promote entrepreneurship while also managing the energy and resource challenges of rapid urbanization. Such institutional development is often a multigenerational endeavor that presents a challenge for policy makers as the benefits are not immediately visible and may accrue indirectly and over the very long term.

The highest priority for the last group—which includes economies from Tajikistan to Nepal—must be to accelerate growth and join the group of convergers. That requires reducing inequality, improving the quality and spread of education, developing infrastructure, strengthening institutions, and adopting pro-business policies that promote domestic growth and external trade.

Need for enhanced resilience

Asia's rise will almost certainly not be smooth. History teaches that. In the past 40 years, for example, financial crises have occurred roughly once every decade. It is most likely that there will be major crises—economic or political—between now and 2050. Fortunately in the past, with each successive crisis, Asia has demonstrated a growing capacity to manage their effects. An enhanced resilience to external shocks was demonstrated vividly during the Great Recession of 2007–2009 (Boorman et al., 2010). Asia was the first region to recover, rebounding sharply and leading global growth since (Kohli and Sharma, 2010). But the region must not become complacent. It must continue to reinforce its resilience by following prudent macroeconomic, fiscal, and monetary policies and by making financial systems more robust. The adaptability, flexibility, and capacity to respond to a fast-changing global economic landscape will carry a high premium.

Box 16.1 | Avoiding the Middle Income Trap

Few countries sustain high growth for more than a generation, and even fewer continue high growth once they reach middle-income status. The biggest difference between middle-income growth strategies and those of low-income countries is the need for the former to focus more on demand. Domestic demand and new export demand become more important engines of growth in middle-income economies and a transition must take place toward services firms. Innovation and product differentiation to meet the needs of the market become increasingly important since cost-competitiveness declines with higher wages.

Three strategic issues face policy makers in middle-income countries. First, unlike low-income countries where diversification is the key process, middle-income countries (at least in the upper ranges) start to specialize in production. Specialization is a key ingredient in redeploying resources from low- to higher-productivity activities. That implies continuing to address rigidities that can arise from vested interests, inappropriate regulations, imperfect information, discrimination, and other barriers to effective competition. Developing good social safety nets and skill-retraining programs are policy ingredients that can help ease the pain of the restructuring that accompanies specialization.

Second, the education system must be reformed for an innovation economy. Advanced secondary and tertiary education is required to equip the labor force with the skills to generate ideas and to develop new technology to fit the changing world. Institutions of higher learning to produce skilled professionals cannot be created overnight but require long-term investment and planning. To be successful and accumulate a critical mass of professionals, middle-income countries must be enjoyable places to live.

Third, innovation must accompany investment and capital accumulation. But individuals and firms in middle-income countries face large obstacles in becoming more innovative. They have few options for financing other than family and friends. Large, well-connected firms often dominate their sectors, limiting scope for growth of start-up companies. Barriers to entry and exit are high. Universities and research institutes do not have incentives to encourage knowledge workers to link to the business community. These barriers will have to be eliminated

Beyond these three issues, middle-income strategies—by focusing on demand—might also require a change in mind-set for social programs. For low-income countries, social policy is equated with efforts to reduce poverty and improve opportunities for poor people. This is important for welfare reasons, but poverty reduction itself does not generate the large consumer markets nor the investments in education and institutionalized savings that are needed to sustain growth. They require social policy to target the middle class. In many countries, failure of the middle class to develop slows growth. The alternative to net export

> ### Box 16.1 — Avoiding the Middle Income Trap
>
> demand, domestic consumption, does not expand at the required rate without a strong middle class. Targeting social policy for creating and satisfying the middle class is quite different from that required in low-income countries. It may mean low-cost housing for first-time home buyers in cities, or programs to ensure that recent graduates have suitable employment opportunities. It can mean paying more attention to public goods like safety, urban transport, and green spaces.

Cost of missing the Asian Century

Failure to achieve the Asian Century implies the second of the two scenarios set out: falling into the Middle Income Trap. This would bring a very different set of outcomes for the well-being, happiness, and lifestyles of generations of Asians—and for other societies around the world—by 2050.

The pie charts in Figure 16.1 illustrate the differences in the basic economic parameters in the two scenarios. The differences are dramatic (Table 16.1). Asia's GDP per capita (in PPP terms) in the Middle Income Trap scenario is about half ($20,600) that in the Asian Century scenario ($40,800). Asian GDP at market exchange rates in 2050 reaches only $65 trillion, or 31 percent of global GDP, as compared with $174 trillion, or 52 percent of the global economy. The opportunity cost of not realizing the Asian Century scenario is huge, especially in human terms.

The human dimension: Quality of life

In the Asian Century scenario, almost 3 billion additional Asians—roughly 90 percent of the region's inhabitants—would enjoy the fruits of an affluent society at least one generation earlier than in the Middle Income Trap scenario. In either scenario Asia scores well in eradicating absolute poverty and more than achieves the income poverty threshold of the Millennium Development Goals. However, there do exist large differences between the two scenarios with respect to non-income factors such as the access to basic infrastructure services.

Provision of basic infrastructure services[1]

Access to clean and safe drinking water is a striking example. In the Asian Century scenario in 2050, 98 percent of Asians have access to improved water supplies, leaving 82 million in need (Figure 16.2). Falling into the Middle Income Trap leaves as many as 222 million Asians without

---

1 The models used in this section to project the road-network density and population without access to improved water sources build upon the growth model used for this book (described in Appendix 2). Their methodology and data definitions are given in Kohli and Basil (2011), which specifies for these sectors certain structural equation models based on instrumental variables. However, the variables chosen and corresponding coefficients used there are based on data for only Latin America. Here we employ global models generated using data for 174 countries, with the variable choices and coefficients given in Kohli and Mukherjee (2011), from which the following discussion is taken.

Figure 16.1 | Asian Century vs. Middle Income Trap

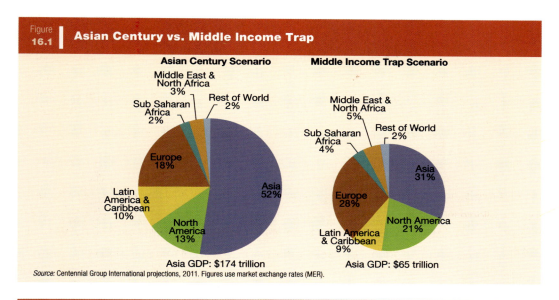

Asian Century Scenario
- Middle East & North Africa 3%
- Rest of World 2%
- Sub Saharan Africa 2%
- Europe 18%
- Latin America & Caribbean 10%
- North America 13%
- Asia 52%

Asia GDP: $174 trillion

Middle Income Trap Scenario
- Middle East & North Africa 5%
- Rest of World 2%
- Sub Saharan Africa 4%
- Europe 28%
- Latin America & Caribbean 9%
- North America 21%
- Asia 31%

Asia GDP: $65 trillion

Source: Centennial Group International projections, 2011. Figures use market exchange rates (MER).

Table 16.1 | Economic 2050 outcomes in two scenarios— Asian Century and the Middle Income Trap

Share of global GDP (%), MER	Asian Century	Middle Income Trap
Asia	52	31
PRC	20	10
India	16	7
United States	12	18
GDP ($ trillions, MER)		
Asia	174	65
PRC	68	20
India	53	14
United States	38	38
World	333	208
GDP per capita ($ PPP)		
Asia	40,800	20,600
PRC	52,700	23,500
India	40,700	17,900
United States	94,900	94,900
World	37,300	25,600

Note: MER = market exchange rates.

Source: Centennial Group International projections, 2011.

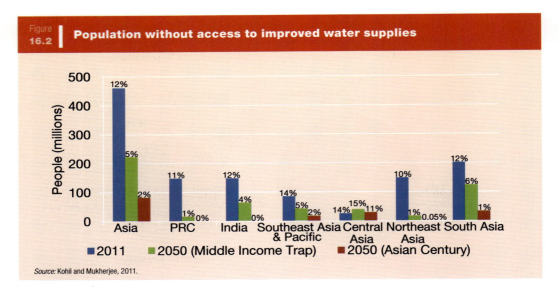

Figure 16.2 | Population without access to improved water supplies

Source: Kohil and Mukherjee, 2011.

access to them.

A loss of potential economic growth would also create shortcomings in other areas of basic infrastructure, including access to paved roads. Research shows distance from roads is one of the indicators most closely tied to infant death rates (Ombok et al., 2010; Huang et al., 1997). Increased proximity to roads also increases family and leisure time by decreasing transportation time, and rehabilitating roads raises aggregate crop indices and agricultural wages, better develops local communities, decreases reliance on farming for primary income, and increases food availability and primary and secondary school completion rates (Khandker et al., 2006; Mu and van de Walle, 2007; Calderón et al., 2008).

In the Asian Century scenario, non-urban road density across the region is 21 percent higher than in the Middle Income Trap, and is 25 percent higher in PRC, 23 percent higher in India, and 21 percent higher in Southeast Asia. Figure 16.3 compares the expansions of the road networks over time in each scenario.

For comparisons for the sanitation, port, and airport sectors, see Kohli and Mukherjee (2011).

The intangibles

Admittedly, the three-pronged agenda—national, regional, and global—is daunting. But the promise of an Asian Century is a great prize. It more than justifies the extraordinary effort, discipline, and enlightened leadership required.

The policy and strategic changes required together with the related institutional reforms have long gestation periods extending over decades, but their impact must be seen well before 2050 to set the path to prosperity.

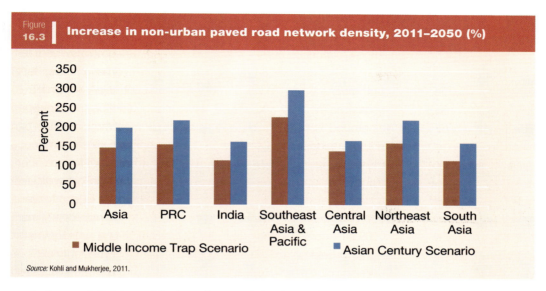

Figure 16.3 Increase in non-urban paved road network density, 2011–2050 (%)

Source: Kohli and Mukherjee, 2011.

Actions of Asia's political, policy, and business leaders today—and their successors tomorrow—will determine whether the Asian Century becomes reality, or remains a tantalizing promise.

As important as the intergenerational issues and related policy agenda highlighted in Chapters 7–15 are four overriding intangible factors that will determine Asia's ability to resolve these issues and shape its long-term destiny.

First is a requirement for leadership with unwavering focus on the long term, regardless of relentless short-term problems and shifts in comparative economic advantages. This is critical if the current level of momentum is to be sustained for another 40 years. Second, Asians must be willing to adopt and pursue pragmatic, rather than ideological, policies and put an emphasis on the results these policies deliver. Third is the need for much greater mutual trust that is essential for effective regional cooperation. And fourth is a commitment by leaders to modernize governance and institutions, improving transparency and accountability.

Asia's future is in its own hands.

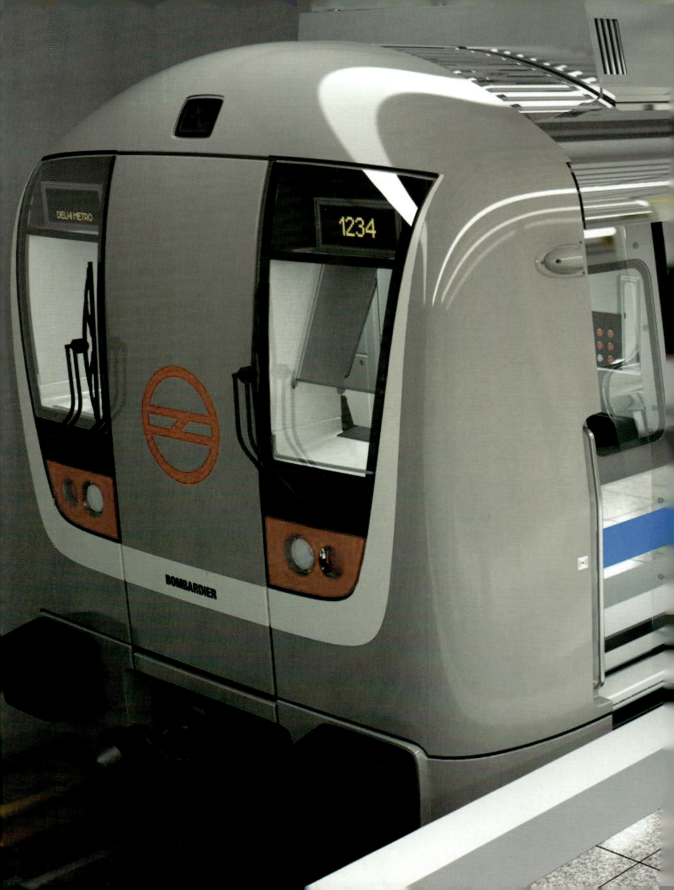

Appendix 1

Demographic Changes in Asia's Regions by 2050[1]

By 2050, Asia will constitute about 52 percent of the global population, a little smaller than its 57 percent share in 2010, but with roughly 822 million more people than today.

Northeast Asia's share in all of Asia's population will have fallen from nearly 40 percent in 2010 to 31 percent in 2050. What is concealed in this general number is the fact that Japan and Republic of Korea's populations will continue to fall, and by 2050, will have fallen by 14 percent and 2 percent, respectively. New population projections, released by the United Nations Statistics Division, in May 2011, estimate that by 2050 PRC's population will have fallen by 3.4 percent, which represents 46 million fewer people than in 2010.

Southeast Asia is expected to grow faster than the Asia average and to have added about 164 million people by 2050. In the period 2010 to 2050, Indonesia will have grown by 22 percent, adding 54 million people to its total, and Viet Nam by over 18 percent with 16 million more.

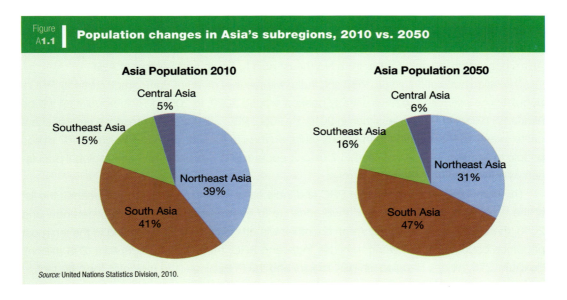

Figure A1.1 Population changes in Asia's subregions, 2010 vs. 2050

Source: United Nations Statistics Division, 2010.

1 This appendix was written by Natasha Mukherjee.

Table A1.1 | Population changes in Asia, 2010–2050

Population (in millions)	2010	Projected 2050	Change in population (millions)	change (%)
Asia	3,933	4,755	822	20.9
Japan	127	109	-18	-14.2
Republic of Korea	48	47	-1	-2.4
PRC	1,341	1,296	-45	-3.4
Viet Nam	88	104	16	18.3
Indonesia	240	293	54	22.3
India	1225	1692	467	38.2
Pakistan	174	275	101	58.3
Afghanistan	31	76	45	142.7

Source: UN Statistics Division, 2011.

Central Asia will add around 78 million people by 2050. It will be growing from relatively smaller absolute numbers—but in percentage terms this sub-region, especially Afghanistan and Iran, will be growing dramatically. It is estimated that Afghanistan's population will skyrocket from its current 31 million to 76 million; Iran will add about 11 million to its total population.

In 2050, Asia will be heavily influenced by the relative demographic weight of South Asia. South Asia (with India) is already more populous than Northeast Asia (which includes PRC). By 2050, just Pakistan will have added 100 million more people to the total Asian tally. The balance of Asia's population will shift further from Northeast Asia to South and Southeast Asia.

The Asian population giants, PRC and India, will see very different demographic trends. PRC's population is estimated to have already peaked around 2029; in 2050, PRC's population will be nearly 1.3 billion, 45 million less than in 2010. By 2050, PRC will thereby represent a smaller share of the total global population than before. India, on the other hand, will have grown by 467 million people to a total population of nearly 1.7 billion people in 2050; its share of the total global population will have grown to nearly 20 percent.

The demographic dominance of PRC and India notwithstanding, in the next decades the list of the largest countries in the world will continue to be dominated by Asia. Between now and 2050, there will be five additional Asian countries with the distinction of belonging to the ten most populous countries in the world: besides India and PRC, there will be, Indonesia (293 million), Pakistan (275 million), Bangladesh (194 million) and the Philippines (155 million) in the "top ten".

Table A1.2 — Projected growth of Asia's elderly population (number of people, age 65 and above, in millions)

	2010	2020	2030	2040	2050	% increase 2010–2050
Northeast Asia	147	215	286	380	395	168
South Asia	78	110	160	221	298	284
Southeast Asia	33	48	76	107	137	312
Central Asia	9	12	19	26	38	312

Source: UN Statistics Division, 2011.

Asia's aging trends

The demographic figures for Asia in 2050 impress by the sheer numbers of its growing population: in 40 years from now, Asia will have nearly 5 billion people. Projections on how many of these people will be officially classified as 'elderly' are just as impressive: in 2050, more than 860 million Asians will be 65 years and older.

What is especially striking about this phenomenon is the relative speed of the process of aging in Asia, and the fact that the 'greying' of Asia is occurring at all levels of the economic spectrum, i.e. even in low-income countries.

Asia's 3-speed aging world

In the context of demographics, it is tempting to borrow the differential-speed economic growth framework that is used in the economic model that underlies the book.

The three-speed demographic taxonomy in Asia occurs around distinct groups: one, the aging countries in North East Asia (notably, PRC and the Republic of Korea; from now on referred to as Speed 1 or Old Asia), two, the countries in South East and South Asia that are approaching the demographic transition (called Speed 2 or Young Asia. This group covers a wide spectrum of countries such as Thailand and Indonesia that are relatively older, and other countries that are roughly 10 years further behind, such as India and Viet Nam), and three, the youngest countries in Asia that are still growing, much further away in their demographic transitions, such as Pakistan and Afghanistan, for instance—referred to as Speed 3 or Very Young Asia.

By tracing the population figures for some of the major (already large) Asian countries, it becomes evident that PRC's population begins to decline around 2029, the Republic of Korea in 2026, Thailand will begin shrinking in 2033, Viet Nam in 2045. Japan's demographic descent has already begun; its population reached its peak in 2009; India's demographic inflection point occurs only after 2050; the same applies to Indonesia, Bangladesh, Pakistan and Afghanistan.

Tracing the percentage of the total population that is of a working age (defined as 20–64

Table A1.3 | Asia's differential-speed demographic inflection years

	Total population	Working age population
Speed 1: Old Asia		
Japan	2009	1997
Republic of Korea	2026	2018
PRC	2029	2018
Speed 2: Young Asia		
Thailand	2033	2022
Viet Nam	2045	2035
Indonesia	Post 2050	2038
Bangladesh	Post 2050	2044
India	Post 2050	Post 2050
Speed 3: Very Young Asia		
Pakistan	Post 2050	Post 2050
Afghanistan	Post 2050	Post 2050

Source: Centennial Group International calculations based on data from United Nations Statistics Division, 2011.

years of age) also reveals different and differently timed inflection points: for Speed 1 countries, the old countries of Asia, the working age population has already peaked and is now declining (as in Japan) or is about to do so (as in Republic of Korea). Working age populations in the Speed 2 countries ("Young Asia") trail the Speed 1 countries by about 20–25 years (e.g., Indonesia, Thailand, Bangladesh). These inflection points are an important indicator of demographic windows of opportunity and potential demographic dividends that countries could exploit to their advantage.

An important, valid concern is that a rapidly ageing population is antithetical to achieving high-income status. The fear that a country might become too old before it becomes rich enough has two elements: with high old age-dependency ratios, investments to achieve higher factor productivity are difficult to achieve; and meeting the needs of an elderly population will entail costly economic and social institutions that are needed to achieve income security, adequate health care, and other needs (Lee, Mason, and Cotlear, 2010).

Table A1.4 — Projected GDP per capita (PPP) vs. share of aging population, 2050

	GDP pc (PPP) in 2050	Share of population (%) 65+ in 2050
Afghanistan	2,456	4.1
Nepal	3,548	11.5
Myanmar	5,275	17.6
Pakistan	8,530	10.4
Tajikistan	16,913	9.0
Bangladesh	19,300	15.9
Iran, Islamic Rep.	23,696	23.5
Philippines	27,208	10.7
Mongolia	30,144	14.0
Cambodia	30,280	12.8
Sri Lanka	33,385	21.6
Viet Nam	34,139	23.1
Lao PDR	37,875	12.6
India	40,715	13.4
Bhutan	41,928	16.9
Armenia	42,160	21.8
Indonesia	42,176	19.2
Azerbaijan	52,174	17.1
PRC	52,681	25.6
Kazakhstan	60,847	13.6

Source: Centennial Group International Growth Model, 2011.

Model for Developing Global Growth Scenarios[1]

Appendix 2

This book estimates GDP as a function of labor force, capital stock, and total factor productivity for 185 countries between 2011–2050 under two different growth scenarios that we call the "Asian Century" and "Middle Income Trap". This section offers an abbreviated description of the model; a more detailed exposition, in Kohli, Szyf, and Arnold (2012), is available on request.

As seen in equation (1), a Cobb-Douglas function with constant returns to scale is assumed, with α equal to two-thirds:

$$GDP = TFP \times L^{\alpha} \times K^{1-\alpha} \quad (1)$$

GDP figures are generated for three different measures: real GDP (constant 2010 prices); GDP PPP (constant 2010 PPP prices); and GDP at expected market exchange rates, which incorporates expected exchange rate movements and serves as this book's best proxy for nominal GDP.

The model first estimates yearly real GDP growth for each country between 2012 and 2050. These estimates are applied to the previous values of real GDP, GDP PPP, and nominal GDP deflated by US inflation (on which GDP at market exchange rates is based) to derive the full series. Finally, to derive GDP at market exchange rates, real exchange rate changes are calculated and multiplied by nominal GDP (deflated by inflation) to obtain GDP at market exchange rates.

Labor force growth stems from population growth and from changes in labor force participation rates. Population growth is based on the 2010 Revision of the UN's World Population Prospects, while labor force participation rates are projected separately, by gender, for seven age cohorts (15–19, 20–24, 25–29, 30–49, 50–59, 60–64, and 65+) to better capture cohort-specific trends. Male rates are projected directly; female rates are derived by projecting the difference between male and female rates for each age group. Labor force participation rates from 1980 through 2011 are taken from the International Labor Organization.

The cross-country, cohort-specific equations to forecast male rates are simple autoregressions of the following form:

$$\ln(M_{age,t}) = m_{age} \times \ln(M_{age,t-1}) \quad (2)$$

---

[1] This appendix was written by Harpaul Alberto Kohli.

where M_{age} is the percent of males in age group *age* who are active in the labor force and m_{age} is a constant that varies for each age group.

The cross-country, cohort-specific equations to forecast the differentials between male and female participations rates are:

$$\ln(D_{age,t}) = d_{age} \times \ln(D_{age,t-1}) \quad (3)$$

where D_{age} equals the difference between the percentage of males in age group *age* in the labor force and the percentage of females in age group *age* in the labor force, and d_{age} is a constant that varies by age group. In both male and female models, for certain cohorts, rough upper or lower bounds are incorporated to address outliers. Observations that begin in 2011 beyond these bounds are not governed by the regressions but instead gradually converge over time towards the bounds.

Capital stock growth, based on an initial capital stock and yearly investment rates and depreciation, is defined as:

$$(1 + K\,Growth_t) = \frac{K_t}{K_{t-1}} = \left(\frac{I_{t-1}}{K_{t-1}}\right) - 0.06 \quad (4)$$

where K is the capital stock, 0.06 represents the yea_+rly depreciation of 6%, and I_{t-1} is the capital investment from the previous year, which is defined as the previous year's GDP (measured in constant 2010 PPP dollars) multiplied by the investment rate as a share of GDP.

The initial capital stock is calculated using the Caselli method (Kharas 2010b), with the following equation:

$$K_0 = \frac{I_0}{g + 0.06} \quad (5)$$

where K_0 is the initial capital stock, g is the average GDP growth over the subsequent ten years, 0.06 is the depreciation rate, and I_0 is the initial year's investment. For I_0, for each country, the earliest year for which there exists capital investment data (year y) is identified. The average of the investment rate values for year y and the two subsequent years is computed and treated as the initial investment rate. This smoothing out of fluctuations in the initial investment rate is necessary to yield better estimates for certain countries in which there is much volatility in the earliest investment rate values. This rate is then multiplied by the GDP in year y to determine I_0. The earliest year possible is chosen for this estimate because the longer the timeframe before the projections commence the more the yearly depreciations will reduce the effects on the model of any initial imprecisions in capital estimates.

The model is calibrated by calculating total factor productivity (TFP) for an initial year (2011) based on labor force, capital stock, and historical GDP, with GDP and capital stock measured in purchasing-power-parity dollars at constant 2010 PPP prices. For subsequent years, TFP is projected.

For the TFP projections, we differentiate four tiers of countries: rich or developed; converging; non-converging; and fragile.

All countries begin with a default TFP growth rate of 1.3 percent per annum derived from past studies (Kharas 2010b). This parameter is close to the 100-year TFP growth rate of the US, and is treated as the global standard. In our model, this is the fixed rate of productivity growth for non-converging, non-fragile countries.

Research shows that some growth differences between developing countries can be successfully modelled by separating them into two groups: converging (Tier 2) and non-converging (Tier 3) countries (Gill et al 2007; Jones 2002; Kharas 2010a; Kharas 2010b; Wolfensohn 2007).

A country is deemed to be converging if its per-capita income has rapidly converged over a 20-year period to that of best practice economies; the lower its productivity relative to the global best practice, the more quickly it converges. This convergence reflects technology transfers from richer innovating countries, technology leapfrogging, the diffusion of management and operational research from more developed countries, and other ways that a country can shortcut productivity-improvement processes by learning from economies that are already at the productivity frontier.

In the model, the lower the country's productivity relative to that of the US, the larger the boost, and the quicker the catch-up.[2] The productivity growth of rich (Tier 1) countries is treated the same as that of Tier 2 countries. On the other hand, non-converging (Tier 3) countries have only a 1.3 percent yearly productivity growth and no boost. The general equation for TFP growth is:

$$TFPGrowth = 1.3\% + CB - FP \qquad (6)$$

where CB is the convergence boost benefiting "converging" countries and FP is the productivity growth penalty suffered by failing or fragile states.

---

[2] TFP is used in the convergence term instead of the per-capita income used by others for three reasons: first, if the equation were to use GDP per capita, over time the TFP of a converging country would not converge to that of the US but instead to other values. Also, since the convergence equation represents convergence of TFP, we use TFP in order to make the equation consistent with its purpose. Third, using the convergence coefficient from past research in tandem with an income-based convergence term yields large discrepancies with the recent historical data for TFP growth for many countries; using TFP yields a better fit.

The convergence boost is defined as follows:

$$CB = c \times 2.33\% \times \ln\left(\frac{TFP_{USA,t-1}}{TFP_{i,t-1}}\right) \quad (7)$$

where i is the country, 2.33 percent is the convergence coefficient (derived from historical data), TFP is the total factor productivity, and c takes a value between 0 and 1 and identifies whether a country is treated as a converger ($c=1$) or as a non-converger or fragile state ($c=0$), or in an intermediate state of transition between being a converger and non-converger ($0 < c < 1$).

The failed-state penalty FP is defined as:

$$FP = f \times 1.8\% \quad (8)$$

where f plays a role analogous to that of c in equation (7) above. For each fragile (Tier 4) nation, f is set equal to 1, corresponding to a penalty in productivity growth of 1.8 percent, so that its yearly productivity is assumed to fall by 0.5 percent a year. The coefficient of negative 1.8 percent and the list of such fragile states is derived by identifying state failures and debilitating wars prior to the global financial crisis that lasted at least 2 consecutive years in 44 nations.

The projections of GDP growth are concluded by applying the labor growth, capital deepening, and productivity changes to each country over the period 2012–2050.

The measure of GDP at expected market exchange rates adjusts the GDP estimate by expected changes in the real exchange rate. First, an equation is derived to establish a theoretical relationship between a country's real exchange rate and its PPP income relative to that of the US. Then, the country's modelled exchange rate converges towards the value that corresponds to its income in this theoretical equation. These relationships are not linear, and the countries for which increases in GDP PPP per capita most appreciate their real exchange rates are the countries whose incomes are between a third and two-thirds that of the United States, and not the poorest or richest countries.

The model also projects the sizes of the low, middle, and high-income populations, again following Kharas (2010b), by measuring the number of people in each country with living standards—in PPP terms—within a certain absolute range. An income distribution for each country is derived from the World Bank's International Comparison Program.

The book makes separate projections for the Asian Century and Middle Income Trap scenarios. The difference between the scenarios is how countries are classified, either as converging, non-converging, or failed, and how countries gradually transition between classifications.

For the first scenario (the Asian Century), the starting point is the countries' statuses in 2010: 38 countries (7 Asian) are rich, 31 (11 Asian) converging, 112 (29 Asian) non-converging, and 14 (2 Asian) failed.[3] For 145 countries, the classification is taken from the "Four-Speed World" classification used by Kharas. The remaining 50 countries are classified using a similar analysis of recent historical data.[4] The Asian Century scenario assumes the following: all eleven currently converging, middle-income economies in Asia will continue to converge; eleven Asian (and six non-Asian economies) will gradually also become convergers; and all failed states will gradually stop failing beginning in 2021 and fully graduate to the third group in 2025. The convergence of the six non-Asian non-convergers and the fact that all failing states eventually stop failing in this scenario results from the shared prosperity of the Asian Century scenario that benefits the entire world.

The second scenario is the "Middle Income Trap Scenario". Here, all currently converging Asian countries with a GDP PPP per capita in 2010 below $20,000 are assumed to fall into the Middle Income Trap. They gradually stop converging beginning at varying income-dependent points between 2015–2026, and remain non-convergers for the rest of the time-frame.

In both scenarios, the transition of individual countries between converging and non-converging, or from failed to non-converging, is gradual. That is, countries are made to adopt an intermediate state between failed and not-failed, or between converging and non-converging, by varying the values of f and c in equations (7) and (8).

---

3 Projections could not be made for 10 of these 195 countries because the required data is not available.
4 However, unlike the Kharas classification, this book does not distinguish between middle income non-convergers and poor non-convergers. We argue that during the next forty years many poor or lower-middle income countries will graduate to middle income status.

Asia's Technology Landscape

Appendix 3

Ramesh Mashelkar and Vinod Goel

Predicting the future

As the first decade of the 21st century draws to a close, it is interesting to ponder the future that lies four decades hence. To be fair, we would not have been able to predict today's technological landscape four decades ago. At the time, there was no Internet, no World Wide Web, no laptops, no mobile phones, no network of communications satellites, no iPods or iPads, and no stem cell technology; yet, today all of these items impact—if not dominate—our lives. Thus, it is a very difficult exercise to predict the technological landscape of Asia four decades from now. However, this note attempts a best guess as to what the future state of technology could look like and how such a picture might influence events in Asia. With the current pace of technological change, one can easily conceive of major technological breakthroughs appearing before 2050 (and beyond). As a result, the Asian Century may not only be marked by a shift of economic power to the region, but a shift that extends to technology as well.

Rapidly changing Asia

In terms of technological innovation, Asia has progressed unevenly over the past 4 decades. Following the end of World War II, Japan raced ahead to become a technological superpower, joining the Organisation for Economic Cooperation and Development (OECD) in 1962. Within another one to two decades, the Republic of Korea and Taipei,China had achieved the status of technologically advanced countries due to an emphasis on and investment in higher education, science, and technology. Singapore eventually joined this club by carving out a niche in specific areas such as biotechnology and making innovative changes in public policy to welcome foreign nationals who had achieved eminence in science and technology elsewhere. In this way, Singapore avoided suffering from the disadvantage of having a small human capital base.

India faced two adversities along its journey of technological innovation following independence in 1947. First, as a poor country lacking financial resources, India had to resort to "frugal engineering," which meant creating more from less. Second, India lacked access to a variety of technology, ranging from satellites to nuclear power to supercomputers.

The lack of competition in the Indian economy prior to liberalization, which did not begin in earnest until the early 1990s, resulted in technological development that was driven solely by a policy of import substitution. A closed economy also meant a lack of access to foreign direct investment (FDI) and foreign technology. Once it began pursuing a policy of liberalization starting in 1991, India made rapid gains in technological innovation.

The People's Republic of China (PRC) opened its economy two decades earlier than India did and reaped huge benefits as a result. PRC remains ahead of India today in all areas of technology, with the exception of information technology services and computer software development. PRC's prowess in high-technology areas such as advanced space, aerospace, and nuclear technologies is well known, with achievements ranging from high-speed bullet trains and advanced fighter jets, to naval aircraft carriers and advanced nuclear reactors. Furthermore, massive investments in clean technology are already returning a rich dividend, and PRC has acquired the second position behind the United States in nanotechnology even after its late start. Meanwhile, PRC has taken a huge lead over India in supercomputers. The recently announced list of the world's top 500 supercomputers shows PRC topping the global list with 41 indigenously developed supercomputers, compared with four from India.

Biotechnology

It is widely agreed that the 21st century will be the century of biology just as the 20th century was dominated by information and communication technology (ICT). Together, these two technologies will have game-changing influence on human development over the next four decades. What will be Asia's position in this century of modern biotechnology? It is plausible that Asia could be a biotechnology leader by 2050 with a dominant position in a variety of frontier fields including stem cell technology, synthetic biology, and pharmaco-genomics.

Stem cell technology has moved from preventive (vaccines) and curative (antibiotics) medicine, to predictive (gene therapy) and regenerative (stem cell therapy) medicine. Several Asian countries have taken an early lead in the development of stem cell technology. Today, the Republic of Korea and Singapore are considered among the leaders in this field of science. India and PRC are beginning to build on the promise of stem cell technology through judicious investments in human capital and infrastructure.

More than 20 research centers in India are carrying out basic stem cell research to develop therapies for cancer, diabetes, heart disease, and brain disorders such as Alzheimer's disease. Although PRC has less than 10 major stem cell research centers, in Taizhou a spinoff of Beijing University known as Beike Bio Technology is already using stem cells to treat more than 250 patients for diseases ranging from cerebral palsy to optic nerve damage. Many of their patients come from the US, where therapies based on stem cell research are difficult to find due to legal restrictions.

An early advantage has been gained by Singapore, Republic of Korea, PRC, and India, which have forged ahead through less restrictive policies concerning stem cell research. Asia has the competitive advantages needed to become a leader in stem cell technology and therapies. This unique positioning in regenerative medicine could have interesting consequences for medical tourism, with a potential explosion in the numbers of Americans coming to PRC seeking stem cell therapies.

Asia could also lead the new age of pharmaco-genomics, or personalized medicine, in which physicians select the drugs that are most likely to help a specific patient, while at the same time ensuring the absence of unwanted side effects. There are two factors that favor Asia in this field: affordability and diversity. First, the costs of sequencing an organism's genetic material have plummeted dramatically; the dream of sequencing an individual's genetic makeup in as little as 15 minutes at a cost of only US$15 is not far off. Affordability can lead to ready access to such sophisticated technologies in learning centers across Asia.

Second, Asia's vast genetic diversity aids research in pharmaco-genomics. Gene-based prevention, diagnosis, and treatment has the potential to revolutionize the treatment of HIV/AIDs, cancer, and other deadly diseases. Genetic sequencing may be particularly useful in combating infectious diseases through a process of reverse vaccinology, which refers to the design of vaccines based on computer analysis of a pathogen's genome. This approach has recently delivered success in the production of a vaccine against Group B meningococcus, which had escaped conventional vaccine production methods for over 40 years. Remarkably, the development of this vaccine took only 18 months, which was far faster—and at a cheaper cost—than previous techniques. The bulk of vaccine production is shifting to countries such as India. Aided by affordable advanced technologies, Asia could be a world leader in the research and production of modern vaccines.

The field of synthetic biology is developing new ways to build living organisms. Simple bacteria can be made routinely by inserting synthetic genomes into empty cells. These organisms do not merely duplicate their natural predecessors but also incorporate whatever new traits their designers wish to include in them. From triggering an immune system response, to conveying new generic material into human cells, to repairing hereditary diseases, to carrying out industrially useful chemicals, the promise of synthetic biology is awesome. Although the US has a clear lead in this field, it would not be surprising if India or PRC took a leading position starting in 2010–2020.

The replacement of traditional chemistry by processes that are modeled on biology will lead the way to bio-mimetic synthesis. Closely related to this is bio-manufacturing—the use of cells to produce medically and industrially useful compounds. Cells will be genetically engineered to deliver compounds that nature overlooked. Scientists have already produced universally acceptable blood from stem cells. Medical researchers have successfully altered complex organs in the human body such as the skin, liver, heart, and pancreas. By 2050, it is entirely possible that organs will be grown in a laboratory from the recipient's own tissue, after appropriate genetic repair and then inserted into the recipient's body.

Another advance will come from combining knowledge of engineering and electronics with biology to make complex systems. One example is the recent work on creating artificial retinas for the blind that can link to the optic nerve and send messages to the brain. Other experiments involve using cells as the serving elements in detectors for pollution, bacteria, and nerve agents.

Bio-genealogy, which is the study of the fundamental processes of ageing, could lead to considerable progress in preventing, delaying, or reversing the ageing process by 2050. Asia will see a dramatic extension in life expectancy as both economic conditions and sanitary standards improve, more effective treatments become available for infectious diseases, and as the results of a concerted effort to treat biological ageing as a preventable disease materialize.

The following life-extending developments are expected to be available by 2050.
- Almost everyone will have their own DNA sequence that can be compiled into a database comprising health risks, therapies, and best practices based on the characteristics of an individual's genes.
- Mitochondrial DNA damaged by disease or ageing will be replaceable.
- Most genetic disorders will be curable through gene therapy.
- Immune systems weakened by age will be replaced using fresh cells grown from the patient's own bone material.
- To replace diseased or failing organs, doctors will grow new ones from patients' own cells.
- Tissue regeneration will take place without rejection by creating, manipulating, and transplanting pristine cells from another part of a patient's body.

These and other anti-ageing therapies will make life spans of over 100 years commonplace. More importantly, based on animal-based studies underway at the moment, the "quality of life" will not suffer with ageing as it does today. This development could have a profound effect on the impacts of a "demographic dividend in some Asian countries.

Information and communications technology

In the 1960s, Gordon Moore predicted that computer power would double every year, which he later amended to a doubling every two years. Subsequent computer experts have so suggested that this uncannily accurate law may not survive beyond 2020 because transitions will have reached limits of miniaturization at the atomic level. While it took 42 years from 1959 to 2001 for computer speed to increase by a factor of 1 million, according to Denis Bushnell, Chief Scientist at NASA's Langley Research Center, computer power is only likely to grow by a factor of 100 between 2001 and 2030.

Meanwhile, today's silicon chips will no longer be relevant by 2020. They will have been supplanted by newer, much faster technologies, including optical computers, molecular computers, bio-computers, and perhaps even quantum computers. Before the end of the first decade of the 21st century, IBM launched its petaflop machine, which is capable of performing 1 million billion floating point operations per second. But within a year, PRC announced that it was joining the race with a petaflop supercomputer of its own. By 2050, India may also have consolidated its position as a leader in supercomputing.

An evolutionary change in human society in recent decades has been the proliferation of the Internet, facilitated by growing bandwidth. By 2020, it is predicted that a combination of fiber optics, satellite-based Internet backbone services, and universal high speed "last mile" connections will shift all electronic communications to the Internet. Traditional telephones will have been replaced by voice over internet protocols (VOIP). The use of natural user interface (NUI) technologies, which do not employ a keyboard but instead respond to gestures or touch, will bring further dramatic shifts. Similarly, early successes in conversational computing will occur in narrowly focused applications such as toys and pre-school computer tutors. Within 5 years, many professional and technical workers will likely be carrying a chatty cyber-assistant in their cell phones, capable of responding to a large number of routine verbal instructions and work-related requests. Conversational computers will commonly be used in customer service lines, tracing lost luggage, citizen complaints, public crime reporting, and warranty fulfillment. By 2050, humans can expect to have regular conversations with their cars, appliances, and houses, as conversational computer technology further improves with mature artificial intelligence (AI).

Concurrently, the challenges of labor shortages in countries with ageing populations are being addressed through the use of robotic technology. The governments of Japan and the Republic of Korea are each promoting research and development (R&D) in the field of robotics for the specific purpose of reducing dependence on immigrant labor. Sectors such as agriculture, transportation, and healthcare are expected to rely heavily on robots in the future.

Similarly, AI is now used on a limited but growing basis in specialized applications such as medical diagnostics, interpretation of photo-imagery, and student counseling. By 2050, AI-based systems will have displaced a range of technical and para-professional workers, whose jobs involve routine applications of normative and cognitive skills. The evolution of such systems has the potential to significantly reduce the amount of labor devoted to offshore routine customer support services and back office financial service operations, among other activities.

It is conceivable that by 2050 integrated robotics, AI, and conversational computer capabilities will have measurably reduced labor requirements in agriculture, food processing, manufacturing, factory-built housing, transportation, and services. This job displacement will have two potential effects: (i) in mature industrial economies, it will free up scarce labor for high-value jobs; and (ii) in much of Asia, it will take away jobs from semi-skilled functionaries, thereby eliminating a comparative advantage that many Asian countries have enjoyed to date.

The changing landscape of science, technology, and innovation

There are clear indications that the center of gravity of scientific research and technological innovation is shifting toward Asia.

First, in recent years there has been a massive expansion of educational and research institutions in parts of the Asia, most notably in PRC and India.

Second, in the past decade, there has been a steep rise in the level of the advanced economies' R&D funding in the rapidly expanding economies in Asia.

Third, an abundant availability of scientific talent at a low cost in Asia has meant that international companies are setting up their R&D centers in countries like India and PRC. In India, over 760 international companies have set up R&D centers, employing around 130,000 scientists, engineers, and technologists. These centers have begun to generate significant amounts of intellectual property for their parent organizations.

Fourth, with educational and employment opportunities expanding in leading Asian countries, the well-known phenomenon of "brain drain" is beginning to reverse itself. A significant number of employees of multinational R&D centers are returning Asians who have been trained in some of the best centers of excellence in scientific research in the world. Improved economic conditions in their native countries have led to the availability of more sophisticated equipment for R&D. Advances in ICT have also translated into more productive interactions with overseas peers.

Finally, tighter intellectual property laws in most Asian countries are allowing scientists to create innovative products, such as entirely new drug molecules, rather than simply reverse engineering existing products.

Exciting economic and social developments, as well as intellectually stimulating challenges, have reversed the process of brain drain from Asia to one of "brain gain." Several governments have even adopted proactive strategies to facilitate the return of talented scientists. For example, Taipei,China was able to secure the return of Nobel Laureate Professor Y.T. Lee by making an extraordinary offer of employment and appointing him the Minister of Science and Technology. PRC has designed schemes to draw top minds back from overseas by creating special high technology facilities to maximize their talents and offering differentiated privileges and remuneration packages. Singapore has drawn some of the world's leading researchers by offering world class facilities and lucrative compensation packages.

These and other proactive incentive schemes are helping to set the stage for Asia to become a leader in science, technology, and innovation by 2050.

Potential game-changing technological breakthroughs

Technological revolutions that have yet to be foreseen might also bring major changes to the lives of entire generations born in the Asian Century.

One of the fundamental mega-challenges the world faces is ensuring a sustainable supply of energy, while at the same time mitigating climate change risks. Some progress is being made through incremental technological innovations, including increasing the cost effectiveness of solar thermal- and solar photovoltaic-based energy systems.

The transport sector, a huge energy consumer and major producer of carbon emissions, has been the focus of research resulting in some progress on energy conservation. For example, by 2035, 50 percent of all vehicles are expected to run on either electricity or hydrogen. By 2050, it has been predicted, 30 percent of all transport will run on alternative fuels, compared with nearly total dependence on fossil fuels today, and 30 percent of all liquid fuels will be bio-fuels.

These forecasts might even change dramatically in the face of innovations that are transformative rather than merely incremental. A research group at the Massachusetts Institute of Technology has already achieved a breakthrough in splitting water molecules at room temperature. Tata Motors from India is partnering with this group to examine the feasibility of on-board hydrogen generation by splitting water molecules, possibly to enable the world's cheapest car, the Tata Nano, to run on water!

Meanwhile, the Nobel Prize winning research of J. George Bednorz and K. Alexander Müller from IBM labs in Zurich has raised expectations about superconductors that can function at ambient temperatures. If such a breakthrough were to occur, superconductors operating at room temperature could power levitating trains that would outperform any of today's high-speed trains.

With regard to climate change, the environmental risks that emanate from the burning of fossil fuels can only be tackled through technological innovation. Physical carbon sequestration could be aided significantly by bio-sequestration, the process of using carbon dioxide-dependent microalgae to convert carbon dioxide, water, and nutrients into lipids through photosynthesis. The lipids, in turn, are converted into bio-fuels. The successful application of this technology could lead to coal-based power plants in which bio-sequestration produces a closed-loop system without any carbon dioxide emissions.

Technological revolutions might occur in other areas as well. For example, even with only incremental innovations between now and 2050, agriculture will become increasingly automated. Robots will appear on farms and in fisheries to replace human laborers. Sensor-based and electronic tagging systems can already monitor growth rates, nutrient levels, and circulation processes. The results produce models, which study plant structures from root to tip to determine their growth patterns. This technology will lead to continued productivity improvements in agricultural output that will help meet the demands of an ever-growing global population that is estimated to reach 9 billion people by 2050. Furthermore, as land and water become scarcer in the decades ahead, modern biotechnology will continue to make advances in crops that can be grown under saline conditions while using a fraction of the water and nutrients needed today.

The most significant scientific discoveries and breakthroughs of the 20th century came exclusively from the developed economies of the EU, Japan, and North America. These included (i) integrated circuits, which led to the ICT revolution that has changed the world; and (ii) the discovery of the structure of DNA, which has led to recombinant DNA technology, a true game-changer for humanity. Given the evolving landscape of science, technology, and innovation today, the potential game-changing breakthroughs of the future may well come from Asia!

Asia as an inclusive innovation leader by 2050

Despite the rise of Asia as an economic power, income inequalities and a lack of opportunity for a vast number of Asians remain important challenges. Asia must aim for inclusive growth and inclusive innovation. Enterprises have always sought to get more (performance) from less (resources) for more (profit). A new paradigm should seek to get more (performance) from less (resources) to meet the needs of more and more (people) at the bottom of the development pyramid. This new paradigm constitutes the essence of inclusive innovation.

Examples of inclusive innovation comprise products and services such as the world's cheapest car, the Tata Nano, which is priced at only US$2,500; the world's cheapest mobile phone sets priced at US$20; mobile phone call rates just over US$0.01 per minute compared with US$0.08 in the US; cataract surgery that costs US$30 compared with US$3,000 in the US; and laptop computers costing just US$35. These are not dreams, but accomplishments that have resulted from ingenious innovations in technology, business processes, and work flow. Such achievements bode well for Asian-led inclusive innovation.

Inclusive innovation is not only good for Asia, it is also good for the whole world through reverse innovation (Immelt et al 2009). For example, the General Electric (GE) medical team in India has developed a portable electro cardiogram machine at a fraction of the cost of a similarly performing machine in developed economies. Similarly, the GE medical team in PRC has developed a portable ultrasound machine at a fraction of the cost of a similarly performing machine in developed economies. GE has found that a market is emerging for these machines in the developed world, reflecting a reversal of the traditional paradigm in which researchers in advanced economies would develop an expensive medical machine and make it affordable to the developing world only after dropping certain high-cost features. There is widespread recognition that the old paradigm is now reversing itself as Asian countries such as PRC, India, and others are undoubtedly going to be sources of global innovation in the future.

Whether it is reverse innovation or inclusive innovation that will shape the future, or a combination of both, it is clear that Asian businesses are well-positioned to lead. This evolving reality should form the cornerstone of the vision of Asia's technology and research landscape in 2050.

Driving Productivity and Growth

Appendix 4

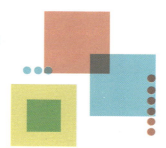

Table A4.1 — Asia: GDP growth and TFP growth, 1970–2010

	Real GDP growth (avg. % annual)				Real TFP growth (avg. % annual)			
	1970–1980	1980–1990	1990–2000	2000–2010	1970–1980	1980–1990	1990–2000	2000–2010
North America	3.3	3.2	3.4	1.7	0.8	1.1	1.6	0.1
Europe	3.3	2.5	1.7	1.8	1.4	0.7	1.2	0.3
Latin America & Caribbean	6.4	1.4	3.2	3.3	1.8	-1.9	0.4	0.8
Asia	5.5	6.7	5.4	5.5	1.2	2.4	0.8	1.9
Central Asia	NA	NA	0.5	6.7	NA	NA	-2.1	2.5
Northeast Asia (excl. PRC)	5.4	5.6	2.3	1.5	1.2	2.7	0.2	1.0
South Asia (excl. India)	3.3	5.2	4.4	5.1	1.1	1.2	0.7	1.3
Southeast Asia	7.2	5.7	5.0	5.2	0.8	0.3	1.4	2.3
PRC	6.2	9.3	10.4	10.5	0.7	3.8	6.0	6.2
India	2.7	5.6	5.6	7.5	-0.9	1.9	2.0	3.1
High Income	5.5	5.6	2.4	1.6	1.2	2.7	0.3	1.0
Converging	5.8	8.1	8.3	9.1	0.8	3.1	3.3	5.0
Non-converging	3.7	3.7	3.4	5.1	0.3	0.1	-0.3	1.4

Table A4.2 Asia: Composition of growth, 1970–2010

	Share of TFP (%)				Share of labor (%)				Share of capital (%)			
	1970–1980	1980–1990	1990–2000	2000–2010	1970–1980	1980–1990	1990–2000	2000–2010	1970–1980	1980–1990	1990–2000	2000–2010
Central Asia	NA	NA	-172.4	49.1	NA	NA	139.3	27.0	NA	NA	133.8	22.0
Northeast Asia (excl. PRC)	24.8	50.4	7.9	65.4	22.5	17.2	24.1	-2.8	51.2	30.7	66.9	36.6
South Asia (excl. India)	26.9	19.3	18.7	26.9	31.0	37.4	38.3	34.9	41.0	41.7	41.6	36.6
Southeast Asia	22.1	12.1	18.3	46.8	26.9	38.3	32.4	26.9	48.8	47.9	47.8	24.7
PRC	11.4	41.2	57.0	58.9	24.6	18.7	7.4	5.3	62.4	37.4	32.9	33.3
India	-32.0	33.6	36.1	41.5	54.1	28.8	25.4	17.6	77.9	35.9	36.8	38.5
High Income	24.6	49.9	10.1	62.8	22.5	17.5	24.3	1.8	51.4	31.0	64.6	34.6
Converging	12.5	33.3	47.6	55.5	28.7	24.6	13.1	8.8	57.2	39.7	36.9	33.3
Non-converging	6.8	9.0	-1.2	36.6	38.7	53.7	55.8	37.1	53.6	36.3	44.5	24.8

A New Approach to Urbanization

Appendix 5

Table A5.1 | Fifty fastest growing cities in Asia

City/Urban Area	Country	Average growth annual 2050	Population (in thousands)
Beihai	PRC	10.58	145
Ghaziabad	India	5.20	969
Surat	India	4.99	4,168
Kabul	Afghanistan	4.74	3,731
Faridabad	India	4.44	1,055
Chittagong	Bangladesh	4.29	4,962
Nashik	India	3.90	1,588
Dhaka	Bangladesh	3.79	14,800
Patna	India	3.72	2,321
Rajkot	India	3.63	1,357
Jaipur	India	3.60	3,131
Gujranwala	Pakistan	3.49	1,652
Delhi	India	3.48	17,000
Pune (Poona)	India	3.46	5,002
Indore	India	3.35	2,173
Faisalabad	Pakistan	3.32	2,849
Rawalpindi	Pakistan	3.31	2,026
Peshawar	Pakistan	3.29	1,422
Khulna	Bangladesh	3.24	1,682
Suwon	Republic of Korea	3.23	1,132
Karachi	Pakistan	3.19	13,000
Lahore	Pakistan	3.12	7,132

Source: City Mayors Statistics.

Table A5.1 | Fifty fastest growing cities in Asia

City/Urban Area	Country	Average growth annual 2050	Population (in thousands)
Asansol	India	3.11	486
Multan	Pakistan	3.06	1,659
Jakarta	Indonesia	3.03	9,700
Palembang	Indonesia	2.94	1,244
Agra	India	2.93	1,703
Hyderabad	Pakistan	2.91	1,590
Bandung	Indonesia	2.90	2,412
Wenzhou	PRC	2.90	2,659
Wuhan	PRC	2.87	7,681
Amritsar	India	2.85	1,297
Meerut	India	2.83	1,494
Changsha	PRC	2.80	2,415
Bangalore	India	2.79	7,218
Heze	PRC	2.78	1,830
Shantou	PRC	2.77	3,502
Ahmadabad	India	2.73	5,717
Lucknow	India	2.72	2,873
Bhopal	India	2.69	1,843
Ujung Pandang	Indonesia	2.63	1,294
Ludhiana	India	2.63	1,760
Zhanjiang	PRC	2.59	1,007
Karaj	Iran	2.59	1,584
Jamshedpur	India	2.59	1,387
Vadodara	India	2.55	1,872
Davao	Philippines	2.53	1,519
Kanpur	India	2.53	3,364
Shenzhen	PRC	2.51	9,005
Srinagar	India	2.50	1,216
Coimbatore	India	2.49	1,807
Yangon	Myanmar	2.46	4,350
Dhanbad	India	2.46	1,328

Source: City Mayors Statistics.

Table A5.2 | World mega cities with population over 10 million for 2010, 2030, and 2050

2010		2030		2050	
Tokyo	36.1	**Tokyo**	36.4	**Mumbai**	40.3
Mumbai	20.1	**Mumbai**	29.1	**Tokyo**	36.4
Sao Paulo	19.6	**Delhi**	24.9	**Dhaka**	35.5
Mexico City	19.5	**Dhaka**	24.8	**Delhi**	34.6
New York-Newark	19.4	**Kolkata**	22.8	Kinshasa	33.9
Delhi	17	**Karachi**	21.7	**Karachi**	33.3
Shanghai	15.8	Sao Paulo	21.6	**Kolkata**	32.3
Kolkata	15.6	Mexico City	21.2	Lagos	23.0
Dhaka	14.8	New York-Newark	20.8	Cairo	22.1
Karachi	13.1	**Shanghai**	20.1	Sao Paulo	22.1
Buenos Aires	13.1	Kinshasa	19.9	**Shanghai**	21.7
Los Angeles-Long Beach-Santa Ana	12.8	Lagos	17.4	Mexico City	21.6
Cairo	12.5	Cairo	16.9	New York-Newark	21.2
Rio de Janeiro	12.2	**Manila**	15.8	**Manila**	19.4
Manila	11.7	**Beijing**	15.0	**Lahore**	19.2
Beijing	11.7	Buenos Aires	13.9	**Beijing**	16.3
Osaka-Kobe	11.3	Los Angeles-Long Beach-Santa Ana	13.9	**Jakarta**	16.2
Lagos	10.6	Rio de Janeiro	13.5	**Chennai**	15.6
Moscow	10.5	**Jakarta**	13.2	Los Angeles-Long Beach-Santa Ana	14.3
Istanbul	10.5	Istanbul	12.4	Buenos Aires	14.1
Paris	9.9	**Guangzhou**	12.2	Rio de Janeiro	13.8
Seoul	9.8	**Lahore**	12.0	Istanbul	13.4
Jakarta	9.7	**Osaka-Kobe**	11.4	**Guangzhou**	13.4
Guangzhou	9.4	**Chennai**	11.2	**Shenzhen**	11.5
Kinshasa	9.1	**Shenzhen**	10.6	**Osaka-Kobe**	11.4
Shenzhen	8.1	Moscow	10.5	Moscow	10.5
Chennai	7.6	Paris	10.0	Paris	10.0
Lahore	7.1	**Seoul**	9.7	**Seoul**	9.7
Asia:	184.4		266.2		340.7
Total:	307.9		473.2		577.1
Asia/Total	59.9%		56.3%		59.0%

Source: ADB, 2010a.

Table A5.3 | Rates of urbanization by country: 2010 and 2050

Economy	2010	2050
PRC	46.96	73.23
Hong Kong, China	100.00	100.00
Macao, China	100.00	100.00
Dem. People's Republic of Korea	60.22	74.53
Japan	66.83	80.08
Mongolia	62.03	79.53
Republic of Korea	82.96	90.83
Afghanistan	22.60	47.00
Bangladesh	28.07	56.41
Bhutan	34.71	64.17
India	30.01	54.23
Iran	70.75	85.52
Kazakhstan	58.51	75.87
The Kyrgyz Republic	34.55	53.58
Maldives	40.10	73.12
Nepal	18.62	47.56
Pakistan	35.90	59.37
Sri Lanka	14.31	31.34
Tajikistan	26.32	46.40
Turkmenistan	49.50	71.60
Uzbekistan	36.25	56.01
Brunei Darussalam	75.65	87.21
Cambodia	20.11	43.83
Indonesia	44.28	65.95
Lao People's Democratic Republic	33.18	68.03
Malaysia	72.17	87.85
Myanmar	33.65	62.87
Philippines	48.90	69.36
Singapore	100.00	100.00
Thailand	33.96	59.96
Timor-Leste	28.12	54.92
Viet Nam	30.38	58.99

Source: UN Population Division.

References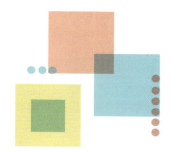

Acemoglu, D, Johnson, S & Robinson, J 2001, 'The Colonial Origins of Comparative Development', *American Economic Review*, vol. 91, no. 5.

Acemoglu, D, Aghion, P, Burstyn, L & Hemous, D 2010, *The Environment and Directed Technical Change*, FEEM Working Paper no. 482, Fondazione Eni Enrico Mattei, Milan.

Acharya, A 2005, 'Do Norms and Identity Matter? Community and Power in Southeast Asia's Regional Order', *The Pacific Review*, 19, no. 1, pp. 95–118.

—— 2010, 'Democracy or Death? Will Democratisation Bring Greater Regional Instability to East Asia?', *Pacific Review*, vol. 23, no. 3, pp. 335–358.

Acs, Z J & Szerb, L 2011, *Global Entrepreneurship and Development Index*, 2011, Edward Elgar Publishing, Cheltanham, UK.

Acs, Z J & Audretsch, D B 1988, 'Innovation in Large and Small Firms: An Empirical Analysis', *American Economic Review* 78(4), pp. 678–690.

Adelman, A & Watkins, G 2008, 'Reserve Prices and Mineral Resource Theory', *Energy Journal*, Special Issue.

Ahluwalia, MS 2011, 'Prospects and Policy Challenges in the Twelfth Plan', *Economic & Political Weekly*, vol. 4–6, no. 21, pp. 88–105.

Ahmed, Z S & Bhatnagar, S 2008, 'Interstate Conflicts and regionalism in South Asia: Prospects and Challenges', *Perceptions*, Spring-Summer, pp. 1–19.

Ahmedabad Municipal Corporation & Ahmedabad Urban Development Authority 2006, City Development Plan: *Ahmedabad, 2006–2012*, Jawaharlal Nehru National Urban Renewal Mission, New Delhi.

Alburo, F A 2009 'Regional Cooperation on Trade and Transport Facilitation', *Impact of Trade Facilitation on Export Competitiveness: A Regional Perspective*, ESCAP, Studies in Trade and Investment 66.

Alesina, A & Rodrik, D 1994, 'Distributive Politics and Economic Growth', *Quarterly Journal of Economics*, vol. 109, no. 2, pp. 165–90.

Ali, I & Zhuang, J 2007, *Inclusive Growth toward a Prosperous Asia: Policy Implications*, ERD Working Paper no. 97, Asian Development Bank, Manila.

Alkemade, R, van Oorschot, M, Miles, L, Nellemann, C, Bakkenes, M & ten Brink, B 2009, 'GLOBIO3: A Framework to Investigate Options for Reducing Global Terrestrial Biodiversity Loss', *Ecosystems*, vol. 12, no. 3, pp. 374–90.

Alm, J 2010, *Municipal Finance of Urban Infrastructure: Knowns and Unknowns*, The Brookings Institution, Washington, DC.

Anandaram, S 2010, 'The Case for Early Stage Funds', *India Chief Mentor*, WSF Blogs.

Ando, M 2009, 'Impacts of FTAs in East Asia: CGE Simulatin Analysis', *RIETI Discussion Paper Series 09-E-037*, Tokyo.

Angel, S, Sheppard, S C & Civco DL 2005, *The Dynamics of Global Urban Expansion*, The World Bank, Washington, DC.

Aon Benfield UCL Hazard Research Centre, China Dialogue & Humanitarian Futures Programme 2010, *The Waters of the Third Pole: Sources of Threat, Sources of Survival*, University College London and King's College London, London, <http://www.abuhrc.org/Publications/Third%20Pole.pdf>.

Arnell, N 2006, 'Climate Change and Water Resources: A Global Perspective', in H Schellnhuber, W Cramer, N Nakicenovic, T Wigley & G Yohe (eds), *Avoiding Dangerous Climate Change*, Cambridge University Press, Cambridge, UK, pp. 167–75.

Arond, E & Bell, M 2010, *Trends in the Global Distribution of R&D Since the 1970s: Data, their Interpretation and Limitations*, STEPS Working paper 39 for STEPS Centre, Brighton, UK.

Arrighi, G, Hamashita, T & Selden, M 1996, *The Rise of East Asia in World Historical Perspective*, Background paper for Planning Workshop, Fernand Braudel Center, SUNY Binghampton.

Asian Development Bank 2003, 'Competitiveness in Developing Asia: Taking Advantage of Globalization, Technology and Competition', in *Asian Development Outlook*, Asian Development Bank, Manila.

—— 2008a, *Managing Asian Cities*, Asian Development Bank, Manila.

—— 2008b, *Education and Skills: Strategies for Accelerated Development in Asia and the Pacific*, Asian Development Bank, Manila.

—— 2009a, *The Economics of Climate Change in Southeast Asia: A Regional Review*, Asian Development Bank, Manila.

—— 2009b, *Understanding and Responding to Climate Change in Asia and the Pacific*, Asian Development Bank, Manila.

—— 2009c, Changing Course: *A New Paradigm for Sustainable Urban Transport*, Asian Development Bank, Manila.

—— 2010a, *Focused Action: Priorities for Addressing Climate Change in Asia and the Pacific*, Asian Development Bank, Manila.

—— 2010b, *Human Capital Accumulation in Emerging Asia, 1970–2030*, Asian Development Bank, Manila.

Asian Development Bank & Asian Development Bank Institute 2009, *Infrastructure for a Seamless Asia*, Asian Development Bank Institute, Tokyo.

Asian Disaster Preparedness Center 2010a, *ADPC Brochure*, Asian Disaster Preparedness Center, Bangkok, <http://www.adpc.net/v2007/About%20Us/Brochures/ADPC_Brochure2010.pdf>.

Asian Disaster Preparedness Center 2010b, Implementing National Programs on Community-Based Disaster Risk Reduction in High Risk Communities—Lessons Learned, Challenges, and Way Ahead, RCC Working Paper Version 2, Asian Disaster Preparedness Center, Bangkok.

—— 2010b, *Joint Ministerial Statement*, Ninth Ministerial Conference on Central Asia Regional Economic Cooperation, Cebu, Philippines, 2 November 2010.

—— 2010c, *Transport and Trade Facilitation Progress Report and Work Plan (later 2010–2011)*, Senior Officials' Meeting, Cebu, Philippines, 31 October 2010.

Asia Policy Forum 2009, *Recommendations of Policy Responses to the Global Financial and Economic Crisis for East Asian Leaders*, <http://www.adbi.org/files/2009.03.18.keydocs.policy.recommend.global.financial.crisis.east.asian.leaders.pdf>.

Assuncao, J & Chein, F 2008, *Climate Change, Agricultural Productivity, and Poverty*, World Bank, Washington, DC.

Azis, I J 2009, *Crisis Complexity and Conflict: Contributions to Conflict Management, Peace Economics and Development, Volume 9*, Emerald, Bedfordshire, United Kingdom.

Azis, I J 2011, *Reshaping Global Economic Governance and the Role of Asia in the Group of Twenty (G20)*, Prepared under Asian Development Bank's Technical Assistance 7501 Asia's Strategic Participation in the Group of Twenty for Global Economic Governance Reform, Asian Development Bank, Manila.

Balassa, B & Williamson, J 1987, *Adjusting to Success: Balance of Payments Policy in the East Asian NICs*, Institute for International Economics, Washington DC.

Banerjee, A, Coleman, S & Duflo, E 2005, 'Bank Financing in India', in *India's and China's Recent Experience with Reform and Growth*, IMF and Palgrave McMillan Washington DC.

Bannister, J 2005, *Manufacturing Employment and Compensation in China*, US Department of Labor, Bureau of Labor Statistics, Washington, DC.

Barker, J J 1997, *Governance and Regulation of Power Pools and System Operators, An International Comparison*, Technical Paper no. 382, World Bank, Washington, DC.

Barro, RJ 1999, *Inequality, Growth, and Investment*, NBER Working Paper No. 7038, National Bureau of Economic Research, Cambridge, Massachusetts.

Barro, R and Lee, J W (eds.) 2011, *Costs and Benefits of Economic Integration in Asia*, Oxford University Press, Oxford.

Baru, S 2010, *Early Steps towards Regionalism in South Asia: SAARC and Other Arrangements*, Background paper for Institutions for Regional Integration: Toward an Asian Economic Community, Asian Development Bank, Manila.

Batelle 2010, 'Global R&D Funding Forecast', *R&D Magazine*, <http://www.battelle.org/aboutus/rd/2011.pdf>.

BBC News 2010, *Finishing School for Indian IT Graduates*, 7 March 2010, <http://news.bbc.co.uk/2/hi/8547327.stm>.

Beckman, R 2010, *South China Sea: How China Could Clarify Its Claims*, RSIS Commentaries no. 116/2010, S. Rajaratnam School of International Studies, Singapore.

Berg, A, Ostry, JD & Zettelmeyer 2008, *What Makes Growth More Sustained?*, IMF Working Paper no. 08/59, International Monetary Fund, Washington, DC.

Bertaud, A 2003, *The Spatial Structures of Cities: International Examples of the Interaction of Government, Topography, and Markets*, presentation, <http://alain-bertaud.com/AB_China_course_part3_PPT_%20.ppt>.

—— 2010, *Land Markets, Government Interventions, and Housing Affordability*, Wolfensohn Center for Development Working Paper no. 17, The Brookings Institution, Washington, DC.

Bhattacharyay, B 2010, *Estimating Demand for Infrastructure in Energy, Transport, Telecommunications, Water and Sanitation in Asia and the Pacific: 2010–2020*, ADBI Working Paper 248, Asian Development Bank Institute, Tokyo.

Bin, P 2009, 'Enhancing Export Competitiveness through Trade Facilitation in Asia', in *Impact of Trade Facilitation on Export Competitiveness: A Regional Perspective*, United Nations Economic and Social Commission for Asia and the Pacific, Bangkok, Studies in Trade and Investment no. 66, pp. 1–17.

Blanford, G, Richels, R & Rutherford, T 2009, 'Feasible Climate Targets: The Roles of Economic Growth, Coalition Development, and Expectations', *Energy Economics*, vol. 31, Supplement 2, pp. S283-93.

Bloomberg BusinessWeek 2010, *India to Raise $535 Million from Carbon Tax on Coal*, <http://www.businessweek.com/news/2010-07-01/india-to-raise-535-million-from-carbon-tax-on-coal.html>.

Bolt, R 2004, *Accelerating Agriculture and Rural Development for Inclusive Growth: Policy Implications for Developing Asia*, ERD Policy Brief Series no. 29, Asian Development Bank, Manila.

Boorman, J, Fajgenbaum, J, Bhaskaran, M, Kohli, H A & Arnold, D 2010, *The New Resilience of Emerging Market Countries: Weathering the Recent Crisis in the Global Economy*, Paper presented at the ADB Regional Forum on the Impact of the Global Economic and Financial Crisis: Impact of the Global Crisis on Asia, Lessons Learned, Policy Insights, and Outlook, Manila, 4 November 2010.

Bosetti, V, Carraro, C & Tavoni, M 2009, 'Climate Change Mitigation Strategies in Fast-Growing Countries: The Benefits of Early Action', *Energy Economics*, vol. 31, Supplement 2, pp. S144–51.

Boston Consulting Group 2009, *The 2009 BCG 100 New Global Challengers*, BCG, Boston, MA.

Bourguignon, F, Ferrerira, FH & Walton, M 2006, *Equity, Efficiency, and Inequality Traps: A Research Agenda*, John F. Kennedy School for Government Faculty Research Working Paper no. RWP06–025, Harvard University, Cambridge, MA.

Bowen, A & Ranger, N 2009, *Mitigating Climate Change Through Reductions in Greenhouse Gas Emissions: The Science and Economics for Future Paths for Global Annual Emissions*, Policy brief, Grantham Research Institute on Climate Change and the Enviornment and Centre for Climate Change Economics and Policy, London, UK.

British Petroleum 2010, *BP Statistical Review of World Energy*, London, United Kingdom.

Brohan, P, Kennedy, J, Harris, I, Tett, S & Jones, P 2006, 'Uncertainty Estimates in Regional and Global Observed Temperature Changes: A New Data Set from 1850', *Journal of Geophysical Research*, vol. 111, no. D12, p. D12106.

Brooks, D & Ferrarini, B 2010, *Changing Trade Costs between the People's Republic of China and India*, ADB Economics Working Paper no. 203, Asian Development Bank, Manila.

Brooks, D & Stone, S (eds) 2010, *Trade Facilitation and Regional Cooperation in Asia*, Asian Development Bank, Manila.

Burke, E, Brown, S & Christidis, N 2006, 'Modeling the Recent Evolution of Global Drought and Projections for the Twenty-First Century with the Hadley Centre Climate Model', *Journal of Hydrometereology*, vol. 7, no. 5, pp. 1113–25.

Calderón, C, Serven, L & World Bank 2008, *Infrastructure and Economic Development in Sub-Saharan Africa*, Policy research working paper 4712, The World Bank, Washington, DC.

Camilleri, J A 2003, *Regionalism in the New Asia-Pacific Order: The Political Economy of the Asia-Pacific Region, Volume II*, Edward Elgar, Cheltenham, United Kingdom.

Carbonpositive 2009, *Brazil Cuts Deforestation, Sets Emission Target*, <http://www.carbonpositive.net/viewarticle.aspx?articleID=1732>.

Cardia, N 2000, *Urban Violence in Sao Paulo*, Comparative Urban Studies Occasional Paper no. 33, Woodrow Wilson International Center for Scholars, Washington, DC.

Carroll, R 2010, *US Union Challenges China over Clean Tech at WTO*, <http://www.pointcarbon.com/news/1.1473202>.

Castells, M 2000, 'The Information City, the New Economy, and the Network Society', in A Teokesessa Kasvio, V Laitalainem, H Salonen & P Mero (eds) *People, Cities, and the New Information Economy*, proceedings from conference held at Helsinki, Finland, 14–15 December 2000.

Centennial Group 2006, *Regional Cooperation and Integration: Lessons from Experience of Europe and the Americas*, Washington, DC.

Central Asia Regional Economic Cooperation 2010a, *Collective View of the Multilateral Institutions*, Ninth Ministerial Conference on Central Asia Regional Economic Cooperation, Cebu, Philippines, 2 November 2010.

Chandra, R & Kumar, R 2008, *South Asian Integration Prospects and Lessons from East Asia*, ICRIER Working Paper no. 202, Indian Council for Research on International Economic Relations, New Delhi.

Chandy, L & Gertz, G 2011, *Poverty in Numbers: The Changing State of Global Poverty from 2005 to 2015*, Global Views Policy Brief no. 97, The Brookings Institution, Washington, DC.

Chatterjee, S, Ja, R & Mukherjee, A 2010, *Approaches to Combat Hunger in Asia and the Pacific*, ADB Sustainable Development Working Paper no. 11, Asian Development Bank, Manila.

Chinese Academy of Social Sciences 2010, *Global Urban Competitiveness Report*, Edward Elgar Publishing, United Kingdom.

Chu, Y and Huang, M 2007, *A Synthetic Analysis of Sources of Democratic Legitimacy*, Working Paper Series no. 41.

Churchman, A 1999, 'Disentangling the concept of density', *Journal of Planning Literature*, vol. 13, no. 4, pp. 389–411.

Clarke, L, Edmonds, J, Krey, V, Richels, R, Rose, S & Tavoni, M 2009, 'International Climate Policy Architectures: Overview of the EMF 22 International Scenarios', *Energy Economics*, vol. 31, Supplement 2, pp. S64–81.

Clean Technology Fund 2009, *Investment Plan for CSP Scale up In the MENA Region*, World Bank, Washington, DC.

Club of Rome 1972, The Limits to Growth, Macmillan, New York, NY.

Cohen, R 2008, *Disaster Standards Needed in Asia*, Brookings Northeast Asia Commentary no. 20, The Brookings Institution, Washington, DC, <http://www.brookings.edu/opinions/2008/06_disaster_standards_cohen.aspx>.

Coleman, J 1996, 'Japanese Call for Overhaul of Education System—Rote learning, Focus on Exam Take a Big Toll', *The Seattle Times*, <http://community.seattletimes.nwsource.com/archive/?date=19961117&slug=2360255>.

Commission on Growth and Development 2008, *The Growth Report, Strategies for Sustained Growth and Inclusive Development*, Washington, DC.

Corporación Andina de Fomento 2008, 'Special Report: Roads to the Future--Infrastructure Management in Latin America, *Annual Report 2008*, CAF, Caracas.

Costello, B 2010. *When Creativity Rules the World*, <www.makingmindsmatter.com>.

Das, RU, Vadusev, R & Gupta, M 2011, *Regional Integration and Cooperation in Asia: An Indian Perspective*, Centennial Development Advisory Services, India.

Davies, H 2010, 'Global Financial Regulation after the Credit Crisis', *Global Policy*, vol. 1, no. 2, pp. 185–90.

De, P 2009, 'Enhancing Asia's Trade: Transport Costs Matter', in *Impact of Trade Facilitation on Export Competitiveness: A Regional Perspective*, United Nations Economic and Social Commission for Asia and the Pacific, Bangkok, Studies in Trade and Investment no. 66, pp. 19–70.

De, P 2010, *Governance, Institutions, and Regional Infrastructure in Asia*, Asian Development Bank Institute, Tokyo.

De, P, Sumudram, M & Moholkar, S 2010, *Trends in National and Regional Investors Financing Cross-Border Infrastructure Projects in Asia*, ADBI Working Paper no. 245, Asian Development Bank Institute, Tokyo.

Debroy, B 2009, Linking South and East Asian Economies: Markets and Institutions, Background paper for *Institutions for Regional Integration: Toward an Asian Economic Community*, Asian Development Bank, Manila.

Dechezleprêtre, A, Glachant, M, Hascic, I, Johnstone, N & Ménière, Y 2011, 'Invention and Transfer of Climate Change Mitigation Technologies: A Global Analysis', *Review of Environmental Economics and Policy*, forthcoming.

Dent, CM 2009, *Organizing the Wider East Asia Region*, Background paper for *Institutions for Regional Integration: Toward an Asian Economic Community*, Asian Development Bank, Manila.

De Soto, H 2000, *The Mystery of Capital: Why Capitalism Triumphs in the West and Fails Everywhere Else*, Basic Books, New York City.

Dickie, M 2011, 'Rethinking Japan's White-Collar Hiring', *Financial Times*, 25 Januray 2011, <http://www.ft.com/cms/s/0/17da40e2-28a4-11e0-aa18-00144feab49a.html#ixzz1FHvahuAQ>.

Dobbs, R, Lund, S, Roxburgh, C, Manyika, J, Kim, A, Schreiner, A, Boin, R, Chopra, R, Jauch, S, Kim, H, McDonald, M & Piotrowski, J 2010, *Farewell to Cheap Capital? The Implications of Long-Term Shifts in Global Investment and Saving*, McKinsey Global Institute, <http://www.mckinsey.com/mgi/publications/farewell_cheap_capital/pdfs/MGI_Farewell_to_cheap_capital_full_report.pdf>.

Dodman, D & Satterthwaite, D 2009, 'Are Cities Really to Blame?', *Urban World*, vol. 1, no. 2, pp. 12–3.

Dolan, P, Layard, R & Metcalfe, R 2010, *Measuring Subjective Well-being for Public Policy: Recommendations on Measures*, Centre for Economic Performance, London School of Economics, London.

Dollar, D, Shi, A, Wang, S & Xu, LC 2004, *Improving City Competitiveness through the Investment Climate: Ranking 23 Chinese Cities*, The World Bank, Washington, DC.

Duval, Y & Utoktham, C 2010, *Intraregional Trade Costs in Asia: A Primer*, Staff Working Paper no. 01/10, United Nations Economic and Social Commission for Asia and the Pacific, Bangkok.

Earle, L & Scott, Z 2010, *Assessing the Evidence of the Impact of Governance on Development Outcomes and Poverty Reduction*, Issues Paper, UK Department for International Development through the Emerging Issues Research Service of the Governance and Social Development Resource Centre, University of Birmingham, UK.

Earth Policy Institute 2010, *Annual Solar Photovoltaics Production by Country, 1995-2009*, <http://www.earth-policy.org/index.php?/data_center/C23/>.

Easterly, W R 2001, *The Elusive Quest for Growth: Economists' Adventures and Misadventures in the Tropics*, MIT Press, Cambridge, MA.

Economics of Climate Change Adaptation Working Group, 2009, *Shaping Climate-Resilient Development: A Framework for Decision-Making*, Economics of Climate Adaptation, <http://www.mckinsey.com/App_Media/Images/Page_Images/Offices/SocialSector/PDF/ECA_Shaping_Climate%20Resilent_Development.pdf>.

El-Arian, M A & Spence, M 2008, *Growth Strategies and Dynamics: Insights from Country Experiences*, Working Paper No. 6 for the Commission on Growth and Development.

Emerging Markets Forum 2010. *Is Early Action on Climate Change in Self Interest of Emerging Market Economies?*, Centennial Group International, Washington, DC.

Energy Information Agency (EIA) 2007a, *Cost and Performance Baseline for Fossil Energy Plants*, Department of Energy, Washington, DC.

—— 2007b, *Natural Gas Market Review: Security in a Globalizing Market to 2015*, Department of Energy, Washington, DC.

—— 2008, *Global Energy Trends to 2030*, Department of Energy, Washington, DC.

—— 2009, *World Energy Outlook*, Department of Energy, Washington, DC.

—— 2010a, *Energy Technology Perspectives*, Department of Energy, Washington, DC.

—— 2010b, *World Energy Outlook*, Department of Energy, Washington, DC.

—— 2010c, *Country Brief Analysis for various Asian Countries*. Department of Energy, Washington, DC.

—— 2011, *Country Information*, Department of Energy, Washington, DC, <www.eia.doe.gov>.

ESMAP 2008, *Potential and Prospects for Regional Energy Trade in the South Asia Region, Energy Sector Management Assistance Program and the South Asia Regional Cooperation Program*, World Bank, Washington, DC.

European Commission 2009, *Mediterranean Solar Plan Strategy Paper*, European Commission, Brussels.

European Renewable Energy Council 2006, *Re-thinking 2050: A 100% Renewable Energy Vision for the European Union*, European Renewable Energy Council, Brussels.

Farhoomand, A 2005, *Innovation in Asia with Patent Data*, Asian Case Research Center, Hong Kong, China.

Fay, M, Toman, M, Benitez, D & Csordas, S 2011, 'Infrastructure and Sustainable Development', in S Fardoust, Y Kim & C Sepulveda (eds), *Postcrisis Growth and Development: A Development Agenda for the G20*, World Bank, Washington, DC, pp. 329–82.

Fei, J, Ranis, G & Kuo, S 1979, *Growth with Equity*, Oxford University Press, New York, NY.

Felipe, J 2010, *Inclusive Growth, Full Employment, and Structural Change: Implications and Policies for Developing Asia*, Anthem Press and Asian Development Bank, London and Manila.

Feng, Z 2004, *Asian Axis Would Benefit All*, <http://english.peopledaily.com.cn/200405/19/eng20040519_143750.html>.

Ferguson, N 2007, *The Evolution of Financial Services*, Oliver Wyman, New York City.

Financial Crisis Inquiry Commission 2010, *Shadow Banking and the Financial Crisis*.

Florida, R 2002, 'The Economic Geography of Talent', *Annals of the American Association of Geographers*, vol. 92, no. 4, pp. 743–55.

Florida, R, Gulden, T & Mellander, C 2007, *The Rise of the Mega Region*, The Martin Prosperity Institute, University of Toronto School of Management, Toronto, <http://www.rotman.utoronto.ca/userfiles/prosperity/File/Rise.of.%20the.Mega-Regions.w.cover.pdf>.

Food and Agriculture Organization 2008, *Food Insecurity in the World*, United Nations, Rome.

Francois, J, Manchin, M & Pelkmans-Balaoing, A 2009, 'Regional Integration in Asia: The Role of Infrastructure', in J Francois, P Rana & G Wignaraja (eds), *Pan Asian Integration: Linking East and South Asia*, Palgrave, London, pp. 439–86.

Freeman, C & Soerte, L 2004, *Economics of Industrial Innovation, 3rd Edition*, MIT Press, Cambridge, Massachusetts.

Freemark, Y 2010, *Shanghai's Metro, Now World's Longest, Continues to Grow Quickly as China Invests in Rapid Transit*, The Transport Politic, 15 April 2010.

Friedman, M 1955, 'Memo to the Government of India', in *Western Economists and Eastern Societies: Agents of Social Change in South Asia, 1950–1970*. Oxford University Press, Delhi.

Fuchs, R 2010, *Cities at Risk: Asia's Coastal Cities in an Age of Climate Change*, Asia-Pacific Issues no. 96, East-West Center, Honolulu.

Gallini, N & Scotchmer, S 2001, *Intellectual Property: When is it the Best Incentive System?*, Working paper no. E01–303, Department of Economics, University of California, Berkeley.

Gao, J & Jefferson, G H 2005, *Science and Technology Takeoff in Theoretical and Empirical Perspective*, Manuscript, Brandeis University, Waltham, MA.

Garnaut, R, Song, L & Woo, WT 2009, *China's New Place in a World Crisis: Economic, Geopolitical, and Environmental Dimensions*, ANU E-Press, Canberra.

Garcia Fontes, W 2005, *Small and Medium Enterprises Financing in China*, Universytat Pompeu Fabra, Barcelona.

Gasparini, L & Gluzmann, P 2009, *Estimating Income Poverty and Inequality from the Gallup World Poll: The Case of Latin America and the Caribbean*, ECINEQ, Society for the Study of Economic Inequality, Palma de Mallorca, Spain.

Geethanjali, N 2007, *Infrastructure Challenges in South Asia: The Role of Private-Public Partnerships*, ADBI Discussion Paper no. 80, Asian Development Bank Institute, Tokyo.

Gill, I S, Kharas, H & Bhattasali, D 2007, *An East Asian Renaissance: Ideas for Economic Growth*, World Bank, Washington, DC.

Glaeser, E, Sheinkman, J & Shleifer, A 1995, 'Economic Growth in a Cross-Section of Cities', *Journal of Monetary Economics*, vol. 36, no. 1, pp. 117–143.

Glaeser, EL & Kahn, ME 2008, *The Greenness of Cities: Carbon Dioxide Emissions and Urban Development*, NBER Working Paper no. 14238, National Bureau of Economic Research, Boston.

Gosling, L, Narayanan, R, Patkar, A & van Norden, H 2011, Equity and Inclusion in Sanitation and Hygiene in South Asia: A Regional Synthesis Paper, Water Supply and Sanitation Collaborative Council, Geneva.

Government of Cambodia 2011, *National Social Protection Strategy for the Poor and Vulnerable*, Government of Cambodia, Phnom Penh.

Government of PRC 2007, *China Statistical Yearbook 2006*, Government of PRC, Bejing.

Government of the People's Republic of China 2010, Full Text of President Hu Jintao's Speech at the Fifth APEC Human Resources Development Ministerial Meeting, <http://pib.nic.in/newsite/erelease.aspx?relid=60623>.

Government of Singapore 2001, *Economic Development Board, 2001 Annual Report*, Government of Singapore, Singapore.

Government of the United Kingdom 2003, *Sustainable Development in Government: Second Annual Report 2003*, London.

Grenville, S 2010, *An Asian Perspective on Financial Crises*, <http://www.eastasiaforum.org/2010/04/24/an-asian-perspective-on-financial-crises>.

Gros, D 2010, *EMF in IMF*, Brussels.

Grossman, A & Helpman, E 1991, *Innovation and Growth in the Global Economy*, MIT Press, Cambridge, Massachusetts.

Guo, R 2010, *Territorial Disputes and Seabed Petroleum Exploitation: Some Options for the East China Sea*, CNAPS Visiting Fellow Working Paper, Center for Northeast Asia Policy Studies, The Brookings Institution, Washington, DC.

Haggard, S 2009, *The Organizational Architecture of the Asia-Pacific: Insights from the New Institutionalism*, Background paper for *Institutions for Regional Integration: Toward an Asian Economic Community,* Asian Development Bank, Manila.

Hales, S, de Wet, N, Maindonald, J & Woodward, A 2002, 'Potential Effect of Population and Climate Changes on Global Distribution of Dengue Fever: An Empirical Model', *Lancet*, vol. 360, no. 9336, pp. 830–34.

Hamilton, K 2010, *Scaling up Renewable Energy in Developing Countries: Finance and Investment Perspectives*, Chatham House, London.

Haub, C 2010, 'Demographic Dynamics of Asia', in B Stiftung (ed.), *Asia: Changing the World*, Bertelsmann Stiftung, Gutersloh, pp. 26–7.

Heathcote, J, Perri, F & Violante, G 2010, 'Unequal We Stand: An Empirical Analysis of Economic Inequality in the United States, 1967–2006', *Review of Economic Dynamics*, vol. 13, pp.15–51.

Hellman, J & Kaufmann, D, 'Confronting the Challenge of State Capture in Transition Economies', *Finance & Development*, vol. 38, no. 3.

Hernandez, J & Taningco, AB 2010, *Behind-the-Border Determinants of Bilateral Trade Flows in East Asia*, 8010, ARTNeT Working Paper no. 8010, Asia-Pacific Research and Training Network on Trade, Bangkok.

Hertel, T, Hummels, D, Ivanic, M & Keeney, R 2004, 'How Confident Can We Be in CGE-Based Assessments of Free Trade Agreements?, *NBER Working Paper*, Washington, DC.

Hettne, B & Soederbaum, F 2006, 'Regional Cooperation: A Tool for Addressing Regional and Global Challenges', in International Task Force on Global Public Goods (ed.), *Achieving Global Public Goods*, Foreign Ministry, Stockholm, pp. 179–244.

High-Powered Expert Committee 2011, *Report on Indian Urban Infrastructure and Services*, Indian Council for Research on International Economic Relations, New Delhi.

Hill, H and Menon, J 2011a, ASEAN Economic Integration: Features, Fulfillments, Failures and the Future, ADB Working Paper Series on Regional Economic Integration no. 69, Asian Development Bank, Manila. <aric.adb.org/pdf/workingpaper/WP69_Hill_Menon_ASEAN_Economic_Integration.pdf>.

—— 2011b, 'Reducing Vulnerability in Transition Economies: Crises and Adjustment in Cambodia', *ASEAN Economic Bulletin* 28 (3).

HSBC 2010, *Sizing the climate economy*.

Hu, A G Z & Jefferson, G H 2004, 'Returns to Research and Development in Chinese Industry: Evidence from State-Owned Enterprises in Beijing', *China Economic Review*, 15(1), pp. 86–107.

Hu, A G Z, Jefferson, G H & Qian, J 2005, 'R&D and Technology Transfer: Firm-level Evidence in Chinese Industry', *Review of Economics and Statistics*, 87(4), pp. 780–786.

Huang, Y 2008, *Capitalism with Chinese Characteristics: Entrepreneurship and the State*, Cambridge University Press, Cambridge, Massachusetts.

Huang, W et al 1997, 'Infant Mortality Among Various Nationalities in the Middle Part of Guizhou, China', *Soc Sci Med*, 45(7), pp. 1031–40.

Huang, Y & Qian, Y 2010, 'Is Entrepreneurship Missing in Shanghai?', in *International Differences in Entrepreneurship*, National Bureau of Economic Research, University of Chicago Press.

Huang, Y 2011, *Cross Border Labor Mobility—Governance Framework*, unpublished draft.
Iimi, A 2005, 'Urbanization and Development in East Asian Region', *JBICI Review*, no. 10, pp. 88–109.

Immelt, J, Govindarajan, V & Trimble C 2009, 'How GE is Disrupting Itself', *Harvard Business Review*, <http://hbr.org/2009/10/how-ge-is-disrupting-itself/ar/1>.

Intergovernmental Panel on Climate Change 2001, *Climate Change 2001: Impacts, Adaptation and Vulnerability*, Cambridge, UK.

Intergovernmental Panel on Climate Change 2007, *Climate Change*, Intergovernmental Panel on Climate Change, Geneva.

International Energy Agency 2009, *World Energy Outlook 2009*, International Energy Agency, Paris.

—— 2010, *China Overtakes the United States to Become World's Largest Energy Consumer*, <http://www.iea.org/index_info.asp?id=1479>.

International Monetary Fund 2009, *Lessons of the Financial Crisis for Future Regulation of Financial Institutions and Markets and for Liquidity Management*, Monetary and Capital Markets Department, International Monetary Fund, Washington, DC.

International Monetary Fund 2011, *IMF Performance in the Run-Up to the Financial and Economic Crisis: IMF Surveillance in 2000–07*, Independent Evaluation Office, International Monetary Fund, Washington, DC.

Johnson, S, McMillan, J & Woodruff, C 2002, 'Property Rights And Finance,' *American Economic Review*, vol. 92, pp. 1335–1356.

Jomo, KS 2006, *Growth with Equity in East Asia?*, DESA Working Paper No. 33, United Nations, New York, MY.

Jones, C & Williams, J C 1999, *Too Much of a Good Thing: The Economics of Investment in R&D*, Working paper no. 99015, Economics Department, Stanford University, Palo Alto, CA.

Jones, C I 2002, *Introduction to Economic Growth*, W. W. Norton, New York, NY.

Kanbur, R & Spence, M (eds) 2010, *Equity and Growth in a Globalizing World*, Commission on Growth and Development, Washington, DC.

Kang, K & Miniane, J 2008, 'Global Financial Turmoil Tests Asia', *Finance and Development*, vol. 45, no. 4, pp. 34–36.

Kao, J 2009, 'Tapping the World's Innovation Hot Spots', *Harvard Business Review*, <http://hbr.org/hbr-main/resources/pdfs/comm/fmglobal/tapping-worlds-innovation-hotspots.pdf>.

Kar, D & Curcio, K 2011, *Illicit Financial Flows from Developing Countries: 2000-2009, Update with a Focus on Asia*, United Nations Development Programme, New York, NY.

Karacadag, C, Sundararajan, V & Elliot, J 2003, 'Managing Risks in Financial Market Development: The Role of Sequencing', in RE Litan, M Pomerleano & V Sundararajan (eds), *The Future of Domestic Capital Markets in Developing Countries*, International Monetary Fund, Washington, DC, pp. 233–72.

Kaufmann, D, Kraay, A & Mastruzzi, M 2006, 'Measuring Corruption: Myths and Realities', *Global Corruption Report 2007*.

Kawai, M 2009, *Reform of the International Financial Architecture: An Asian Perspective*, ADBI Working Paper no. 167, Asian Development Bank Institute, Tokyo.

Kawai, M & Wignaraja, G 2010, Free Trade Agreements in East Asia: A Way toward Trade Liberalization, ADB Briefs no. 1, Asian Development Bank, Manila.

Kemp, A G & Kasim, A S 2008, 'A Least-Cost Optimization Model of CO_2 Capture Applied to Major Power Plants Within the EU-ETS Framework', *Energy Journal*.

Kennedy, S 2011, *Greece Default with Ireland Breaks Euro by 2016 in Global Poll*, <http://www.bloomberg.com/news/2011-01-25/greece-default-with-ireland-breaks-euro-by-2016-in-global-poll.html>.

Khandker, S R, Bakht, Z & Koolwal, G B 2006, *The Poverty Impact of Rural Roads: Evidence from Bangladesh*, Policy Research Working Paper, Poverty Reduction and Economic Management Division, The World Bank Institute, Washington, DC.

Kharas, H 2010a, 'India's Promise: An Affluent Society in One Generation', in *India 2039: An Affluent Society in One Generation*, pp. 9-28, Sage, New Delhi.

—— 2010b, 'Latin America: Is Average Good Enough?', in *Latin America 2040: Breaking Away from Complacency: An Agenda for Resurgence*, pp. 71–100, Sage, Thousand Oaks, California.

Kim, Y J & Terada-Hagiwara, A 2010, 'A Survey on the Relationships between Education and Growth with Implications for Developing Asia', Background paper, *ADB Economics Working Paper Series No. 236*, Asian Development Bank, Manila.

King, A A & Tucci, C L 2002, 'Incumbent Entry into New Market Niches: The Role of Experience and Managerial Choice in the Creation of Dynamic Capabilities', *Management Science*, 48 (2), pp. 171–86.

Kohli, H & Sood, A (eds.) 2010, *India 2039: An Affluent Society in One Generation*, Sage, New Delhi.

Kohli, H, Loser, C & Sood, A (eds.) 2010. *Latin America 2040—Breaking Away from Complacency: An Agenda for Resurgence*, Sage, New Delhi.

Kohli H & Sharma A (eds.) 2010, *A Resilient Asia Amidst Global Financial Crisis: From Crisis Management to Global Leadership*, Sage, New Delhi.

Kohli, H & Ahmed, J (eds.) 2011, *Islamic Finance: Writings of V. Sundararajan*, Sage, New Delhi.

Kohli, H A & Basil, P 2011, 'Requirements for Infrastructure Investment in Latin America Under Alternate Growth Scenarios: 2011–2040', *Global Journal of Emerging Market Economies* 3(1).

Kohli, H A & Mukherjee, N 2011, 'Potential Costs to Asia of the Middle Income Trap', *Global Journal of Emerging Market Economies* 3(3).

Kohli, H A, Szyf, Y A & Arnold, D 2012, 'Possibilities for the World's Economies through 2050 Using a Revised Growth Model for 185 Countries', *Global Journal of Emerging Market Economies* 4(1).

Krueger, AO 1995a, *Trade Policies and Developing Nations*, The Brookings Institution, Washington, DC.

Krueger, A O 1995b, 'The Role of Trade in Growth and Development: Theory and Lessons from the East Asian Experience', in R Garnaut, E Grilli & J Riedel (eds), *Sustaining Export-Oriented Development: Ideas from East Asia*, Cambridge University Press, Cambridge, pp. 1–30.

Kumhof, M & Ranciere, R 2010, *Inequality, Leverage and Crises*. Working paper no. 10/268 for the International Monetary Fund, Washington, DC.

Kursten, B 2004, *Cross-Border Transnational Urban Economic Regions*, <http://www.globalurban.org/GUD%20Transnational%20MES%20Report.pdf>.

Lamia, K-C & Roberts, A (eds) 2009, *Competitive Cities and Climate Change*, Regional Development Working Paper no. 2, Organisation for Economic Co-operation and Development, Paris.

Langguth, G 2003, 'Asian Values Revisited', *Asia Europe Journal*, vol. 1, pp. 25–42.

La Rovere, E & Pereira, A 2007, *Brazil and Climate Change: A Country Profile*, Science and Development Policy Briefs, 14 February 2007 <http://www.scidev.net/en/policy-briefs/brazil-climate-change-a-country-profile.html>.

Lee, J W & Francisco, R 2010, 'Human Capital Accumulation in Emerging Asia, 1970–2030', *ADB Economics Working Paper Series No. 216*, Asian Development Bank, Manila.

Lee, R, Mason, A, & Cotlear, D 2010, *Some Economic Consequences of Global Ageing*, World Bank, Washington, DC.

Legatum Institute 2010, *Legatum Prosperity Index*, <http://www.prosperity.com/>.

Lerner, J & Schoar, A 2010, 'International Differences in Entrepreneurship,' in *National Bureau of Economic Research Book*, University of Chicago Press, Chicago.

Levine, M 2010, *Energy Use in Chinese Buildings: Views of an Outsider Looking In*, First U.S.-China Energy Efficiency Forum, Beijing.

Levine, R 2004, 'Finance and Growth: Theory and Evidence', in P Aghion & S Durlauf (eds), *Handbook of Economic Growth*, Elsevier Science, Amsterdam, vol. 1, pp. 865–934.

Lewis, J 2010, Building a National Wind Turbine Industry: Experiences from China, India and South Korea, *Int. J. Technology and Globalisation*, vol. 5, no. 3/4, pp. 281–305.

Linn, JF & Tiomkin, D 2007, 'Economic Integration of Eurasia: Opportunities and Challenges of Global Significance', in A Aslund & M Dabrowski (eds), *Europe after Enlargement*, Cambridge University Press, Cambridge, UK, pp.189–228.

Linn, JF & Pidufala, O 2008, *The Experience with Regional Economic Cooperation Organizations: Lessons for Central Asia*, Wolfensohn Center for Development Working Paper no. 4, The Brookings Institution, Washington, DC.

Linn, JF 2010, *Connecting Central Asia and the Caucasus with the World*, Eurasia Emerging Markets Forum, Thun, Switzerland, 23–25 January 2010, background paper.

Lynch, JP & Butiong, RAQ 2009, *Greater Mekong Subregion (GMS): Review of Transport Projects along GMS Corridors*, Thirteenth Meeting of the GMS Subregional Transport Forum, Siem Reap, Cambodia, 27-28 October 2009, presentation, <http://www.adb.org/Documents/Events/Mekong/Proceedings/STF13-Appendix8.pdf>.

Madan, T 2006, *Energy Security Series: India*, Brookings Foreign Policy Studies, Brookings Institution, Washington, DC.

Mahbubani, K 2008, *The New Asian Hemisphere: The Irresistible Shift of Global Power to the East*, PublicAffairs, New York, NY.

Mao, J 2008, *Status and Development of China's Electric Power*, Asia Clean Energy Forum, Manila.

MasterCard Worldwide 2008, *Global Centers of Commerce Index*, MasterCard Worldwide, Purchase, NY.

Masud, J 2007, *Energy for All: Addressing the Energy, Environment and Poverty Nexus in Asia*, Asian Development Bank, Manila.

McKinsey & Company 2009a, *China's Green Revolution: Prioritizing Technologies to Achieve Energy and Environmental Sustainability*, McKinsey & Company, Shanghai.

—— 2009b, *Pathways to a Low Carbon Economy for Brazil*, McKinsey & Company, Sao Paulo. McKinsey & Company 2009c, *Roads toward a Low Carbon Future*, McKinsey & Company, Boston.

McKinsey and Company 2009d, *Capturing the India Advantage*, Working paper, Pharma Summit 2009, Delhi, 30 November 2009, <http://www.indiapharmasummit.com/downloads/reports/Capturing%20the%20India%20Advantage.pdf>.

McKinsey Global Institute 2010, *Farewell to Cheap Capital? The Implications of Long-term Shifts in Global Investment and Saving*.

Meehl, G & Stocker, T 2007, 'Global Climate Projections', in S Solomon, D Qin, H Manning, Z Chen, M Marquis, K Averyt, M Tignor & H Miller (eds), *Climate Change 2007: The Physical Science Basis, Contribution of Working Group I to the Fourth Assessment Report of the Intergovernmental Panel on Climate Change*, Cambridge University Press, Cambridge, UK and New York City, pp. 747–846.

Menon, J and Warr, P 2008, 'Does Road Improvement Reduce Poverty? A General Equilibrium Analysis for Lao PDR', in D Brooks and J Menon (eds.), *Infrastructure and Trade in Asia*, London: Edward Elgar, pp. 115–42.

Menon, J 2009, 'Dealing with the Proliferation of Bilateral Free Trade Agreements', *World Economy*, vol. 32, pp. 1381–407.

Merrill Lynch & Capgemini 2008, *World Wealth Report 2008*, Merrill Lynch and Capgemini, <http://www.capgemini.com/insights-and-resources/by-publication/world_wealth_report_2008/>.

Mestl, S, Aunan, K, Jinghua, F, Seip, H, Skjelvik, J & Vennemo, H 2005, 'Cleaner Production as Climate Investment—Integrated Assessment in Taiyuan City, China', *Journal of Cleaner Production*, vol. 13, no. 1, pp. 57–70.

Miller, J 2004, *The Roots and Implications of East Asian Regionalism*, Background paper for *The Asia-Pacific Center for Security Studies Occasional Paper Series*, Honolulu, HI.

Mogilevsky, R 2010, *Trends and Determinants in Inter-Regional Trade in CAREC*, CAREC Institute, Manila.

Mohan, R 2006, *Keynote Address*, Conference on Land Policies and Urban Development, Cambridge, Massachusetts, 5 June 2006.

Morck, R, Stangeland, D & Yeung, B 2000. 'Economic Effects of Concentrated Corporate Ownership: Inherited Wealth, Corporate Control, and Economic Growth—The Canadian Disease?,' in *Concentrated Corporate Ownership*, National Bureau of Economic Research, Boston, MA, pp. 319–372.

Moses, S, Blanchard, JF, Kang, H, Emmanuel, F, Paul, SR, Becker, ML, Wilson, D & Claeson, M 2006, *AIDS in South Asia: Understanding and Responding to a Heterogeneous Epidemic*, World Bank, Washington, DC.

Mu, R & van de Walle, D 2007, 'Rural Roads and Poor Area Development in Vietnam', *Policy Research Working Paper Series*, The World Bank, Washington, DC.

Müller, C, Bondeau, A, Popp, A, Waha, K & Fader, M 2009, *Climate Change Impacts on Agricultural Yields*, World Bank, Washington, DC.

Musalem, AR & Tressel, T 2003, 'Institutional Savings and Financial Markets: The Role of Contractual Savings Institutions', in RE Litan, M Pomerleano & V Sundararajan (eds), *The Future of Domestic Capital Markets in Developing Countries*, The Brookings Institution, Washington, DC.

Nathan, A J 2007, *Political Culture and Diffuse Regime Support in Asia*, Working Paper Series no. 43.

National Science Foundation 2010, *Science and Engineering Indicators 2010*, <http://www.nsf.gov/statistics/seind10/>.

N'Diaye, P 2010, Transforming China: Insights from the Japanese Experience of the 1980s, IMF Working Paper no. 10/284, International Monetary Fund, Washington, DC.

Nehru, V 2010, 'East Asia and the Pacific Confronts the 'New Normal'', *Economic Premise*, no. 24, pp. 1–9.

Nicholls, R, Hanson, S, Herweijer, C, Patmore, N, Hallegatte, S, Corfee-Morlot, J, Chateau, J & Muir-Wood, R 2007, *Ranking Port Cities with High Exposure and Vulnerability to Climate Extremes: Exposure Estimates*, OECD Working Paper no. 1, Organisation for Economic Co-operation and Development, Paris.

Nishimura, K 2011, *This Time May Truly Be Different—Balance Sheet Adjustment under Populating Ageing*, American Economic Association Annual Meeting, Denver, 7 January 2011, speech.

Nordhaus, W & Boyer, J 2000, *Warming the World: Economic Models of Global Warming*, MIT Press, Cambridge, MA.

Nordhaus, W 2010, 'Economic Aspects of Global Warming in a Post-Copenhagen Environment', *Proceedings of the National Academy of Sciences*, vol. 107, no. 26, pp. 11721–6.

Normile, D 2007, 'Japans Picks Up the "Innovation" Mantra', *Science*, vol. 316, no. 5882, pp. 186, <http://www.sciencemag.org/content/316/5822/186.full?sid=657eeac2-9e26-4405-922c-9352396fe239>.

O'Connor, D, Zhai, F, Aunan, K, Berntsen, T & Vennemo 2003, *Agricultural and Human Health Impacts of Climate Policy in China: A General Equilibrium Analysis with Special Reference to Guangdong*, OECD Development Centre Technical Paper no. 206, Organisation for Economic Co-operation and Development, Paris.

OECD 2007, 'Basic Statistics on Scientific and Technological Activities', in *OECD Reviews of Innovation Policy—China Synthesis Report*, OECD, Paris.

—— 2010, *PISA 2009 Results*, OECD, Paris.

OFDA/CRED International Disaster Database 2010, *EM-DAT*, Brussels.

Olcott, MB 2010, *Central Asia's Oil and Gas Reserves: To Whom Do They Matter*, Eurasia Emerging Markets Forum, Thun, Switzerland, 23-25 January 2010, background paper.

Ombok, M et al 2010, 'Geospatial Distribution and Determinants of Child Mortality in Rural Western Kenya 2002–2005', *Trop Med Int Health*, 15(4), pp. 423–33.

Organisation for Economic Cooperation and Development (OECD) 2008, *Growing Unequal? Income Distribution and Poverty in OECD Countries*, OECD, Paris.

Organization for Economic Cooperation and Development (OECD) 2009, *Integrating Climate Change Adaptation into Development Cooperation*, OECD Paris.

Organization of Oil Exporting Countries (OPEC) 2009, *World Energy Outlook*, OPEC.

Ostrom, E 1998, 'A Behavioral Approach to the Rational Choice Theory of Collective Action: Presidential Address, American Political Science Association, 1997', *American Political Science Review*, vol. 92, no. 1, pp. 1–22.

Panagariya, A 2006, *Pursuit of Equity Threatens Poverty Alleviation*, Financial Times, 3 May.

Pangestu, M and Gooptu, G 2004, 'New Regionalism Options for East Asia', in K Krumm and H Kharas (eds.) *East Asia Integrates: A Trade Policy Agenda for Shared Growth*, World Bank and Oxford University Press, Washington, DC.

Pearson, N O 2010, *India to Raise $535 million from Carbon Tax on Coal*, <http://www.businessweek.com/news/2010-07-01/india-to-raise-535-million-from-carbon-tax-on-coal.html>.

Pempel, T J 2005, 'Introduction: Emerging Webs of Regional Connectedness', in *Remapping East Asia: The Construction of a Region*, Cornell University Press, Ithaca, New York, pp. 1–28.

Pirikh, K & Binswanger, H 2011, *Structural Change and Prospects and Constraints for Indian Agriculture*, Report prepared for Centennial Group International, forthcoming.

Pistor, K & Wellons, P 1999, *The Role of Law and Legal Institutions in Asian Economic Development 1960-1995*, Prepared for the Asian Development Bank, Oxford University Press, NY.

Planning Commission of India 2006, *Report of the Expert Committee on Integrated Energy Policy*, Planning Commission of India, New Delhi.

Pomfret, R 2010, *Regionalism in East Asia: Why Now and Where To?*, unpublished manuscript.

Porter, M 1998, 'The Microeconomic Foundations of Economic Development', in *Global Competitiveness Report*, World Economic Forum, Geneva.

Porter, M & Bond, G 1999, *Innovative Capacity and Prosperity: The Next Competitiveness Challenge*, Unpublished manuscript.

Pozsar, Z, Adrian, T, Ashcraft, A & Boesky, H 2010, *Shadow Banking*, Federal Reserve Bank of New York Staff Report no. 458, Federal Reserve Bank of New York, New York.

Prahalad, C K & Mashelkar 2010, 'Innovation's Holy Grail', *Harvard Business Review*, <http://hbr.org/2010/07/innovations-holy-grail/ar/1>.

Press Information Bureau, Government of India 2010, *PM Inaugurates Civil Services Day*, 2010, http://pib.nic.in/newsite/erelease.aspx?relid=60623

Rajan, R 2009, *Crises, Private Capital Flows, and Financial Instability in Emerging Asia*, UNESCAP Working Paper no. 09/06, United Nations Economic and Social Commission for Asia and the Pacific, Bangkok, <http://www.unescap.org/pdd/publications/workingpaper/wp_09_06.pdf>.

Rajasekharan, K 2011, *Reducing Corruption in Public Governance: Rhetoric to Reality*, <http://www.sidb.com>.

Ravallion, M & Chen, S 1997, 'What Can New Survey Data Tell Us about Recent Changes in Distribution and Poverty?', *The World Bank Economic Review*, vol. 11, no. 2, pp. 357–82.

Ravenhill, J 2009, *The Political Economy of Asian Regionalism, Background paper for Institutions for Regional Integration: Toward an Asian Economic Community*, Asian Development Bank, Manila.

Razavi, H 2009, 'Natural Gas Pricing in the Countries of the Middle East and North Africa', *The Energy Journal*, vol. 30, no. 3.

—— 2010, Unleashing an Energy Revolution, in *India 2039: An Affluent Society in One Generation*, Sage, New Delhi.

Reichenmiller, P, Spiegel, A, Bresch, D & Schnarwiler, R 2010, *Weathering Climate Change: Insurance Solutions for More Resilient Communities*, Swiss Reinsurance Company Ltd., Zurich.

Reinhart, CM & Rogoff, KS 2009, *This Time is Different: Eight Centuries of Financial Folly*, Princeton University Press, Princeton, NJ.

Republic of Singapore 2003, 'Bites of the Week', *MITA News*.

Roberts, B & Kanaley, T (eds) 2006, *Urbanization and Sustainability in Asia: Case Studies of Good Practice*, Asian Development Bank, Manila.

Roberts, E & Eesley, C (2009), *Entrepreneurial Impact: The Role of MIT*, Paper prepared for the Kauffman Foundation, Kansas City, MO.

Robins, N, Clover, R & Singh, C 2009, *A Climate for Recovery: The Colour of Stimulus Goes Green*, HSBC Global Research, London.

Robins, N, Clover, R, Singh, C, Knight, Z & Magness, J 2010, *Sizing the Climate Economy*, HSBC Global Research, London.

Rodrik, D 1999, *Where Did All the Growth Go? External Shocks, Social Conflict, and Growth Collapses*, Journal of Economic Growth, vol. 4, no. 4, pp. 395–412.

Rogers, J 2006, *Scenarios for CO_2 Emissions from the Transport Sector in Asia*, Presentation.

Roland-Holst, D 2006, *Infrastructure as a Catalyst for Regional Integration, Growth, and Economic Convergence*, ERD Working Paper no. 91, Asian Development Bank, Manila.

Romer, P M 1990, 'Endogenous Technological Change—Part 2: The Problem of Development: A Conference of the Institute for the Study of Free Enterprise Systems, *The Journal of Political Economy*, vol. 98, no. 5, pp. S71–S102.

Royal Society 2005, *Ocean Acidification Due to Increasing Atmospheric Carbon Dioxide*, 12/05, Royal Society, London.

Saez, E 2004, 'Reported Incomes and Marginal Tax Rates, 1960–2000: Evidence and Policy Implications', in *Tax Policy and the Economy*, vol. 18, pp. 117–174, National Bureau of Economic Research, Boston.

Sahmed, S, Kelagama, S & Ghani, E 2010, *Promoting Economic Cooperation in South Asia: Beyond SAFTA*, Sage Publications, New Delhi.

Saxenian, A 2006, *The New Argonauts: Regional Advantage in a Regional Economy*, Harvard University Press, Cambridge, Massachusetts.

Schadler, S, Carkovic, M, Bennett, A & Kahn, R 1993, *Recent Experiences with Surges in Capital Inflows*, Occasional Paper no. 108, International Monetary Fund, Washington, DC.

Schadler, S 2008, *Managing Large Capital Inflows: Taking Stock of International Experiences*, ADBI Discussion Paper no. 97, Asian Development Bank Institute, Tokyo.

Scheper-Hughes, N 2004, 'Dangerous and Endangered Youth: Social Structures and Determinants of Violence', *Annals of the New York Academy of Sciences*, vol. 1036, pp. 13–46.

Scotchmer, S 1991, 'Standing on the Shoulders of Giants: Cumulative Research and the Patent Law', *The Journal of Economic Perspectives*, vol. 5, no. 1, pp. 29–41.

Securities Industry and Financial Markets Association, 2009, *SIFMA Fact Book*, Securities Industry and Financial Markets Association, New York, NY.

Severino, RC 2009, *Regional Institutions in Southeast Asia: The First Movers and their Challenges*, Background paper for *Institutions for Regional Integration: Toward an Asian Economic Community*, Asian Development Bank, Manila.

Shahin, S 2004, *India, Japan Eye New Axis*, <http://www.atimes.com/atimes/South_Asia/FH24Df03.html>.

Shanker, V 2003, *Towards an Economic Community: Exploring the Past*, Background paper for the Research and Information System for the Non-Aligned and Other Developing Countries, New Delhi.

Shapiro, N 2010, *Addressing the Global Challenge of Financial Inclusion*, International Finance Corporation.

Sheng, A 2009, *From Asian to Global Financial Crisis*, Cambridge University Press, London.

—— 2010, 'The Regulatory Reform of Global Financial Markets: An Asian Regulator's Perspective', *Global Policy*, vol. 1, no. 2, p. 10.

—— 2011, *Out with the Tiger, In with the Rabbit*, <http://biz.thestar.com.my/news/story.asp?file=/2011/2/5/business/7926843&sec=business>.

Shirakawa, M 2009, *Reforming the Framework of Financial Regulation and Supervision: An International and Asian Perspective*, Bank Negara Malaysia-Bank for International Settlements High-Level Seminar, Malaysia, 11 December 2009, speech, <http://www.boj.or.jp/en/announcements/press/koen_2009/ko0912b.htm/>.

Shvidenko, A, Barber, C, Persson, R, Gonzalez, P, Hassan, R, Lakyda, P, McCallum, I, Nilsson, S, Pulhin, J, van Rosenburg, B & Scholes, B 2005, 'Forest and Woodlands Systems', in R Hassan, R Scholes & N Ash (eds), *Ecosystems and Human Well-being: Current State and Trends*, Island Press, Washington, DC, pp. 585–621.

Simon, C 1998, 'Human Capital and Metropolitan Employment Growth', *Journal of Urban Economics*, vol. 43, no. 2, pp 223–43.

Sohn, I 2008, 'Learning to Co-operate: China's Multilateral Approach to Asian Financial Co-operation', *The China Quarterly*, vol. 194, pp. 309–326.

Song, W 2007, 'Regionalization, Inter-regional Cooperation, and Global Governance', *Atlantic Economic Journal*, vol. 5, no. 1, pp. 67–82.

Soros, G 2009, *The Crash of 2008 and What It Means: The New Paradigm for Financial Markets*, PublicAffairs, New York, NY.

Stern, N 2007, *The Stern Review: Economics of Climate Change*, Cambridge University Press, Cambridge, UK.

—— 2008, 'The Economics of Climate Change, Richard T. Ely Lecture', *American Economic Review: Papers & Proceedings*, vol. 98, no. 2, pp. 1–37.

Stiglitz, J E, Sen, A & Fitoussi, J P 2009, *Report by the Commission on the Measurement of Economic Performance and Social Progress*, OECD, Paris.

Subnational Doing Business 2009, *Doing Business in Indonesia 2010*, World Bank and International Finance Corporation, Washington, DC.

Sustainability Institute 2010, *Climate Scoreboard*, <http://climateinteractive.org/scoreboard/scoreboard-science-and-data/current-climate-proposals-1/april-2010/Proposals%20Summary%20Apr10.pdf>.

Szwarcwald, C, Bestos, F, Viacava, F & de Andrade, C 1999, 'Income Inequality and Homicide Rates in Rio de Janeiro, Brazil', *American Journal of Public Health*, vol. 89, no. 6, pp. 845–50.

Tandon, A & Zhuang, J 2007, *Inclusiveness of Economic Growth in the People's Republic of China: What Do Population Health Outcomes Tell Us?*, ERD Working Paper no. 47, Asian Development Bank, Manila.

Tanser, F, Sharp, B & le Sueur, D 2003, 'Potential Effect of Climate Change on Malaria Transmission in Africa', *The Lancet*, vol. 362, no. 9398, pp. 1792–8.

Taylor, R 2008, *Financing Energy Efficiency: Lessons from Brazil, China, India, and Beyond*, World Bank, Washington, DC.

TeamLease Services 2009, India Labour Report 2008—TeamLease Services 2008, *India Labour Report 2008—The Right to Rise: Making India's Labour Markets Inclusive*, Bangalore, India.

Tett, G 2011, 'So Who's Top of the Class Now?', *Financial Times*, <http://www.ft.com/cms/s/0/20904748-2423-11e0-a89a-00144feab49a.html#ixzz1FHhB8hRC>.

Thomas, V 2007, 'The Difference Inclusive Growth Makes', *Latin America Emerging Markets Forum 2007 Discussion Draft*, Emerging Markets Forum, Washington, DC.

UNDP 2005, *Central Asia Human Development Report*, New York.

United Nations 2005, *World Population Prospects: The 2004 Revision*, United Nations, New York, NY.

—— 2010, *Joint Statement by Heads of UN Entities for the Launch of the International Year of Youth*, United Nations, New York, NY.

—— 2011a, *World Population Prospects: The 2010 Revision*, United Nations, New York, NY.

—— 2011b, *Education For All: Global Monitoring Report, 2011*, United Nations, New York, NY.

United Nations, Department of Economic and Social Affairs 2009, *World Urbanization Prospects: The 2009 Revision*, United Nations, New York, NY.

United Nations Development Programme 2005, *Central Asia Human Development Report*, New York, NY.

UN Habitat 2010, *The State of Asian Cities 2010/11*, United Nations, New York, NY.

United States Energy Information Administration 2002, *South China Sea Region*, <http://www.eia.doe.gov/emeu/cabs/schina2.html>.

United States Financial Crisis Inquiry Commission Report 2011, *Financial Crisis Inquiry Commission Report*, <http://www.fcic.gov>.

US Department of State 2003, *Country Reports on Human Rights Practices, Burma*, 31 March 2003, <http://www.state.gov/g/drl/rls/hrrpt/2002/18237.htm>.

van Dingenen, R, Dentener, F, Raes, F, Krol, M, Emberson, L & Cofala, J 2009, 'The Global Impact of Ozone on Agricultural Crop Yields under Current and Future Air Quality Legislation', *Atmospheric Environment*, vol. 43, no. 3, pp. 604–18.

Veron, N 2010, *An Update on EU Financial Reforms*, Policy Brief no. PB10-30, Peterson Institute for International Economics, Washington, DC.

Wade, R 2007, *Global Finance: A New Global Financial Architecture?*, New Left Review, <http://newleftreview.org/?view=2681>.

Wadhwa, Vivek 2004, 'Is the U.S. Brain Drain on the Horizon? Immigrants Now See Better Prospects at Home', *Yale Global*, December 8, 2009.

Walton, M 2007, Poverty Reduction in the New Asia and Pacific: Key Challenges of Inclusive Growth, Technical Note, Asian Development Bank, Manila.

—— 2010, 'Tackling Structural Inequities,' in Kohli and Sood (eds.) *India 2039: An Affluent Society in One Generation*, Sage, New Delhi.

Wang, Y 2009, *Evolving Asian Power Balances and Alternative Conceptions for Building Regional Institutions*, Background paper for *Institutions for Regional Integration: Toward an Asian Economic Community*, Asian Development Bank, Manila.

Ward, K 2011, *The World in 2050—Quantifying the Shift in Global Economy*, HSBC Global Research, London.

Warr, P 2009, 'Poverty Reduction Through Lon-term Growth: The Thai Experience', *Asian Economic Papers*, vol. 8, no. 2, pp. 51–76.

Warr, P, Menon, J & Yusuf, A 2010, 'Regional Economic Impacts of Large Projects: A General Equilibrium Application to Cross-Border Infrastructure', *Asian Development Review*, vol. 27, no. 1, pp. 104–34.

Warren, R, Hope, C, Mastrandrea, M, Tol, R, Adger, N, & Lorenzoni, I 2006, *Spotlighting the Impacts Functions in Integrated Assessment Models*, Tyndall Centre for Climate Change Research, Norwich, UK.

Webster, D 2004, *Urbanization Dynamics and Policy Frameworks in Developing East Asia*, World Bank, Washington, DC.

Weerakoon, D 2010, 'SAFTA: Current Status and Prospects', in S Ahmed, S Kelegam & E Ghani (eds), *Promoting Economic Cooperation in South Asia: Beyond SAFTA*, World Bank, Washington, DC, pp. 71–88.

Weitzman, M 2009, 'On Modelling and Interpreting the Catastrophic Consequences of Climate Change', *Review of Economics and Statistics*, vol. 91, no. 1, pp. 1–19.

Wessel, I & Wimhofer, G 2001, *Violence in Indonesia*, Abera-Verl, Hamburg.

White House 2009, *Progress Report: The Transformation to a Clean Energy Economy*, White House, Washington, DC, 15 December 2009, <http://www.whitehouse.gov/sites/default/files/administration-official/vice_president_memo_on_clean_energy_economy.pdf>.

White House, Office of the Press Secretary 2010, *Obama's State of the Union Address*, White House, Washington, DC, 27 January 2010, <http://www.america.gov/st/texttrans-english/2010/January/20100127234716SBlebahC0.8334728.html>.

Wigley, T & Raper, S 2001, 'Interpretation of High Projections for Global-Mean Warming', *Science*, vol. 293, no. 5529, pp. 451–4.

Wigley, T 2005, 'The Climate Change Commitment', *Science*, vol. 307, no. 5716, pp. 1766–9.
World Bank 2005, *Malaysia Firm Competitiveness, Investment Climate, and Growth*, The World Bank, Washington, DC.

World Bank 2006, *World Development Report 2006*, World Bank, Washington, DC.

—— 2007, *Cost of Pollution in China: Economic Estimates of Physical Damages*, World Bank, Washington, DC.

—— 2009a, *Education for the Knowledge Economy*, The World Bank, Washington, DC.

World Bank 2010a, *Ease of Doing Business, 2010*, The World Bank, Washington, DC.

—— 2010b, *Entrepreneurship Database*, The World Bank, Washington, DC, <http://econ.worldbank.org/WBSITE/EXTERNAL/EXTDEC/EXTRESEARCH/0,,contentMDK:21164814~pagePK:64214825~piPK:64214943~theSitePK:469382,00.html>.

—— 2010c, 'New Firm Creation', *Viewpoint*, The World Bank, Washington, DC.

—— 2010d, *Knowledge Economy Index*, The World Bank, Washington, DC.

—— 2010e, *Doing Business in Pakistan 2010*, World Bank and International Finance Corporation, Washington, DC.

—— 2010f, *Doing Business in Indonesia 2010*, World Bank and International Finance Corporation, Washington, DC.

—— 2010g, *Economic Integration in the Maghreb*, Middle East and North Africa Region, Washington, DC.

World Bank & United Nations International Strategy for Disaster Risk Reduction 2008, *South Eastern Europe Disaster Risk Mitigation and Adaptation Programme*, United Nations International Strategy for Disaster Reduction Secretariat and The World Bank, Geneva and Washington, DC.

World Economic Forum, 2008, *Convergence of Insurance and Capital Markets*, Geneva.

—— 2010, *Global Gender Gap Report, 2010*, World Economic Forum, Geneva.
Wolfensohn, J 2007, 'Summit of the Eight III: The four circles of a changing world', *New York Times*, June 4, 2007, New York.

Wu, S, Dai, E, Huang, M, Shao, X, Li, S & Tao, B 2007, 'Ecosystem Vulnerability of China under B2 Climate Scenario in the 21st Century', *Chinese Science Bulletin*, vol. 52, no. 10, pp. 1379-86.

Yanev, Pl *Avoiding the Next Earthquake Catastrophe in East Asia and the Pacific*, presentation, <http://siteresources.worldbank.org/INTEAPREGTOPHAZRISKMGMT/Resources/drm_peter_yanev.pdf>.

Young, T 2010, *China to Launch Domestic Carbon Trade in Five Years*, <http://www.business-green.com/business-green/news/2266875/china-launch-domestic-carbon>.

Yuan, WJ & Murphy, M 2010, *Regional Monetary Cooperation in East Asia: Should the United States Be Concerned?*, Report of the CSIS Freeman Chair in China Studies, Center for Strategic and International Studies, Washington, DC.

Yusuf, S 2007, *Urban Mega Regions: Knowns and Unknowns*, Policy Research Working Paper no. 4252, World Bank, Washington, DC.

Zacher, M W 2001, 'The Territorial Integrity Norm: International Boundaries and the Use of Force, *International Organization*, vol. 55, no. 2, pp. 215–25.

Zhang, S 2011, Unpublished note prepared at MIT Sloan School of Management based on <http://www.nanowerk.com/nanotechnology/Nanotechnology_Companies_in_China.php>.

Zhuang, J, De Dios, E & Lagman-Martin, A 2010, 'Governance and Institutional Quality and the Links with Growth and Inequality: How Asia fares', *Poverty, Inequality, and Inclusive Growth in Asia: Measurement, Policy Issues, and Country Studies*, Asian Development Bank, Manila.

Zhung, J 2010 (ed.), *Poverty, Inequality, and Inclusive Growth in Asia: Measurement, Policy Issues, and Country Studies*, Anthem Press and Asian Development Bank, London and Manila.

About the Editors, Authors, and Contributors

The Editors

Harinder S. Kohli is the Founding Director and Chief Executive of Emerging Markets Forum as well as President and CEO of Centennial Group International, both based in Washington, D.C. He is the Editor of Global Journal of Emerging Markets Economies, and serves as Vice Chairman of the institution-wide Advisory Group of Asian Institute of Technology (Thailand). Prior to starting his current ventures, he served some 25 years in various senior managerial positions at the World Bank. He has written extensively on the emergence of Asia and other emerging market economies, financial development, private capital flows, and infrastructure. He is co-editor of "India 2039: An Affluent Society in One Generation" (2010), "Latin America 2040—Breaking Away from Complacency: An Agenda for Resurgence" (2010), "A Resilient Asia amidst Global Financial Crisis" (2010), and "Islamic Finance" (2011).

Ashok Sharma is the Senior Director of Asian Development Bank's Office of Regional Economic Integration. He is the chair of the community of practice for regional cooperation and co-chairs the community of practice for finance of ADB. He also served as Senior Advisor of the South Asia Department of ADB and Director of Financial Sector, Public Management and Trade Division of South Asia Department. He has worked extensively on project and knowledge products on financial sector development, fiscal and governance reforms, infrastructure financing, and enabling public-private partnerships. He is the co-editor of "A Resilient Asia Amidst Global financial Crisis" (2010).

Anil Sood is Chief Operating Officer of Centennial Group International. In his 30-year career at the World Bank, he occupied many senior positions including Vice President, Strategy and Resource Management, and Special Advisor to the Managing Directors. He has since advised chief executives and senior management of a number of development organizations including the African Development Bank, the Islamic Development Bank, the United Nations Development Program, and the United Nations Economic Commission of Africa, on matters of strategy and development effectiveness. He is the co-editor of "India 2039: An Affluent Society in One

Generation" (2010), and "Latin America 2040—Breaking Away from Complacency: An Agenda for Resurgence" (2010).

The Authors

Drew Arnold graduated from Georgetown University in 2010 with an undergraduate degree in International Economics and an honors certificate in International Business Diplomacy. He is currently pursuing a master's degree in Applied Economics and a certificate in Forecasting Practice from John Hopkins University. He has been working at Centennial Group International since 2009, and currently works as an Economic Analyst. He has contributed to papers involving wealth lost during the 2008 financial crisis and the recent resilience of certain emerging market economies.

Cameron Hepburn is a Director of Vivid Economics Ltd. and Senior Research Fellow at the London School of Economics (Grantham Research Institute). He is an expert in market economics, commercial strategy, and environmental economics and ethics. He has advised governments and international institutions on environmental and climate policy, and has worked with a range of private sector clients on environmental and climate strategy. He also holds Research Fellowships at Oxford University and serves as a member of the Economics Advisory Group to the UK Secretary of State for Energy & Climate Change, and as a member of the Academic Panel, UK Department of Environment, Food and Rural Affairs. He is an Associate Editor of the Oxford Review of Economic Policy.

Yasheng Huang is professor of political economy and international management and holds International Program Professorship in Chinese Economy and Business at Sloan School of Management, Massachusetts Institute of Technology. He also holds a special-term professorship at School of Management, Fudan University and an honorary professorship at Hunan University. His previous appointments include faculty positions at the University of Michigan and at Harvard University. He is a member of MIT Entrepreneurship Center, a fellow at the Center for China in the World Economy at Tsinghua University, a research fellow at Shanghai University of Finance and Economics, a fellow at William Davidson Institute at Michigan Business School, and a World Economic Forum Fellow. Professor Huang has numerous publications to his credit, including Capitalism with Chinese Characteristics which was selected by The Economist magazine as one of the best books published in 2008.

Shigeo Katsu is President of the Nazarbayev University in Kazakhstan and Chair of the USA Board of Restless Development, a UK-based youth-oriented international NGO. Prior to these ventures, he had a 30-year career at the World Bank, where he held many senior positions, including Vice President for Europe and Central Asia (ECA) and Special Advisor to the Managing Directors. He now also advises governments and a number of international organizations on different issues related to development.

Homi Kharas is a Senior Fellow and Deputy Director of the Global Economy and Development program at the Brookings Institution in Washington, D.C., has been a member of the Working Group for the Commission on Growth and Development, chaired by Michael Spence, a nonresident Fellow of the Organization for Economic Cooperation and Development's (OECD) Development Centre, and a member of the National Economic Advisory Council to the Prime Minister of Malaysia. He spent 26 years at the World Bank. His research interests are now focused on the global middle class, Asian growth and development, and international aid for the poorest countries. He has numerous publications to his credit.

Harpaul Alberto Kohli is the Manager of Information Analytics at Centennial Group International and Emerging Markets Forum, where he is responsible for all modeling, econometrics, databases, statistics, and technology management. He earned a degree with honors in Mathematics and Philosophy from Harvard University, where he served as co-president of both the Society of Physics Students and the Math Club. He earned his MBA at Georgetown University, with emphases on psychology and on financial markets and public policy. He is also a Microsoft Certified Technology Specialist.

Johannes F. Linn is a Senior Resident Scholar at the Emerging Markets Forum and a Non-resident Senior Fellow at the Brookings Institution in Washington, D.C. During his 30-year career at the World Bank, he held many senior positions, including Vice President for Europe and Central Asia (ECA) and Staff Director of the World Development Report 1988. A collection of his speeches were published under the title 'Transition Years—Reflections on Economic Reform and Social Change in Europe and Central Asia' (World Bank, 2004). In 2004/5, he was the lead author of the United Nations Development Program's Central Asia Human Development Report. He recently edited (with Werner Hermann) the volume 'Central Asia and The Caucasus: At the Crossroads of Eurasia in the 21st Century (Sage, 2011).

Jayant Menon is Principal Economist in the Office for Regional Economic Integration at the Asian Development Bank. He was the co-task manager of the Asia 2050 study. Prior to joining ADB, he was Senior Research Fellow at the Centre of Policy Studies at Monash University in Melbourne, Australia. He has also worked at the University of Melbourne and Victoria University, and has held visiting appointments at the Australian National University, Institute of Southeast Asian Studies in Singapore, and American University in Washington, DC. He holds adjunct appointments at the Australian National University, University of Nottingham, and the Cambodian Institute for Cooperation and Peace. He is co-editor of the ASEAN Economic Bulletin, and serves on editorial boards of several academic journals. He is the author or co-author of more than one hundred academic publications, mostly on trade and development, and particularly as they relate to Asia.

Sabyasachi Mitra is a Senior Economist in the Office of Regional Economic Integration (OREI) of the Asian Development Bank. He was the co-task manager of the Asia 2050 study and was also the task manager of the ADB flagship study 'Institutions for Regional Integration: Toward an Asian Economic Community.' He participates in ASEAN+3's Asian Bond Market Initiative (ABMI) and other regional financial initiatives. In his current capacity, he is responsible for the ADB's research on local currency bond markets and works on financial market integration and regional cooperation issues. Prior to joining the ADB, he worked as an international financial journalist with Reuters for over ten years in London; Hong Kong, China; Malaysia; and India.

Anthony Pellegrini is a partner and member of the Board of Centennial Group International. He is a former Director of Transportation, Water and Sanitation and Urban Development at the World Bank. Mr. Pellegrini is a past chairman of the International Advisory Board of Paranacidade, a Brazilian development fund that lends to local governments. Mr. Pellegrini has extensive international experience in the field of urban development and infrastructure. He chaired the Transportation, Water and Sanitation and Urban Development Sector Boards of the World Bank which brought together all regional sector managers in the Bank responsible for policy issues in these sectors. Mr. Pellegrini's recent clients have included the Asian Development Bank, the European Investment Bank, the International Fund for Agriculture Development, Japan Bank for International Cooperation, the World Bank, US Trade and Development Agency, USAID, and as well as private companies and governments.

Hossein Razavi is the former Director of the Energy and Infrastructure Department of the World Bank. During his 25-year tenure at the World Bank he served a number of managerial and professional positions including the Chief of Oil and Gas Division, the Director of the Energy Department, and the Director of Private Sector Development. Dr. Razavi's main research interest is on structuring financial vehicles suitable to the energy sector. He trains government officials and oil and gas executives on the subjects of energy finance, private sector development, and infrastructure policy. His publications include several books and numerous papers on project finance, economic planning; and energy and environment. He serves on the editorial boards of the Energy Journal and Energy Economics.

Andrew Sheng was Chairman of the Securities and Futures Commission, Hong Kong, from October 1998 to 30 September 2005. He has served in various positions with Bank Negara Malaysia, the World Bank, and the Hong Kong Monetary Authority. He has chaired/co-chaired the Working Party on Transparency and Accountability (one of the three Working Parties formed under the Group of Twenty-two Finance Ministers and Central Bank Governors), the Financial Stability Forum's Task Force on Implementation of Standards (1999), and the Technical Committee of IOSCO, the International Organization of Securities Commission (2003-2005). In May 2003, he was appointed Convenor of the International Council of Advisers and Chief Adviser to the China Banking Regulatory Commission. He became Chairman, OECD-ADBI Roundtable on Capital Markets in October 2005 and concurrently Adjunct Professor, Graduate School of Economics and Management, Tsinghua University, Beijing and Faculty of Economics and Administration, University of Malaya.

Y. Aaron Szyf is a Policy Analyst at Centennial Group International where he focuses on analyzing projected debt sustainability and country risks for selected emerging economies. He graduated from the Fletcher School of Law and Diplomacy in Massachusetts with a Master of Arts in International Affair and concentrations in Development Economics (MALD) and International Business. In addition, Aaron holds a Master of Arts in Modern Jewish History from Yeshiva University in New York. He earned his Bachelor of Science in Finance Summa Cum Laude from the Sy Syms School of Business of Yeshiva University in 2003.

John Ward is a Principal at Vivid Economics where he specializes in environmental economics, industrial organization, finance and the application of economics to public policy issues. He has led much of Vivid Economics' work on climate change in developing and emerging economies and the advice that Vivid Economics provided to the African Development Bank on the UN High Level Advisory Group on Climate Change Finance. He has managed projects for a diverse portfolio of clients including numerous companies, government departments and regulatory bodies, as well as the European Commission, World Bank, IEA and UNEP.

With contributions from:
Amitav Acharya is Professor in the School of International Service, American University in Washington DC, and the UNESCO Chair in Transnational Challenges and Governance and Chair of the ASEAN Studies Center. Previously, he was Professor of Global Governance at the University of Bristol, Professor at York University, Toronto, and at Nanyang Technological University, Singapore, Fellow of the Harvard University Asia Center, and Fellow of Harvard's John F. Kennedy School of Government. His recent books include *Whose Ideas Matter?* (Cornell, 2009); *Beyond Iraq: The Future of World Order* (co-edited, World Scientific, 2011); *Non-Western*

International Relations Theory (co-edited, Routledge, 2010); and *The Making of Southeast Asia* (Cornell, 2011).

Hans P. Binswanger-Mkhize is a development economist who has conducted research on a wide range of topics related to agriculture. In his 25 years at the World Bank, he was a manager in the World Bank's central Rural Development Department, as well as in the Latin America and Africa Regions. He assisted a number of countries in the development of agricultural and rural development strategies, and in the design of Community-Driven Development Programs and HIV/AIDS programs. He was the architect and writer of the 1997 Rural Development Strategy of the World Bank. He is a fellow of the American Association for the Advancement of Sciences and of the American Association of Agricultural Economists, as well as a recipient of the Elmhirst Medal of the International Agricultural Economics Association.

Vinod Goel, a former World Bank official, is Head of Global Knowledge and Innovation Practice at Centennial Group International, and consultant for the World Bank and other international organizations. He is also the CEO and President of the Lagom Group. Mr Goel is a leading expert on private and financial sector issues and is well known in the international community for his pioneering work on higher education, technology and innovation, including publishing books on the subject. His global experience includes countries in Asia, Europe, Africa and Latin American Regions. He has a PhD and MBA from Cornell University, USA and Masters of Technology from National Dairy Research Institute, India.

Natasha Mukherjee is the Deputy Editor of the Global Journal of Emerging Market Economies. She has held numerous positions in regional and international financial institutions (SADC, the Southern African Development Community, World Bank), academia (University of Zimbabwe) and non-governmental organizations (IFRPI, the International Food Policy Research Institute, Southern African Regional Poverty Network), and has worked on a variety of topics in the fields of agricultural, environmental, trade and development economics. She holds a Ph.D. in environmental economics from the Johns Hopkins University in Baltimore, USA.

Ramesh Mashelkar is the President of the Global Research Alliance, a network of public research institutions globally. He is Chairman of the National Innovation Foundation and the Reliance Innovation Council in India. He serves on the boards of several companies and educational and research organizations. He served for 11 years as the Director General of the Council of Scientific and Industrial Research. He is a Fellow of the Royal Society (U.K.) and Foreign Associate of the National Academy of Science (U.S.), and Foreign Fellow of the National Academy of Engineering (U.S.). He lectures widely and consults for national and international organizations on innovation and restructuring public research and development (R&D) institutions worldwide. He has received more than 50 awards and medals including the Padma Shri and Padma Bhushan, two of India's highest civilian honors.

Index

Academic Ranking of World Universities, 118
action agenda, for economic development in
    Asian countries, 88–89
    climate change, 93–94
    governance, 93
    growth and jobs, 89–91
    interventions and distribution policies, 91–93
Agency for Science, Technology and Research (ASTAR), Singapore, 104
aging trends, in Asia, 301
air pollution, 214–215
air quality, 214, 215, 235
Alzheimer's disease, 312
ASEAN Free Trade Agreement (AFTA), 261
ASEAN+3 Macroeconomic Research Office (AMRO), 173, 174, 263
ASEAN Regional Forum (ARF), 12, 252
Asia
    aging trends in, 301
    annual export growth, 13
    capital stock, 32–33
    creative thinking deficit, 116
    development performance in 21st century, 13
    differential-speed demographic inflection years, 302
    economic and social prospects, 12–13

energy consumption, historical perspective of, 182–184
    ASEAN countries, 186–187
    Central Asia, 187–188
    PRC, 185–186
    high-income, 184–185
    India, 186
    Iran, 188
    past and projected energy demand and supply, 183
energy demand and supply scenarios, 193
foreign exchange reserves, 13
future prospects, basic assumption
    effective global action on climate change, 45–46
    open global trading system, 44–45
    peaceful and orderly restructuring, 43–44
    stable global financial system, 44–45
GDP growth (1990–2015), 23
Great Recession, 22
income inequality in, 55–56
innovation scores, 122
intra subregional trade costs in, 256
investment rates, 13
meaning of, 10–13
Millennium Development Goals, 77
net inflows of private capital, 13
non-income inequalities, 73

productivity and entrepreneurship in, 102–105
projected GDP per capita (PPP) *vs.* share of aging population, 303
ranking on Ease of Doing Business indicators, 113
share of
   global R&D expenditure, 120
   world researchers, 121
three-speed demographic taxonomy in, 301
urban population, 135
working age population, 32
Asia Disaster Preparedness Center, 266
Asia-7 economies, 48, 63, 227
Asia–Europe Meeting (ASEM), 271
Asian Bond Fund Initiative, 159
Asian Bond Market Initiative (ABMI), 263, 271
Asian Capital Market Initiative, 271
Asian Century scenario
   actions at three levels, 2
   assumptions, 46
   cost of missing, 292–294
   econometric model for, 46
   global agenda, 5
   global output footprint, 46–48
   intangibles, 6
   makings of, 2
   middle class consumption in advanced countries, 33
   vs. Middle Income Trap, 5–6, 293
   national action agenda, 2–4
   regional cooperation, 4–5
Asian Development Bank, 113, 169, 174, 207, 262
Asian economy
   decline and reemergence (1700–1970), 19–20
   globalization dividend (1970–2010), 20–24
Asian finance. *See also* Islamic finance
   alternative scenarios of, 153–155
   current reform proposals for, 158
   future scenario, 160–161
   as global leader, 178
   global reserve currency, 159–160
   Great Recession (2007–2009), 157–158
   implications of Asian Century for, 155–157
   and importance of using global best practice, 176–178
   institutional structure. *See* financial institutional structure, models for
   international financial architecture and, 158–159
   Middle Income Trap scenario, 155
   priority action plan for, 174–176
   regional cooperation and global financial leadership, 172–174
   rise of, 151–153
   transformational changes for serving real sector, 161–162
   two-scenario projections for, 155
Asian financial crisis (1997–1998), 3, 12, 20–21, 66, 123, 154
Asian financial safety net, 173
Asian financial system, 151, 160–161, 172
Asian identity, proponents of, 11
Asian Monetary Fund (AMF), 173, 271
Asian Monetary System, 159
Asian NATO, 59
Asian values, concept of, 11
Asia-Pacific Economic Cooperation (APEC), 262, 280
Asia's global role
   climate change, 278
   communications channels, 277–278

in development assistance and private capital flows, 279–280
financial system, 278
global commons, 277
in global governance, 280–281
impact of national and regional policies on others, 280
implications of, 276–277
peace and prosperity, 278–279
and relations with other parts of world, 279
shipping lanes, 277–278
trading routes, 277–278
trading system, 277
"Asia 2050" study, purpose of, 9–10
asset management, 163, 166–168
Association of Southeast Asian Nations (ASEAN), 12, 59
  Bond Market Initiative, 174
  corporate banking, 165
  Economic Community Blueprint, 174
  electricity demand, 187
  energy consumption, 186–187
  energy security, 184
  Free Trade Area, 225
  Plus Three, 12
  Power Grid, 197
  Roadmap on Monetary and Financial Integration, 174
  Trans-ASEAN Gas Pipeline, 197
Australian Stock Exchange, 172

balance-of-payments deficits, 159
Bank for International Settlements, 173, 177, 280
banking system
  commercial, 162–164, 168
  investment, 165
  retail, 162–164
Basel III requirements
  for bank capital and liquidity, 45
  for global financial institutions, 175
basti improvement program, 130
Bay of Bengal Initiative for Multi-Sectoral Technical and Economic Cooperation (BIMSTEC), 270
Beike Bio Technology, 312
bilateral trade agreements, 45
bio-fuels, 95, 317
biotechnology, 312–314
Brazil
  macroeconomic crises, 21
  political and economic policies, 54
"business as usual" (BAU) scenario, for energy demand, 192
business environment, in Asia, 112–113

Calcutta Metropolitan Development Authority (CMDA, now KMDA), 130–131
Cambodia
  Gini coefficient for income distribution, 90
  inclusive growth in policy planning, 90
  income distribution, 90
  national social protection strategy, 90
  urban population, 133
capital
  flows, 23, 45, 157, 159
  global reallocation of, 24
  stock, 32
capital–labor ratio, 32
capital markets, 166–168
  difference with insurance products, 170
capital stock growth, definition of, 306
carbon capture and storage (CCS), 191, 199
carbon emissions, 135, 136, 181, 192, 200

Caselli method, for calculation of initial capital stock, 306
Caspian gas pipeline, 198
catch-up entrepreneurship, 99, 105–107, 112, 123
Central Asia
    energy demand, 187–188
    gas demand and import dependency, 190
    HIV/AIDS prevalence rates, 266
    income disparities, 56
    oil demand and import dependency, 189
    population changes, 299
    regional energy integration, 197–198
    transcontinental oil and gas pipelines, 264
    triple integration opportunity, 259
    urban population, 135
Central Asia Regional Economic Cooperation (CAREC), 259, 262
Chiang Mai Initiative Multilateralization, 159, 173, 174, 263
Club of Rome (1972), 55
coal, 184
    consumption, 192
    electricity generation, 186
Cobb–Douglas function, for developing global growth scenarios, 305
commercial banking, 162–164, 166, 168
Commission on Growth and Development, 25, 226
communications revolution, economic implications for Asia, 36–38
compact city, concept of, 138
competition, for finite natural resources, 55
conflicts flashpoints, 43–44, 266–267
consumption, by global middle class, 33–34
converging economies, 2–4, 6, 25, 46, 57, 64, 67–68, 99–100, 104, 126–127, 235, 239, 285, 286, 288

corruption, 230–233, 240
Council of Asian Cooperation, 271
creative thinking, deficit in Asia, 116
Credit Guarantee and Investment Facility, 263
cross-border conflict, risk of, 58–59
cross-border production networks, 136
crude oil, 184
current income distribution, parameters for, 36

debt management, 237
debt market capitalization, 152
Declaration on the Conduct of Parties, 265
Declaration on the South China Sea, 265
disaster mitigation, 148
Doha Development Round, 44
domestic capital markets, measures for supporting growth of, 177
domestic exchange rates, 161

Ease of Doing Business indicators, 112
East Asia
    exports in sectors with increasing returns to scale, 253
    parts and components trade in, 254
    tribute-trade system, 12
    uneven economic integration, 254
East Asia and Pacific Central Banks (EMEAP), 174
East Asia Summit, 12, 252
Easterlin, model for economics of happiness, 39
e-business, 113–114
e-Choupal, 106
eco-compact city, concept of, 141
economic development, technology and innovation-based, 121, 123
economic growth in Asia
    classic drivers of

capital deepening, 32–33
demography and labor force, 31
technological change and productivity,
    29–31
global agenda, 69–70
national economic and social policy agenda
    entrepreneurship, innovation, and
        technological development, 67
    financial transformation, 65–66
    governance and institutional
        development, 67–68
    growth and inclusion, 65
    growth and well-being, 68
    reduction in intensity of energy and
        natural resource use, 66–67
    strategy to manage urbanization, 66
regional cooperation, 68–69
three dimensions of, 63–65
economic integration
    drivers of, 256–257
    prospects for further, 257–258
Economic Review and Policy Dialogue (2000),
    263
Economics of Climate Adaptation Working
    group, 171
Economist Intelligence Unit, 113, 121
education
    education indices, 116
        Educational Attainment indicator, 117
        Legatum Prosperity Index, 115
        World Bank Knowledge Assessment
            Methodology (KAM), 115
    enrollment rates in high-income countries in
        Asia, 117–118
    facilities in Asian countries, 84–85
    human capital requirements, 114–117
    research and development, 117–122

secondary, 115
tertiary, 117–122
TFP levels, 115
Educational Attainment indicator, 117
electricity demand, in ASEAN countries, 187
EMEAP Monetary and Financial Stability
    Committee (2007), 174
EMEAP Roadmap on Regional Financial
    Cooperation, 174
energy and natural resource use, intensity of, 3
energy consumption, 135, 136
    historical perspective of, 182–184
        ASEAN countries, 186–187
        Central Asia, 187–188
        PRC, 185–186
        high-income, 184–185
        India, 186
        Iran, 188
        past and projected energy demand and
            supply, 183
energy demand and supply in Asia
    "business as usual" (BAU) scenario, 192–193
    past and projected, 183
energy efficiency and diversification (EED), 3,
    137, 184, 192, 194–196, 198–199, 215
energy imports, 3, 184, 197
energy security, 67
    ASEAN countries, 184
    and climate change, 213–214
    implications of energy consumption on,
        188–191
    improvement through efficiency and
        diversification, 192–194
        energy efficiency, 194–196
    priorities for domestic action
        emerging energy technologies, 199–200
        energy efficiency and diversification,
            198–199

public and private sector roles, 200
priorities for regional cooperation, 201
role of natural gas in, 189
sudden supply disruptions, policies for reducing
    regional energy integration, 197–198
    strategic petroleum stocks, 196–197
energy supply and use
    composition of, 192
    global revolution in, 191
    in transport sector in PRC, 185
entrepreneurship
    key elements of
        business environment, 112–113
        education, 114–117
        physical and technological infrastructure, 113–114
        tertiary education and R&D, 117–122
    overall policy framework, 122–125
    priorities and action agenda, 125–127
    rights in PRC and India, 105–108
        broad policy reforms, 111
        foreign direct investment (FDI), 108–109
        knowledge production, 110–111
        policy focus, 109–110
        R&D, 109
    TFP levels, 101
    types of, 99
Entry Density indicator, 112
environmental sustainability, and risk management, 147–148
ESCAP initiative, 262
EU finance sector, two-scenario projections for, 156
European Commission, 138, 268
European Financial Stability Fund, 173

fast-growing converging economies, 2–4, 6, 25, 46, 57, 67–68, 286, 288
financial institutional structure, models for
    asset management, 166–168
    capital markets, 166–168
    development finance and policy-based financial institutions, 168–170
    exchanges and clearing systems, 171–172
    insurance, 170–171
    investment banking, 164–165
    retail and commercial banking, 162–164
financial institutions
    Islamic finance, 161
    policy-based, 168–170
Financial Stability Board, 45, 173, 177
food security, 95–96
foreign direct investment (FDI), 108–109, 247, 251, 312
foreign exchange, 13, 23, 107, 123, 151–152, 161–162, 171, 276
fossil fuels, 186, 187, 193, 204, 317
    impact of combustion, 215
free regional trade and investment, 5
free trade agreements (FTAs), 261
frontier entrepreneurship, 99, 109, 112, 117, 123, 124
Fujita, model for spatial allocation of economic activity, 39

gas and electricity networks, regional interconnections of, 197–198
gas pipelines
    Iran–Pakistan–India pipeline, 198
    Turkmenistan–Afghanistan–Pakistan–India pipeline, 198
gas security, 190
gas supply, security of, 190

gender inequality, 88
General Electric (GE), 318
Gini coefficient, 90
    for measurement of income inequality in Asia, 80
    for measurement of urban inequality, 83
    urban, 140
Glaeser, arguments for dense city planning, 39
global agenda, 5, 69–70
global capital markets, 166
global emissions, emerging economies' contributions to, 203–204
Global Entrepreneurship and Development Index (GEDI), 100
global finance sector indicators, 152
global financial system, 44–45
global investment banks, 165
global middle class spending, in western countries, 34
global reserve currency, 159–160
global trading system, 44–45
global warming, 56–57, 171
governance and institutions, in Asia
    challenges in Asia, 226–230
    corruption issues
        grand corruption, 231
        petty corruption, 230–231
        state capture, 231–233
    drivers for change in
        demographics, 233–235
        expanding middle class and communications revolution, 236–237
        urbanization, 235–236
    impact on development outcomes, 222
    for improvement of equality, 93
    and institutional capacity, 3, 57–58
    key actors of, 237–238
    principles and priorities, 239–242
Grameen Bank, 161
Greater Mekong Subregion (GMS) Program, 248, 262
Great Recession (2007–2009), 3, 13, 22, 154, 157–158, 165, 172
greenhouse gases, 191, 215
green technology, 107, 125, 165, 213
gross domestic product (GDP), 1, 2, 204, 250
gross R&D expenditures (GERD), 123
Gulf Cooperation Council Grid, 198

"happiness" surveys, 38
health care, facilities in Asian countries, 85–87
high-income economies, 4, 24–25, 127
HIV/AIDS prevalence rates, 266
housing ownership, 35
human capital development, 99, 126, 147
Human Development Index, 83
hydropower, 186–187, 195, 264

import substitution, policies for, 74
inclusive growth, meaning of, 78–79
inclusive policies for urban management, development of, 147
income inequality, in Asia, 55–56, 79
    current status in, 80–84
        spatial inequality, 81–84
        urban inequality, 81
    Gini coefficient for measurement of, 80
India
    energy consumption, 186
    energy mix in, 195
    energy-related carbon emissions, 182
    entrepreneurship and innovation rights in, 105–111
    food demand, 95

growth of middle class, 36
growth of wind power capacity in, 194
inclusive growth in policy planning, 90
Internet usage, 37
level of education of
    men, 85
    women, 85
mobile phone subscriptions, 37
models of innovation development, 107
percentage point share of global GDP per decade, 47
pharmaceutical industry, 106–107
spatial inequality, 90
technological innovation, progress in, 311–312
urban inequality in, 81
Indonesia
    Hepatitis B vaccination coverage, 87
    Jakarta, urbanization of, 134
    TransJakarta express bus lane system, 146
industrial revolution, 1, 15, 19, 44, 212
inequalities, types of, 80
information and communication technology (ICT), 270, 312, 314–315
Information Highway Project, 270
infrastructure finance
    design framework, 170
    environment for, 169
    impediments to private sector financing, 169
infrastructure planning, and land use, 146
innovation development
    key elements of
        business environment, 112–113
        education, 114–117
        physical and technological infrastructure, 113–114
        tertiary education and R&D, 117–122
    models of, 107
    overall policy framework, 122–125
    priorities and action agenda, 125–127
INSEAD's Global Innovation Index, 121
institutional development, in Asia's nonbank sector, 153
Institutions for Regional Integration: Toward and Asian Economic Community (ADB), 271
insurance, 170–171
insurance-linked securities, 170
intellectual property
    laws, 316
    rights, 44, 112, 127, 224
International Comparison Program, World Bank, 308
International Energy Agency (IEA), 181
    decarbonization scenario, 192
International Labor Organization, 305
International Monetary Fund (IMF), 13, 173
international monetary system, 159–160, 278
International Organization of Securities Commissions, 173, 177
Internet, usage in Asia, 37
inter-regional cooperation initiatives, 270
intracountry inequality, 51, 73
intraregional financial service trade, 172
investment banking, 165, 170, 175
Iran–Pakistan–India pipeline, 198
Islamic finance, 161

Jakarta, urbanization of, 134
Japan
    Bank for International Cooperation, 184
    domestic energy resources, 196
    energy security, 184

energy strategy, 184
keiretsu system of corporate governance, 224

Knowledge Assessment Methodology (KAM), World Bank, 115
Kyoto Protocol, 203, 207, 208

labor force, 31
  from low to higher-productivity activities, 52
labor-intensive manufacturing exports, 20
labor-intensive production, 75
labor rights, 92
land markets, 136, 146
land reforms, 76
Legatum Prosperity Index, 115
liquefied natural gas (LNG), 184, 187, 191
Lomborg, role of price mechanism for management of resource scarcity, 39
low- and lower-middle-income economies, 4
low-income countries, growth strategies in, 52

market exchange rates, 2, 6, 19–20, 22, 54, 153, 292, 305, 308
market incentives, for better urban design, conservation, and green energy development, 144
mass public transport, 137, 146
mega-challenges and risks, for sustaining growth momentum in Asia
  disparities across countries and subregions, 55–56
  expanding global footprint, 58
  finite natural resources, competition for, 55
  global warming and climate change, 56–57
  governance and institutional capacity, 57–58
  inequality within countries, 51
  Middle Income Trap
    low-income countries, 52
    middle-income countries, 52–54
    political leadership, 54–55
  risk of conflict, 58
microfinance, 161
Middle and Long-Term Program for Science and Technology Development (2006–2020), 110
middle class
  emergence and impact on economic growth of Asia, 33–36
  growth of, 34
middle-income countries, growth strategies in, 52–54
Middle Income Trap, 1, 4, 9, 14, 51, 68, 155, 225, 239, 290–292
  vs. Asian Century, 5–6, 293
  and entrepreneurial development, 100
  low-income countries, 52
  middle-income countries, 52–54
  political leadership, 54–55
  scenario, 46
  vulnerability of middle-income countries, 25
Millennium Development Goals (MDGs), 73
  for poverty reduction, 77–78
Minsky, warning against moral hazard in banking system, 39
Multimedia Super Corridor, Malaysia, 139
municipal development funds (MDFs), 144

nanotechnology, 107, 110, 132, 312
national action agenda, Asia
  for achieving growth with inclusion, 285–286
  for making a financial transformation, 287

for managing massive urbanization, 287
for mitigating and adapting to climate change, 288
for productivity, entrepreneurship, and technological development, 286
for reducing energy intensity and natural resource use, 287–288
for transforming governance and quality of institutions, 288

National High Tech R&D Program (863 Program), PRC, 110

National Key Technologies Program, PRC, 110

National Science and Technology Board, Singapore, 104

natural gas, 184
role in Asia's energy security, 189

natural resources
competition for, 55
strategy for reducing intensity of using, 66–67

natural user interface (NUI) technologies, 315

net private financial capital flows, 23

newly industrialized economies (NIEs), 10, 20, 151, 249
characteristic of economic performance of, 75–76

non-converging economies, 99–100, 117, 126

non-income equality, status of Asian countries in
education, 84
gender inequality, 88
health, 85–87
sanitation, 87–88

non-revenue-earning infrastructure, 143

nuclear energy, 184, 186, 191–193, 195, 200

official development assistance (ODA), 139, 224

oil demand and import, past and projected, 189

oil security, 189

open regionalism, policy of, 5

Organisation for Economic Co-operation and Development (OECD) Program, 13, 311

Pakistan
nutritional status of children in, 86
sanitation facilities, 87

Patent Act (1970), 106
Patent Act (2005), 107
patents, 13, 121
Patents and Design Act (1911), 106
pension schemes, 167

People's Republic of China (PRC)
alternative energy projects, 109
energy consumption, 185–186
energy-related carbon emissions, 182
entrepreneurship and innovation rights in, 105–111
green technology, 107, 125
growth of middle class in, 35
growth of wind power capacity in, 194
household consumption expenditure, 35
inclusive growth in policy planning, 90
Internet usage, 37
mobile phone subscriptions, 37
models of innovation development, 107
National High Tech R&D Program (863 Program), 110
National Key Technologies Program, 110
percentage point share of global GDP per decade, 47
pharmaceutical industry, 107
"973 Program" (mechanism for funding allocations), 109

progress in tertiary education and research, 119
Project 211 (1996), 110
Project for Funding World-Class Universities, 110
share of India's imports of manufactured goods, parts and components, 255
Spark Program, 110
Torch Program, 110
trends in scientific publications, 111
urban income deciles, 82
urban inequality in, 81
urbanization strategy, 135
cities, of the future, 135–138
    city building, dimensions of, 138–139
    compact city, concept of, 138
    small and medium-sized towns and cities, management of, 139
    sustainable development policy for, 138
    vision for, 137
city building, dimensions of, 138–139
city centers, modernizing/retrofitting of, 138
city management, 137, 145. *See also* urban planning
city-to-city logistics chains, 144
civil service, 241–242
clearing houses, 171–172
climate change, 3, 67
    adaptation and risk management for
        climate change resilience in agriculture, 217
        development planning, 216–217
        disaster risk finance, 217
        disaster risk reduction and management, 217
        increasing resilience of sector strategies and projects, 217
        reducing vulnerability, 216

    adaptation types and examples by sector, 218
    Asia's stance on, 278
    global action on, 45–46
    global burden sharing, 217
    global warming and, 56–57
    impact, business-as-usual scenario, 204–205
        economic impact, 206–207
        health impact, 207
        physical impact, 205
        sea-level rise, 205–206
    impact, complementary mitigation actions, 208–210
    impact, mitigation by developed countries only scenario, 207–208
    implications of energy consumption on, 191–192
    mitigation of risks associated with, 56
    negative impacts of, 93–94
    and transition to low-carbon economies, 210–216
pharmaceutical industries, 106–107
    "supply chain" of, 107
pharmaco-genomics, 312, 313
Philippines
    constructive regional cooperation, 252
    gender inequality, 88
    Gini coefficients of rising inequality, 81
    population living on less than $1.25 (PPP) per day, 75
    prenatal care provision in, 86
    rapid aging of societies, 13
    skilled and unskilled labor, export of, 56
physical and technological infrastructure, in Asia, 113–114
Physical Infrastructure Index, 113

population changes
    in Asia (2010–2050), 300
    in Asia's subregions (2010 vs. 2050), 299
    projected growth of Asia's elderly people, 301
poverty reduction, 13, 36
    in metropolitan Kolkata, 131
    and Millennium Development Goals, 77–78
    in selected Asian countries, 74
power grids, 197
private–public sector partnerships, 168
private sector financing, of infrastructure, 169
process innovation, 107–108, 111
product innovation, 107–108, 110, 118
Project 211 (1996), PRC, 110
Project for Funding World-Class Universities, PRC, 110
public administration reform, 222
public financial management (PFM), 222, 237
public-private partnerships (P-PPs), 66, 94, 142–144, 169, 287
public services, pressure of population growth on, 130
public transport, 130, 132, 136–138, 185
purchasing power parity (PPP), 1, 2, 13, 307, 308

real estate developments, 139
Recovery Act, USA, 212
regional cooperation, for economic prosperity, 4–5
    agenda for, 288–289
    ASEAN countries, 252
    vs. conflict, 247–249
    contours of future, 258–261
    economic fortune and disarray, 249
    economic integration
        drivers of, 256–257
        prospects for further, 257–258
    importance of, 246
    priority areas for facilitating
        access to natural resources, 264–265
        conflict prevention, 266–267
        macroeconomic cooperation on integration and financial stability, 262–264
        responding to common regional threats, 265–266
        setting priorities, 267–268
        trade policy and role of free trade agreements, 261–262
        transport and trade facilitation, 262
    prospects and institutional options, 269–272
    regional economic integration (1970–2010), 249–256
    six reasons for, 68–69
regional trade agreements, 45
regional trade network, 12
renewable energy, 186, 192–196, 198–199, 201
Republic of Korea
    domestic energy resources, 196
    economic growth, strategy for, 21
    Export–Import Bank, 185
    nuclear generation capacity, 185
    science and technology, 123
    Seoul metropolitan area, 132
    Songdo International Business District, 139
    stem cell technology, 312
research & development (R&D), 109
retail banking, 160, 162–164
Romer, models for growth as an innovative process using knowledge, 39
rural development, 65, 90, 133–135, 286

rural–urban migration, 167

Saez, model for income concentration at top level, 39
sanitation facilities in Asia, provisions for, 87–88
Schumpeter, Joseph, 101
sea-level rise, 205–206
    emerging market action, impact of, 210
secondary education, 92, 115
Sen, Amartya, 38
Seoul metropolitan area, 132
Shanghai Cooperation Organization (SCO), 12, 267
Silk Road, 11
Singapore Exchange, 172
slow- or modest-growth aspiring economies, 4, 25
small and medium-sized enterprises (SMEs), 139, 161
    financing of, 164
    International Accounting Standards, 176
small and medium-sized towns and cities, management of, 139
social safety net programs, 92
social security network, 167
social transformation in Asia, new drivers of
    communications revolution, 36–38
    emerging middle class, 33–36
    growth and social well-being, 38–40
solar energy, 194, 199
solar technology, 199, 201
Songdo International Business District, Republic of Korea, 139
South Asia
    evolution of parts and components trade, 255
    sanitation facilities in, 86–87

South Asia Growth Quadrangle (SAGQ), 270
South Asian Association of Regional Cooperation (SAARC), 270
South Asian FTA (SAFTA), 261
South Asia Subregional Economic Cooperation (SASEC), 270
South Asia Tourism Infrastructure Development Project, 270
Spark Program, PRC, 110
spatial inequality, 81–84
    Human Development Index, 83
    in India, 90
Special Drawing Rights, 39
stem cell technology, 311–313
Stiglitz Commission, 40
stock exchanges, 171–172
stock market capitalization, 151–152
stock market price-earnings ratios, 153
strategic petroleum stockpiling, 196–197
"supply chain," of pharmaceutical industry, 107
sustainable development, 138
synthetic biology, 312–313

Tamil Nadu Urban Fund, 144
tax credits, 123
technological landscape of Asia
    Asia as an inclusive innovation leader by 2050, 318
    biotechnology, 312–314
    information and communications technology, 314–315
    predicting the future, 311
    science, technology, and innovation, 316
    technological breakthroughs, 316–318
    technological innovation, progress in, 311–312
tertiary education, 117–122

    progress of PRC in, 119
thermal power generation, 187
Torch Program, PRC, 110
total factor productivity (TFP), 99, 307
    high growth in converging countries, 100
trade barriers, 74, 253
trade disputes, 44
Trans-ASEAN Gas Pipeline, 197
TransMilenio system, 146
Transparency International's Corruption Perceptions Index, 241
Triffin, warning against short-term national interest and long-term international interests, 39
Triumph of the Cities (Glaeser), 39
Turkmenistan–Afghanistan–Pakistan–India pipeline, 198

UN Economic and Social Commission on Asia and the Pacific for a Trans-Asian Energy System, 264
United Kingdom
    economic power, 44
    "happiness" surveys, 38
urban development, 133–135
    local government, recommendations for
        attractiveness to private investment, 145
        city management, 145
        development of inclusive policies, 147
        environmental sustainability and risk management, 147–148
        infrastructure planning and land use, 146
        land markets and resolution of land title disputes, 146
    national government, recommendations for
        cross border, city-to-city mega regions, 144
        effective decentralization, 142–143
        market incentives for better urban design, 144
        national frameworks for financing urban infrastructure, 143–144
        visionary leadership for, 148
urban Gini coefficient, 83, 140
urban inequality, 81
    Gini coefficients of, 83
urban infrastructure deficit, 143–144, 169
urbanization
    benefits of, 135
    of Jakarta, 134
    major risks, management of
        breakdown of social cohesion, 139–140
        environmental risks, 141–142
        growth of slums, 139–140
        inequality, 139–140
        poorly planned infrastructure and land use, 141
        unmet expectations of expanding middle class, 141
    priority agenda for better urban future
        recommendations for local government, 145–148
        recommendations for national government, 142–145
    quality and efficiency of, 3
    strategy for management of, 66
urban planning
    basti improvement program, 130
    inter-municipal projects, 131
    self-financing scheme, 131
    Seoul metropolitan area, 132
    sustainable development policy, 138
urban settlement, 131
urban transport technology, 146
US finance sector, two-scenario projections for, 156

US Glass–Steagal legislation, 165
utility systems, 136

visionary leadership, for urban growth and development, 148
vocational education and training (VET), 92, 117
Voice over Internet Protocol (VoIP), 315

water cycle, 205
wealth management, 163, 167, 173
wind power, 186
    growth in India and PRC, 194
World Bank, 164, 207
    International Comparison Program, 308

World Economic Forum
    Gender Gap Report, 117
    Global Gender Gap Report, 88
World Health Organization (WHO), 106
World Intellectual Property Organization, 13
World Trade Organization (WTO), 23, 45, 259
Worldwide Governance Indicators (2009), 227, 232, 239, 241
Wuxi Suntech, 107

Xiaochuan, Zhou, 39
Xiaoping, Deng, 107, 109

zero involuntary unemployment, 89